Bloom's Modern Critical Views

Bloom's Modern Critical Views

Alexander
  Solzhenitsyn
Sophocles
John Steinbeck
Tom Stoppard
Jonathan Swift
Amy Tan
Alfred, Lord Tennyson
Henry David Thoreau
J.R.R. Tolkien
Leo Tolstoy

Ivan Turgenev
Mark Twain
John Updike
Kurt Vonnegut
Derek Walcott
Alice Walker
Robert Penn Warren
Eudora Welty
Edith Wharton
Walt Whitman
Oscar Wilde

Tennessee Williams
Thomas Wolfe
Tom Wolfe
Virginia Woolf
William Wordsworth
Jay Wright
Richard Wright
William Butler Yeats
Emile Zola

Bloom's Modern Critical Views

EMILE ZOLA

Edited and with an introduction by
Harold Bloom
Sterling Professor of the Humanities
Yale University

CHELSEA HOUSE
PUBLISHERS
A Haights Cross Communications Company
Philadelphia

Library of Congress Cataloging-in-Publication Data
Emile Zola / edited and with an introduction by Harold Bloom.
      p. cm. — (Bloom's modern critical views)
   ISBN 0-7910-7663-6
   1. Zola, Emile, 1840-1902—Criticism and interpretation. I. Bloom,
Harold. II. Title. III. Series.
   PQ2538.E46 2003
   843'.8—dc22
                                        2003016889

Chelsea House Publishers
1974 Sproul Road, Suite 400
Broomall, PA 19008-0914

http://www.chelseahouse.com

Contributing Editor: Janyce Marson

Cover designed by Terry Mallon

Cover photo by © Bettmann/CORBIS

Layout by EJB Publishing Services

Contents

Editor's Note

My Introduction meditates upon the shocker, *Thérèse Raquin*, in which Zola first emerged as himself.

The novelist Angus Wilson charts the series of the Rougon-MacQuart, emphasizing Zola's avoidance of preoccupation with singular characters.

An astute analysis by the critic F.W.J. Hemmings centers upon *Germinal*, certainly Zola's most eminent novel, while William J. Berg brings together Zola's "poetics of vision" and his naturalistic presuppositions.

Zola's fantasy, *Le Rêve*, is judged by Robert E. Ziegler as being the author's attempt to escape from bodily fat and emotional famine, after which Jonathan F. Krell engages *Nana*, Zola's great vision of sexual power and its huge destructiveness.

Frederick Brown, Zola's definitive critical biographer, offers the most lucid sketch we have of "the master plan" of *Les Rougon-MacQuart*, while Hollie Markland Harder confronts the marble woman of Zola's *La Faute de l'abbé Mouret*.

P.M. Wetherill shows us Paris evolving through Flaubert, Proust, and Zola, after which the inevitable Walter Benjamin is hauled in by Nicholas Rennie to sanctify Zola.

Zola's dark side is evoked by Marie-Sophie Armstrong, while Michelle E. Bloom analyzes the fantasist in Zola.

Anthony Savile attempts to rescue Zola from his own naturalism, after which Henri Mitterand concludes this volume by placing Zola among the surrealists.

HAROLD BLOOM

Introduction

Time hallows Zola's greatness, as novelist and as person, though increasingly we see that he transcended his naturalistic aesthetic. Frederick Brown, his crucial scholar-critic, surmises that the novelist's death at sixty-two, by asphyxiation, *may* have been murder, a final revenge by the proto-Fascist anti-Dreyfusards against the leader of those who had exonerated Dreyfus.

Zola, far more even than Balzac, needs to be read in bulk: no single novel carries his full greatness, not even the sequence of *L'Assommoir* (1877), *Nana* (1880), *Pot-Bouille* (1882), *Germinal* (1885), *La Terre* (1887), *Le Rêve* (1888), *La Bête humaine* (1890), *Le Débâcle* (1892), and *Le Docteur Pascal* (1893). Those nine carry through his "Master Plan," as set forth by Frederick Brown in a chapter of his *Zola: A Life* (1995), which I have reprinted in this volume.

Here I wish to consider only *Thérèse Raquin*, the starting point of his art, published in 1867, and written when he was just twenty-six, strongly influenced by Balzac, and perhaps also by Stendhal and by Victor Hugo. Defending his novel in a preface to the second edition (1868), Zola fiercely absolves himself of all charges of immorality and pornography:

> In *Thérèse Raquin* my aim has been to study temperaments and not characters. That is the whole point of the book. I have chosen people completely dominated by their nerves and blood, without free will, drawn into each action of their lives by the inexorable laws of their physical nature. Thérèse and Laurent are human animals, nothing more. I have endeavoured to follow these animals through the devious working of their passions, the compulsion of their instincts, and the mental unbalance resulting from a nervous crisis. The sexual adventures of my hero and heroine are the satisfaction of a need, the murder they commit a consequence of their adultery, a consequence they accept just as

1

wolves accept the slaughter of sheep. And finally, what I have had
to call their remorse really amounts to a simple organic disorder,
a revolt of the nervous system when strained to breaking-point.
There is a complete absence of soul, I freely admit, since that is
how I meant it to be.

A disciple of Taine, Zola calls his enterprise "scientific," or
"sociological" in our current language. Hippolyte Taine himself, though he
admired the novel, urged Zola to work on a more panoramic scale. It is true
Thérèse Raquin is a closed-in nightmare; Brown usefully stresses that Zola's
own recurrent nightmare was to be buried alive, as in Poe's dreadful fantasy.

The novel is the story of the half Algerian Thérèse, her sickly husband
whom she does not love, and of Laurent, her lover, who murders the weak
husband, Camille, by pushing him into the Seine. The result is the victim's
triumph over his murderers, who eventually share the same glass of poison.

The novel remains grimly memorable, and far more of a
phantasmagoric than a realistic work. Though it failed to gain Zola a public,
it is a presage of a greatness to come. Like so much of Nineteenth Century
"realism" and "naturalism," Zola seems now a visionary fantasist, akin to the
sublime Balzac.

ANGUS WILSON

Les Rougon-Macquart: The Form of Expression

Artistry and journalism in Zola's work—his assaults upon his readers' emotions—impressionist writing—careful balance of character and incident—'atmospheric' devices—analysis of his 'black' poetry—too great concern with exact detail—animal symbols—adherence to unities of time and place—cinematic quality of Zola's work—his preoccupation with the human will—no preoccupation with single characters until Rougon-Macquart series was complete.

After the publication of *L'Assommoir*, with its phenomenal, scandalous success, Flaubert, while praising the novels highly, was moved to protest against Zola's increasing use of publicity. To this, Zola was quick to reply that he was not only artist but journalist, and that both personalities must find expression. There is a certain disingenuousness in this answer, of which Zola himself may not have been fully conscious, for it implied that the artist expressed himself in the novels, the journalist in pamphlets and articles. Zola had learnt the value of publicity from his early career as a shock leaderwriter, and he never ceased to use such shock methods to force his work on the public. But it was not only by publicity that the Rougon-Macquart novels were turned into best-sellers and their author into a very rich man. Readers might have been brought to the novels by preparatory newspaper articles, correspondence and prearranged controversy, they would not have been

From *Emile Zola: An Introductory Study of His Novels.* © 1952 by Angus Wilson.

persuaded to stay. Then, as now, the average reader wanted a saccharine, a sugar-cake world; it could only be by bludgeoning and violence that he would be persuaded to assist at a black mass in which his sacred bourgeois creeds were recited backwards, his angels of virtue revealed as seven deadly sins, and the very Host of his self-esteem was spat upon. The strength of the greatest Rougon-Macquart novels lay in exactly this kind of assault and battery; an attack, planned with the greatest care and conscientious artistry by a writer whose devotion to the creed of art for art's sake was by no means lip service, and carried out by a journalist of genius, who frequently failed to see that his literary devices were stale and obvious, but whose force of expression was great enough to prevent the reader from seeing it too. Though artist and journalist were frequently at loggerheads, in the earlier novels, they gradually learnt to work together to form a novelist who was unique.

The optimistic, cocksure bourgeois world of the 'forties and 'fifties was giving way to fin-de-siècle, melancholy and ennui; all but the most obtuse felt the rotten boards creak beneath their feet, saw the scaffolding tremble above their heads. Zola, in his luxury and success, was seldom unconscious of these rumblings and groanings, and by his art, his force, his hatred, compassion and vulgarity, he drove the public to pile up his fortune as they queued to peer at the very hell they had spent most of their lives in avoiding. The peepshows were: cleverly labelled—the Sanctity of the Family, the Honour of the Army, the Virtues of the Poor, the Ideals of the Artist, the Traditions of the Peasantry, the Splendour of the Church, the Soundness of Finance—and in each there lay a putrescent corpse, far more terrible than the skeleton the poor reader had shut away so carefully in the cupboard of his own guarded conscience. Even now, the greatest of the novels— *L'Assommoir*, *La Terre*, *Germinal*—have the quality of nightmares; how much more appalling must they have been for the contemporary reader. And, as from nightmares, there was no means of escape. Each world of horror was air-tight, a little cell, like that where Coupeau danced his delirium tremens, carefully secured and locked, carefully padded but not too much; Zola the artist saw to that. After the victim had come out, of course, he would cry triumphantly 'Life isn't like that. Realism, indeed! Why, no peasant talks like that. Spontaneous combustion, insanity, haemophilia all in one chapter, ridiculous! Five deaths from drink in one novel, absurd!' But he would always remember that it was real while it lasted, and that somewhere inside himself there was a twin horror which had been exposed. If there were moments when Zola the artist failed to convince, when the detail was too careful, when a chink of sunlight crept into the black room, then before the reader could stir himself, wake and declare that he knew it hadn't happened, Zola the journalist was ready with a truncheon, some vast episode of peculiar force or horror, to bludgeon him into submission—Françoise making her way past the endless sea of ripe, golden corn, beneath the baking sun of *La Terre*, suddenly and brutally assaulted by Buteau, less brutally, less completely by Jean—the reader's credulity wavers. The atmosphere, the scene, the growing lust of the men, Zola the artist has built these up with complete surety, but two rapes in the afternoon? No we can't quite take that. All right, says the journalist, what about that cry from the centre of the cornfield—Palmyre, the pathetic cripple girl, the beast of burden, has broken beneath her load, a blood-vessel burst in the glare of the sun, and then, in case the reader is still resisting, the tall, gaunt figure of La Grande, the aged peasant woman, advances and prods the body with her stick, 'Dead', she says, 'well, that's better than a wretched burden on others.' The episode is complete, the life of the peasantry, one feels sure, is like that—hard, mercenary, brutal. 'Il faut avoir la passion,' said Zola, 'un souffle, un et fort, qui emporte le lecteur jusqu'à la fin.'

Zola's whole artistic approach made him particularly fitted to carry out this task. He saw each novel as a separate picture, planned the whole shape in advance as would a painter. We have already said that the Rougon-Macquart series as a whole with its science, its heredity, even its social analysis, was always subordinate to the needs of the individual novels, equally the internal considerations of each novel—characters, events, time, place— were all subject to the demands of the logic of the total book.

From the earliest notes made for the series, it is clear that Zola realized his need to ensure this air-tight quality in his novels if they were to succeed. He affirms his decision to avoid Balzac's methods of presenting more than one group of society in any particular book. It is only in the later books like Paris that the very poor and the very rich are shown together, and it is clear from the unsuccessfully crude contrast, with its obvious moralising flavour, that his earlier decision was, a wise one. His cuts into society were, in general, horizontal, and not vertical. Within these horizontal sections, he planned each succeeding chapter as a separate step in the progressive logic of the whole. His own words describe this method very exactly: 'Instead of the flowing analysis of Balzac, establish fourteen or fifteen powerful masses, within this framework analysis may be made step by step, but always from above. Everybody in the world analyses in detail nowadays, I must react against this through the solid reaction of masses, of chapters, through the logic, the thrust of the chapters, succeeding each other like superimposed blocks; by the breath of passion; animating all, flowing from one end to another of the work.' Logical steps fused into a whole by passion, and by another quality which he does not mention, acute atmospheric sensitivity. A solidly established formal scheme given movement by emotional force and life by shimmering atmosphere—an Impressionist painting of the highest order. It is not 'Naturalism' but impressionistic technique which explains Zola's greatness.

The neurotic obsessions of artists are often a clue to their greatest gifts. We have seen that Zola's acute fears of death reflect the inner theme of his great work. In 1881 and 1882, when the serious nervous tension of his life came nearest to a breakdown, a number of symptoms showed themselves. Delusions of clouds of birds relate probably to the importance of animals in his work, which will be discussed later in this chapter, but there was also revealed a strong obsession with numbers, their relationships, and the good auguries of certain primary numbers and their various multiplications. Such numerical and counting obsessions are familiar pathological features of nervous disorders. A supreme example of their control of a writer almost to the point of insanity is to be found in the work of the Marquis de Sade, and the effect upon his work is direct—each sexual exploit is repeated in a series in which progressive numbers of persons participate until the whole is reduced to a catalogue which can only be regarded as a written version of the repeated touching of objects for luck, one of Freud's examples of the pathology of everyday life. Zola's obsession with numbers was only a distortion of the strong proportional sense which is the underpin of his whole fictional structure. Each character, each aspect, each symbol must be given an exactly related stress in the novel. After reading the preparatory notes for *L'Assommoir*, for example, it becomes apparent that every incident in the book has been prepared and fitted into the frame like the pieces in a jigsaw puzzle. Inevitably, on occasion, this 'made' aspect of the book manifests itself to the reader, for if Zola had great artistic force, he had less artistic taste. But, if the central symbol of the old undertaker and his conversations with Gervaise concerning the comfort of the grave for the poor are too obvious a preparation for the final scenes in which he removes her mouldering, forgotten corpse, there are other aspects of the same careful prearrangement which are so well contrived within the narrative and so swept along by the force of the novel that it would require a very detached reader to detect them. Gervaise, for example, asks no more of life than a small corner in which to lay her bones in old age, the little country retreat of the poor slum-dweller, and the reader is so struck by the pathos of this simple wish, and the actual horror of her decline, that he is unlikely to notice the heightening effect that is given to it by the use of the same language to describe her ultimate pauper's grave. An obvious, theatrical trick, one would suppose, but it succeeds. Again the horror of Gervaise's death is led up to by those other deaths of the poor—Maman Coupeau and Papa Bru. The little note of gaiety in Gervaise's character in the days of the laundry's success which is shown in her simple power to amuse by imitation is to have horror in its sequence when she earns a drink or two by mimicking her husband in the padded cell. Coupeau's fear of drink, because his father, also a builder, had fallen to his death when drunk, is strangely fulfilled in reverse when his own fall leads to a convalescence that turns him into a drunkard. The two great humorous scenes in a novel full of a terrible ironic humour are neatly balanced in detail—the wedding feast and the feast of Nana's first communion. Though the whirring of the mechanism still distracts us on occasion in *L'Assommoir*, in *Germinal* and the later great novels it has been reduced to a ticking which enhances the reality of the atmosphere on which it has ceased to obtrude.

If the nervous undercurrent in Zola's life was made manifest spasmodically by mental obsessions and delusions, it was evidenced throughout his life by a physical hyperaesthesia which, like his obsession with numbers, is another great cornerstone of his creative powers. He saw, heard and, above all, smelt his surroundings more intensely than the normal person. To judge from his work we would suspect it was many years before this excess of physical sensitivity was integrated with the rest of his personality. It was responsible for the development within him of a poet— not the derivative, Romantic imitator of his youth, but a poet whose detailed powers of natural description allied him more to the Parnassian school, and who converted the natural phenomena he felt so intensely into images and shapes that finally give this side of his work a close link with the Symbolists. But the first emergence of this poetry in his novels, for example the famous descriptions of the food shops in *Le Ventre de Paris*, 1873, of which the symphony of the cheeses became notorious, was in the form of interspersed, lyrical passages of considerable power but quite unintegrated into the body of the novel. He attempted to overcome this technical difficulty by relating each 'food poem' to a particular character in the book, but the device is clumsy and did not solve the problem any better than the relation of the famous descriptions of hot-houses and aquaria which accompany the various steps of Renée's affaire with Maxime in *La Curée* (1872). These interpolated, ornate prose poems, repeated in the description of Paris in *Une Page d'Amour* (1878), look forward to work like Huysmans' *A Rebours*. Zola was to develop a means of using his poetry which was a far more remarkable technical achievement.

There was, it would seem, at the outset of his career, a barrier between the general, acute observation which went into the ordinary 'Realistic' narrative of his novels, and the more immediate violent accesses of aesthetic reaction which found their expression in the prose poem passages. The first was always informed with intellectual control, checked by carefully collected observations from outside sources, subordinate to the narrative and the formal demands of the novels. The second was a more powerful, concentrated, almost intuitive observation, which, however apparently disconnected with the surface theme of the novel in hand, had for Zola a deeper, more subconscious relation to it. Certain sounds, smells, sights would strike a response in him which made them a total pictorial symbol of the general theme on which he was engaged. This aspect of Zola's creative ability may perhaps be best compared with the active discipline of memory which Proust in his 'madeleine' passages makes the basis of artistic creation: It was not with Zola, of course, a conscious process, and in any case was less reminiscent than immediate. Proust, with his natural distaste for the dogma of Naturalism, seems never to have seen the extent to which his most cherished gift was shared by Zola; like so many critics who were misled by the stated Naturalist creed of Zola's school, he saw only a pedantic and ridiculous subordination to realism. If Zola had been forced to rely upon the more intellectually controlled observation which was the basis of the main narrative of his works, he would have been no more than such critics declared him, an academical realist painter, a sort of lesser Courbet. This is the competent level which he reached in some of his early novels—*La Fortune des Rougon*, *La Conquête de Plassans*—in which the influence of Balzac is less assimilated, the likeness to minor, realistic writers like Champfleury most marked. But the great lyrical descriptions of *La Curée* and *Le Ventre de Paris* already pointed to a wider, more original achievement, and by hard work and discipline he achieved the fusion of the surface and deep levels of observation which made him the great 'black poet' of *La Terre*, the great impressionistic realistic novelist of *Germinal* and *La Débâcle*, the Manet of despair.

The first steps towards this fusion can be seen in the publication of the first of his idyllic novels, *La Faute de l'Abbé Mouret* (1875). In this near fantasy of the young priest Serge Mouret's natural, Rousseauesque love idyll in the ruined garden, Zola attempted a whole novel drawn from his 'poetic' side. Effective though much of it is, the strain placed upon the fancy, the violent momentary imagination, by sustaining it at such length, was too great. Much of the book seems forced and laboured, nor was he to attempt such a thing again except in the short failure *Le Rêve*. But in order to give shape to the Abbé's tragic story he was forced to fill it in with a picture of village life that was drawn from his more immediate powers of observation. The possibility of fusion realized, the gates were opened that could let the fairy Ninon into the black, sterile world of the Rougon-Macquarts. The result of this union was the first of his great novels, *L'Assommoir* (1877).

In this, in many ways the most brutal of his works, the poetry has been diffused over the whole in symbol, humour, above all in the creation of a special language which fills the story of Gervaise with a peculiar fanciful character,[1] and yet seems only to heighten the realistic horror of the theme. The language spoken by his Parisian slum-dwellers was criticized then and since on the grounds that it was long since out of date and even then inexact. This justifiable charge was partly due to the naïve academicism which allowed Zola quite contentedly to take 'life' from dictionaries and textbooks. But the charge is really irrelevant, for however outdated the argot Zola so transforms it and weaves it into the book that it flows over from the speech of the characters, into his own narration. This, perhaps, was excessive, and he did not attempt it again, but in this general fusion of his poetry, by symbol, humour and language he had found the colour with which to paint his great impressionist canvases. Each of the great novels was to have its own groups of words, partly symbolic, partly colouring, which recur in ever-changing patterns and varying intensity, like the dominating hues of a Monet or a Whistler.

This desire to give a predominating colour to each novel had, however, a certain danger. It encouraged the rather naïve academicism which has already been noticed. Zola's conscious adherence to realism, though fortunately swept on one side by the unconscious force of his creative needs, made him preternaturally anxious concerning correct detail, and his inferiority feelings about his education increased this desire to be scholarly and exact. Zola down the mines, in the fishmarket, riding with the engine driver, talking to retired tarts, writing notes on his cuff at bankers' receptions, the whole character of the militant Naturalist on the warpath, according to the Goncourt receipt, is a well-known figure. In part, it belonged to his somewhat ill-judged publicity campaigns, but in part it was his genuine method of approach to his material. As the notebooks show, only a small proportion of the vast information he amassed was used, but even so, it often stuck together like indigestible, undercooked lumps in a pudding, obstructing the easy flow of the narrative, upsetting the careful proportions of the form. This was particularly common with details derived from books or Government reports, for which Zola had especial reverence. The description of the goldsmith's work and of the forge in *L'Assommoir* are examples, as are medical details of anaemia in *Une Page d'Amour*, the information about seaweed in *La Joie de Vivre* and almost the whole of the organization of Paris finance in *L'Argent*.

More satisfactory, but still often insufficiently assimilated, were the symbols frequently drawn from the animal world which are used to generalize the narrative. The fat satisfaction of Mouton, the ginger cat of *Le Ventre de Paris*, the continual frustrated maternalism of Manouche, the cat of *La Joie de Vivre*, the strange life of the pit ponies in *Germinal*, the mating of the cattle and the birth of the calves in *La Terre*, are examples of this means by which Zola reached towards and eventually attained a content within his novels over and above, indeed eventually more important than the history of the personages who appear in their pages.

The whole history of the Rougon-Macquart is the development of a detailed, realistic canvas into a statement of a mood, an atmosphere of a certain place and time within the same limited confines. It is as though Frith's 'Derby Day' broke and dissolved into a vast pattern of colour, sound and movement like some gigantic peopled Monet. Zola's earlier novels, however, for all their detail and precision, are never static like the realism of Frith, his later panoramas never totally abstracted, sheer moods like Monet's scenes. Some critics, indeed, objected to the obtrusion of an individual character in such novels of mass movement as *Germinal* and *La Débâcle*. The crowd is the hero of such epics, they declared, and the formal narrative of individual lives only dissipates their force. But for Zola the crowd and the leading personages were one and the same, each was needed as the expression of the other. He could not even make the division into chorus and characters that Hardy did, though there is a great similarity between such profound melodramas as *La Terre*, *The Return of the Native*, *Germinal* and *Far from the Madding Crowd*. He was largely conscious of this movement of the focal point from individuals to groups, groups to institutions, institutions to the mass and the army, but he knew that the strength of his work lay in the pouring of huge vats of new material into the frames he had moulded so carefully and so long. Such changes of shape as were needed would come from the sheer force of the impact, not from a destruction of the old forms or a conscious search for outlines in which to encase an ocean.

Changes of shape were, however, constantly battered out as the great wave of new ideas—institutional cross currents of jealousy, mob anxieties and hopes, the strange intuitive telegraphy and the hysteria of speculators or armies—poured in. But however overwhelming the flow, Zola still saw his work as single pictures, and it was this formal discipline that gave his vast conceptions their artistic supremacy.

The wider the field and the louder the vibration of the mass overtones to his individual themes, the more strict the limits he imposed upon his picture. It is not surprising that he hankered after success as a playwright, for it was exactly the theatre's conventional limits of time and place, its external observation of character, its customary climaxes that were the source of his success. The author of *La Joie de Vivre* or *La Bête Humaine* might well have expected to do the work of Ibsen, but he could only have achieved such success by continuous development of his symbolism and such development could only have been at the expense of his unique verbal impressionism. It has been said more than once that Zola's great novels are the forerunners of the epic cinema—of D. W. Griffiths, of Jean Duvivier or of Pabst—but excellent films though many of them would make, such a view ignores the fact that Zola's greatness lies in his use of words. He was a pictorial artist, but to say that his world would be better represented by the camera is the result of an age-old confusion of means and results in the arts.

His inclination towards unity of time and place within individual novels is almost as marked as the homogeneity of tone and language by which he built up the atmosphere of each fictional world. He often held to such formal unities against the demand of realism. The natural climax which history contributed to his great series by the fall of the Second Empire in 1870 imposed upon him, in fact, a longer time scheme than he had in fact originally planned. The most striking example of such enforced change, of course, is the setting of Jean Macquart's war adventures in the Franco-Prussian War of 1870 rather than in the Italian campaigns of 1859 and 1860, but many of the other original schemes were equally affected. The treatment of *Nana* for which a dramatic ending was provided by the departure of the army from Paris in 1870 as the courtesan is dying, illustrates Zola's distaste for broken or prolonged time schemes. The death of Nana is in many respects a less successful climax than might be expected. This is partly due to Zola's curious choice of smallpox as the fell disease instead of the obvious syphilis, but it is also the result of the shadowy, unsuccessfully managed disappearance of Nana from the Paris scene for some years before she returns to die. These years of absence are necessary to the realism of the total time scheme as the fall of the Empire dictated it, but the break in continuity seems to have meant a break in Zola's intensity of interest. He naturally preferred a short and compact time scheme for, as in many of the great nineteenth-century novels, his characters, as we shall see later, did not develop.

If the unity of time which he tried to preserve in face of the demands of realism was a handicap, his unity of locality was a source of strength. Only by confining the movements of his characters was he able to build up the overpowering, inescapable atmosphere, the sense of hopeless imprisonment by which he holds the reader. Each class of society, each group of characters is shown within its own district, the very buildings and streets of which seem filled with the clashes of will, the frustrations of lust, the hopeless, creeping decay of the lives within them. For the poor this geographical prison is a symbol not only of their submerged lives but of their ignorance, the isolation to which the prudence of society has consigned them lest their infection should spread. From it they emerge—Gervaise's wedding party wandering round the Louvre, the strikers in the luxurious home of the manager, the peasants visiting the lawyer's office—like medieval voyagers to the land of Prester John, bewitched, awed, suspicious, and finally tired and bewildered. For the middle classes the locality is often, and purposely, I think, even narrower. It is the prison of the home—fat, prosperous, self-satisfied and treacherous like the well-filled shops of *Le Ventre de Paris*, stifling, priest-ridden, threatened by the undercurrents of hysteria and insanity, like the house of François Mouret in *La Conquête de Plassans*, rent with close-quartered hatreds and infidelities like the apartments of *Pot-Bouille*, or sunk in the muds of despair and melancholy like the Tchechovian home of *La Joie de Vivre*. The hopeless idylls of *La Faute de l'Abbé Mouret* and *Une Page d'Amour* do not leave the confines of their forbidden gardens. Even the rich suffocate in their overfurnished, overheated rooms as Renée and Maxime are overpowered by the force of their incestuous passion bred of ennui. Only in *L'Argent*, one of the last of the Rougon-Macquart novels, does Zola forsake his early expressed determination not to move from one section of society to another in the same book. The result is a confusion and a dissipation of energy which make this book, for all its greater cleverness and wider sympathy, one of the weakest of the series. We are already looking forward to that failure in power, bred of a greater liberality of emotion, which will be described in the account of the series *Les Trois Cités* (Chapter VI). Once, however, before the great creative impulse finally died in him, Zola managed to survey a wide scene with something of the intensity of his earlier novels. The army of Napoleon fights and retreats across vast areas of the East of France, but nevertheless *La Débâcle* does not fail to hold the attention as does *L'Argent*, or the post–Rougon-Macquart novels. In fact, the adventures of the broken, disillusioned French army, the final climax of hollow cruel comedy of the Second Empire, are for Zola an extension of the bewildered mood of Gervaise and her fellow revellers as they wander among the treasures of the Louvre and the whole novel is largely sustained on the note of prisoners released for an unhappy moment into a wider world from which they only long to return to their prison that has now fallen in pieces behind them.

If Zola's presentation of time and place supplies some key to the compulsion of his novels, his treatment of character gives the final answer. Zola was intensely interested in the physiological, medical approach to the human personality which the science of his youth propounded; one may well believe that the theories of Jeannet or Bergson would have attracted him as much as they did Proust, or that the views of Freud would have dominated him as they have later novelists. It is, however, very difficult to imagine a Freudian Zola, far more difficult to conceive a Freudian Flaubert or Tolstoy, let alone a Freudian George Eliot, Dostoevsky or Stendhal. As we have already noted, Zola began, like Dickens or Balzac, with characters that were largely humours. If he developed them, it was not by the enlargement of intellectual or emotional sympathy as George Eliot did, but by the unconscious infusion of his own personality into them. The Impressionist approach which he used could have led to a development of the interior monologue, as it did for Tolstoy, or to the tracking of memory as it did for Proust, but Zola's impressionism remained entirely fictional and external. Only one aspect of personal psychology really interested him deeply—the human will. It was probably this interest that attracted him to the works of Stendhal, at that time a neglected writer, and it is this interest that is predominant in his two 'psychological' horror stories, *Thérèse Raquin* and its later counterpart *La Bête Humaine*.

For the rest, character was for him merely a part of the general statement of his novels. Starting with a Balzacian realist approach, which was never entirely happy, he developed his humours in two directions; the central characters tended to be hardened into symbols, the others dissolved into 'humanity', crowds, groups. The family chronicle in the hands of most writers has tended to become a series of novels dominated by certain characters; indeed, the weakness of the later novels of many such family chronicles is that they are vehicles for developing some individuals with whom the author has become obsessed, addenda on Soames Forsyte, the Thibault father or Judith Herries, which are without shape as individual works of art. For Zola such an obsession, usually the mark of second-rate writers, was an impossibility. The simple 'humour' might gain force and energy as a symbol as Nana dominates her world, otherwise there can only be multiplication of characters to fill out the theme of the novel. Such a treatment of character is, of course, most successful where the world is a simple one, and it is for this reason that Zola's novels on the poor are his greatest. There are no more characters in *Pot-Bouille* than in *Germinal* or in *Son Excellence Eugene Rougon* than in *La Terre*, but the middle class and ruling class worlds demand a sophistication of character which, if it is granted, confuses, and if it is not, fails to convince.

Central characters exist in all his novels, but they are a convention like the much advertised tenets of naturalism which he only supported one moment to deny the next. The approach to the scene is always external, and if that external viewpoint is sometimes for the sake of convenience labelled Gervaise or Étienne, the scenes in which they are present merge happily and easily into those in which they are not: the observer is always Zola's five senses. The characters grow in number and in intensity, but never in intricacy, until, at last, in *La Débâcle*, they have dissipated into a vast, bewildered nation, through which move two moods, or symbols—despair labelled Maurice, and solid French character in whom the future lies—Jean Macquart. It was only when the long-planned series was ended and the long-sustained impulse flagged, that a dominating character appears—Abbé Froment of the trilogy—and with this domination of personal beliefs and anxieties comes a dissipation of energy which is marked by repetition, moralizing and ill-digested theory.

NOTE

1. It may be compared to the masterly language invented by Dickens for such characters as Mrs. Gamp.

F . W . J .   H E M M I N G S

Cry from the Pit

La joie de vivre, was published in February 1884. On 2 April Zola began writing *Germinal*. He finished it on 23 January of the following year.

Almost since its first appearance, *Germinal* has been considered by the bulk of critical opinion everywhere as probably the most important single contribution Zola made to literature. In his own country it does not seem to have been the most sought after of his novels: Charpentier's catalogues in the year of Zola's death and twenty-five years later show that at both dates *Germinal* comes only sixth in order of popularity, after *Nana*, *La Terre*, *La Débâcle*, *L'Assommoir*, and *Lourdes*;[1] but Gide's choice of it for inclusion in the 'Dix Meilleurs Romans Français' series brought out a few years ago, and the fact that, until very recently, it was the only novel of Zola's in translation which was kept in print in this country—these are some indications of the peculiar esteem it has won. No critic drawing up his 'short list' of the books of Zola he would recommend, however short he may make it, will omit *Germinal*. For Henry James, the 'productions in which [Zola] must most survive' are *L'Assommoir*, *Germinal*, and *La Débâcle*; Denis Saurat, with characteristic trenchancy, dismisses everything save *Germinal* and *La Débâcle*; while Havelock Ellis suggests that *Germinal* 'begins to seem the only book of his that in the end may survive'.[2]

Whether *Germinal* should be placed on a lonely pinnacle of excellence, or whether it should share this eminence with two, three, or more

From *Émile Zola*. © 1953 by F.W.J. Hemmings.

masterpieces is not, perhaps, a question that need greatly concern us. But as we continue to consider Zola's literary career in terms of a gradual perfecting of the realist formula, we are bound to place *Germinal* in a class by itself. Here, the impersonal treatment of the theme is unexceptional: Flaubert's principle, *faire et se taire*, was observed to the letter, as it had already been in *L'Assommoir*. But between *L'Assommoir* and *Germinal* the balance tips slightly in favour of the second book. There is, in *L'Assommoir*, a certain chilliness in the relentless march to catastrophe, which in *Germinal* is dissipated by the heat of dramatic friction. Gervaise has to fight her losing battle in desperate isolation and against forces many times too strong for her; Étienne and the miners at least have the comfort of fellowship and the strength of their numbers, and they do not succumb without inflicting terrible damage on their adversary: their defeat, moreover, is anything but irrevocable. The generous fervour and the final—if deceptive—surge of optimism in *Germinal* humanize the austerely dispassionate handling of the subject.

In the compositional technique adopted, *Germinal* differs altogether from *L'Assommoir* and, in fact, from all previous novels Zola had written. For the first time he employed a method of presentation which Balzac, notably, had favoured but which was not practised by Zola's other model, Flaubert. This method involves the use of an extremely lengthy prologue, filling at least a quarter of the novel, in order to develop the desired atmosphere for the subsequent dramatic action. The most frequently quoted instance, in Balzac, is *Eugénie Grandet*, a novel with probably no other analogies with *Germinal*. The description of the miser's house and family circle at Saumur, and the account of the disturbance set up by the arrival of Grandet's nephew from Paris, take up rather more than half the entire book. This prologue covers the events of a little less than twenty-four hours; the story proper that follows extends over some ten years or more.

The more traditional or conventional type of novel can be represented as travelling steadily and without much resistance down the stream of time. *Le Rouge et le Noir* or *Madame Bovary* or *War and Peace* could be taken as examples of this method, which we can regard as the normal one. *L'Assommoir* belongs to the same class: along the course of Gervaise's life certain distinct points are selected by the author, who focuses our attention on them for the space of a chapter or less; but the impression of the unhurried and uninterrupted progress of time never leaves us. In *Eugénie Grandet*, on the other hand, and in many other novels of *La Comédie humaine*, interest is heaped up mountain-high at the beginning, and thereafter the author, as it were, needs merely to send his reader careering down the slope he has artificially raised. Balzac puts a brake on time at the outset, and we watch characters who are new to us gesturing, speaking, and acting with preternatural slowness; then, suddenly, he releases the spring: the clock-hands revolve at their ordinary speed, then, accelerating as though they had accumulated momentum while he held them in check, the days, the months, and the years start flitting past at an ever-increasing rate.

This is not quite what Zola did in *Germinal*; *Eugénie Grandet* remains the classic instance of this kind of artificial manipulation of time. But one cannot fail to notice the immense industry with which in his first ten chapters (there are thirty-six in all) Zola piles up a huge pyramid of characters and atmosphere. These ten chapters cover the twenty-four hours between the arrival of Étienne Lantier in the mining district and the end of his first day's work underground. Then, halfway through the eleventh chapter, a paragraph opens with the words: 'The next day, and the following days, Étienne resumed work in the pit ...'. The next paragraph begins: 'And day followed day, weeks, months passed by ...'.

Externally, there is no difference between the form of *Germinal* and that of a characteristic novel by Balzac; but each writer had a different purpose in adopting this form. Balzac needs time, in his exposition, in order to paint the back-cloth against which his drama is to evolve; without the rich and sombre colouring he uses, the plot (in the case of *Eugénie Grandet* particularly) would seem petty, a domestic tussle of no special account. But in *Germinal* the drama needed no such setting off; it was moving enough in its own right. The function of the first ten chapters is simply to accumulate the mass of impressions needed for the creation of a setting so far removed from the ordinary as to be almost otherworldly. Zola passes from one point to another in the grimy landscape and in the hot, damp galleries of the mines, registering wherever he goes brief visions of miners' cottages seen from outside and inside, introducing us into one where a family of nine is shown sleeping in one bedroom and on the landing outside, waking at four in the morning, dressing hastily and breakfasting meagrely; of other cottages emptying as men and girls, almost indistinguishable in their identical costume, tramp off to work; of the pithead in the half-light of dawn, a 'hall vast as a cathedral nave, dimly lit and peopled by large, floating shadows', noisy with the rumble of trollies full of fresh-hewn coal; of cage-load after cage-load of workers dropping plumb into the depths of the earth under a continual patter of water oozing from an underground lake; of gangs of workers toiling at the seam in semi-darkness, stripped almost naked because of the heat 'spectral forms' lit by an occasional lamp, which shone on 'the curve of an axe, a stringy arm, a fierce-looking head bedaubed as though for a crime'; of the soft hiss and cobwebby smell of fire-damp. Then, returning to the surface and to daylight, we are shown 'the sky earth-coloured, the walls sticky with a greenish moisture, the roads covered with clammy mud, a mud peculiar to coal-mining areas, black with soot in suspension, thick and so sticky that clogs came off in it'; the bridle-path alongside a canal, 'in the midst of plots of waste land, enclosed by moss-covered fences'; more roads with, on either side, 'little brick houses, daubed with paint to brighten the scene, some yellow, some blue, some black, the last no doubt to waste no time in coming to the ultimate, inevitable black', an occasional brick church, like 'a new type of blast-furnace, with its square belfry, soiled already by the floating coal-dust', and, above all, taverns and beer-shops, 'so many that for a thousand houses there were more than five hundred taverns'; and finally, in the evening, the 'soup', the baths in the cottages, the miners gardening, chatting, or drinking, the children at play, the adolescents strolling in couples or mating in the waste ground round a disused mine.

When he has reached the end of this prologue, the reader has the impression of being completely enveloped by the atmosphere, of being himself a denizen of this narrow world. With a little imagination he finds himself breathing the air laden with coal-dust, feeling on his shins and shoulders the sore places rubbed by the jutting pieces of schist, experiencing the nausea of hard physical labour on inadequate rations. There is remarkably little plain description in all this: Zola has progressed since *Le Ventre de Paris* and *La Faute de l'Abbé Mouret*. Everything is shown as seen and felt by one character or another; dozens are introduced, though it is principally through Étienne's observations that the mosaic is built up—since he is new to the mines, his impressions are more acute and more varied. Descriptive writing gives place to the technique of accumulating scores of minor incidents which merge into a general picture of 'a corner of nature'.

In the remaining parts of the book, the single dramatic conflict between the strikers and the management predominates. On two occasions it rises to a climax: the first, when a mob of starvelings spreads havoc over the countryside, smashing machinery and taking murderous vengeance on blacklegs and enemies like the grocer who had refused them credit; the second, when, several weeks later, they try to prevent a Belgian labour force from going down the pits, and clash bloodily with the military. There is one crowning catastrophe at the end, when an act of sabotage causes the pits to flood after the beaten strikers have resumed work. In the intervals between these three major incidents, Zola shows the gradual sinking of the miners' hopes, their bickerings among themselves, the hunger and cold they endure, the whole siege of misery, in a succession of brief but significant episodes.

The form of *L'Assommoir*, as we have seen, could be illustrated by a curved line, rising to a zenith and then sinking again; but *Germinal* has more than one dimension: it has to be described in terms of cubic capacity, of the balance of weights and counterweights. In *Germinal* Zola constructs, where before he had simply painted.

IN ANOTHER respect *Germinal* may be thought superior to *L'Assommoir*. The merit of a work of art may up to a point be measured by the artist's skill in solving the difficulties set him by his subject. In a sense *L'Assommoir* and *Germinal* deal with the same subject, or at any rate with the same problem— that of social injustice; and for a writer with even the dullest social conscience, the temptation to extract from that theme a momentarily successful but ephemeral *roman à thèse* is almost irresistible. In *L'Assommoir*, as we have seen, the danger was met by suppressing the factor of social strife; in *Germinal*, however, Zola had the courage to give this factor full weight. In his preliminary notes,[3] he defined his novel as 'the struggle between capital and labour', adding that this question was 'the most important one the twentieth century will have to face'. Both the helots and their lords would be given equal place in the economy of the work, and none of the horrors of the class war would be glossed over. Zola's secret for preserving impartiality was to absolve both parties in the conflict from guilt: the root of the evil was to be left buried, and the author would refuse to point to scapegoats or to venture into any specific dialectical analysis of the situation.

> In order to obtain a strong effect, I must make the cleavages plain and sharpen them to the maximum intensity possible. So, to begin with, all the sufferings, all the fatalities that weigh on the collier. This must be done by producing facts, without pleading a cause. He must be shown crushed, underfed, ill-educated, suffering in his offspring, sunk in a veritable inferno; and yet no persecution, no deliberate wickedness on the part of the bosses— he is simply crushed by the social system itself. On the contrary, the bosses must be shown to be humane so long as their interests are not threatened; I must not be trapped into making foolish demands for reform (*ne pas tomber dans la revendication bête*)....

Thus everything must follow on logically, starting from little factual details, from the original unhappiness and suffering, the cause of which is universal, and traceable to the unknown social factor, the god Capital, crouching in its temple like a fat, glutted beast, monstrous in satiety; all that taking place not by the desire of the masters that I show on the stage, but arising from a state of affairs beyond their control and determined by the age.

THE 'GOD CAPITAL' alluded to here in these preliminary notes is more than a passing figure of speech. The embodiment of everything that Zola preferred, for reasons of art, to leave unexplained, it is introduced into the narrative whenever too sharp a diagnosis of social ills seems to threaten. In the first chapter Étienne Lantier, who has wandered into the mining district in search of work, is shown in conversation with Bonnemort, a veteran of the mines, the eldest member of the Maheu family who have worked underground, father and son, mother and daughter, ever since extraction began in the area. Étienne has asked him who owns the pits.

> 'Eh? who owns it all? ... Couldn't say. Lots of people.'
> And, with a wave of his hand, he indicated an indistinct point in the darkness, an unknown, distant spot, where those people lived for whom the Maheus had been hewing at the seam for over a century. His voice had dropped into a tone of religious awe, as if he had spoken of an inaccessible tabernacle, where squatted the gorged and hidden god to whom they all sacrificed their flesh and whom they had never seen.

This modern Moloch is a true symbol, an abstraction having the force of a natural law but made more terrible by the tangible image of it Zola offers to our imagination. He invokes it as an impenetrable First Cause, deaf to supplication and unamenable to reason. It looms up again during the miners' interview with Hennebeau, the manager, when they ask him if it would not be possible to make their grievances known in person, instead of having to transmit them through him.

> M. Hennebeau kept his temper. A smile even passed over his face. 'Ah! well now, things get complicated, if you don't trust me ... You would have to go yonder.'
> The delegates had followed the vague motion of his hand, pointing to one of the windows. What did he mean—yonder? Paris, they supposed. But they were not quite certain, it backed away into a terrifying distance, into an inaccessible, sacred country where the unknown god sat enthroned, crouching at the back of his tabernacle. They would never see him, they felt him only as a power bearing from afar on the ten thousand coalminers

of Montsou. And when the manager spoke, this was the power he had behind him, occult and delivering oracles.

This power is no more consciously malevolent than that which, in *Au Bonheur des Dames*, causes the ruin of the small shopkeepers driven out of business by the competition of the big modern store created by Octave Mouret. 'The Company does not control the level of wages', Hennebeau reminds the delegates; 'it bows to the law of competition, else it would be ruined. Blame the facts, not the Company.' Mouret uses the same argument to Denise, after he has reduced her uncle Baudu to bankruptcy: Baudu was doomed from the start and he, Mouret, was only an agent of the power—the power of economic progress—which has crushed him. Mouret needed to ruin Baudu in order to make the profits which permitted him to enlarge and brighten his premises, satisfy the shoppers with a wider and cheaper range of goods, and house his employees more comfortably. The greater well-being of the many is secured at the cost of pauperizing a few: 'this manure of misery was necessary for the well-being of the Paris of the future.... Some blood had to be spilt, every revolution demanded its martyrs, each step forward had to be made over dead bodies.' The conclusion here quoted is Denise's: Mouret's rhetoric has prevailed over her compassion.

In both *Au Bonheur des Dames* and *Germinal* (and later, in *La Terre* also) the dilemma is the same: the path of free competition is the path of progress; but, since competition is simply the right of the stronger to devour the weaker, there will be stretched by the wayside the bodies of many an innocent victim. In *Au Bonheur des Dames* Zola was able to endorse this process, at least for its ends if not for its means; but when, turning from a purely internal struggle within the commercial class, he looked at the major clash between the possessors and the dispossessed, his complacency was shattered.

A FEW WEEKS before he began writing *Germinal*, on 21 February 1884, a strike broke out at Anzin, one of the biggest collieries in the north of France. Thanks to the protection of Alfred Giard, a radical deputy, Zola was able to visit the district and mingle with the strikers. He saw for himself the conditions in which they worked underground and in which they were housed on the surface; he was able to observe the stigmata of malnutrition and of occupational diseases, and the stunting of their spirit by the ugliness of the surroundings in which they lived. The victims were not a handful of impoverished shopkeepers, but an entire population. Moreover, this was no passing crisis, these were not the growing-pains of a new social order; such things were inherent in the economic order as it existed, and as it would continue to exist unless and until it was deliberately, and perhaps violently, altered.

Yet Zola was quite honest, and even accurate, in declaring as he did that 'Germinal is a work of compassion, not a revolutionary work'.[4] It escapes being revolutionary, however, only by a hair's breadth. There are occasions when the phantom of revolutionary purpose is starkly apparent. When Hennebeau speaks the words quoted a page or two back: 'Blame the facts, not the Company', adding impatiently: 'But you won't listen to me, you won't try to understand', Étienne, a member of the delegation, answers him:

> Yes, we understand quite well that there can be no possible improvement for us, so long as matters continue the way they are, and it is just for that very reason that the workers will see to it, one of these days, that they are changed.

However, such threatening asides are exceptional, and no more permit us to call Germinal a seditious work than certain voluptuous scenes in Nana would justify us in calling Nana a salacious work. It was not in Zola to write a book preaching revolution: not altogether because he was temperamentally averse to revolutionary violence; nor even because, as a Marxist critic like Lukács will suggest, he was by the circumstances of his class origins opposed to revolutionary change; but chiefly because to admit the feasibility of progress through revolution would have meant repudiating his faith in the evolutionary interpretation of social growth borrowed from Darwinism. He preferred, as he would continue all his life to prefer, 'a "scientific" method in which society is conceived as a harmonious entity and the criticism applied to society formulated as a struggle against the diseases attacking its organic unity, a struggle against the "undesirable features" of capitalism'.[5]

But the social injustice he recorded in Germinal was so monstrous, and seemed so immovably lodged in the social system, that it was only by omitting all discussion of causes and remedies that Zola succeeded in keeping up appearances as an impartial social chronicler. He could not dream of disguising the need for social reform: Germinal was an urgent warning to laissez-faire economists who blinked this need; but he was equally anxious not to seem to side with socialists of any description who proposed to substitute a new economic order which would be immune from the abuses of the old. His method was to remove the whole problem from the realm of economic argument and treat it in its human aspect alone.

The mining community he observed at Anzin and depicted in *Germinal* is a race of men and women deformed in body and soul by the controlling conditions of their lives. They inherit a debilitated physique from many generations of underground workers, all starved and stunted. Untaught, they are in consequence brutal, sensual, sometimes vicious or criminal; housed in one-bedroom cottages, made to work together in the mines without distinction of sex,[6] they are almost inevitably promiscuous in their habits; having no fate to fear worse than the life they habitually lead, they plunge into frenzied violence when their situation becomes unendurable. Deneulin, a small colliery-owner brought to ruin by the rioting miners who wreck his machinery, cannot find any hatred in his heart for the saboteurs: 'he was conscious of the complicity of everyone, of the universal, age-long fault. Brutes they may have been, but brutes illiterate and dying of hunger.'

It is a miracle that in such a fetid atmosphere some human virtues survive—that Maheu, for instance, on a rare occasion when his wife has been able to afford a piece of meat, scolds her for not giving the younger children their share, and sits them on his knees to feed them; that Chaval, the brutal and tyrannical lover of Catherine Maheu, comes to her rescue when she swoons in an overheated gallery, and finds kind words of sympathy to encourage her when she recovers; that Zéphyrin, never greatly attached to his sister, works like a demon to deliver her when she is trapped in the flooded pit, and is killed by an explosion of fire-damp brought about by his reckless haste. The miner is not flattered, and certainly he is no hero. He is the product, quite simply, of a degrading environment which smothers in him all except the most elementary social instincts.

But though not heroic in any moral sense, the miner is undeniably the true hero in the literary acceptance of the word. He is depicted in representative types—four or five of them have just been named, and there are a dozen more in the book—but above all he is presented in the mass. This method was an innovation, and one which Zola found so suited to his genius that he brought it into regular use in subsequent novels—notably in *La Débâcle, Lourdes, Paris, Travail*, and *Vérité*. Towards the end of his life it became a recognized cliché that 'the crowd was often his unique, and always his favourite, character', or even that 'the crowd was his hero, in whom he placed all the hope, all the warmth of enthusiasm that he refused to the individual'.[7] Both these observations overstate the case.

Crowd-scenes had been attempted in the earlier novels—in *La Fortune des Rougon*, for instance, and in *Le Ventre de Paris*; *L'Assommoir* opens with a striking panoramic view of the army of workers descending into Paris in the early morning from the slums that ring the city. But not until he wrote

Germinal did it occur to Zola what might be made out of a study of the behaviour of crowds; the book contains a series of instances of the type-phenomena of mass-psychology, as they have been catalogued since by trained investigators. There are crowds bent on amusement (the description of the *ducasse*, the miners' holiday, a scene of open-air jollity); crowds swayed by oratory (the forest meeting of the strikers); crowds enraged and out of control (the march to Jean-Bart, Deneulin's colliery, with its sequel; the clash between the miners and the troops); crowds in a panic (the escape of the blackleg workers from Jean-Bart after the strikers cut the cables). Nearly all these scenes illustrate the truth that Zola intuitively grasped, that people in the aggregate are more ferocious, and yet more cowardly, than each separate component of the group. Singly, his miners are on the whole as decent a lot of men as their circumstances and upbringing will allow them to be; but, like certain radioactive elements, once they are packed together in sufficient quantities a catastrophic qualitative change takes place. Négrel, who knows his workers well, is startled when he sees them pass, three thousand strong, on the road to Montsou, vengeful and furious,

> a compact mass moving in a single block, jammed together in tight-packed disorder, so that it was impossible to distinguish the faded trousers or the ragged woollen pull-overs, blurred in the same earthy uniformity. Their eyes were blazing, nothing could be discerned beyond the black caverns of their mouths singing the *Marseillaise*, its verses lost in a dull roar which was accompanied by the hammering of clogs on the hard earth ...
> 'What frightful faces!' stammered Mme Hennebeau.
> Négrel muttered under his breath:
> 'The devil take me if I can recognize one of them. Where have they sprung from, then, the brigands?' ... Négrel, usually most courageous, felt himself turn pale too, gripped by a terror stronger than his will, one of those terrors that are wafted from the unknown.

It is not only Négrel, in *Germinal*, who recoils before a crowd which has got out of hand. Étienne Lantier who sees the strength the miners possess in their numbers and tries to fashion them into an instrument of political power, learns to his cost how treacherous and unmanageable such an instrument can become. He is an engine-man who has lost his job on the railways for an act of insubordination and only by chance becomes a miner. In making him the ringleader of the strike, Zola took account of the secular passivity and resignation of the Flemish miner. It was not from their ranks that the firebrand was to be taken; their natural leader, ousted by Étienne, is the innkeeper Rasseneur, whose cautious policy aims at the progressive betterment of conditions by mutual agreement between workers and owners.[8]

The stages in Étienne's political education constitute a study of considerable psychological interest, and one which implies, besides, a formidable indictment of revolutionary activity.

The first lessons are received in the shape of a kind of correspondence course in socialism provided by Pluchart, his foreman at Lille, now a propagandist for the (First) International. Encouraged by Pluchart's letters, Étienne begins to read; and 'a stock of obscure ideas, lying dormant inside him, started to stir and unfold'. Zola attributes his thirst for knowledge not so much to the desire to find solutions to the problems that puzzle him as to the humiliation of knowing himself to be uninstructed. So he studies whatever comes to his hand, pamphlets, newspapers, technical treatises, 'with the unmethodical zeal of the ignorant intoxicated by knowledge'—in precisely the same way (the resemblance is not pointed out by Zola and may not have occurred to him) as his distant relative Silvère Mouret, whose fervour for the popular cause was narrated, with its tragical consequences, in *La Fortune des Rougon*.

The Maheu family provides him with an admiring and uncritical audience for his half-baked utopianism, and the next phase in his political evolution occurs when he realizes the power that his ideas, chaotic and contradictory though they still are, exert over his uneducated listeners. For Étienne discovers in himself an unsuspected talent for demagogic oratory.

As the days pass, the circle of his listeners widens; and the respect the colliers pay him swells his vanity and inflames his ambition. The decision to strike is taken largely on his initiative, though a cut in the miners' wages plays into his hands. The privations they endure do not at first weaken their will to resist, nor in any way curtail Étienne's popularity. His self-assurance steadily increases, and his pride is fed continually by the consciousness of power. At this point Zola drops the first hint of what will eventually deprive Étienne of the right to represent his own class: the success he enjoys among his fellows in itself causes him to lose sympathy with them—'he was climbing on to a higher rung, he was entering that detested bourgeoisie through the private gratification of his intelligence and instinctive love of comfort'. It is true that his culminating triumph has still to come, when, in the forest meeting, he defeats the moderate Rasseneur, and has a resolution passed to make the strike general. For the first time he holds a crowd in the palm of his hand, and tastes power 'as it were materialized in these three thousand breasts whose hearts he set beating with a single word'. But the following day's events destroy his illusions. He puts himself at the head of an army of strikers to ensure that the mines still open shall be closed; but the crowd slips out of his control, committing acts of sabotage and vengeance which he had never envisaged or intended. The pride of authority withers, and there remains only a sour distaste for the undisciplined horde which he had believed he could lead into the promised land. After the day's rioting he hides from the police in a disued pit, from which he is in no hurry to escape if it means returning to the village.

> How revolting they were, those wretches living cooped up together, feeding at the communal trough! Not one of them with whom he could discuss politics seriously, all living like cattle, always breathing the same stifling air reeking of the smell of onions! He longed to widen their horizons, lift them to the level of well-being and good breeding of the bourgeoisie by making them the masters; but what a time it would take! and he no longer felt he had the courage to await the victory in this famished convict-prison.

He decides that if he has the chance he will join Pluchart in Paris, 'give up working with his hands and devote himself entirely to political work, but on his own, in a clean room, on the pretext that using one's brains takes up all one's time and requires a great deal of quiet'.

At the end of the book this is what he does, though not before he has experienced to the full the fickleness of the crowd, who turn on him and stone him when the strike is finally broken. His reflections after this incident show the bankruptcy of the demagogue and his fundamental impotence. He had never really been their leader; on the contrary it had always been the pressure of the mob behind that had guided his hand.

> He felt at the end of his tether, he was not even at one with his comrades now, he was frightened of them, of the enormous, blind, irresistible mass of the common people, rushing on like a force of nature, sweeping everything before it, in defiance of rules and theories. Gradually he had become detached from them by his aversion for them, by the malaise of his increasingly refined tastes, by the slow climb of his whole individuality up to a higher social level.

Étienne Lantier, typifying the socialist who rises from the depressed classes, is a failure, in spite of the high hopes with which Zola allows him to depart, 'his education completed ... armed, a rational soldier of the revolution, who had declared war on society such as he saw it and condemned it'. The process is simple: under the compulsion to acquire knowledge so as to fit himself to be the leader of his class, he becomes coated with a thin layer of culture which is sufficient to open his eyes to the brutishness of the starvelings he champions. His gorge rises against them, and though he will continue to fight their cause, this is only because he has identified it with his own personal aspirations. He might well become, in the future, a noted political figure,[9] but like them all, like Eugène Rougon before him, he will find his driving force mainly in the lust for power.

IN SOUVARINE, ZOLA introduced a second and a very different example of the militant socialist. Instead of being, like Étienne, a worker in instinctive revolt, he represents the intellectual *déclassé* of aristocratic origin. He is not intended to enlist our sympathy any more than Étienne.

In many ways Souvarine is a puzzling figure, best accounted for, perhaps, by Zola's wish to stress the explosiveness of the industrial situation. The presence of a Russian anarchist in France under the Second Empire is, for a start, something of an anachronism. Russian political *émigrés* during this period congregated in London or Switzerland for preference, and only after the fall of the Empire came to Paris; in Russia itself, moreover, the political terrorism of the Nihilists did not become widespread until well after 1870. The Russian critic M. K. Kleman, in a study of Zola which deserves translation into a language better known in Zola's own country, has brought to light a number of similarities between Souvarine's career in Russia, as related in *Germinal*, and various outrages committed by Russian terrorists between 1878 and 1881.[10] The presumption is that these details were communicated to Zola by Turgenev, possibly during the *dîners des Cinq*, before and after the death of Flaubert. In the west Turgenev enjoyed the reputation of being exceptionally well informed about the Russian revolutionary movement; his novel *Virgin Soil*, translated into French in 1877, was looked on as a source-book, especially when historical fact came to corroborate his fiction: the assassination, on 24 January 1878, of Trepov, the governor of St. Petersburg, by the woman terrorist Vera Zasulitch appeared to have been prefigured in the history of Turgenev's heroine, Marianne Sinetzkaya.

Turgenev's picture of what he himself had named 'the Nihilist' was adopted unquestioningly by Zola. But this picture was not copied from

Turgenev's fictional heroes (Bazarov in *Fathers and Sons*, Nezhdanov in *Virgin Soil*); it arose out of suggestions made by the Russian author in private conversation. During the last years of his life (he died in 1883) Turgenev was planning a fresh book on the Russian revolutionary movement, which he never had time even to start; his English translator Ralston has, however, left a record of the theme of the book, as Turgenev communicated it to him. Turgenev planned to call attention in his new work to the divergencies he detected between the development of socialism in Russia and in the west, divergencies which were to come dramatically to a head in the quarrel between the Russian, Bakunin, and the German, Marx; ultimately this conflict was to result in the foundation by the latter of the Second International in 1889, some years after Turgenev had died and after the publication of *Germinal*. It seems as though Zola, in *Germinal*, carried out to a small degree Turgenev's intention, by stressing the opposition between the viewpoints of Étienne and Souvarine and attributing this, by implication, to differences in race.

Souvarine is a follower of Bakunin, afire with all the fanatical mysticism which is traditionally credited to the Slav. He backs Étienne in his plans to enrol the miners in the International, believing that Bakunin will be able to make it an instrument of his policy. But this policy, and even more so the methods of implementing it which Souvarine, on occasion, expounds ('a series of frightful crimes must terrorize the rulers and arouse the people'), horrifies the French socialist.

> 'No, no!' Étienne murmured, banishing these abominable visions with a broad wave of his hand. 'We haven't reached that stage, here in this country. Fire and murder, never! It's monstrous, unjust; every worker would rise to strangle the criminal!'
>
> And besides, the idea was not clear to him, the instincts of his race rebelled against this dark dream of the extermination of the world, scythed like a field of rye, leaving nothing but stubble.

It is due to Souvarine that the strike does not end altogether as it might have, with the workers beaten and the Company in a stronger position than ever. At the risk of his life, he descends the ladders and with a saw and a screwdriver weakens the lining of the main shaft so that on the following day (the day when the miners return to work) the water underground sweeps the wooden planks away and floods the entire pit. The earth subsides, all the pithead machinery is engulfed, and a nearby canal breaks its banks and empties into the crater. From a neighbouring hillock Souvarine watches the destruction he has caused, and then,

> throwing away his last cigarette, without casting a single glance backwards, he walked off into the gathering night. Far away, his shadow shrank, merging into the darkness. He was walking into the distance, making for the unknown. With his harmless appearance, he was going to wreak destruction wherever there was dynamite to be had to blow up cities and men. He will be there, no doubt, when the last of the bourgeois hear beneath them, at each step they take, the paving-stones in the streets exploding.

The bomb-throwing Russian terrorist is a figure which Turgenev may have elaborated for Zola, but which it is certain he did not initiate. The Crimean War started when Zola was at the impressionable age of thirteen, and who knows what strange stories of the half-Asian Empire and its inhabitants, retailed in the press of the time or brought back by combatants, were still lurking in his memory from that period? As a schoolboy at Aix he had known a young Russian student at the Faculty of Law, and he never forgot finding in his room a grey-covered pamphlet written in Russian which the student translated for him. It was a treatise on the best way to blow up Paris, compiled by a Russian officer domiciled in France at the end of the eighteenth century. The plan was soberly devised: the catacombs were to be entered outside the city, filled with explosives, and the whole left bank would have been destroyed.[11] In the making of Souvarine, a distrust of the Russian character which reached down into Zola's subconscious merged with a more recent aversion from the Russians as the principal advocates of a theory of violent social change.[12] Souvarine emerges as a bugbear, evidently meant to make our flesh creep. Zola's first socialist, Étienne, is contemptible; his second is execrable. They are the bad apostles of a possibly just cause; but they are determined principally as human products of race and environment, the rights and wrongs of their political programmes taking second place.

IF NOW WE turn to the representatives of the threatened middle class, we shall find that Zola presents them in exactly the same way.

He takes three main types: Deneulin, the small capitalist who owns his own mine and exploits it with hired labour; Hennebeau, the salaried manager of a colliery administered by a joint-stock company; and Grégoire, a shareholder in this company.

The Grégoires, being avowedly comic characters, represent a new departure for Zola. Humour is scarcely observable in his earlier works. In *Germinal* it finds a first timid outlet, and we shall see it flowing much more exuberantly in *La Terre*. This humour has its source in irony, which Havelock Ellis called 'the soul of Zola's work', the thing that gives it 'distinction and poignant incisiveness'. It is an irony, however, which disturbs more than it amuses, being morose, tinged at moments with a sardonic savagery, in fact little different from Flaubert's *grotesque triste*, which, as its inventor declared, 'does not call forth laughter, but prolonged meditation'.

The appearance of the Grégoires almost anywhere in the book is a signal for this *grotesque triste*. We are introduced to them at the beginning of the second part: Mme Grégoire 'short, stout, fifty-eight years old', preserving a 'broad, rosy, babyish face under the dazzling whiteness of her hair'; M. Grégoire 'ruddy too, in spite of his sixty years, with large, good-natured, kindly features under the snow of his curly hair'. This Pickwickian couple have a single daughter, Cécile, whom they adore and for whom their indulgence is boundless. 'She was not pretty, too healthy, too robust, fully developed at eighteen; but she had superb flesh and a milky complexion, chestnut hair, a round face and a pert little nose sunk in her cheeks.' Her parents 'saw her as perfect, not in the least over-fat, never well enough fed'. The few servants are contented, the house itself 'had a good smell of good food. The stable-racks and the larders were stuffed to overflowing with provisions.'

Into this cosy atmosphere shuffles the miner's wife, La Maheude, with two of her younger children. She has tramped over through the March wind and mud in expectation of charity. The Grégoires are charitable—intelligently so, never giving cash, 'for it was a well-known fact that as soon as a poor man has a penny he spends it on drink'. La Maheude, who has not the money to give her husband and elder children a meal when they come in from work, is sent away with a parcel of warm clothes for the children, while Cécile unconsciously acts on the legendary proposal of Marie-Antoinette and pushes a *brioche* into their hands. 'The two little mites, who had no bread, went away, holding this cake respectfully in their tiny hands numb with cold.'

The Grégoires are not hypocritical; they are a couple of amiable innocents. Léon Grégoire's great-grandfather had invested a portion of his life-savings, 10,000 francs, to buy a share in the Montsou colliery at the beginning of its history. Rather less than a century later, this initial investment is yielding annually five times the value of the principal. The share has thus been the family providence, enabling it through three generations to live in idleness and ease, and promising the same sybaritic existence to Cécile, her children and her children's children. The arrangement seems so natural to the Grégoires, they are so convinced of their right to their income, that when Négrel, Cécile's fiancé, amuses himself by proving them to be social parasites marked down for liquidation in the next revolution, the old man gasps with indignation.

> The childlike calm, the serene self-satisfaction in which he lived was gone in a twinkling.
> 'Stolen money, my fortune! Did not my great-grandfather earn, and dearly too, the money he originally invested? Have we not incurred all the risks of the enterprise? Do I put my income to a bad use today? ... Ah! I don't deny there are some shareholders who go too far. For instance, I have been told about ministers who have received shares as rewards for services rendered to the Company. And there is that noble lord whose name I shall not mention, a duke, the richest of our shareholders, who lives a life of scandalous prodigality, squandering millions on women, in riotous living and useless luxury ... But we, we who live quietly, like the honest folk we are! we who do not speculate, who are content to live healthy lives with what we possess, giving a portion to the poor! ... Really now! your workmen would have to be downright robbers to steal a pin from us.'

Grégoire's hints of millions wasted in lavish living and political jobbery take us back to *La Curée*, to *Son Excellence Eugène Rougon*, and to Nana, one of whose lovers, the financier Steiner, 'had associated himself with the owner of an ironworks in Alsace; far away in a remote province there were workmen black with coal, dripping with sweat, who day and night strained their muscles and heard their joints crack, toiling to minister to the pleasures of Nana'. The evidence of the earlier books is enough to show that Zola was perfectly aware of the extent to which social injustice was liable to flourish under a system of uncontrolled capitalism. If, in *Germinal*, he was content to make no more than a passing reference to the more disgraceful of these abuses, this was for reasons of art: in order to preserve the illusion of impartiality his *rentiers* had to be made as humanly sympathetic as was consistent with truth. Their *naïveté* acquits them of deliberate villainy.

This *naïveté* occasionally touches the upper registers of comedy. Thus the incident in which, at the height of the rioting at Montsou, the Grégoires placidly walk up the main street and are allowed to pass unharmed by the disconcerted rabble, provides an unexpectedly ludicrous scene in an act of bestial violence. M. Grégoire's subsequent comment on the bloodthirsty yells: 'Bread! Bread! Death to the bourgeois!' is worthy of being coupled with the historic remark of a queen of France already recalled: 'Why, of course [he says], they don't mean any harm really. When they have shouted themselves hoarse, they will go home and eat their supper with all the more appetite.'

Zola miscalculated in punishing the Grégoires so heavily at the end. When the strike is all over and the miners beaten into submission, Cécile is strangled by a Bonnemort now in his dotage, one day when she is making a round of charity visits. This extinction of the line of the *rentiers* by the grimy hands of the ancient industrial serf was perhaps intended as a piece of prophetic symbolism; but if so, the symbolism, it has to be admitted, starts uncomfortably out of the picture, and weakens the caricatural unity of the Grégoire figures. More probably, Zola felt under compulsion not to leave any of his characters unscarred by suffering.

DENEULIN'S END, ON the other hand, is both apt and typical. An owner-manager, he is a survival from an earlier phase of the growth of capitalism. When the strike, spreading to his own employees, ruins him, he is forced to sell out to the big joint-stock company and become one of its paid servants.

Zola gave Deneulin many virtues: an excellent manager of men, courageous, hard-working, and far-sighted, he bears little resemblance to the blood-sucking exploiter of convention and legend. His mine is better equipped than those belonging to the Montsou syndicate, and his workers are attached to him. Between socialism itself, believed unattainable, and monopolistic capitalism, condemned as inhuman, this middle term of paternally administered private enterprise appears to have commended itself most to Zola; but it was already under sentence of strangulation, and in showing his small *entrepreneur* devoured by a cartel, Zola was accurately reflecting the trend of economic development in his day.

OF THE THREE main opponents of the workers in revolt, the most carefully drawn is Hennebeau. Unlike Grégoire and Deneulin, he enjoys no inherited wealth, and has worked his way up from very humble beginnings by sheer industry and intelligence. He has, it is true, made a rich marriage, but his personal income is fixed by the directors he serves. 'I am a wage-earner like the rest of you', he tells the deputation of strikers; 'I have no more power to do as I wish than the youngest of your pit-boys. I receive orders, and my job is simply to see that they are properly carried out.'

Once again it is the human aspect rather than the social that Zola puts first. Through Hennebeau more than through any other character, the drama is lifted out of the political and economic context and raised to the plane of universal truth. 'It seemed to me necessary', Zola told Rod, in answer to some criticism from his disciple, 'to place above the eternal injustice of class oppression the eternal pain of passion.' In the same letter he explained that the only reason for the 'commonplace adultery' between Hennebeau's wife and Négrel was 'to provide me with the scene in which Hennebeau proclaims his human anguish in face of the yelling clamour of social suffering'.

The scene in question is situated in one of the most celebrated chapters in *Germinal*, that in which the maddened strikers scour the countryside smashing machinery and punctuating a discordant rendering of the *Marseillaise* with the cry for food. The responsibility for calling up troops to quell the riot rests on Hennebeau; and Zola, with his usual instinct for dramatic suspense, chooses that moment to deprive him of the power to act. His wife has left the house with Négrel to fetch Cécile and Deneulin's daughters who have been invited to lunch; and a chance discovers to him the intrigue that has been going on under his roof. His jealousy is that of the man still passionately in love with his wife, but repulsed by her, and tolerating her perverse infatuations for a succession of temporary lovers. But Négrel is his own nephew, and this time his fury and despair pass all bounds. Zola achieves impressive drama of quite a new kind by stationing the frenzied mob outside his window, shouting insults up at him and threatening to storm his house, while he watches them from behind a shutter, envious of their freedom from spiritual torment.

> He would cheerfully have made them a present of his fat salary if he could have had what they had, a thick hide and the ability to mate without inhibition or compunction. Why could he not seat them at his table and stuff them with pheasant, while he went and fornicated behind the hedges, tumbling the girls and not caring a straw for those who had tumbled them before him? He would have given everything, his education, his comfort, his luxury, his managerial authority, if he could have been, just for one day, the lowest of the wretches to whom he gave orders, one whose instincts were unfettered, who was churl enough to hit his wife and take his pleasure with his neighbour's. And he longed too to go hungry, to have an empty stomach, to be twisted with cramps which would unsettle and stupefy his brain; perhaps that would

have killed the eternal pain. Ah! to live like a brute, possess nothing at all, roam the cornfields with the ugliest, filthiest haulage-girl, and be able to be satisfied with her!

'Bread! Bread! Bread!'

Then he grew exasperated, he shouted in fury through the din: 'Bread! Is that enough, you fools?'

For his part, he had enough to eat, but that did not stop him groaning with anguish. His ravaged household, his whole aching existence rose to his throat in a deathly shudder. All was not mended by a loaf of bread. Who was the idiot who placed the happiness of this world in the fair distribution of wealth? These revolutionary dreamers might tear up the social fabric if they liked and manufacture a different one, they would not add one joy to humanity, they would not relieve it of one sorrow by cutting every man his slice of bread. In fact, they would increase the unhappiness of the earth, they would make the very dogs howl one day in despair, when they had made them look farther than the calm satisfaction of instincts and raised them to the unappeasable suffering of passions. No, the only happiness was to cease to be, or if that was not possible, then to be the tree, the stone, less still, the grain of sand which the heel of the wayfarer cannot bruise.

The problem here so strikingly dramatized is an old one. Zola may have learnt at school how La Bruyère stated it, with the important rider which is not to be found in *Germinal*:

> One wonders whether, in comparing the different conditions of men, their hardships and advantages, one might not observe a mixture or a sort of compensation of good and evil which would establish equality between them, or which would at least bring it about that the one condition should be hardly more desirable than the other. He who is powerful, rich, and lacks nothing, may frame this question; but it must needs be left to a poor man to decide it.

Zola, acquainted equally with extremes of poverty and wealth, should have been as qualified as a man might be both to put and decide the question; but he preferred to end his chapter with Hennebeau still in tears at the window and the famished rioters still roaring below.

Zola's answer to the question must be looked for elsewhere than in the novel. In a letter to the editor of *Le Figaro*, Zola defended himself against the reproach made by his reviewer of having 'insulted the lower classes' in *Germinal*. 'My only desire has been to show them such as our society makes them, and arouse such pity, such an outcry for justice, that France will at last cease to allow herself to be devoured by a handful of ambitious politicians, and devote herself to the health and happiness of her children.' This position is the same as that which Zola took up in 1868, when he set it down in the preliminary notes to his novel-cycle: 'It will be open to legislators ... to take my work, to draw conclusions from it and to see that the wounds I shall lay bare are dressed.'[13] The refusal to intervene in political issues, a refusal based on a cardinal tenet of the realist aesthetic, was as firm as ever in 1885.

The result is a work which is a masterpiece of realist literature but which, being carefully and intentionally neutral, evades the immediate significance of the social issues while it makes their existence blindingly plain. The exposure in itself, however, almost constituted a revolutionary act at the time. *Germinal* 'made the ghosts of the damned of the earth walk the streets of the capitals. It revealed to every passer-by their physical shapes. with eerie frightfulness, and their existence—if not their destiny—to the marrow. And thus it spread an uneasiness that is the nightmare of revolutionary truth.'[14] I have known one socialist who dates his conversion from a first reading of this book; there must be hundreds like him in this country, thousands in France. But any such effects must be counted accidental. The most that can properly be claimed for *Germinal* is that its picture of social conditions was such that no reader save the most callous could remain complacent.

Yet even when so much is admitted, there remain the figures of Étienne Lantier and Hennebeau which cancel any over-optimistic estimations of the practicability and ultimate value of deliberately engineered social changes. *Germinal*, in short, is neither revolutionary nor counter-revolutionary; it is not primarily a vehicle for extra-literary concerns, and thus ought not to be judged, as too often it has been judged, by its accuracy as a social document, still less by its effectiveness as a piece of propaganda. The only standards of evaluation which can properly be applied are aesthetic ones.

NOTES

1. See Deffoux, 'Émile Zola et ses éditions depuis 1902', *Le Figaro*, 1 Oct. 1927.

2. James, *Notes on Novelists*, p. 43; Saurat, *Perspectives*, p. 133; Ellis, Introduction to the translation of *Germinal* in Everyman's Library.

3. B.N. MS. *Nouv. acq. franç.* 10307, fols. 402 ff.

4. Prefatory note written for a serialized reprinting of the novel, undertaken by *Le Petit Rouennais* in 1886.

5. Lukács, *Studies in European Realism*, p. 86.

6. The employment of female labour in the mines had been made illegal in 1874, but *Germinal* is of course set in the pre-1870 period, when women still worked extensively below ground.

7. The first of these sentences occurred in Abel Hermant's oration over Zola's grave, which was published in *La Petite République*, 7 Oct. 1902; the second is taken from an obituary article by Gabriel Trarieux which appeared in *Pages libres*, 18 Oct. 1902.

8. It was at the Havre Congress of Workers, in 1883 (two years before *Germinal*), that Paul Brousse's group of 'possibilists', advocating the gradual introduction of desirable social reforms when the moment seemed opportune, broke away from the Marxian socialists led by Guesde. Rasseneur is a *possibiliste avant la lettre*.

9. In point of fact, as we learn in *Le Docteur Pascal*, Étienne takes part in the Commune, is arrested, condemned to death, then pardoned and exiled to New Caledonia.

10. Kleman, *Emil' Zola, sbornik statey*, pp. 174–5.

11. Zola recalls this in one of his 'Chroniques' in *L'Événement illustré* (9 May 1868).

12. The trial (in 1882) of Prince Kropotkin, implicated in a bomb-throwing episode at Lyons—a trial which was given wide publicity—may have been an additional contributory factor to Zola's russophobia.

13. See above, pp. 55–6.

14. Barbusse, *Zola*, pp. 172–3 in the English translation.

WILLIAM J. BERG

A Poetics of Vision: Zola's Theory and Criticism

Chaque oeil a ainsi une vision particulière. Enfin, il y a des yeux qui ne voient rien du tout. (Each eye has its own vision. Still, there are some eyes that see nothing at all.)

—Zola, *Le Roman expérimental* (167)

Vision dominates Zola's theories and criticism—both for the visual arts, where one might expect it to, and for the novel, where one might not. Neither corpus of criticism predominates in its influence on the other; rather, the prime role of vision precedes and shapes both. In effect, Zola evolves a poetics where literature, painting, and science intersect in the realm of the visual.

Approaching Zola's poetics through vision enables one to reassess the underrated theories of *Le Roman expérimental*, not as aberrations grafted onto Zola's critical writings for polemic purposes, but in the context of his overall criticism, where they assume a central position. Furthermore, the role of vision in Zola's theoretical program shows itself to be emblematic of the positivist thought of his times, which posits the potential of a scientifically analytic yet imaginative visual process capable of combining freshness of vision with the sophistication of an "educated eye."

From *The Visual Novel: Emile Zola and the Art of His Times.* © 1992 The Pennsylvania State University Press.

VISION AND PAINTING

Although his articles, along with his ardor, began to wane around 1880, Zola's writings on painting span a period of thirty years, from 1866 to 1896, his most dynamic and controversial output occurring at the beginning of his career. Zola's attacks on the established painters exhibiting in the 1866 Salon and his defense of Manet, in particular, in the newspaper *L'Evénement* elicited the violent public reaction described by his disciple Paul Alexis: "Some fanatics went so far as to rip up the paper right on the boulevard, in front of the newsstands. The salon critic for *L'Evénement* received up to thirty letters a day, some containing words of encouragement, most insults; he almost had a duel."[1] After the tumultuous effect of his articles in the late sixties, Zola's art criticism diminished considerably until he was asked by the Russian newspaper *Viestnik Evropy* (*Messenger from Europe*) to chronicle the Salons of 1875 to 1880, a period that, fortunately, paralleled the independent shows of the artists who came to be known as the impressionists, about whom Zola commented in some detail. After a long hiatus, Zola did a final retrospective article on the arts for *Le Figaro*, the paper that, ironically, had replaced *L'Evénement*.

Zola's art criticism is as frustrating as it is fascinating and fruitful, due in part to the loss of the original French version of the Russian articles, but mostly to the evolution of the various painters themselves and of the terms Zola uses to describe them—such as realism, naturalism, positivism, and, finally, impressionism—the relationships among which we shall attempt to unravel as we proceed.

Zola's reasons for appreciating the painting of his times can be reduced to two categories, both pertaining to vision: First, he finds the artists of his generation to be concerned with the purely visual aspects of painting (as opposed, for example, to style or message) considerably more than any other movement in the history of art. For Zola, Manet and, later, the impressionists were able to strip away certain prejudices, not only of technique, but of seeing, and thus attain a far more natural and accurate vision than was previously possible. Second, and somewhat paradoxically, Zola believed that, despite the purely natural, wholly visual nature of their painting, Manet and the impressionists were able to achieve a studied and "scientific" analysis of certain visual effects and of the visual act itself, which was remarkably consistent with the positivist aims of his generation.

The Natural Eye

The repeated recurrence in Zola's theories (particularly in definitions) of visual terms—such as "observation," "seeing," "vision," and "the eye"—not only verifies his conviction that the painters of his generation had initiated what was essentially a visual revolution but also constitutes a concrete link between these theories and those concerning literature. This link is evidenced by the formula Zola uses to end his Salon article of 11 May 1866, entitled "Les Realistes du Salon": "La définition d'une oeuvre d'art ne saurait être autre chose que celle-ci: *Une oeuvre d'art est un coin de la création vu à travers un tempérament*" ("The definition of a work of art could not be other than the following: *A work of art is a corner of creation seen through a temperament*").[2] This formula—where object ("a corner of creation") is welded to observer ("a temperament") through the mediation of observation ("seen")—is repeated on several occasions in Zola's art criticism, just as it assumes a key role in his literary theories. Of course, since painting is a visual art, all painters are concerned to a major degree with seeing, but Zola finds the painters of his generation to possess "une nouvelle vision de la nature" ("a new vision of nature," 261). Indeed, if Edmond Duranty coined the term "new painting" to describe the art of his times,[3] Zola's concept of modern painting might be characterized by the term "new vision," denoting a novel way of seeing based on the rediscovery of the natural eye.

Zola's first assessment of Manet, for example, in an article of 7 May 1866, emphasizes the role of direct perception devoid of visual inheritance: "Le talent de M. Manet est fait de simplicité et de justesse ... il aura refusé toute la science acquise, toute l'expérience ancienne, il aura voulu prendre l'art au commencement, c'est-à-dire à l'observation exacte des objets" ("M. Manet's talent consists of simplicity and accuracy ... he will have refused all acquired knowledge, all former experience, he will have wanted to take art from the beginning, that is, from the exact observation of objects," 67). In his pamphlet on Manet, published the following year, Zola continues his emphasis on unfettered vision, attributing the painter's success to his "facultés de vision et de compréhension" ("faculties of vision and understanding," 87), noting that "il fit effort pour oublier tout ce qu'il avait étudié dans les musées" ("he made an effort to forget everything he had studied in museums," 87) and concluding boldly that "toute la personnalité de l'artiste consiste dans la manière dont son oeil est organisé; il voit blond, et il voit par masses" ("the artist's entire personality consists of the way in which his eye is organized; he sees in blond, and he sees by masses," 91). In 1875, in the first of the "Letters from Paris" for his Russian public, Zola defends Manet's original use of color in *Argenteuil* by stressing, not the role of color on the surface of the canvas, or the interaction of various colors, or their symbolic value, but solely their visual accuracy: "Le peintre a vu ce ton, j'en suis persuadé" ("The painter saw this tone, I'm convinced of it," 158; see also 67). If Manet does have a weakness, as Zola contends in his "Letter" of 1879, it is one of technique, not of vision:

> Je n'ai pas nommé Edouard Manet, qui était le chef du groupe des peintres impressionnistes. Ses tableaux sont exposés au Salon. Il a continué le mouvement après Courbet, grâce à son oeil perspicace, si apte à discerner les tons justes. Sa longue lutte contre l'incompréhension du public s'explique par la difficulté qu'il rencontre dans l'exécution—je veux dire que sa main n'égale pas son oeil.... Si le côté technique chez lui égalait la justesse des perceptions, il serait le grand peintre de la seconde moitié du XIXe siècle.

> (I have not [yet] named Edouard Manet, who was the leader of the group of impressionist painters. His paintings are exhibited in the Salon. He continued the [naturalist] movement after Courbet, thanks to his perceptive eye, so apt in discerning precise tones. His long struggle against lack of public understanding can be explained by the difficulties he encounters in producing—I mean that his hand doesn't equal his eye.... If his technical side equaled the accuracy of his perceptions, he would be the great painter of the second half of the nineteenth century. 227)

Zola repeats this clear distinction between visual mastery and technical inadequacy in his preface to the catalogue for an exhibition of Manet's works, shortly after the painter's death in 1884: "Les doigts n'obéissaient pas toujours aux yeux, dont la justesse était merveilleuse" ("His fingers didn't always obey his eyes, whose accuracy was marvelous," 260).

Zola's concept of a "new vision" was not confined to Manet, whom he considered, nonetheless, to be the greatest (if not "the great") artist of his times. A similar visual revolution was evident in French landscape art, the "glory" of modern French painting, according to Zola, who assessed its break with classic landscape art as follows: "... des artistes révolutionnaires ... emportèrent leur boîte de couleurs dans les champs et les prés, dans les bois où murmurent les ruisseaux, et tout bêtement, sans apprêt, ils se mirent à peindre ce qu'ils voyaient de leurs yeux autour d'eux" ("... revolutionary artists ... carried their boxes of colors into the fields and meadows, into the woods where streams babble, and quite simply, without adornment, they began to paint what they saw around them with their eyes," 166; see also 68, 86, and 241). Zola alludes here primarily to Courbet, Theodore Rousseau, Millet, and Corot, whom he often calls "naturalists"[4] and considers forerunners of the "impressionists," painters whom he also defines according to their visual prowess.

Zola first used the term "impressionist" in his "Letter from Paris" of 1876, shortly after if was coined, pejoratively, by the critic Louis Leroy upon seeing Monet's *Impression: Sunrise* in 1874, and adopted, defiantly, by the group of painters who had undertaken independent shows rather than risk further rejection by the Salon jury. In this group Zola places, among others, Monet (whom he names as their leader), Renoir, Pissarro, Degas, Caillebotte, Morisot, Sisley, Guillaumin, Cassatt, and even Cézanne, but not Manet, whom Zola calls a "realist and positivist" in his 1875 letter (158) and a "naturalist" in his 1880 article "Le Naturalisme au Salon" for *Le Voltaire* (244).[5] In 1868, Zola had applied the term "naturalist," again defined by the key role of vision, to both Pissarro—"il n'est ni poète ni philosophe, mais simplement naturaliste, faiseur de cieux et de terrains. Revez si vous voulez, voilà ce qu'il a vu" ("he is neither a poet nor a philosopher, but simply a naturalist, a maker of skies and terrains. Dream if you want, here is what he saw," 127)—and Manet—"je le félicité encore davantage de savoir peindre, d'avoir un oeil juste et franc, d'appartenir à la grande école des naturalistes" ("I congratulate him even more for knowing how to paint, for having an eye that is accurate and free, for belonging to the great school of naturalists," 132). Of course, Zola did not yet have the term "impressionism" at his disposal, but even in 1880 he links the two movements, through the notion of modernism: "c'est que le naturalisme, l'impressionnisme, la modernité, comme on voudra l'appeler, est aujourd'hui maître des Salons officiels" ("it's [clear] that naturalism, impressionism, modernity, however one calls it, is today master of the official Salons," 244).

For Zola, impressionism is an offshoot of naturalist painting, since both involve the direct observation of nature through the natural eye. However, the impressionists form a distinct group, based precisely on a common "vision"—"Ce qu'ils ont de commun entre eux, je fai dit, c'est une parenté de vision. Ils voient tous la nature claire et gaie" ("What they have in common, as I said, is a kindred vision. They all see nature as light and gay").[6] It is their studies of light that distinguish the impressionists from Manet and the naturalists, but, like their forerunners, they too are characterized by the importance of freshness of vision:

Les artistes dont je parce on été appelés "des impressionnistes,"
parce que la plupart d'entre eux s'efforcent visiblement de
communiquer avant tout l'impression véridique donnée par les
choses et les êtres; ils veulent la saisir et la reproduire
directement, sans se perdre dans les détails insignifiants qui ôtent
toute fraîcheur à l'observation personnelle et vivante. Mais
chacun, par bonheur, a son trait original, sa façon particulière de
voir et de transmettre la realite.

(The artists I'm talking about have been called "impressionists,"
because most of them clearly aspire to communicate above all the
true impression produced by things and beings; they want to
seize [the impression] and reproduce it directly, without getting
lost in the small details that remove all freshness from the
personal, living observation. But each of them, fortunately, has an
original trait, his or her own way of seeing and transmitting
reality. 194)

In short, Manet, the naturalists, and the impressionists have been able to
divest their painting and their seeing of the lessons of the past, of such
aquired concerns as composition, design, line, and perspective. They have
managed to achieve a more natural eye, one whose approach to reality is
fresh and directed at the visual essence of experience.

Zola attributes this same visual freshness to Claude Lantier, the
painter-hero of *Le Ventre de Paris* (1873) and *L'Oeuvre* (1886). Claude
frequently expresses the wish to free his eyes from the blinders of the past,
noting that "on doit apprendre son métier. Seulement, ce n'est guère bon de
l'apprendre sous la férule de professeurs qui vous entrent de force dans la
caboche *leur* vision à eux" ("one has to learn one's trade. But it's no good
learning it under the iron rule of professors who force *their* vision into your
noggin").[7] Claude wishes to liberate his sight, even from the influence of
those painters he most admires; he says of Courbet: "ce fameux réalisme
n'était guère que dans les sujets; tandis que la vision restait celle des vieux
maîtres" ("this famous realism was solely in his subjects; while his vision
remained that of the old masters," 45)—and adds of Delacroix: "Nom d'un
chien, c'est encore noir! J'ai ce sacré Delacroix dans l'oeil" ("Doggone it, it's
still black! I've got that damned Delacroix in my eye," 47). Of the great
painters in the Louvre, Claude believes that their vision does not adequately
translate what the eye encounters in reality: "Il en arrivait à déclamer contre
le travail au Louvre, il se serait, disait-il, coupe le poignet, plutôt que d'y

retourner gâter son oeil à une de ces copies, qui encrassent pour toujours la vision du monde ou l'on vit" ("He began to declaim against the works in the Louvre; he said he'd rather cut his wrists than go back there and spoil his eye on one of those copies, which foul up one's vision of the world where one lives," 43–44; see also 109 and 124). Finally, after a lengthy apprenticeship "unlearning" the lessons of the past, Claude manages to attain the same natural virginity of sight that Zola attributes to Manet and the impressionists: "Son long repos à la campagne lui avait donné une fraîcheur de vision singulière" ("His long rest in the countryside had given him a singular freshness of vision," 204).

For Zola, then, the principal characteristic of impressionism, the one that defines the movement and determines its main directions, is the purely visual nature of its approach to reality, the immediacy of the "impression," the primacy of the "natural eye." Nor does Zola's evaluation appear to be overly simplified or idiosyncratic. Although technical innovations like the accentuated brush stroke and the use of a pale ground are sometimes considered as the principal innovations of late nineteenth-century art,[8] many critics, both at that time and today, see a new conception of visual sensation, returning to the primitive, nonabstract eye, as a major legacy of the impressionist movement.

The French critic Georges Rivière, writing in 1877, characterizes the impressionists as having a "virgin eye,"[9] while Diego Martelli, an Italian critic writing in 1880, further confirms Zola's position in stating that "*Impressionism* is not only a revolution in the field of thought, but is also a physiological revolution of the human eye. It is a new theory that depends on a different way of perceiving sensations of light and of expressing impressions."[10] Jules Laforgue, writing in 1883, proposes the following definition of impressionism, again insisting on the qualities that define the painter's eye: "The Impressionist is a modernist painter who—endowed with uncommon ocular sensitivity, forgetting the paintings amassed over centuries in museums, forgetting the optical education of schooling (drawing and perspective, coloring), by dint of living and looking openly and primitively in the luminous spectacles of the open air (that is, outside the studio lit at a forty-five-degree angle), whether it be in the street, the countryside, or inside—has managed to recreate a natural eye, to see naturally and paint naively as he sees."[11] Thus, the first and foremost characteristic of impressionism, identified by Zola and substantiated by other art critics of his era, is its purely visual nature, its break with the abstractions of the past and its rediscovery of the natural eye.

The Analytic Eye

After freshness of vision, Zola identifies as the second major characteristic of Manet, the naturalists, and the impressionists their rigorous analyses, their sophisticated "studies" of nature. This notion may seem somewhat at odds with the first, and yet many modern painters appeared to assume a scientific and analytic approach to their subjects while remaining purely visual; they seemed to possess a type of vision that was at once "virgin and abstract," as Mallarmé put it in reference to Monet's eye.[12]

Indeed, in Zola's art criticism the term "observation," whose occurrence we have just studied, is often coupled with "analysis," as in the following judgment concerning Manet, from Zola's pamphlet of 1867: "Il est un enfant de notre âge. Je vois en lui un peintre analyste. Tous les problèmes ont été remis en question, la science a voulu avoir des bases solides, et elle en est revenu à l'observation exacte des faits" ("He is a child of our era. I see in him an analytic painter. All issues have been reevaluated, science has sought solid bases, and it has returned to the exact observation of facts," 92). In 1880 Zola links this coupling "of observation and analysis" (251) to the triumph of naturalism in landscape art and goes so far as to proclaim that "tout artiste de talent s'appuie aujourd'hui sur l'observation et l'analyse" ("any talented artist relies today on observation and analysis," 254).

Zola greatly admired the "study" of light effects that Manet achieved in his painting, while remaining faithful to the principle of direct observation:

> Ce qui me frappe avant tout dans ses tableaux, c'est l'observation constante et exacte de la loi des valeurs. Par exemple, des fruits sont posés sur une table et se détachent contre un fond gris. Il y a entre les fruits, selon qu'ils sont plus on moins rapprochés, des différences de coloration, formant toute une gamme de teintes, et il faut dire à l'honneur de Manet qu'il s'est soucié constamment de l'étude de ces teintes, dont l'existence n'est evidemment pas soupçonnée des élèves de l'Ecole des Beaux-Arts.

> (What strikes me above all in his paintings is the constant and precise observance of the law of values. For example, various fruits are set on a table and detach themselves from a gray background. Among these fruits, depending on their distance, there are differences in coloration, forming an entire range of tints, and it must be said to Manet's credit that he has constantly been concerned with the study of these tints, the existence of

which is clearly not suspected by students of the Ecole des Beaux-Arts. 191; see also 90)

Zola was particularly interested in the way Manet was able to study the effect of this decomposed, analyzed light, color, and atmosphere on the objects and people they enveloped, as he noted in 1884: "Une seule règle l'a guidé, la loi des valeurs, la façon dont un être ou un objet se comporte dans la lumière qui dessine autant qu'elle colore, c'est la lumière qui met chaque chose à sa place, qui est la vie même de la scène peinte" ("A single rule guided him, the law of values, the way in which a being or an object behaves in light, which contours as much as it colors; it is light that puts each thing in its place, that is the very life of the painted scene," 260).

Indeed, Zola considers this investigation of light and atmosphere to be the defining characteristic of the impressionist group, as he states in his Russian Letter of 1879: "Les impressionnistes ont introduit la peinture en plein air, l'étude des effecs changeants de la nature selon les innombrables conditions du temps et de l'heure" ("The impressionists introduced open air painting, the study of the changing effects of nature according to the innumerable conditions of climate and time," 226). He goes on to use the term "analysis" in describing their efforts in this area: "ils poussent l'analyse de la nature plus loin, jusqu'à la décomposition de la lumière, jusqu'à l'étude de fair en mouvement, des nuances des couleurs, des variations fortuites de l'ombre et de la lumière, de tous les phénomènes optiques qui font qu'un horizon est si mobile et si difficue à rendre" ("they push the analysis of nature even further, up to the decomposition of light, to the study of air in movement, of color nuances, of random variations in shadow and light, of all the optical phenomena that render a horizon so mobile and so difficult to depict," 226–27).

As of 1880, coinciding (perhaps not coincidentally) with the publication of *Le Roman expérimental*, Zola's praise for the impressionists extends beyond their study of light itself to include its relationship with and its effect on the objects and people of reality. He uses phrases such as "peindre les figures dans fair où elles vivent" ("painting figures in the air where they live," 252) to describe their achievements and begins to apply the term "milieu," at the core of his theories of determinism, to the air and light that the painters were examining through direct observation: "On voit tous les jeunes talents, tous ceux qui ont un besoin de vie et de succès, venir à la nouvelle formule, aux sujets modernes, à l'observation exacte de la nature, a cette peinture du plein air qui baigne les personnages dans le milieu de lumière vraie où ils vivent" ("We see all the young talent, all who need life and success, come to the new formula, to modern subjects, to the exact observation of nature, to this open air painting that bathes figures in the milieu of real light where they live," 249; see also 254).

Zola finds the studies undertaken by the "new" painters to be eminently scientific, rivaling those of the chemist and physicist and conforming closely to determinism's ideal of identifying the causes and effects of natural phenomena:

> Aujourd'hui nos jeunes artistes ont fait un nouveau pas vers le vrai, en voulant que les sujets baignassent dans la lumière réelle du soleil, et non dans le jour faux de l'atelier; c'est comme le chimiste, comme le physicien qui retournent aux sources, en se plaçant dans les conditions mêmes des phénomènes. Du moment qu'on veut faire de la vie, il faut bien prendre la vie avec son mécanisme complet. De là, en peinture, la nécessité du plein air, de la lumière étudiée dans ses causes et ses effets.

> (Today our young artists have taken a new step toward truth, in wanting their subjects to bathe in the real light of the sun, and not in the false light of the studio; it's like the chemist, like the physicist returning to their sources, placing themselves within the very conditions of phenomena. From the moment that one wants to represent life, one has to take life with its complete mechanism. Whence, in painting, the necessity of open air, of light studied in its causes and its effects. 241)

In short, Zola finds, within the visual arts, direct confirmation of the central premise of naturalism—the causal determination of natural and human phenomena by the physical milieu. Small wonder that he should embrace impressionism so firmly, both through natural inclination and for polemic purposes.

If Zola does eventually find fault with Monet, it is precisely because, at a certain point, the latter seems to have abandoned his scientific pretensions and promise: "Les impressionnistes sont précisément, selon moi, des pioniers. Un instant ils avaient mis de grandes espérances en Monet; mais celui-ci parait épuisé par une production hâtive; il se contente d'a peu près; il n'étudie pas la nature avec la passion des vrais créateurs" ("The impressionists are precisely, in my judgment, pioneers. For a moment they had put high hopes in Monet; but he seems worn out by hasty production; he's content to be close; he doesn't study nature with the passion of true creators," 227). Zola felt that Monet and others of the impressionist group had begun to exhibit a nonscientific approach to visual sensation, and, while these painters continued to maintain their purely visual approach, they had failed to achieve the analysis of cause and effect, the synthesis with scientific method, that Zola admired in Manet.[13]

It is in fact the relationship of sensation and science that best informs Zola's conception of the painter Claude Lantier in *L'Oeuvre*, especially concerning the extent to which Claude's failure constitutes a condemnation of impressionism, as is often alleged.[14] Claude is originally intended to reflect the visual and scientific characteristics attributed in Zola's *Salons* to naturalism and, for a time, to impressionism. Zola notes, in the *ébauche* (sketch) for the novel: "Maintenant, il faudrait bien régler mon Claude, J'en fais naturellement un naturaliste" ("Now I should sort out my Claude; naturally I'll make him a naturalist")—and he later adds: "Je prendrai en outre pour Claude quelques théories des impressionnistes, le plein air, la lumière décomposée, toute cette peinture nouvelle qui demande *un génie pour être réalisée*" ("In addition, I'll give Claude some of the theories of the impressionists, open air, decomposed light, all this new painting that demands *a genius to be achieved*"). Zola conceives Claude initially as critical of his would-be "impressionist" followers, and the novelist uses the same word "hasty" that had been applied to Monet: "Mais je reviens aux impressionnistes: Claude s'élèvera contre leur travail hâtif, le tableau fait en deux heures, l'esquisse qui contente" ("But I return to the impressionists: Claude will rise against their hasty work, the painting done in two hours, the sketch that suffices").[15]

At the outset, Claude embodies the positivist/determinist synthesis of the purely visual and the scientific. He exclaims, early in the novel, that his painting must represent the effect of light on the objects and people that it envelops: "les choses et les êtres tels qu'ils se comportent dans de la vraie lumière" ("things and beings as they behave in real light," 45). He later develops his visual faculties and painterly techniques to achieve a scientifically accurate representation of these effects in his art: "Après cette année de repos en pleine campagne, en pleine lumière, il peignait avec une vision nouvelle, comme éclaircie, d'une gaieté de tons chantante. Jamais encore il n'avait eu cette science des reflets, cette sensation si juste des êtres et des choses, baignant dans la clarté diffuse" ("After this restful year in the countryside, in the open air, he painted with a new vision, as if enlightened, with a singing gayness of tones. Never before had he had this knowledge of reflections, such an accurate sensation of beings and things, bathing in diffuse light," 45).

However, Claude, like his eponym Monet, falls prey to the "hasty impression" and fails to realize his analytic and scientific potential, as his friend Sandoz, the novelist and *porte-parole* par excellence, concludes:

> Non, il n'a pas été l'homme de la formule qu'il apportait. Je veux dire qu'il n'a pas eu le génie assez net pour la planter debout et l'imposer dans une oeuvre définitive.... Et voyez, autour de lui, après lui, comme les efforts s'éparpillent! Ils en restent tous aux ébauches, aux impressions hâtives, pas un ne semble avoir la force d'être le maître attendu. N'est-ce pas irritant, cette notation nouvelle de la lumière, cette passion du vrai poussée jusqu'à l'analyse scientifique, cette evolution commencée si originalement, et qui s'attarde, et qui tombe aux mains des habiles, et qui n'aboutit point, parce que l'homme nécessaire n'est pas né? ... Bah! l'homme naîtra, rien ne se perd, il faut bien que la lumière soit.
>
> (No, he wasn't man enough for the formula he discovered. I mean that he didn't have a clear enough genius to plant it upright and impose it in a definitive work.... And look around him, after him, how their efforts are scattered! They're all stuck on sketches, on hasty impressions, not a one appears to have the force to be the long-awaited master. Isn't it irritating, this new notation of light, this passion for truth pushed to [the level of] scientific analysis, this evolution begun so originally, which is lagging, falling into profiteering hands, and is leading nowhere, because the right man isn't born? ... Bah! he'll be born, nothing is lost, the light won't fail. 359)

Indeed, during the course of *L'Oeuvre*, Claude progressively loses his directly analytical vision and turns to abstract notions such as the theory of complementary colors:[16]

> Il en tirait cette conclusion vraie, que les objets n'ont pas de couleur fixe, qu'ils se colorent suivant les circonstances ambiantes: et le grand mal était que, lorsqu'il revenait maintenant à l'observation directe, le tête bourdonnante de cette science, son oeil prévenu forçit les nuances délicates, affirmait en notes trop vives l'exactitude de la théorie; de sorte que son originalité de notation, si claire, si vibrante de soleil, tournait à la gageure, à un

renversement de toutes les habitudes de l'oeil, des chairs violâtres sous des cieux tricolores. La folie semblait an bout.

(He drew this true conclusion, that objects don't have a fixed color, that they are colored according to surrounding circumstances: and the great misfortune was that, when he returned now to direct observation, his head buzzing with this knowledge, his prejudiced eye exaggerated the delicate nuances, confirmed the accuracy of the theory in notes that were too vivid; so that his originality of notation, so light, so vibrant with sunlight, became impossible, turned into a reversal of all ocular habits, violet flesh under tricolored skies. Madness seemed inevitable. 248)

It is clear that the French word "science" here means prior knowledge and principle, not the scientific analysis that results from direct observation. Zola alludes, of course, to the neo-impressionists (particularly Seurat, Signac, and even Pissarro), for whom pointillist technique and color theory were replacing the direct analytical observation of reality. Ten years after the publication of *L'Oeuvre*, Zola expresses his disapproval of current trends in his final Salon:

Mais où ma surprise tourne à la colère, c'est lorsque je constate la démence à laquelle a pu conduire, en trente ans la théorie des reflets.... Très justement, nous soutenions que l'éclairage des objets et des figures n'est point simple, que sous des arbres, par exemple, les chairs nues verdissent, qu'il y a ainsi un continuel échange de reflets dont il faut tenir compte, si l'on veut dormer a une oeuvre la vie réelle de la lumière. Sans cesse, celle-ci se décompose, se brise et s'éparpille.... Seulement rien n'est plus delicat a saisir et à rendre que cette décomposition et ces reflets, ces jeux du soleil où, sans être déformées, baignent les créatures et les choses. Aussi, des qu'on insiste (dès que le raisonnement s'en mêle), en arrive-t-on vite à la caricature. Et ce sort vraiment des oeuvres déconcertantes, ces femmes multicolores, ces paysages violets et ces chevaux oranges, qu'on nous donne, en nous expliquant scientifiquement qu'ils sont tels par suite de tels reflets ou de telle décomposition du spectre solaire.

(But where my surprise turns to anger is when I see the madness stemming, in thirty years, from the theory of reflections.... Quite rightly, we contended that the lighting of objects and figures is

not at all simple, that under trees, for example, nude flesh
becomes greenish, that there is a continual play of reflections that
one must acknowledge, if one wants to lend a work the real life of
light. Constantly it decomposes, breaks up, and scatters....
However, nothing is more difficult to grasp and represent than
this decomposition and its reflections, this play of sunlight where
creatures and things bathe, without being deformed. Thus, as
soon as one stresses this [as soon as reason intervenes], caricature
quickly ensues. And these are truly disconcerting works, these
multicolored women, these violet landscapes with orange horses
that they're giving us, explaining scientifically that things are thus
due to such and such a reflection or such and such a
decomposition of the solar spectrum. 267)

Again the word "scientifically" is used ironically, to suggest the abuse of
precept and prejudice rather than to convey a link with the experimental
method based on direct observation and analysis, to which Zola and the
positivists were committed.

In essence, the criticism that emerges from *L'Oeuvre* concerns the
"dosage" of science in vision: Monet and the mainstream impressionists,
after promising beginnings, turned out to have too little; Seurat and the neo-
impressionists (Cézanne no doubt among them)[17] too much. Claude
Lantier's evolution—from having a balanced "dosage," to too little, to too
much—is meant to reflect, not that of one painter, or even one movement,
but that of the painting of his era.[18] *L'Oeuvre* is not a condemnation of
impressionism but of its aftermath. In fact, throughout his final Salon, Zola
confirms his appreciation for the impressionists as they once were and his
belief that their "new vision" was being undermined by the neo-
impressionists' emphasis on technique at the expense of observation. Precept
had replaced the natural eye; principle had replaced the analytic eye. The
visual artist, like the novelist, must maintain a correct proportion between
sensation and science in order to achieve stability and solidity.

Again, Zola's description of the scientific analysis initally inherent in
impressionist vision finds considerable support among art critics, both his
contemporaries and ours.[19] Edmond Duranty contends of the "new
painters" that "from the standpoint of ocular precision, the subtle
understanding of coloring, the result is completely extraordinary. The most
learned physicist could fault nothing in their analyses of light."[20] Armand
Silvestre, writing in 1876, finds in impressionism "a sort of analytic
impression ... outside of the longstanding conventions of modern landscape

art, [impressionism] discovered certain unexplored aspects of things, analyzed them with infinite subtlety, and thus expanded the field of pictorial research."[21] Perhaps the most striking depiction of the impressionists' synthesis of sight and science comes again from the pen of Laforgue, who explains clearly why he thinks the impressionist eye is both "natural" (visual) and "refined" (analytic):

> Thus a natural eye (or refined, since, for this organ, before going forward it must become primitive again by getting rid of tactile illusions), a natural eye forgets tactile illusion and its convenient dead language—drawing—and acts solely through its faculty of prismatic sensitivity. It manages to see reality in the living atmosphere of forms, decomposed, refracted, reflected through beings and things, with its endless variations. This is the primary characteristic of the impressionist eye.[22]

French critics were not alone in recognizing the positivist solution to the dualism between fresh seeing and refined thinking. The extent to which impressionist vision, if not painting, extends throughout late nineteenth-century Europe is evident in the writings of Conrad Fiedler (1841–95), the German art critic whose major works include *On Judging Works of Visual Art* (1876), *Modern Naturalism and Artistic Truth* (1881), and *On the Origin of Artistic Activity* (1887). After stating that "it is to the independent and free development of perceptual experience that we must look for the peculiar power of artistic talent,"[23] Fiedler adds that "only he will be able to convince himself of the infinite possibilities for the visual comprehension of the world who has advanced to the free and independent use of his perceptive faculties" (*On Judging*, 41). He notes, however, that a meaningful relationship with the world, a learning one, involves conceptualizing and abstraction, and "each time that abstract concepts appear, perception (i.e., pure sensory experience) vanishes" (*On Judging*, 37). This paradox within the act of seeing has a solution, however, which Fiedler expresses by noting: "It should be understood that man can attain the mental mastery of the world not only by the creation of concepts but also by the creation of visual conceptions" (*On Judging*, 40). He concludes that "it is the essential characteristic of the artist's nature to be born with an ability in perceptual comprehension and to use that ability freely" (*On Judging*, 42), and it is precisely this ability that joins modern painting with the scientific discoveries of the postivist era: "Art as well as science is a kind of investigation, and science as well as art is a kind of mental configuration" (*On Judging*, 46).

At the very root of positivism, then, is a combination of the purely visual and the scientific, an amalgamation that involves an analytic way of seeing, a creative vision that Mallarmé, Duranty, Laforgue, Fiedler, and numerous other critics join Zola in locating at the root of late nineteenth-century painting. Zola distinguishes himself from many of his contemporaries, however, in finding this same conjunction to be operable in literature; the writer must also combine observation and analysis to achieve a "new vision" that is direct and immediate yet "experimental."

Vision and Literature

For Zola, painting and literature merge precisely at the point where seeing is necessary to each. Obviously, the two art forms are governed by different sign systems—the visual and the verbal. My purpose here is not to explore the bonds and boundaries between these sign-systems but the extent to which Zola finds vision essential to each. At the stage of creation, he describes painting and writing identically (see Chapter 5); at the stage of representation, he recognizes the necessity of "translating" the visual into verbal terms, but, given Zola's faith in the referential function of language, this is not an undertaking that is problematic by nature but rather a question of finding an adequate "translation" (see Chapter 4).

Zola undertakes in literature a visual revolution like that of Manet and the impressionists in painting—against the precept and prejudice of abstract thought, which, he maintains, has long dominated the arts, verbal as well as visual. He notes as early as 1864 that "les règles n'ont leur raison d'être que pour le génie, d'après les oeuvres duquel on a pu les formuler; seulement, chez ce génie, ce n'étaient pas des règles, mais une manière personnelle de voir" ("rules are applicable only to the genius from whose works they were formulated; except that, for the genius, they weren't rules, but a personal way of seeing," *Correspondance*, 252). Zola frequently speaks of creative vision as the single most essential attribute of the artist, noting that "le don de voir est moins common encore que le don de créer" ("the gift of seeing is even less common than the gift of creating," *Roman expérimental*, 169). He goes so far as to characterize his times by phrases such as "c'est l'heure de la vision nette" ("it's the hour of clear seeing," *Roman ex.*, 79).

To Zola, unfettered vision and the return to direct observation become the highest goals to which the author, like the painter, can aspire. Consequently, the words "observe," "vision," "see," and "eye" permeate his literary theories, just as they do his art criticism, and assume within them the important positions by which they come to define many of the major components of naturalism. Seeing is inseparable from knowing and creating in Zola's following description of his aspirations: "Je voudrais coucher l'humanité sur une page blanche, tout voir, tout savoir, tout dire" ("I would like to lay humanity out on a white page, see all, know all, tell all").[24] He uses strictly similar terms in praising the work of his contemporaries at a banquet for students in 1893: "ma génération … s'est efforcée d'ouvrir largement les fenêtres sur la nature, de tout voir, de tout dire" ("my generation … attempted to open wide the windows onto nature, to see all, to tell all," *Mélanges, prefaces et discours*, 286).

Zola frequently stresses the importance of the visual aspects of verbal representation, as in his renowned definition of a work of art as a "corner of creation seen through a temperament," which was cited in relation to his Salons. The same formula appears throughout his literary criticism, as in the following example from *Mes Haines*, where visuality is emphasized:

> Ainsi, il est bien convenu que l'artiste se place devant la nature, qu'il la copie en l'interprétant, qu'il est plus ou moins réel selon ses yeux, en un mot, qu'il a pour mission de nous rendre les objets tels qu'il les voit, appuyant sur tel détail, créant à nouveau. J'exprimerai toute ma pensée en disant qu'une oeuvre d'art est un coin de la création vu à travers un tempérament.

> (Thus, it is agreed that the artist places himself before nature, that he copies it while interpreting it, that his mission is to represent objects as he sees them, insisting on a given detail, creating anew. I will express my whole thought in saying that a work of art is a corner of creation seen through a temperament. *Mes Haines*, 176)

Zola stresses the importance of visual concerns in his assessment of specific writers as much as in his theoretical pronouncements. He notes of the predecessor he admired most that "Balzac regarde et raconte; le choix de l'objet sur lequel tombent ses regards lui importe peu, il n'a que le souci de tout regarder et de tout dire" ("Balzac looks and recounts; the choice of object on which his eyes fall matters little to him; his only concern is to look at everything and tell everything," *Mes Haines*, 146). He says of Daudet that he records human experience, "ayant tout vu avec ses yeux de myope, jusqu'aux petits détails qui auraient échappé à de bons yeux" ("having seen everything with his nearsighted eyes, even the fine details that would have escaped the best of eyes," *Les Romanciers naturalistes*, 216). The following quotation, concerning the Goncourts, illustrates Zola's understanding of the way a painterly vision came to characterize their perception of reality and, thus, the nature of their writing:

> Ils ont commencé par être tellement sensibles au monde visible, aux formes et aux couleurs, qu'ils ont failli être peintres.... Même, plus tard, quand ils ont eu à faire une description capitale, ils sont allés prendre une vue de l'horizon, ils ont rapporté, dans leur cabinet, une aquarelle, comme d'autres rapportent des notes manuscrites sur un agenda.... A chaque page, on retrouvera ainsi la touche vive et sentie, le croquis de l'artiste.

> (They began by being so sensitive to the visible world, to shapes and colors, that they almost became painters.... Indeed, later, when they had an important description to do, they would go and locate a view of the horizon, they would take a watercolor back to their study, much as others use handwritten notes.... Thus on every page one will find the lived and felt touch, the artist's sketch. *Les Romanciers naturalistes*, 192–93)

Zola makes the same link to painting in describing a forerunner whose work he did not particularly admire: "en somme, Théophile Gautier avait foeil d'un peintre, et telle était sa qualité maîtresse. Toute sa vie littéraire, toute son oeuvre découlait de là. Il écrivait comme on peint, avec le seul souci des lignes et des couleurs" ("in short, Théophile Gautier had a painter's eye, and this was his predominant trait. All of his literature, all of his work stemmed from that. He wrote, much as one paints, with the sole concern for lines and colors," *Documents litteraires*, 115).

The coupling of "painter" and "observer" is applied to his disciple J.-K. Huysmans (*Une Campagne*, 205) and even to Petronius![25] These were two of the most complimentary epithets in Zola's repertoire; in 1868, he wrote for the first time to Flaubert, whom he admired above all other living novelists, sending him a copy of *Madeleine Férat*: "Veuillez accepter le volume ci-joint comme un hommage à votre talent d'observateur et de peintre" ("Please accept the enclosed volume as a hommage to your talent as an observer and painter," *Correspondance*, 353).

Of the many visual terms recurring in Zola's definitions of art, "observer" and "observation" are the most common and significant. Zola regarded naturalism, in literature as in painting, as being essentially a "new vision," a return to direct observation: "On me demande pourquoi je ne me suis pas contenté du mot réalisme, qui avait cours il y a trente ans; uniquement parce que le réalisme d'alors était une chapelle et rétrécissait l'horizon littéraire et artistique. Il m'a semblé que le mot naturalisme élargissait, au contraire, le domaine de l'observation" ("I've been asked why I wasn't content with the word realism, which was being used thirty years ago; solely because realism was a hallowed realm narrowing the literary and artistic horizon. It seemed to me that the word naturalism, on the other hand, expanded the domain of observation," *Le Naturalisme au théâtre*, 147). He insisted on characterizing himself as "simplement un observateur qui constate des facts" ("simply an observer who confirms facts," *Roman ex.*, 92), and he spoke categorically of "le roman naturaliste, le roman d'observation et d'analyse" ("the naturalist novel, the novel of observation and analysis," *Roman ex.*, 166).

Zola believed that the ability to observe correctly and critically was a contemporary phenomenon (Petronius notwithstanding!), contending that "l'observation, l'étude de la nature, est devenue aujourd'hui une méthode qui était a peu près inconnue au XVIIe siècle" ("observation, the study of nature, has become today a method that was more or less unknown in the seventeenth century," *Nat. au théâtre*, 80). In fact, with characteristic temerity, he located its inception in the eighteenth century: "On partait d'un fait observé, on avançait ainsi d'observation en observation, en évitant de conclure avant de posséder les éléments nécessaires. En un mot, au lieu de debuter par la synthèse, on commençait par l'analyse" ("One began with an observed fact and then proceeded from observation to observation, avoiding concluding before possessing the necessary elements. In a word, instead of beginning with synthesis, one began with analysis," *Roman ex.*, 94)—and its flourishing in the nineteenth century with thinkers like Taine[26] and writers like Balzac (*Documents littéraires*, 199–200) and Daudet (*Une Campagne*, 309).[27]

Although the words "observation" and "observer" may have other connotations, Zola is careful to qualify them in such a way as to ensure that only their most concrete, visual meanings could be inferred by the reader. In the following passage, for example, he links the word "observation" to the critic's eyesight: "Le critique est semblable au médecin ... il note ses observations au fur et à mesure qu'il les fait, sans se soucier de conclure ni de poser des préceptes. Il n'a pour règle que l'excellence de ses yeux et la finesse de son intuition" ("The critic is like the doctor ... he notes his observations as he makes them, without concern for concluding or postulating precepts. His only rule is the excellence of his eyes and the insight of his intuitions,"

Mes Haines, 164). In another remark, made to a scientific congress, Zola directly associates the term "observation" with a number of clearly visual expressions: "La vie fiévreuse et emportée de Paris déjoue les délicatesses de l'observation.... Que les jeunes écrivains qui ont de bons yeux se mettent donc à l'oeuvre. Ils n'ont qu'a regarder autour d'eux et dire ensuite ce qu'ils ont vu" ("The feverish and excessive pace of Paris thwarts the insights of observation.... Let the young writers with good eyesight go to work. They have only to look around and then recount what they have seen").[28]

The term "observation," then, in its most visual sense, is virtually synonymous with "naturalism" and recurs in many of Zola's theories, definitions, and critical judgments concerning modern literature. We frequently find the epithet "observer" linked with those of "painter," "analyst," and "creator," but, by far the most common coupling, especially after the publication of *Le Roman expérimental* in 1880, is with the word "experimenter." Zola notes, for example, that "le romancier est fait d'un observateur et d'un expérimentateur" ("the novelist is made of an observer and an experimenter," *Roman ex.*, 16), and it is precisely these two terms that ultimately come to characterize naturalism: "Seulement, je constate la grande évolution d'observation et d'expérimentation qui caractérise notre siècle, et j'appelle naturalisme la forme littéraire amenée par cette évolution" ("However, I note the great evolution of observation and experimentation that characterizes our century, and I call naturalism the literary form brought on by this evolution," *Nat. au théâtre*, 149).[29]

As "observation" (the most recurrent of the many words denoting vision in Zola's theories) becomes increasingly linked to the term "experimentation," this formula comes to figure in most of Zola's definitions concerning naturalism. Consequently, following the thread of visual concerns through Zola's theoretical works leads inevitably to *Le Roman expérimental*, where Zola defines these key terms, delineating the relationships between them.

CREATIVE VISION IN THE EXPERIMENTAL NOVEL

The sheer number of Zola's remarks related to observation and vision confirms the extent to which vision had penetrated and even dominated his poetics, but few cited thus far have offered any precise definition of visual terms. It is in *Le Roman expérimental* that Zola systematically describes his concept of observation. By adopting the theories of the French experimental scientist Claude Bernard, Zola is able to define a type of creative, analytic vision capable of yielding significant discoveries in the arts as well as the sciences. This concept of seeing, when related to the innovations of Manet and the impressionist painters and to Zola's own descriptive and imaginative techniques in literature, will facilitate a reassessment of the role and reputation of *Le Roman expérimental*, called "embarrassingly naive"[31] and "unbelievably naive" by critics today and which elicited a cry of "Poor Claude Bernard!"[32] at the time of its publication.

Zola's frequent linking of observation with some other quality, particularly analysis or experimentation, seems to indicate a realization on his part that pure observation does not alone constitute a meaningful approach to art or experience. In fact, he had recognized the necessity for "cheating" against the principle of direct observation as early as 1868, while he was planning the Rougon-Macquart series; he tells himself in the preliminary notes:

> Avoir surtout la logique de la déduction. Il est indifférent que le fait générateur soit reconnu comme absolument vrai; ce fait sera surtout une hypothèse scientifique, empruntée aux traites médicaux. Mais lorsque ce fait sera posé, lorsque je l'aurai accepté comme un axiome, en déduire mathématiquement tout le volume, et être alors d'une absolue vérité.

> (Use deductive logic especially. It is unimportant that the initial fact be recognized as absolutely true; this fact will mainly be a scientific hypothesis, borrowed from medical treatises. But once this fact is in place, once I have accepted it as an axiom, deduce the whole volume from it mathematically, and thus be of absolute truth.)[33]

Zola increasingly found observation to be either too passive, thus degenerating into a merely photographic and purely representational faculty, or too personal and subjective, thus becoming no more than an orgy of visual sensation, self-satisfying but sterile.

Basically, two novelistic needs propel Zola beyond the boundaries of pure observation—the need for scientific analysis and experimentation on the one hand and for fictional freedom on the other. Zola's naturalism differs from what he terms "photographic realism" precisely because of the naturalist's proposal to study, in scientific fashion, the influence of heredity and milieu on the human being and because of its highly figurative language and imaginative rendering of characters and events. Within this context, it is

easy to imagine why Zola must have been struck by the first words of
Bernard's essay on experimental medicine: "Man can only observe the
phenomena surrounding him within highly restrictive limits; the majority
escapes his senses naturally, and observation is insufficient.... man does not
limit himself to seeing; he thinks and wants to know the meaning of
phenomena whose existence was revealed to him by *observation*."[34]

According to Bernard, observation alone does not constitute scientific
procedure; it must be complemented by hypothesis and analysis. The doctrine
of determinism, for example, exacts a strict analysis of each phenomenon in
terms of the causal relationships that it establishes with other phenomena.
Zola paraphrases Bernard's conception of this doctrine as follows:

> Il appelle "déterminisme" la cause qui determine (apparition des
> phénomènes. Cette cause prochaine, comme il la nomme, n'est
> rien autre chose que la condition physique et matérielle de
> l'existence ou de la manifestation des phénomènes. Le but de la
> methode expérimentale, le terme de toute recherche scientifique,
> est donc identique pour les corps vivants et pour les corps bruts:
> il consiste à trouver les relations qui rattachent un phénomène
> quelconque à sa cause prochaine, ou autrement dit, à déterminer
> les conditions necessaires à la manifestation de ce phénomène.
>
> (He calls "determinism" the cause that determines the
> occurrence of phenomena. This immediate cause, as he terms it,
> is nothing other than the physical and material condition for the
> existence or manifestation of phenomena. The aim of the
> experimental method, the goal of all scientific research, is
> therefore identical for living bodies and for inanimate bodies: it
> consists of finding the relationships that link a given
> phenomenon to its immediate cause, or otherwise stated, of
> determining the conditions necessary for the manifestation of
> that phenomenon. *Roman ex.*, 13)

A "relationship" is a bond between two observable phenomena but is not
itself observable, so that the scientist is inevitably forced to extend analyses
beyond the visible and into the realm of the abstract. Bernard further
explains that the complexity of such relationships necessitates the
implementation of analytic experimentation in addition to observation:
"However, in the experimental sciences these relationships are surrounded
by numerous phenomena that are infinitely complex and varied, which hide

them from our eyes. With the help of experimentation, we analyze, we dissociate these phenomena, in order to reduce them to progressively simpler relationships and conditions" (*Introduction*, 78).[35]

Like the scientist for Bernard, the novelist, according to Zola, must not be content with mere observation but must set further goals: "Il lui faudra voir, comprendre, inventer" ("he has to see, understand, invent," *Roman ex.*, 19); "voir n'est pas tout, il faut rendre" ("seeing isn't everything; one has to depict," *Roman ex.*, 171). Zola must seek, then, to mold the principal tenet of naturalism, the return to direct observation, to conform with the exigencies of analysis and imagination—faculties required by both scientist and artist— and, indeed, the novelist comes to ask himself, "en littérature, où jusqu'ici l'observation paraît avoir ete seule employée, l'expérience est-elle possible?" ("in literature, where observation alone appears to have been used up to now, is experimentation possible?" *Roman ex.*, 14).

This question is at the very root of positivism, because it expresses the fundamental disparity between the movement's methodology, based on direct observation, and its chief goal, scientific knowledge. The solution to this basic rift in the tenets of positivism preoccupied thinkers during the second half of the nineteenth century and was often on Zola's mind as well as those of his closest friends. In fact, Cézanne's objective has been described as "preserving sensibility's essential role while substituting conscious reflection for empiricism,"[36] and, as has been shown, the synthesis of the natural and the analytic was the principal legacy of impressionist painting, according to Zola and numerous contemporaries. Although this synthesis was reflected in the thought of many of the great minds of the late nineteenth century, Zola found its most cogent expression and most applicable resolution in Bernard's treatise.

The experimental method, as described by Bernard, solves the dualism between observation and experiment by wresting the latter from the abstract, reflective position it had previously occupied in scientific thought and making it primarily external and observational. In short, Bernard, as quoted by Zola, resolves the disparity between the basic components of positivism by asserting that "l'expérience n'est au fond qu'une observation provoquée" ("basically, an experiment is only an induced observation," *Roman ex.*, 12). Zola's paraphrase of Bernard continues with a description of the sophisticated, dialectical process by which the experimenter becomes observer, by which thought becomes visual and external:

L'observateur constate purement et simplement les phénomènes qu'il a sous les yeux.... Il doit être le photographe des

phénomènes; son observation doit représenter la nature.... Mais
une fois le fait constaté et la phénomène bien observe, l'idée
arrive, le raisonnement intervient, et l'expérimentateur apparaît
pour interpréter le phénomène.... Dès le moment où le résultat
de l'expérience se manifeste, l'expérimentateur se trouve en face
d'une véritable observation qu'il a provoquée, et qu'il faut
constater, comme toute observation, sans idée précongue.
L'expérimentateur doit alors disparaître ou plutôt se transformer
instantanément en observateur.

(The observer notes purely and simply the phenomena in front of
his eyes.... He must be the photographer of the phenomena; his
observation must represent nature.... But once the fact is noted
and the phenomenon well observed, thought arrives, reasoning
intervenes, and the experimenter appears in order to interpret the
phenomenon.... From the moment when the result of the
experiment occurs, the experimenter finds himself before a
veritable observation that he has induced, and that he must note,
as with any observation, without preconception. The
experimenter must then disappear or, rather, transform himself
instantly into an observer. *Roman ex.*, 15)

For Bernard, the experimental method is not primarily reflective, but occurs
simultaneously with observation; the seemingly disparate processes of
observation and experimentation, and, indeed, the rift between the visual and
scientific aspects of positivism, are synthesized into one direct, immediate,
visual process: "With experimental reasoning, the experimenter is not
separate from the observer ... he must himself be at once observer and
experimenter" (*Introduction*, 37; see also *Roman ex.*, 15–16).[37]

The experimental method, as outlined by Bernard, thus enabled Zola
to proceed beyond "photographic realism," while remaining faithful to its
doctrine of direct observation, by incorporating analysis and
experimentation into the act of seeing: "Un reproche bête qu'on nous fait, a
nous autres écrivains naturalistes, c'est de vouloir être uniquement des
photographer.... Eh bien! avec l'application de la méthode expérimentale au
roman, toute querelle cesse. L'idée d'expérience entraîne avec elle l'idée de
modification" ("A stupid criticism made against us naturalist writers is that
we want to be merely photographers.... Well! with the application of the
experimental method to the novel, debate ceases. The idea of
experimentation entails with it the idea of modification," *Roman ex.*, 18). In

a later example, Zola again denies the title "photographer," here on the grounds of the role of imagination in his art:

> Les gens qui ont fait la naïve découverte que le naturalisme n'était autre chose que de la photographie, comprendront peut-être cette fois que, tout en nous piquant de réalité absolue, nous entendons souffler la vie a nos reproductions. De là style personnel, qui est la vie des livres. Si nous refusons l'imagination, dans le sens d'invention surajoutée au vrai, nous mettons toutes nos forces créatrices a donner au vrai sa vie propre.

> (Those who made the naive discovery that naturalism was nothing other than photography will perhaps understand this time that, while priding ourselves on absolute reality, we mean to breath life into our reproductions. Whence personal style, which is the life of books. If we deny imagination, in the sense of invention added on top of truth, we put all of our creative energies into giving truth its own life. *Roman ex.*, 200)

Unlike "invention"—the indulgence in subjective fantasy— "imagination," like experimentation, is a part of the visual process. In fact, the experimental method encourages the liberal exercise of imagination as part of scientific procedure; Bernard notes that "one must certainly refrain from prohibiting the use of hypotheses and ideas in instituting the experiment. To the contrary, one must give full reign to one's imagination" (*Introduction*, 40).[38] Indeed, as one critic has stated, concerning imagination in *Le Roman expérimental*: "Zola follows Bernard closely on the absolute necessity and primary importance of an initial insight derived from observation. For both men, this idea is the special inspiration of genius, without which there can be nothing. The core of Zola's analogy between art and science rests upon this common point, from which one may progress either to the acquisition of new knowledge or to the creative act."[39]

However, the scientific imagination of Zola and Bernard, founded on deduction and hypothesis, must not be confused with pure fantasy. As Zola notes, the scientist's imagination, contrary to that of the idealist, must be firmly grounded in the observable phenomena of external reality: "Comme le dit Claude Bernard: 'L'idée expérimentale n'est point arbitraire ni purement imaginaire; elle doit toujours avoir un point d'appui dans la réalité observée, c'est-à-dire dans la nature'" ("As Claude Bernard says, 'The experimental idea is not at all arbitrary or purely imaginary; it must always have a basis in observed reality, that is, in nature,'" *Roman ex.*, 18–19; see also 23, 36, and 181).

Zola draws the same distinction between types of imagination elsewhere in stating that "l'imagination, j'entends le rêve, la fantaisie, ne peut que vous égarer. L'imagination ... devient de la déduction, de l'intuition" ("imagination, meaning dream or fantasy, can only lead you astray. Imagination ... is becoming deduction and intuition," *Nat. au théâtre*, 201). Far from contradicting reality by offering an alternative to it, an escape from it, imagination must be in the nature of a deduction derived from and remaining faithful to the phenomena of the external world. Imagination, firmly controlled by observation, thus fosters scientific discovery, which understands and affirms reality instead of rejecting it, as Zola felt the idealists did. By making the artist's *eye*, rather than his brain, heart, or spleen, the seat of his imagination, Zola attempts to adapt the personal and deforming qualities of artistic creation to the principal tenet of naturalism, the return to the direct and immediate observation of natural phenomena. By expanding his conception of vision to include imagination, Zola is able to avoid abstraction and invention on the one hand and mere photographic realism on the other. His theories point toward a creative and imaginative visual process that will blend and synthesize the acute observation of the, camera's lens with the poetic recreation of the artist's temperament.

Zola's radically scientific poetics distinguish him from most of his French contemporaries, but his thought on visual creativity rejoins that of Conrad Fiedler, the German art critic who outlined a similar program for creative yet direct vision, which he, too, felt to be at the root of modern artistic activity. Fiedler, like Zola, condemned photographic realism: "The so-called realists are not ... to be blamed because in their works they put the main stress upon sensuous appearance, but on account of the fact that, commonly, they cannot perceive in sensuous appearance anything more than what the most limited perceptive faculty can gain from it" (*On Judging*, 59). Like Zola, Fiedler chastised the idealists for their "invention," which tends to deny nature altogether: "The idealists, however, by neither feeling satisfied with nature as they observe it nor being able to develop their perceptions of nature to ever higher levels, try to remedy the artistic insufficiency of their own creations by giving them a non-artistic content" (*On Judging*, 60). Fiedler, like Zola, contended that true art must remain faithful to visible reality: "The origin and existence of art is based upon an immediate mastering of the visible world" (*On Judging*, 43); thus, it is visual prowess that defines artistic temperament and talent: "It is to the independent and free development of perceptual experience that we must look for the peculiar power of artistic talent" (*On Judging*, 27).

Elsewhere, Fiedler defines the artist in terms of visual acuity and activity:

> Artistically gifted people differ from others only in the ways their eyes function; in every other respect they are equal. Unfolding and developing awareness of reality specializes in a particular manner in the artistically gifted, solely by virtue of the visual faculty. In the artist seeing develops in a way peculiar to him; it exhausts itself neither by aiding in the formation of images and concepts nor by the partially passive function of receiving impressions. Rather, it attaches to this passive function an advancing activity, for basically the behavior of the visual organ cannot be termed passive and purely receptive.[40]

Fiedler concludes, as did Zola, that the seat of artistic creation is solely in the artists *eye*:

> It seems strange that an organ, common to all men and extensively used by all, should be the active center of a performance limited to a few. Men readily admit that the activity of the artist is not only based on the use of the eye, but is unthinkable without it. Nevertheless, they assume a special artistic power apart from the eye and served by it only in an auxiliary capacity. And yet we may peer within the workshop of artistic activity only when we realize that in essence this activity depends entirely on the eye. Only such realization can strip the artistic process both of the semi-mystical character which it possesses for some and of the trivial meaning attributed to it by others. Only such realization reveals it as a natural process which unfolds from the simplest beginning to endless breadth and height.[41]

Thus, Zola's complaint that "the gift of seeing is even less common than the gift of creating" and his contention that creativity was, in fact, "an optical phenomenon," "a personal way of seeing," clearly reflect the spirit of his generation, which Fiedler articulates in Germany, as Zola does in France.[42] Moreover, the importance of creative vision in Zola's theories of imagination adds credence to his claim, cited in the Preface, that he could leap "toward the stars on the springboard of precise observation" and demands attention to his warning that in order to discover the secret of his imagination, the reader must literally be prepared to "take apart the mechanism of [his] eye" (*Correspondance*, 635–36).

ON A PURELY theoretical level, the experimental method marks a synthesis of science and vision, a resolution of a basic disparity in the thought of Zola and the entire positivist movement. *Le Roman expérimental* is Zola's most systematic statement concerning certain visual notions that were always present in his work, and, consequently, this theoretical tract gives unity and direction to the otherwise isolated and underdeveloped theories concerning vision and visual effects that permeate Zola's poetics.

Zola's literary theories express clearly his belief that the eye could embrace, within the act of seeing, the faculties of cognition and imagination required for scientific analysis and literary creation. Nor was he alone in this belief: Conrad Fiedler, the German art critic, and Jules Laforgue, the French poet, along with Claude Bernard, the experimental scientist, expressed similar theories of "pure visuality," and, indeed, Manet and the impressionist painters, whom Zola knew intimately and defended publicly, had manifested this same purely visual, yet analytic and imaginative, manner of seeing in their work. In dissecting the workings of Zola's eye, the traces of analytic vision will be treated in Chapter 4 (description), while the manifestations of creative vision will be dealt with in Chapter 5 (imagination).

NOTES

1. "Des forcenés allèrent jusqu'à déchirer le journal en plein boulevard, devant les kiosques. Le salonnier de *L'Evénement* recevait jusqu'à des trente lettres par jour, contenant quelques-unes des encouragements, la plupart des injures; il faillit avoir un duel." *Emile Zola, notes d'un ami* (Paris: Charpentier, 1882), 68.

2. *Salons*, 73. Unless otherwise indicated, this and further page references to Zola's art criticism are from the volume *Salons*, collected and edited by F.W.J. Hemmings and R.J. Niess (Geneva: Droz, 1959), and will be included parenthetically in the text.

3. *La Nouvelle Peinture*. Paris: Marcel Guérin, 1876.

4. The term "naturalism" was first applied to landscape art as early as 1839 and denotes merely the realistic representation of nature. Zola first applied the term to literature in 1868, extending its meaning to encompass the scientific representation of reality through determinism and, later, the experimental method. (For a recent discussion of Zola's naturalism, see William J. Berg and Laurey K. Martin, *Emile Zola Revisited* [Boston: G. K. Hall, Twayne's World Authors Series, 1992]). In his

references to the painters of his generation, the "new painters," Zola tends to meld the two definitions of naturalism, no doubt relishing the combination for polemic purposes, that is, in order to advance the fledgling notion of naturalism in literature.

5. Although Manet often met with these painters, sometimes worked with them, and briefly adopted their light palette and loose brushwork (see, for example, the rue Mosnier or rue de Berne paintings of 1877–78), his preference for contrasting values and the predominance of line and design distinguish his work from that of mainstream impressionism, as we shall see in further detail in Chapter 4. (It should be noted in passing, however, that many of these same qualities apply, at various times and to varying degrees, to Degas, Cassatt, and Renoir, among others). Cézanne, also a "colorist" according to Zola (see his article, "Une Exposition," cited in note 6 below), is ultimately concerned more with the geometrical forms and planes underlying a landscape than with the play of light on the surface, which caught the impressionists.

6. From an article dated 16 April 1887, entitled "Une Exposition: Les Peintres impressionnistes," first published in *Le Sémaphore de Marseille* on 19 April 1877. In *Mon Salon/ Manet/Ecrits sur l'art*, ed. Antoinette Ehrard (Paris: Garnier Flammarion, 1970), 282.

7. *L'Oeuvre*, 83. This and all further page references to the Rougon-Macquart novels, unless otherwise noted, are from the five-volume Pléiade edition, edited (brilliantly) by Henri Mitterand (Paris: Fasquelle et Gallimard, Bibliothèque de la Pléiade, 1960–67). *L'Oeuvre* is in vol. 4.

8. On the use of a pale ground, see, for example, *Techniques of the World's Greatest Painters*, ed. Waldemar Januszczak (Secaucus, N.J.: Chartwell Books, 1980), especially the entry on Monet, 102–5. Concerning brushwork, see Oscar Reutersvärd, "The Accentuated Brush Stroke of the Impressionists," *Journal of Aesthetics and Art Criticism 10*, no. 3 (March 1952): 273–78.

9. "oeil vierge." In Lionello Venturi, *Les Archives de l'impressionnisme* (Paris: Durand-Ruel, 1939), I, 52. Throughout the twentieth century, art critics have done little to weaken this notion. André Fontainas repeats Zola's distinction between 'pure visual sensation' and 'preconceived rules coupled with prejudiced abstractions' as approaches to painting: "Manet détermine les courants nouveaux. Il ne voit que par les sees, indépendamment de route théorie préconçue et de tout préjugé qu'on lui a enseignés" (*Historie de la peinture française au XIXe et au XXe siècles* [Paris: Mercure de France, 1922], 218). Pierre Francastel adds that the achievement of a pure vision, uninhibited by abstraction, is the real innovation of these painters: "L'Impressionnisme, tel que nous l'avons conçu, apparaissait comme un effort des artistes pour rendre, avec le moins d'abstraction possible, des sensations avant tout optiques; c'est en ce sens seulement que les artistes de la fin du XIXe siècle apportent des nouveautés techniques" (*L'Impressionnisme: Les Origines de la peinture moderne* [Paris, 1937], 183). The editors of *Réalités* speak of the "raw experience of the optical sensation in its instantaneous confrontation with the visible. Now, this is precisely the final aim of the principal Impressionists, namely, to free the mind of all memory, of all visual culture, of all preconceived knowledge of nature" (*Impressionism* [Secaucus, N.J.: Chartwell Books, 1973], 91–92).

10. "Gli Impressionisti," *Impressionism and Post-Impressionism*, ed. Linda Nochlin (Englewood Cliffs, N.J.: Prentice-Hall, 1966), 25.

11. "L'Impressionniste est un peintre moderniste qui, doué d'une sensibilité d'oeil hors du commun, oubliant les tableaux amassés par les siècles dans les musées, oubliant l'éducation optique de l'école (dessin et perspective, coloris), à force de vivre et de voir franchement et primitivement dans les spectacles lumineux en plein air, c'est-à-dire hors de l'atelier eclaire 145°, que ce soit la rue, la campagne, les intérieurs, est parvenu à se refaire un oeil naturel, à voir naturellement et a peindre naïvement comme il voit." "Critique d'art—L'Impressionnisme," in *Mélanges posthumes*, vol. 3 of *Oeuvres complètes*, 4th ed. (Paris: Mercure de France, 1903), 133–34.

12. "vierge et abstrait." In André Fontainas, *Histoire de la peinture française*, 215.

13. Zola is not alone in this view, echoed by a present-day critic of some standing: "They practically never followed out their theories in a logical fashion. If it has been said that Claude Monet 'was only an eye; but great heavens, what an eye!' it has also been said that Impressionism was a vast eye, capable of capturing the subtlest nuances and values but incapable of taking it a stage further and realizing the synthesis between that eye and the intellect. Its fervent masters do not work out logically or scientifically the effects they desired to evoke; they put down their blobs of color as rapidly as they perceived them" (Maurice Sérullaz, *The Impressionist Painters*, trans. W. J. Strachan [New York: Universe Books, 1960], 11).

14. The issue of Zola's intent (or effect) in *L'Oeuvre* has spawned considerable controversy in literary criticism as well as in art history. It is the principal focus of books by the literary critics Patrick Brady (*"L'Oeuvre" de Emile Zola* [Geneva: Droz, 1967]) and Robert Niess (*Zola, Cézanne, and Manet: A Study of "L'Oeuvre"* [Ann Arbor: University of Michigan Press, 1968]), both of which are discussed briefly in the Introduction. Many art historians of the period have also dealt with *L'Oeuvre*, among them John Canaday (*Mainstreams of Modern Art* [New York: Holt, Rinehart and Winston, 1959], 347), Phoebe Pool (*Impressionism* [New York: Praeger Publishers, 1967], 217–18), and John Rewald (*The History of Impressionism* [New York: MOMA, 1973], 4th rev. ed., 534–36). Pool's opinion of *L'Oeuvre*—"The novel in which Zola travestied Impressionism" (217)—is not atypical of the general consensus among art historians. However, our argument here, paralleling especially that of Brady, suggests that some nuancing may be appropriate.

15. Ms. no. 10.316, fols. 276, 300–301, and 302, Département des Manuscrits, Nouvelles Acquisitions Françaises, Bibliothèque Nationale.

16. The principle of complementary colors—developed in the studies of the chemists Chevreul, Maxwell, and Rood—conformed with the discoveries of the physiologists Young and Helmholtz, and was applied by the neo-impressionists, most notably Seurat, Pissarro, and Signac, beginning in 1884 and 1885. Paul Signac, while reading *L'Oeuvre* in the *Gil Blas*, noticed a mistake in Zola's interpretation of this principle and sent him the following letter on 8 February 1886: "Monsieur: Peintre—dit impressionniste—je suis avec enormément d'intérêt votre beau roman sur l'art contemporain. Je vous demande, Monsieur, la permission de vous signaler dans votre feuilleton d'hier une petite erreur sur la théorie des couleurs complémentaires.

Gagnière dit: 'Mon drapeau rouge se détachant sur un ciel bleu devient violet ...' Le ciel étant *bleu* a pour complémentaire de l'orangé. Cet orangé vient s'ajouter an rouge du drapeau, qui au lieu de devenir violet tire an contraire sur le *jaune*. Pour que le drapeau devint violet—comme le dit Gagnière—il aurait fallu que le ciel soit orangé ou jaune" (in *R-M*, IV, 1452). Zola corrected his mistake to conform with Signac's suggestion before *L'Oeuvre* was published in novel form two months later. The irony is, of course, that he did so in order to criticize abuses of the notion.

17. Although Cézanne is by no means a "pointillist" or "divisionist," his use of color to underscore forms and even to create mood is often nonrepresentational, to say the least.

18. This conclusion is hardly new (see especially Patrick Brady, *"L'Oeuvre" de Emile Zola*), but it does incorporate new evidence from a slightly different angle.

19. Among modern critics, André Fontainas sums up the hopes placed in the scientific aspects of impressionism in the following judgment: "Pour la première fois peut-être, a la suite des physiciens, les artistes examinent les fondements de leur métier; d'inépuisables richesses sent issues de ces investigations; un renouveau fécond, une fraîcheur, une vigueur qu'on n'eût osé espérer.... Ces observations scientifiques, un peu ardues, mais aisément vérifiables pour chacun (il suffit de juxtaposer des bandes de papier coloré), sont à la base du metier des impressionnistes; il importait de les enoncer avec le plus de simplicité possible" (*Histoire de la peinture française*, 228–29). Oscar Reutersvärd, speaking of the widespread interpretation of impressionism as a positivist movement, notes also the strange synthesis of visual and scientific at the root of positivism. This proponent of the accentuated brush stroke articulates the position of the visualists with particular cogency: "This doctrine [the positivistic ideology of art] was an offspring of Comte's philosophy and consequently rejected everything creative in art which did not emerge from 'positive experience', from cognizance of the senses. This meant a revolutionizing emphasis being placed on the visual moment in art. The painter was to discover new values with the aid of his eyes and not improvise on the deal with literary subjects which in themselves lacked visual effect. And exactly as in the positivistic epistemology, they made a study of deciding the 'actual subjects' of art, the empirically gained visual phenomena right down to their slightest constituents, and to determine the capability and function of the organ of cognizance—the eye. Thus a sensual aestheticism crystallized, recognizable by its peculiar admixture of physiological and optic-physical principles. Painting was to be upheld by the geniuses of sight who could master the world as a visual appearance and analyse it and reproduce it in detail.... And the impressionists were held up as those who applied the new aesthetic doctrine. Their painting was propounded as being scientific reports of the chromo-luminaristic conditions in nature, the decomposed structure was said to correspond with the disaggregation of sunlight into different prismatic elements, and by fusing on the observer's retina, the impressionists' touches of color would give rise to the same effects as the spectral phenomena in physical reality" ("The Accentuated Brush Stroke," 276–77).

20. "Au point de vice de la délicatesse de foeil, de la subtile pénétration du coloris, c'est un résultat tout a fait extraordinaire. Le plus savant physicien ne pourrait rien reprocher à leurs analyses de la lumière." *La Nouvelle Peinture* (Paris: Marcel Guerin, 1876), 39.

21. "une sorte l'impression analytique ... en dehors de la longue convention du paysage moderne, elle a decouvert certains aspects inexplores des choses, les a analysés avec une subtilité infinie, en a agrandi le champ des recherches picturales." *L'Opinion* (2 April 1876) in Venturi, *Les Archives de l'impressionnisme*, II, 286.

22. "Donc un oeil naturel (on raffiné puisque, pour cet organe, avant d'aller, il faut redevenir primitif en se débarrassant des illusions tactiles), un oeil naturel oublie les illusions tactiles et sa commode langue morte: le dessin-contour et n'agit que dans sa faculté de sensibilité prismatique. Il arrive à voir la réalité dans l'atmosphere vivante des formes, décomposée, réfractée, réfléchie par les êtres et les choses, en incessants variations. Telle est cette première caractéristique de l'oeil impressionniste." "Critique d'art—L'Impressionnisme," 135–36.

23. *On Judging Works of Visual Art*, trans. Henry Schaefer-Simmern and Fulmer Mood (Berkeley and Los Angeles: University of California Press, 1949), 27. Further references to Fielder's work are from the above translation, unless otherwise indicated, and will be cited in the text as *On Judging*, followed by the page number.

24. Quoted in Armand Lanoux, *Bonjour Monsieur Zola* (Paris: Hachette, 1954), 136–37.

25. "Si maintenant j'interroge la littérature latine, je ne trouve guère chez les Romains que deux romanciers, Apulée et Pétrone. Ce dernier fut un véritable romancier, un observateur clairvoyant, un peintre fin et spirituel" (quoted in Guy Robert, "Trois textes inédits de Zola," *Revue des sciences humaines* 51–52 [July–December 1948]: 200).

26. See, for example, *Lettres de Paris*, ed. Phillip Duncan and Vera Erdeley (Geneva: Droz, 1963), 34.

27. But not Stendhal (*Romanciers naturalistes*, 75) and Dumas (*Documents littéraires*, 199–200).

28. In Guy Robert, "Trois textes inédits de Zola," 207. A. David-Sauvageot, an art critic and a contemporary of Zola, uses the term "observation" in the same purely visual, nonabstract way as the author of *Les Rougon-Macquart* when he says: "C'est l'observation qui est le premier et le principal outil. Remarque souvent faite, pour qualifier un bon ouvrage on disait autrefois: bien imaginé; tandis qu'aujourd'hui l'on dit: bien observe. Les yeux des réalistes de toute école sont comme braqués sur la réalité" (*Le Réalisme et le naturalisme* [Paris: Calmann Lévy, 1890], 197).

29. In his criticism he applies these two epithets to the artists he admires most, his disciple Céard (*Une Campagne*, 207), his ancestor Balzac (*Une Campagne*, 104; *Romanciers naturalistes*, 64), and his "master" Flaubert (*Romanciers naturalistes*, 162).

30. Angus Wilson, *Emile Zola: An Introductory Study of His Novels* (New York: William Morrow, 1952), 25.

31. F.W.J. Hemmings, *Emile Zola*, 2nd ed. (Oxford: The Clarendon Press, 1966), 151–52.

32. A. de Pontmartin, *Souvenirs d'un vieux critique* (Paris, 1881) in Le Blond's notes for *Le Roman expérimental*, 345.

33. In Pierre Martino, *Le Roman réaliste sous le Second Empire* (Paris: Hachette, 1913), 283.

34. "L'homme ne peut observer les phénomènes qui l'entourent que dons des limits très restreintes; le plus grand nombre échappe naturellement à ses sens, et l'observation ne lui suffit pas.... l'homme ne se borne pas à voir; il pense et veut connaître la signification des phénomènes dont *l'observation* lui a révele l'existence." *Introduction à l'étude de la médecine expérimentale*, 17. This and all further page references are from the Classiques Larousse edition (Paris: Librairie Larousse, 1951), subsequently referred to parenthetically in the text as *Introduction*, followed by the page number.

35. "Seulement dans les sciences expérimentales ces rapports sont entourés par des phénomènes nombreux complexes et variés a l'infini, qui les cachent à nos regards. A l'aide de l'expérience nous analysons, nous dissocions ces phénomènes, afin de les réduire à des relations et à des conditions de plus en plus simples."

36. Maurice Denis, "Cézanne," *L'Occident* 12 (September 1907), in John Rewald, *The History of Impressionism*, 414.

37. "Dans le raisonnement expérimental, l'expérimentateur ne se sépare pas de l'observateur ... il doit être lui-même la fois observateur et expérimentateur."

38. "il faudrait bien se garder de proscrire l'usage des hypotheses et des idées quand il s'agit d'instituer l'expérience. On doit, au contraire, comme nous le verrons bientôt, donner libre carrière à son imagination."

39. Gordon Dewart, "Emile Zola's Critical Theories on the Novel" (Ph.D. diss., Princeton University, 1953), n, 69.

40. From "Three Fragments," in *From the Classicists to the Impressionists*, ed. Elizabeth Gilmore Holt, vol. 3 of *A Documentary History of Art* (New York: Doubleday Books, 1966), 449.

41. Ibid., 452.

42. Among those late nineteenth-century French artists who embraced a doctrine of "pure visuality" similar to that of Zola and Fiedler were Jules Laforgue, who was, as one critic notes, directly influenced by Fiedler—"En se rattachant à l'esthétique de la 'visualité pure' de Fiedler, Laforgue affirme que la peinture la plus admirable est non pas celle où se retrouvent les chimères d'écoles, mais celle qui révèle l'oeil qui est allé le plus loin dans l'évolution de la visualité 'par le raffiné de ses nuances ou le compliqué de ses lignes'" (Venturi, *Les Archives de l'impressionnisme*, I, 67)—and Paul Valéry, who contended that "Je tiens qu'il existe une sorte de mystique des sensations, c'est-à-dire une 'Vie Extérieure' d'intensité et de profondeur au moins égales à celles que nous pretons aux ténèbres intimes et aux secrètes illuminations des ascètes, des soufis, des personnel concentrées en Dieu" (from "Autour de Corot," *Pieces sur l'art* [Paris: Gallimard, 1946], 147).

ROBERT E. ZIEGLER

Interpretation as Awakening from Zola's Le Rêve

A fictional instance of authorial projection, a predictive "dream" of a fantasized love affair, Zola's 1888 idyll he entitled *Le Rêve* confessionally transposed his frustrated wishes. Biographers of Zola have characterized the writer at the time of his work on *Le Rêve*, describing his fearsome girth and stagnating marriage to the querulous Alexandrine.[1] Yet by restricting his intake of wine and starchy food, he embodied himself in his volume, with critics identifying an early version's protagonist and the author who was starved for affection: "Un homme de quarante ans, n'ayant pas aimé, jusque-là dans la science, et qui se prend d'une passion pour une enfant de seize ans," Zola writes ("Ebauche" 223). The incorporeity of the novel and characters is the result of a Naturalism-free diet, one intended to transform the consumer of labor he reworked and expelled as his texts. Thus, a corpulent, reality-laden book like *La Terre*, which immediately preceded *Le Rêve*, was the textual corollary of the one who had measured "44 inches round what used to be his waist" (Hemmings 139). Having equated this "Moi" with "le travail, la littérature qui a mangé ma vie," Zola says ("Ebauche" 224), he strived to eliminate the empirical method that had left him at once fat and famished. But if his subsequent liaison with Jeanne Rozerot had allowed Zola's dream to come true, most critics have resisted incorporating or swallowing the illusion the romance is based on.[2]

From *Nineteenth-Century French Studies* 21, nos. 1–2 (Fall–Winter 1992–93). © 1993 by The University of Nebraska Press.

Perhaps a reason for the novel's often hostile reception may emerge with a different approach, one that stresses, not the relation of writer to text, but the way the book models its audience. Rather than crediting an impulse toward introjection, orality that is imputed to the author himself, this essay will examine the book's problematizing of how readers take in what they read, and why they distance themselves from the narrated fantasy by interposing interpretive language.

Intratextually, the heroine Angélique is a paradigm for an undissociated reader's complicity, as she refashions and flees from a text of reality that devoured and left her a victim, and escapes into the fictions of legend and fairy tale she absorbs and turns into herself. A self-referential model for his own ideal reader, she is different from Zola's first critics, like Anatole France, who professed being shocked since the book seemed to him out of character: "l'on ne saurait plaire, si l'on n'est plus soi-même," as the latter remarked in *Le Temps*.[3] What the novel's detractors were unable to realize was this was precisely the author's intention: "Je voudrais faire un livre qu'on n'attende pas de moi," Zola states at the start of "L'Ebauche" (223). It is literature's ability to transform that effectively bonds the creator and reader, permitting the ephemeral fulfillment of dreams that are conjugated by two who collaborate. A belief in the miraculous power of fiction is the novel's subject and purpose, changing foundlings to princesses who marry Prince Charming, making lovers of overweight authors, as God heals the faithful who submit to his will: "Si Dieu veut, je veux," says the d'Hautecoeur motto.

"[T]he literary work dreams a dream for us," as Norman Holland has written (75), recreating the dependency of infant on mother in the relation of reader and text. When an audience is "eaten" by the literature that paradoxically left Zola obese and diminished, they find that the word is what is able to nourish the one who expects to be gratified. It is natural that Angélique should turn to her readings as to a matrix of solace, support, *La Légende dorée* a compensatory fantasy dream-book that rewrites her own tale of abandonment. Edited out of the life of her mother, Sidonie, from an earlier volume, Angélique reads herself into de Voragine's text as a virgin protected from evil. Describing Sidonie as "Mauvaise mère, supprimée" ("Ebauche" 224), Zola makes Angélique's past an ellipsis, a lacuna filled in by the narrative dream that her history leaves uncontested. But while authorizing his character to act "as if" she were orphaned, Zola frames her by preceding documents, not genetically determining her by his earlier novels, but defining her as textual cipher.

First encountering the character as an anonymous waif, dressed in tatters, freezing, and homeless, the reader assimilates her to the statue of

Agnes, the virgin who is draped by the snow. Since she is vulnerable, has no sense of a family identity, she becomes the beloved of Jesus, is cuirassed in crystal and wears a mantle of frost that scintillates with the sunlight's embroidery. As one who "phantasies," she is likened to the writer whose wish "finds its fulfillment in the creative work" (Freud 151), her production of chasubles and priestly vestments a vehicle that conveys her ascensional dream.[4] As a result of her vagrancy and exposure to the cold, her original oral needs are refigured, topologically displaced as a wish for asylum in the home of the ones who adopt her. Indeed, the statues of the martyrs with whom Angélique identifies are appendages of the cathedral, "la mère ... énorme au milieu du petit tas des maisons basses, pareille à une couvée abritée ... sous ses ailes de pierre" (19–20). This feeling of fusion or undifferentiation, of bonding with the mother as edifice, is fostered by her sanctuary in the house of the Huberts "où Angélique désormais allait vivre, ... la plus proche de la cathédrale," as the narrator says, "celle qui tenait à sa chair même" (20).

Externally the church is the text of its sculptures, its steeple pointing out of the world, while internally it is the mother brought to life by the prayerful language of those who are lost. Yet before she reenters the peace of God's house, beneath its sheltering wing of dead stone,[5] Angélique must repress, put away what describes her as an outcast unknown to society. When she is first taken into the heart(h) of the mother, fed on Hubertine's warm milk and bread, Angélique is still neurotically attached to the document which has officially classed her as no one. A text that attests to its content's own nullity, a biography whose subject is empty, it objectively confirms for Angélique an identity that is administratively recorded as missing. In clinging so obstinately to a past she ignores, "l'abandon numeroté et classé" (14), Angélique stakes her pride on her success in surviving the misfortunes reality authored. "Le Livre de l'assistance publique," which establishes her subjection to others' neglect, is similar to the documents that Zola would furnish to anchor his fictional children. Maman Nini, who had treated her charge with benevolence, has often admonished the girl: "Tu vois, c'est tout ce que tu possèdes, car, si tu n'avais pas ça, tu n'aurais rien" (16). But as Zola had temporarily forsaken his method of hereditarily fixing his characters, his orphan stops identifying with the book of her nothingness to be the heroines exalted in legend. Defensively clutching beneath her threadbare, soaked dress the papers that describe her abjection, Angélique inadvertently leads the Huberts to think that she suffered some kind of deformity: "Ils la crurent infirme du bras droit, tellement elle le serrait, immobile, sur sa poitrine.... Quand elle eut fini, elle faillit casser la tasse, qu'elle rattrapa du coude ... avec un geste d'estropiée" (13).

It is only by consenting to surrender the book that she is made to seem graceful and healthy, acceding to a level of human autonomy, no longer "un animal" (13), "une chose" (12) as she had been. But as she proceeds to migrate from one text to another, she discredits objective experience, unwilling to measure her dream's viability against the disillusioning lessons of life. Hubertine tries to temper Angélique's grandiose project of marrying Jesus in the guise of a prince by reactivating the memory of her textual origins, leaving the child "anéantie, devant le petit livre" (23). But the "mise en abîme" structure that shows her as a character copying others who are less and less real points out her dismissal of the non-literary world as a bogy that poisons her dream. Distrusting "cette réalité triste dont on lui parlait comme on parle du loup aux enfants déraisonnables" (141), she does not look on literature as a ravenous monster that devours a life like her author's. She sees it, instead, as harmless if it refers to no reality apart from its own, or if, rather than forcing a dream to come true, it allows truth itself to be dreamed.

According to Holland's transactive model, readers dream themselves into a text, and do so in order "to produce a ... unifying interpretation of experience," as Freund has observed (123). Thus, every art work that Angélique sees repeats this "identity theme," establishing her lineage from some mythical ancestor that replaces the absent bad mother. The medieval writings to which the child has recourse, the lives of saints that amaze and console her, tell of "aventures merveilleuses, aussi belles que des romans" (26) and make a fiction of the one who consumes them. Evil is no longer exclusively attributable to guardians who live in the present, but is neutralized and safely contained when assigned to a devil at whom the virtuous scoff. This invisible realm of quotidian miracles is a reflection of her own solipsism: "Cela lui semblait fou, de s'imaginer le monde comme une mécanique, régie par des lois fixes" (65). Unstable images of laughing bronze statues, singing wolves (64), virgins turned into doves, mutilated martyrs who disarm their assassins and, disembodied, ascend into paradise "la ravissaient d'aise, au-dessus du réel" (29) where the book of her past had confined her. Since she is raised in a milieu where time never passes, is uneducated, naive, and imaginative, this mystical world, "elle le créait elle-même, ... il naissait ... des désirs inconscients de sa puberté" (65). In affirming "Tout venait d'elle pour retourner à elle" (65), Zola's narrator privileges the reader, defining her as origin, beneficiary, and locus of the creative act her fantasies trigger. In the home of the Huberts, where chasuble-making had been done for 500 years, Angélique ceases being a discarded child, who was shunned and mistreated by all, and is able to rewrite her history and establish her descendancy from story-book heroines. Even before her immersion in *La Légende dorée*, she graphologically lays claim to her ancestry: "elle avait ... une jolie écriture, élancée et ferme, une de ces écritures irrégulières des grandes dames d'autrefois" (21–2).

What delays the realization of her dream of regression is a complex array of defenses, as her fantasy of marrying the son of the bishop, the noble scion of Jean d'Hautecoeur, is thwarted/legitimized by her sense that fulfillment would wake her, break the spell and so kill her. Ysabeau, Gudule, Yvonne, Austreberthe, the "great ladies" of eras gone by, had preserved both their dreams and their virginity inviolate by succumbing to death opportunely. Assimilated to the saints who were delivered from earth, spared the sexual profanation of love, "toutes les Mortes heureuses" remained enclosed in their legends and were not roused from their sleep to the world. Angélique denies also that her desire for gold compensates for her childhood penury, insisting her wish to marry a prince would make her grateful, more modest, and caring. The practice of charity would not entail, as she sees it, a retroactive gift to the self, her assumption of the duty of philanthropic largesse not meant to benefit a victimized orphan.

As a composite of images of worldly heroines, candid, brave fiancées of the Savior, Angélique is a character fleshed out by the readings that she and others provide. In her initial encounter with her suitor Félicien, they had laid out a sheet on the grass, still distanced by their unwritten "page d'amour": "ce grand linge, d'une blancheur éblouis-sante" (76). It is not with her writing that the unschooled Angélique will embody her inchoate fantasy, but with the needlework that extends the euphemized past she had issued from in her dream. Having alleged the commissioning of a special mitre for the bishop to wear in procession, Félicien calls on Angélique and shows her his sketch "sur la grande feuille qu'il posait devant elle" (89). As pretext both for his visit and for their co-authored romance, his design is an image of Agnes, and when Angélique examines the sheet, she discovers the saint is a likeness of her (91). Enabling the imitation to supersede its own prototype, Félicien gives her an unfinished image, whose completion dismantles a debased former self and constructs a more glorious avatar. No greater love could Félicien show Angélique than to reconfirm her as a reader, reauthorizing her creation of an identity modeled on a character she dreams of becoming.[6] As she weaves gold thread into the saint's flaming hair, which turns into a garment and halo, she has, with her needlework, the means of producing an ethereally transfigured double.

In fact, others' behavior is patterned on Angélique's compulsion to act out a text, as they incorporate her as a character whose presence revises a previously unhappy romance. To alter the outcome of what had before been an unhappy love story, the Huberts, in adopting the child they find, accept the malediction by Hubertine's mother. Having cursed with infertility the couple who had gone on to marry without her consent, the mother, responsible for the death of their first-born, had been thwarted by Angélique's coming. But the return of the "mauvaise mère supprimée" is effected when her authority is finally ratified, with "la mort consentie de l'enfant" Angélique that is accompanied by Hubertine's pregnancy (169). Undoing the consequence of their earlier sin, they second the mother's decision, acquiescing again to the death of their child so that a child might be born in her place. The "mort heureuse" that Angélique covets gives the blessed denouement to both stories: the detour of Angélique from the real world to heaven and her adoptive parents' union reconsecrated.

Indeed, the tale of the bishop is a subtle new variant on the theme of parental intransigeance, the interdiction of passion by an inflexible elder that internalizes the child's fear of fulfillment. Concluding his youthful days of impetuous action, he had fallen in love with a girl, the "miraculously beautiful" Paule de Valençay, who had not survived bearing his son Félicien. As he is dead to the society, to the secular world, Monseigneur is like Hubertine's mother, inexorable in opposing to love's consummation his otherworldly, steadfast rejection. But by conforming to the will of a higher authority, God's design as original text, the bishop sees the dead Angélique come to life and re-enact his earlier marriage. In this way, the acknowledgement and circumvention/appeasement of some vigilant, censoring figure, the acceptance of the death of a guilty relationship resurrected when all is forgiven, gives a satisfactory ending to these unhappy stories by grounding them "in a larger sustaining matrix—the myth" (Holland 260). As the novel concludes with a wedding celebrated in the church's maternal interior, it reaches back, is resituated in its mythical substructure and so facilitates its own introjection. Prolonging the legend of the blessed dead brides, Angélique expires in her kiss, evoking associations of Gnostic unions with loved ones, nuptials hallowed as a flight from the body. "Tout n'est que rêve;" as the narrator comments (208), a regression to an earlier text, from novel to legend to ancestral memory, reading back farther in the unconscious—all intended to postpone the traumatic awakening that comes with the end of the book. In fact, Angélique's life, "ce qu'elle rêve de la vie ... d'après des lectures," as Zola had qualified ("Ebauche" 224), is centered on an ignorance-based avoidance of unmediated experience resulting in death: "la réalisation de son rêve," which leads her to smile, "sachant qu'elle avait la mort en elle" (203–4).

Up until the time Félicien appears in her room and begs Angélique to run away with him, her dream had existed as potentiality, made half-audible by the language of things. The world's permeability to her fantasy of love, its articulating of forbidden desires, had allowed an awareness "des désirs de sa puberté" since its voice spoke to her from outside: "la jeune fille entendait ses rêves qui lui revenaient, ... ce qu'elle avait mis d'elle dans les choses" (105).[7] This is different from the insinuating, vegetal speech that had issued from the Paradou garden, desublimating the amnesiac Serge Mouret's impulses as it drowned out religion's proscriptions. Resisting the temptation of sexual flight, her surrender "au galop des chevaux" (179), Angélique later hearkens less to Félicien's pleas than to the dead virgins' narcotic message. Félicien speaks of crossing a drawbridge at sunset into the restored chateau d'Hautecoeur, of acknowledging the respectful salutations of villagers who kneel as the lovers ride by, and of falling asleep in each other's arms on a couch draped in purple and gold. But his romantic narrative of conjugal joys goes unheeded by Angélique, who listens more closely to "[le] chuchotement d'âmes, ... les vierges qui arrivent, invisibles" (180). While painting a picture of time's circularity, setting their future in "les temps anciens," Félicien cannot offer what the martyred saints do: a sanctuary "dans la Légende" (179). "Je suis celui qui existe, Angélique, et vous me refusez pour des rêves .... Venez, ne mettez plus rien de vous dans les choses, elles se tairont" (181). He learns that for Angélique textual language is more powerful than the flesh in evoking reality, his depictions of love amidst honey-sweet fruits less vivid than storybook pictures, the images conjured up by "les vierges de la Légende ... dont le vol mystique sortait du ... livre" (180). With her legs seemingly paralysed, she resists his entreaties, asking only that her dream speak more clearly, the whispering voices of her phantom-filled room that leave her anxious, still, and attentive. Commenting on the link between a regression to fantasy and inhibited motor activity, Holland relates the absorption in dream to the esthetic stance of a reader, asserting that the ability to sink deep in the text is conditional on one's immobility.[8] So for Angélique's dream to be maintained intact, it cannot be enacted or realized, whence her physical weakness and her staggering to bed "où elle tomba victorieuse et sans souffle" (182).

The ultimate defense against the dispelling of dreams is to sleep and never awaken, and so after Félicien disappears in the night, Angélique lapses into a coma. Motivating her retreat into pure subjectivity is a flight from corrective experience, a fear that her fantasy of marrying a prince might be banished to daylight reality. Her only contact with the external world is through the air she inhales and expels, the breath of the soul that departs when she kisses her husband as they leave the cathedral. It is the mouth from which issues both "parole" and "souffle:" her life, the dream, its expression, so that accompanying the knowledge that makes the fictional world mute are her death and the end of the narrative. Having hungered for illusion, she once had been satisfied with echoing the books she had read from, re-establishing the connection between orality and vision as the channels through which she gained pleasure. But when the bishop anoints with his sanctified oil her unspeaking lips and closed eyes, there are no sins that the sacrament need cleanse or remove since she had never lived first through her senses: "elle ne connaissait d'autre livre que la Légende," says the narrator. "Et, si elle vivait dans l'erreur, c'était son rêve qui l'y avait mise, l'espoir de l'au-delà, la consolation de l'invisible, tout ce monde enchanté que créait son ignorance" (190, 192).

It is the apparent disparity between his previous novels and this magic world fashioned by ignorance, between an experimental method based on reality-testing and the indulgence in "vaporous reveries,"[9] that has long disconcerted critical readers of Zola and made their response to Le Rêve so unfavorable. Having indoctrinated his audience to second the views propounded in La Confession de Claude, Zola leaves critics thinking that his attitude toward Le Rêve must have been one of ironic distancing, or that the novel was so different from his preceding works that it violated the trust of his readers. It is this same sense of intertextual incongruity that prompted Charles Bigot to remark: "Quand un auteur a déjà beaucoup produit, on s'est fait ... une idée de sa manière. On attend de lui certaines choses et pas d'autres. On l'aborde avec un parti pris" (248). The displeasure provoked when expectations are frustrated causes efforts to find explanations, making the audience "step up its ... intellection," says Holland, thus dissociating it from the work (185). Angélique's drive-gratifying experience of reading is the opposite of Zola's own critics', whose impulse is to reconcile an anomalous text with the rest of his fictional corpus. As a result Matthews maintains that Le Rêve still adheres to the method that Zola laid down, emphasizing the "interplay between [Angélique's] passionate nature and the influences of her 'environment'" (190).[10] A. A. Greaves insists similarly that Le Rêve does not signify a contravention of Zola's own principles, but thematically parallels La Faute de l'Abbé Mouret and recapitulates longstanding ideas.[11] In the same way that he classes both books as alike, Greaves makes his response universal: "There is a pattern of similarity to the two novels," he argues, "which evokes the same reaction" in readers (16). Thus, the heroine's denial of the sexual promptings she converts into spiritual dream is mirrored by the defense against an authorial fantasy that the critic sublimates into meaning.[12]

There is agreement among readers that Angélique's story fictionally transposes Zola's wishes and that his emotional investment in the novel's creation "acted like a sedative on his methodical way of working." As a consequence, King adds, "the flights of a young girl's fancies led [Zola] into hours of nonproductive day-dreaming. If [Angélique] could dream, why not he?" as King asks. "If his heroine's dream could come true, why not his?" (King 268). But the novelist's failure to "soften" the character of his personal "day-dreams," says Freud, may result in "the feeling of repulsion" that comes from the clashing egos of writer and reader (Freud 153).

It is only on the last page that Angélique stands on the threshold of diurnal lucidity, accompanied by the church organ's resounding hosannas as she walks toward the crowd in the square. When she emerges from the confines of her darkened dream-chamber to the outer world's sun-flooded openness, the novel-length spell of her triumphal sleep is dispelled and *Le Rêve* is concluded. Even the extra-textual resonances of the dream's prolongation cannot confirm that her wish had been realized, her fantasy, not of being either married or rich, but of dying and dreaming forever: In a way, then, the subject of the novel is meant to sustain the effects of its reading, insuring the persistence of an oneirical vision even when the dream object has faded. But as awareness of dreaming causes the sleeper to waken, the self-designation of the plot as unreal disillusions the reader and turns the fantasy content into the object of his analysis. The disabusing referentiality of the text to itself as conveyed in remarks by the narrator—"Ce n'était qu'une apparence, qui s'effaçait, après avoir créé une illusion" (208)—makes the book less a vehicle than an obstacle to integration in the fantasy matrix. Remembering a virtually identical passage that appeared early on in the narrative—"N'était-ce pas une apparence qui disparaîtrait, après avoir créé une illusion?" (65)—one compares Angélique's questioning her material reality to the novel's dismissing its substance. As he is engaged more in secondary process activity, the reader does not take part in the dream, but interprets it by re-embodying its impalpable contents into the concrete book in his hands. The dream's evanescence and elusive significance prompt efforts to fix and explain them, to bring back to consciousness the "invisible vision" (207) which is glimpsed and, on waking, forgotten.

Angélique was first able to dismantle the textual self inscribed in her booklet, replacing a bureaucratically empty identity with the *Légende*, whose fictions entranced her. She then is the church window's stained glass translucence, the "blancheur vague" Félicien sees at her window (107), a diaphanous confidante of the ghosts of dead saints, the silken radiance of her embroidered self-image. Re-experiencing the process by which books devour life, she becomes Zola's euphemized counterpart, imponderable, wasted by an absorption in fantasy, an angel who evaporates into her medium. Like the gentle aggression of literature, which annihilates the real that it turns into language, Angélique reads herself out of existence, becoming "un rien très doux et très tendre" (207). But even merged with the air, the heavenly bird leaves behind her "une poignée de plumes," the textual residue of a dream that has flown but that can still be explained and interpreted. It is in the giving of meaning, not in the reception of fantasy, that the critic discovers his sustenance, in his work that runs counter to the novel's dynamic and so leads him to censor its dream, by retrieving through writing a book about books consumed and turned into nothing.

NOTES

1. Hemmings, for example, describes Zola as one who, in 1887, "had given up smoking and ever since had put on weight steadily until now, as he sat there trying to plan his next novel in the sad grey light of a November morning, with his pet dog snoring on a sofa in the corner of the room, he felt it altogether grotesque that he should be allowing himself to indulge in so impossible a dream" (139).

2. As Paul Pelckmans remarks: "La critique, le plus souvent, dédaigne *Le Rêve*, dont le ton quasi sulpicien tranche sur le ton global de la série: il ne s'agirait que d'une 'bluette,' qui a tout au plus 'la fadeur touchante des cartes postales d'époque'" (889).

3. Anatole France, "Opinion d'Anatole France," *Le Temps*, October 21, 1888, cited by Maurice Le Blond in "*Le Rêve* et la Critique" ("Notes et Commentaires sur *Le Rêve*" 246).

4. It is worth noting that the only writer specifically mentioned by Freud in his short essay is Zola, whose novels are seen as generally standing "in quite special contrast to the type of the day-dream." Zola's hero, writes Freud, "sees the actions and sufferings of other people pass before him like a spectator," much as a reader reacts to the lives of fictional characters (Freud 151).

5. Catherine Marachi, in discussing the filiation between *La Faute de l'Abbé Mouret* and *Le Rêve*, notes "qu'après sa chute, désormais en proie aux remords et à la honte, Serge s'adressait à Albine en ces termes: 'La petite église deviendra si colossale, elle jettera une telle ombre, que toute ta nature crevera. Ah! la mort, la mort de tout, avec le ciel béant pour recevoir nos âmes, au-des-sus des débris abominables du monde!' La cathédrale du *Rêve* n'est-elle pas justement la concrétisation de la prophétie de Serge, de cette petite église ayant acquis des proportions surnaturelles?" (90–1).

6. "In the unconscious," observes Otto Fenichel, "to look at an object may mean ... to grow like it (be forced to imitate it), or, conversely, to force it to grow like oneself" (376).

7. Of this kind of "speech," Adolfo Fernandez-Zoïla says: "Il s'agit de voix métaphores, figures de style proposees par l'écrivain, pour marquer *le parti pris des choses et la prégnance des lieux et des objets qui font partie d'elle-même*.... Ces énonciations marquent d'une manière très forte l'élaboration d'un monde autour de soi, un *Umwelt*, un monde d'artifices, qui devient une 'bulle' langagière et fantasmatique (en images issues aussi des mots) qui nous entoure" (166).

8. See Holland's remarks on the "connection between motor inhibition and regression to fantasy" (73–74).

9. Charles Bigot, "L'Opinion de M. Charles Bigot," *La République Française*, October 22, 1888, cited by Maurice Le Blond in "*Le Rêve* et la Critique" ("Notes et Commentaires sur *Le Rêve*" 248).

10. "In its final form," says Matthews, "*Le Rêve* is as much an experimental novel as any Zola wrote.... The manuscript notes reveal that he set out constructing his fairy tale in exactly the same way as he prepared *Pot-Bouille* or *Son Excellence Eugène Rougon*: he sketched out the *Ebauche*, in which he decided on the general subject and the development the action would take; he drew up a list of *Personnages* ...; and he finally prepared a *Plan*, by chapters, in which all the scattered elements were brought together before final expression in the text" (193–94).

11. For another comparison of *La Faute de l'Abbé Mouret* with *Le Rêve*, see Marachi *passim*.

12. "Defense, in a literary work, takes one of two general modes: meaning or form. Typically, the unconscious fantasy at the core of a work will combine elements that could, if provided full expression, give us pleasure, but also create anxiety. It is the task of the literary 'work' to control the anxiety and permit at least partial gratification of the pleasurable possibilities in the fantasy. The literary work, through what we have loosely termed 'form,' acts out defensive maneuvers for us ... Meaning, whether we find it or supply it, acts more like sublimation: giving the fantasy material a disguised expression which is acceptable to the ego, which makes sense" (Holland 189).

WORKS CITED

Fenichel, Otto. "The Scotophilic Instinct and Identification." *Collected Papers of Otto Fenichel: First Series*. New York: Norton, 1953.

Fernandez-Zoïla, Adolfo. "Le jeu des imaginaires dans *Le Rêve*," *Cahiers Naturalistes* 62 (1988): 153–70.

Freud, Sigmund. "Creative Writers and Day-dreaming." *The Standard Edition of the Complete Psychological Works of Sigmund Freud*. Vol. 9. London: Hogarth Press, 1959: 141–54.

Freund, Elizabeth. *The Return of the Reader*. London: Methuen, 1987.

Greaves, A.A. "A Question of Life or Death: A Comparison of *Le Rêve* and *La Faute de l'Abbé Mouret*." *Nottingham French Studies* 19.2 (1980): 16–24.

Hemmings, F.W.J. *The Life and Times of Emile Zola*. New York: Scribners, 1977.

Holland, Norman. *The Dynamics of Literary Response*. New York: Oxford University Press, 1968.

King, Graham. *Garden of Zola*. New York: Barnes & Noble, 1978.

Le Blond, Maurice. "Notes et Commentaires." *Le Rêve*. By Emile Zola. Paris: François Bernouard, 1928.

Marachi, Catherine. "La place du Rève dans la serie des Rougon-Macquart. *Cahiers Naturalistes* 58 (1984): 89–95.

Matthews. J. H. "Zola's *Le Rêve* as an Experimental Novel". *Modern Language Review* 3 (1957): 187–94.

Pelckmans, Paul. "Herédité ou mimétisme familiale? Pour une nouvelle lecture du *Rève*." *Cahiers Naturalistes* 57 (1983): 86–103.

Zola, Emile. "Ebauche." *Le Rêve*. Paris: Francois Bernouard, 1928.

———. *Le Rêve*. Paris: François Bernouard, 1928.

JONATHAN F. KRELL

Nana: Still Life,
Nature morte

T owards the end of "Le Roman expérimental," Zola summarizes his "experimental method" of writing and defines clearly the strictly scientific nature of his art. Determined to study human phenomena on a firm base of "solid ground,"[1] he seeks only to discover *how* human beings are formed by a complex array of hereditary and environmental factors and does not propose to ask the dangerous question: *why* do human beings act as they do? Such a query would depart from the logical and methodical sphere of experimental science, and drift towards the invisible stratosphere of the imaginary.

Zola's concept of the experimental novel thus apparently denies any ties to the philosophical, religious, magical or mythical. His naturalism would appear to occupy the last position on a continuum of fictional genres from the most stylized (myths, tales) to the most realistic. This is in fact how naturalism was seen until the advent of archetypal criticism, which underscored the mythical patterns permeating even literature that pretends to ignore the supernatural. Writers who do not believe in gods still have their own imaginations to contend with, and, in spite of themselves, confront what Joseph Campbell calls "that awesome ultimate mystery which is both beyond and within [themselves] and all things."[2] Zola's controversial and much maligned scientific approach, inspired by Claude Bernard's "médecine

From *French Forum* 19, no. 1 (January 1994). © 1994 by The University of Nebraska Press.

expérimentale," envisioned the novelist as a literary surgeon. Such a theory was doomed to failure, for unlike the doctor, writers cannot separate themselves from the object of their experiment. As an early critic of Zola noted, if an author restricts characters to the "inevitable actions" governed by heredity, "[t]he conclusion drawn by a writer from such actions must be open to the retort that he invented the whole himself."[3] Transformed by the imagination, the most mundane facts take on symbolic meaning. Zola of course recognized this; in "Le Roman expérimental" he described the novelist as an experimenter as well as an observer. The "expérimentateur" *invents* a story based on disinterested observations and thus instructs the reader: "il faut que nous produisions et que nous dirigions les phénomènes; c'est là notre part d'invention, de génie dans l'oeuvre" (*Le Roman expérimental* 66). Five years later his language was decidedly less scientific. In letters to Jules Lemaître and Henry Céard, he expressed a pantheistic vision and a cognizance of the vertical nature of metaphor:

> Vous isolez l'homme de la nature, je ne le vois pas sans la terre, d'où il sort et où il rentre. L'âme que vous enfermez dans un être, je la sens épandue partout, dans l'être et hors de l'être, dans l'animal dont il est le frère, dans la plante, dans le caillou.[4]

> J'ai l'hypertrophie du détail vrai, le saut dans les étoiles sur le tremplin de l'observation exacte. La vérité monte d'un coup d'aile jusqu'au symbole. (Letter to Henry Céard, March 22, 1885; *Correspondance* 249)

Zola's scientific rigor bows to his creative imagination, conjuring up gods in gutters, heroic victims in Paris sweatshops, and bewitching goddesses in the form of innocent country girls and street-wise prostitutes. Workers become warriors in Zola's fictional universe, as the author himself declared: "Oui, l'ouvrier qui serre les poings et qui provoque un camarade, sur nos boulevards extérieurs, est un véritable héros d'Homère, Achille injuriant Hector."[5] And Jules Lemaître, in the article that inspired Zola's response quoted above, noted the Homeric quality of the Zolian metaphor, concluding that the *Rougon-Macquart* is "une épopée pessimiste de l'animalité humaine" ("M. Emile Zola. A propos de *Germinal*," *Revue Politique et Littéraire* [*Revue Bleue*] 11 [March 14, 1885] 321–30, quoted in Zola, *Correspondance* 245–46n1).

Northrop Frye's *Anatomy of Criticism* sheds light on the coexistence of the mythical and the naturalistic in Zola's writings. Frye defined five modes—myth, romance, high mimetic, low mimetic, and ironic—which he ordered according to two criteria, the first chronological, the second based on the protagonist's power over both other people and the environment. Thus:

> If superior in *kind* both to other men and to the environment of other men, the hero is a divine being, and the story about him will be a myth.... If inferior in power or intelligence to ourselves, so that we have the sense of looking down on a scene of bondage, frustration, or absurdity, the hero belongs to the *ironic* mode.[6]

Interesting in Frye's analysis is the fact that irony and myth are not polar opposites; one often finds traces of the mythical in irony, which at times appears to be returning to myth, perhaps searching for its own origins: "Irony ... begins in realism and dispassionate observation. But as it does so, it moves steadily towards myth, and dim outlines of sacrificial rituals and dying gods begin to reappear in it. Our five modes evidently go around in a circle" (Frye 42). In the "ironic mode"—Zola's naturalism being for Frye a prime example—myths are displaced, losing their primary (real) significance, and assuming a metaphorical (unreal) meaning. Thus we have two antithetical definitions of the term *myth*: to an insider, myths relate fundamental truths about a society's origins; but to an outsider, they are nothing but fabulous fictions.

What is it in Zola's ironic novels that irresistibly pulls the author, consciously or unconsciously, back to myth? Beyond the scope of the present essay, this vast question has been analyzed brilliantly by Jean Borie[7] and Roger Ripoll.[8] I shall restrict my study to *Nana*, hoping to elucidate just one of the many links between Zola's naturalism and myth: the primacy that each attributes to the female body. I will focus on the body stilled, silenced: frozen as in a painting, a sculpture, or in mute images of events that occurred, as Mircea Eliade writes, *in illo tempore*, before the advent of human history.[9]

THE PRE-EMINENT DOMAIN of myth is the past, "le temps primordial, le temps fabuleux des 'commencements'" (Eliade 16); and when one deals with the origins of life, one necessarily confronts the enigma of the woman's body and the Fall from Paradise. Naomi Schor points out that "The mystery of femininity inevitably leads one back to the mystery, indeed the myth of origins."[10] Courbet graphically unveiled and displayed this unutterable riddle in his scandalous painting of a reclining woman, genitalia looming in the foreground, which he entitled *L'Origine du monde*.[11] Courbet's work was denounced, reports Brooks, as "the visual equivalent of Zola's 'putrid literature'" (22), underlining the shared unmentionable status of the mystery of creation, Zola's naturalistic texts, and the female sex. Zola's own words corroborate this isomorphism; in the following quotation from the "Ebauche de *Nana*," the repetition of *grand* bestows a mythical aura on the female sex organs: "le cul est tout puissant, et c'est lui le grand générateur et le grand destructeur" (quoted in Ripoll 634). For Jean Borie, the ancestral Fall and the hereditary transmission of the obscure transgression that initiated it are keys to the two archetypes underlying Zola's "mythical anthropology" (Borie 43): the cave man, remarkable for his unbridled desire and his savage treatment of women; and the cave woman, almost as brutal in the revenge she takes on her companion (44). Nana is the most lethal of Zola's cave women; the journalist Fauchery describes how the fatal flaw she has inherited from the "Eve" of the Rougon-Macquart family, Tante Dide, manifests itself in her. In his article "La Mouche d'or," Fauchery writes that Nana was

> ... née de quatre on cinq générations d'ivrognes, le sang gâté par une longue hérédité de misère et de boisson, qui se transformait chez elle en un détraquement nerveux de son sexe de femme.... Avec elle, la pourriture qu'on laissait fermenter dans le peuple, remontait et pounissait l'aristocratie.[12]

Zola attributed to this young woman's body all the ills he perceived in her social body: the proletariat. This, Borie believes, is the essential body of Zola's naturalism; infecting the bourgeoisie, itself "en proie au furieux appétit du corps" (26), the proletariat is in large part responsible for the catastrophic Fall of nineteenth-century French society.

Zola's foremost object of study is thus the body of his fallen creatures. He claims, in the letter to Jules Lemaître, that he is not a psychologist, and indeed, many of his characters seem devoid of soul and mind; mere masses of flesh, blood and nerves, their actions are reduced to the satisfaction of primary instincts. Zola describes the bestial nature of the naturalist protagonist in the preface to the second edition of *Thérèse Raquin*; his "two heroes" are nothing more than soulless human brutes without personalities, "souverainement dominés par leurs nerfs et leur sang."[13]

There is much in Zolian characters that brings to mind the tales of Olympus. One may associate myth with the supernatural or the metaphysical, but the bawdy characters of classical mythology, groping for the causes of natural phenomena, closely resemble their counterparts in naturalistic novels. Tales of incest, lechery, and infidelity abound; the distance is slight between the cuckold Vulcan and the innocent brute Goujet of *L'Assommoir*, between the amorous Venus and the insatiable Nana. The genealogy of the Rougon-Macquart and the dubious feats of its "heroes" call to mind a working class version of the Olympian family: the "Arbre généalogique," its twisted branches following the paths of lechery and greed across France and over five generations, recounts the machinations of the same unbridled appetites characteristic of the gods and goddesses of classical mythology. The body, whether it be mortal or immortal, a victim of an inherited flaw or Zeus's rage, takes center stage.

It is the female body that assumes special mythical significance in Zola. The Zolian woman, remarks Borie, "agit surtout par sa présence physique" (48). Clotilde, in *Le Docteur Pascal*, is the figure of a sculpted or painted goddess, "le corps souple, de cette souplesse allongée des divines figures de la Renaissance."[14] Likewise, in the "Ebauche de *La Faute de l'Abbé Mouret*," Zola describes Albine as a "Renaissance virgin,"[15] and elsewhere her life-giving power is closely associated with the sun.

But Nana, of course, represents the apotheosis of the female body in Zola's work; she is "la *chair* centrale" (Zola, "Ebauche de *Nana*," quoted in Ripoll 632), almost deified by the "almighty power" (*Nana* 53) of her flesh. Critics have remarked upon her dual nature: the smiling, robust "bonne enfant" hides a "mangeuse d'hommes" (*Nana* 53), a foul proletarian beast who infects the aristocracy with the malady of her raging sex. It would seem that, despite his desire to ameliorate the wretched conditions of the lower classes, Zola the myth-maker is at odds with Zola the social reformer. For Nana is more demonized than deified; an infernal Venus, she incarnates what Frye calls the "demonic imagery" (147) of the "ironic mode," in which "[t]he demonic erotic relation becomes a fierce destructive passion" (149). Through metaphors characterizing Nana as a sex-crazed beast or a filthy insect, Zola perpetuates contemporary "myths" on hysteria and prostitution, reinforcing some of the very prejudices he desires to overturn. He "underwrites," in the words of Charles Bernheimer, a "conservative patriarchal ideology" which "defines the working class's functions within the social organism as libidinal sexuality, primitive instinct, and excremental release."[16] Bernheimer, commenting on the number of artistic works in nineteenth-century France that treat "the contaminating decomposition of [the prostitute's] sexual ferment" (2), tells of the hygienist Alexandre Parent-Duchâtelet, who felt that his monumental study of prostitution in Paris was but the logical sequel to his research on the city's sewers. And Peter Brooks notes "the equation, typical in Zola, between a strong female sexuality and the lower classes: the body as a source of class confusion, of potential revolution, as an object of fear" (18–19).

Nana embodies the "crisis of the nude" that Brooks (16) and others have perceived in nineteenth century art. Artists wanted to break the shackles of Classicism, which accepted the nude only as part of an exotic environment, usually Classical or Oriental. When depicted in a natural setting, or next to clothed male figures, as in Manet's famous *Dejeuner sur l'herbe*, the female nude loses its exotic distance and moves disturbingly close to the observer. When Nana takes the stage at the beginning of the novel, playing the title role in *Blonde Vénus*, her partial nudity is in accord with the motif of classical mythology. But at the same time, we are witnessing the shattering of a sacred world ("on piétinait sur un monde, on cassait les antiques images" [*Nana* 47]), as the antics of Mars, Venus and Vulcan are grotesquely caricatured, complete with commentary from the "choeur des cocus." Parodies such as this are typical of Frye's naturalistic "demonic imagery:" divine myths are displaced in a human hell. Gods are mocked, and so is "the exuberant play of art by suggesting its imitation in terms of 'real life'" (Frye 147). Olympus falls as myth melts into modernism in *Blonde Vénus*. Brooks observes that the premiere of the play coincides with the opening of the Exposition Universelle of 1867, a showcase for industrial and luxury articles, and he characterizes Nana as a "Second Empire pinup" (9), or again as a "kitsch Venus ... at a moment when the post-sacred world is celebrating its new myths of industrial progress" (2).

The secret of Nana's naked power would seem to lie in her *petrification*. Schor considers the woman in Zola, especially Nana, to be an object of worship, an idol. Nana leaves the quagmire of her class and is mythified, sculpted into a work of art, a quasi-religious image. When she dances and sings in the first act of *Blonde Vénus*, her beauty is rendered less imposing by her awkward movements and bad voice. The audience laughs at the pretty clown, not out of place in this irreverent farce. But then Nana hardens into a goddess. Her triumph—as she lifts her spellbound audience out of the world of kitsch and back to Mt. Olympus—comes in the third act, when, not obliged to sing or dance, she mesmerizes the audience by her mere presence, her *immobility*. Petrified, Nana is the enigmatic and impenetrable sphinx, incarnating what Schor calls the "hieratic code" (44), the feminine variation of Roland Barthes's "hermeneutic code," that network of enigmas the formulation and deferred solutions of which constitute an important group of textual signifiers.[17]

In two final scenes, Nana demonstrates the power of the pose. At the Grand Prix horse races, she is the center of attention, "ses cheveux jaunes envolés, son visage de neige, baigné de soleil." In a gloating gesture, "pour faire crever les autres femmes qu'enrageait son triomphe, elle leva son verre plein, dans son ancienne pose de Vénus victorieuse" (*Nana* 340). Moments later, when the filly named after her wins the Grand Prix, Nana again strikes a silent pose before the cheering crowd: "Nana, debout sur le siège de son landau, *grandie*, crut que c'était elle qu'on acclamait. Elle était réstee un instant *immobile*, dans la *stupeur* de son triomphe" (354, my emphasis).

Nana's final apotheosis is in the play *Mélusine*, in which she plays the legendary fairy. It is worth dwelling for a moment on this role, Nana's last. For it is as Mélusine that Parisian society will remember Nana's body, and it is her embodiment of Mélusine that seals Nana's demonic place in the world of myth. By her very name, Nana is linked to Mélusine, and, indirectly, to Venus as well. *Nana* is a deformation of *Nanaï*, an ancient word for water, and *Tanaïs*, the common etymological root of Astarte and Ishtar, the great Semitic goddesses. The onomatopoeic combination "nana–mama" further reinforces the association between Nana and aquatic mother goddesses such as the Indian Maya and the Egyptian Marica, who in the Occident are assimilated to Mère Lousine, the water spirit of the alchemists, or the fairy Mélusine.[18] As for the link between Mélusine and Venus, the former is associated with the evil Morgan, the latter with Aphrodite, whose names both mean "born from the sea."

Nana incarnates the fairy of many legends crystallized in Jean d'Arras's fourteenth-century novel, *Mélusine*.[19] The celebrated animality of Nana, a woman "something less than human,"[20] her powerful hips and flowing hair inspiring in men the fear of the Beast (*Nana* 216–17) and eliciting comparisons to the horse and the lion (216–17, 349), recalls the animal nature of the fairy. Mélusine transmits her secret fault—she is part serpent—to her sons, nine of whom are born with hideous deformities. Similarly, as David Baguley points out, Nana, the destructive "human beast,"[21] passes on her inherited flaw to her badly cared for and sickly son Louiset; his "sang gâte" (*Nana* 309) brings on his own and his mother's early deaths, demonstrating "the essential naturalist condition" characterized by a "brief, tenuous hold on human existence" (Baguley 213). Such is the condition of Mélusine as well: cursed by her fairy mother[22] for taking upon herself the vengeance for her human father's unwitting breaking of a sacred promise, Mélusine may enjoy human love only as long as her husband Raymondin does not attempt to see her on Saturdays, when she assumes her serpent form. Eventually Raymondin, like Mélusine's father before him, transgresses the pact, and Mélusine disappears from the human world she desperately loves, condemned to wander the fairy world forever as a serpent.

Both Mélusine and Nana employ the mirror as a tool of seduction. Many critics have analyzed the scene of "plaisir solitaire" (*Nana* 217) in which Nana, under the fascinated gaze of Count Muffat, admires her unclothed body in the mirror.[23] Paralleling her stage performance of *Blonde Vénus*, Nana opens her beguiling performance with movement—caressing hands and rotating hips—and then freezes as Muffat contemplates the woman and the mirrored image: "Nana ne bougea plus. Un bras derrière la nuque, une main prise dans l'autre, elle renversait la tête, les coudes écartés" (216). This still-life of Nana framed in her mirror—the power of her nudity increased twofold—transports Muffat back to mythical time: "Il songeait à son ancienne horreur de la femme, au monstre de l'Ecriture, lubrique, sentant le fauve.... [L]'animal reparut au fond des ténèbres, grandi, terrible, exagérant sa posture. Maintenant, il serait là, devant ses yeux, dans sa chair, à jamais" (216–17).[24]

Nana's narcissistic preoccupations recall Mélusine, a water spirit, for whom "le miroir n'était jamais loin."[25] Like Nana, quite proud of her hair, Mélusine is combing her tresses in front of a mirror when Raymondin meets her for the first time (Louis-Combet 30). At their second encounter, she is sitting on the edge of a pool, gazing on the "surface miroitante de la fontaine" (44). She wears a golden dress which alternately veils and reveals her body, becoming transparent as she nears the water, and dark as she moves away. She tells Raymondin: "Il y a là un grand mystère qui me rappelle singulièrement le mystère de l'amour ... Mais je ne saurais vous en dire davantage. Je sais seulement que le miroir est ce qui nous unit" (44).

The reflecting pool's strange effect on the fairy's dress calls to mind the scene from *Nana* referred to above. Even when the Count, with the mirror as accomplice, has a privileged view of her nudity, Nana does not reveal all, for her "cuisses de cavale ... donnaient au sexe le voile troublant de leur ombre" (*Nana* 217). Janet Beizer refers to the "hide and seek" nature of this and other scenes, and argues that "the essence of Nana's seductiveness lies in this play of presence and absence: a presence which is never quite realized, an absence on the eternal verge of becoming present" (46, 49). Nana's seductive "intermittence" characterizes what one might call her fairy nature, full of secrets, delight always threatening disaster and disappearance. The alternating "bonne enfant" and "mangeuse d'hommes" recalls the capacity of all fairies for both divine and demonic acts. Mélusine is the perfect lover and mother until her secret is made public; at that moment her attachment to the world of death becomes permanent. Harf-Lancnet affirms "l'emprise du diable sur le merveilleux féerique"[26] and notes that, despite the loving nature of Mélusine and her great deeds, such as founding the house of Lusignan,

and building fortresses and aqueducts for her descendants, she belongs
ultimately to the forces of evil: "La difformité des fils de Mélusine, la
déchéance du lignage de Lusignan prouvent que dans l'imaginaire médiéval,
la fée reste toujours proche du démon" (178). As one reads the description of
the Muffats's elegant dinner party, which closes with the orchestra playing
Nana's theme, the waltz from *Blonde Vénus*, one might be reminded of
Mélusine transformed into a winged serpent, hovering above her castle
before flying off to the demonic world of death and corruption, forsaking the
noble lineage she had founded:

> Ici, sur l'écroulement de ces richesses, entassées et allumées d'un
> coup, la valse sonnait le glas d'une vieille race; pendant que Nana,
> invisible, épandue au dessus du bal avec ses membres souples,
> décomposait ce monde, le pénétrait du ferment de son odeur
> flottant dans l'air chaud, sur le rythme canaille de la musique.
> (Nana 380)

Always elusive, there and not there, Nana is perhaps at her most graceful
when she is "invisible" and seems to float on the sensuous strains of the
music. The waltz's dizzying rhythm, writes Auguste Dezalay, accentuates the
frenetic activity of the men turning around Nana, whose destructive force is
a "maelström vertigineux," or a "cyclone devastateur."[27] But Nana herself,
oblivious to the commotion around her and to the lives she ruins, stands
always at the unreachable center, the eye of the hurricane.

Nana is a destroyer, seemingly the contrary of most fairies, known
rather as builders.[28] However their "fonction érectrice"[29] is not limited to
manipulating stones and lumber: "Elles manient—on l'a dit—des matériaux
qui, s'ils ne sont pas toujours des matériaux de construction, sont cependant
durs et résistants" (Belmont 403). Phallic figures, fairies like Mélusine are the
precursors of Nana. Louis-Combet notes Mélusine's "grande vigueur" (28),
her "majesté sauvage, violente, une énergie d'amour nourrie de toutes les
puissances de la forêt" (44). Her Gargantuan "puissance dévoratrice" (103)
and her "insatiabilité" (107) call to mind Gervaise Macquart, whose
gluttonous appetite for food is only equaled by her daughter's appetite for
sex. As Mélusine studies her image in a double mirror, one side clear, the
other dark, she contemplates her dual nature: "Généreuse, débonnaire,
toujours prete à donner, ... elle savait et sentait que toute cette part souriante
de son être était mue, en profondeur, par un appétit de possession qui n'avait
d'égal que son appétit de ruine et de perdition" (108). Like Nana, she is
"constructrice destructrice" (108), building an empire of love only to destroy

it, and "nourricière dévorante" (109), bearing children cursed from birth. The Lusignan family had all but died out when Jean d'Arras wrote his novel (Harf-Lancner 176), and as legend credited Mélusine with the earlier brilliance of the lineage, so it blamed her for its tragic decline, said to have been initiated by the fairy's abrupt metamorphosis and departure. Zola echoes the demise of the Lusignan family in the Grand Prix scene, in which the favorite of the race bears the name "Lusignan." The filly Nana defeats the great horse, and that night, Vandeuvres, owner of both horses but financially wiped out by the woman Nana's extravagances and Lusignan's defeat, kills himself and all his horses by setting fire to the stables. Once again, a treacherous fairy has wreaked havoc on a noble family: "Peu à peu, avec ses gros membres, ses rires canailles de faubourienne, elle s'était imposée à ce fils, si appauvri et si fin, d'une antique race" (*Nana* 343).

Let us return to Nana's triumph in *Mélusine*. She has a non-speaking part, which is doubtless one reason for the play's "grand succès": "son rôle était une simple figuration, mais un vrai 'clou,' trois poses plastiques d'une fée puissante et muette" (*Nana* 425). *Clou* can have a triple meaning here: a success, or "hit," because Nana steals the show; an insignificant ornament, which aptly describes Nana's silent part; or a nail, an appropriate metaphor for her fixed "pose plastique." Later, as we learn that Nana has just died of smallpox, a friend tells us a bit more about her semi-nude pose; dominating the stage, Nana gave Paris one last look:

> Oh! épatante, ma chère, lorsqu'elle paraissait au fond de la grotte de cristal! ... Elle ne disaitpas un mot,[30] même les auteurs lui avaient coupé une réplique, parce que ça gênait non, rien du tout, c'était plus grand, et elle vous retournait son public, rien qu'a se montrer.... Autour d'elle, la grotte, toute en glace, faisait une clarté; des cascades de diamants se déroulaient des colliers de perles blanches ruisselaient parmi les stalactites de la voûte; et, dans cette transparence, dans cette eau de source, traversée d'un large rayon électrique, elle semblait un soleil, avec sa peau et ses cheveux de flamme. (429–30)

Nana synthesizes the elements in this final pose. Mélusine is chiefly an aquatic spirit, but as Gilbert Durand points out, like all mother goddesses, she is associated with the fertile earth as well, so her cult "oscille entre un symbolisme aquatique et un symbolisme tellurique" (261). Nana stands motionless in the crystal cave, the prostitute mineralized and purified: stalactites, precious stones, and fountains cascade upon the goddess, illuminated by a great ray of light. She seems the fountainhead of life itself, the alchemist's dream: her inert body is the mercurial passive principle, the ray of light the active soul, out of whose union is born the "*Filius sapientiae*" (Durand 259).

Barthes describes the power of immobility in *S/Z*; the woman is immortalized as art in the motionless statue, or in the writing of a text: "[L]a Femme copie le Livre. Autrement dit: tout corps est une citation: du *déjà-ecrit*. L'origine du désir est la statue, le tableau, le livre" (40). Beauty on its own is mute; one can only understand it through metaphor. Nana thus rises above her human nature, deified in an already conceptualized essence, the work of art. To the Parisian crowds, her beauty is that of the plastic model, defined by the innumerable artistic representations of Venus that have preceded her.[31]

Nana's uncanny power, then, is most impressive when she is mute and motionless: a still life framed in glass, as in her mirror or in the crystal grotto of *Mélusine*. To paralyse, this Medusa must herself be transfixed. Turning again to Barthes, we find the erotics of immobility unveiled. The dance of the striptease euphemizes rather than heightens the eroticism of the act, distracting the audience's attention from the threatening nudity of the dancer, sublimating the sexual into art. In Barthes's words, the dance desexualizes the dancer, acting like "un cosmétique de mouvements" that ward off "la peur de l'immobilité."[32] A gay laughter greets Nana, dressed in a white tunic, as she dances and sings in *Blonde Vénus*; but when she returns in the third act, a marble goddess in a transparent shift, the audience's reaction mirrors her still silence:

> Nana était nue. Elle était nue avec une tranquille audace, certaine de la toute-puissance de sa chair.... Personne ne riait plus, les faces des hommes, sérieuses, se tendaient, avec le nez aminci, la bouche irritée et sans salive. Un vent semblait avoir passé, très doux, chargé d'une sourde menace. Tout d'un coup, dans la bonne enfant, la femme se dressait, inquiétante, apportant le coup de folie de son sexe, ouvrant l'inconnu du désir. (53)

Nana embodies here the menacing aura of the still female nude, a troubling figure that prompted Michel Leiris to make this improbable comparison between museums and brothels: "Rien ne me parait ressembler autant à un bordel qu'un musée. On y trouve le même côté louche et le même côté pétrifié."[33] For Leiris, Venus finds her modern counterpart in houses of prostitution, twentieth-century slave markets whose occupants appear to be frozen in a ritual of stereotyped gestures.

The glory of the goddess is of course ephemeral. As Baguley remarks, the solar hero has no permanent place in naturalism's "entropic vision," and "the sun that is reflected by the naturalist hero in the fallen, subverted order of nature is clearly on the eclipse" (223). The reader cannot forget the mortality of the woman Nana, as references to her horrible death are juxtaposed with the description of her triumph as Mélusine: "Nana morte! ... Etait-ce drôle qu'elle fût morte! ... Maintenant, elle devait être jolie là-haut!" (*Nana* 429–30). Nana's solar goddesses were in fact never far removed from the shades: Venus was a funereal goddess in some traditions (Durand 222); the horse with which Nana is associated, although later a solar creature, was originally assimilated to the "black sun"—a symbol of death (Durand 82); and finally, as serpent Mélusine is the epitome of the chthonian animal. All this negative symbolism converges in the final scene of the novel; Nana's decomposing eyes, the inverse of her still shining hair, seem to incarnate the black sun, symbol of night and the relentless passage of time:

> Un oeil, celui de gauche, avait complètement sombré dans le bouillonnement de la purulence; l'autre, à demi ouvert, s'enfonçait, comme un trou noir et gâté.... Et, sur ce masque horrible et grotesque du néant, les cheveux, les beaux cheveux, gardant leur flambée de soleil, coulaient en un ruissellement d'or. Vénus se décomposait. (Nana 438–39)

This then is our final portrait of Nana; the still life's frozen beauty has melted into a hideous *nature morte*. The mythical element in this novel is, as Frye finds in most works of the "ironic mode," demonic rather than divine: Mélusine's celestial charms could never overcome the dark, threatening nature she observed in her two-sided mirror. As we contemplate the cynical grin that twists Nana's face, it is the petrified prostitutes of Leiris who come to mind, rather than Schor's smiling sphinx. For in the naturalistic novel, petrification finally returns to putrefaction; the radiant golden body which seemed to represent the consummation of the alchemist's dream is now but a "shovelful" of decomposing matter. If Pygmalion's lover seemed for a moment to turn back into marble, she becomes all too human at the end of the novel, and disintegrates: a helpless body, victim of an ancestral flaw, a degraded social body, and above all her author's ironic vision.

NOTES

1. Emile Zola, *Le Roman expérimental* (1880) (Paris: Garnier, 1971) 91.

2. Joseph Campbell, *Creative Mythology* (New York: Penguin, 1968) 6.

3. J.G. Patterson, *A Zola Dictionary* (London: Routledge, 1912) xiii, quoted in Jill Warren, "Zola's View of Prostitution in *Nana*," in *The Image of the Prostitute in Modern Literature*, ed. Pierre L. Horn and Mary Beth Pringle (New York: Frederick Ungar, 1984) 31.

4. Letter to Jules Lemaître," March 14, 1885, *Correspondance*, ed. B.H. Bakker, 5 (Montreal: PU de Montréal, 1985) 245.

5. Emile Zola, *Nos Auteurs dramatiques* (Paris: Bernouard, 1927) 301, quoted in Philip Walker, "Zola's Hellenism," in *The Persistent Voice: Essays on Hellenism in French Literature since the 18th Century*, ed. Walter G. Langlois (New York: New York UP, 1971) 71.

6. Northrop Frye, *Anatomy of Criticism: Four Essays* (Princeton: Princeton UP, 1957) 33–34.

7. Jean Borie, *Zola et les mythes, ou, de la nausée au salut* (Paris: Seuil, 1971).

8. Roger Ripoll, *Réalité et mythe chez Zola*, 2 vols. (Paris: Honoré Champion, 1981).

9. Mircea Eliade, *Aspects du mythe* (Paris: Gallimard, 1963) 24–25.

10. Naomi Schor, "Smiles of the Sphinx: Zola and the Riddle of Femininity," *Breaking the Chain: Women, Theory, and French Realist Fiction* (New York: Columbia UP, 1985) 30.

11. Reproduced in Peter Brooks, "Storied Bodies, or Nana at last Unveiled," *Critical Inquiry* 16 (1989) 21.

12. Emile Zola, *Nana* (1880) (Paris: Garnier, 1968) 215.

13. Emile Zola, *Thérèse Raquin* (1867) (Paris: Garnier, 1970) 59–60.

14. Emile Zola, *Le Docteur Pascal* (1893) (Paris: Garnier, 1975) 54.

15. Emile Zola, "Ebauche," *La Faute de l'Abbé Mouret* (1875) (Paris: François Bernouard, 1927) 420.

16. Charles Bernheimer, *Figures of Ill Repute: Representing Prostitution in Nineteenth Century France* (Cambridge: Harvard UP, 1989) 217.

17. Roland Barthes, *S/Z* (Paris: Seuil, 1970) 26.

18. Gilbert Durand, *Les Structures anthropologiques de l'imaginaire* (1960), 10th ed. (Paris: Bordas, 1984) 257–58.

19. Jean d'Arras, *Mélusine: roman du XIVe siècle*, ed. Louis Stouff (1932; rpt. Geneva: Slatkine Reprints, 1974).

20. Frances McNeely Leonard, "*Nana*: Symbol and Action," *Modern Fiction Studies* 9.2 (1963) 150.

21. David Baguley, *Naturalist Fiction: The Entropic Vision* (Cambridge: Cambridge UP, 1990) 213.

22. Nana too was rejected and cursed by her mother. Ch. 11 of *L'Assommoir* recounts the last months that Nana lived at home. Gervaise, infuriated by her daughter's scandalous behavior, repudiates her: "Oui, ce chameau dénaturé lui emportait le dernier morceau de son honnêteté dans ses jupons sales. Et elle se grisa trois jours, furieuse, les poings serrés, la bouche enflée de mots abominables contre sa garce de fille." Emile Zola, *L'Assommoir* (1877) (Paris: Garnier, 1969) 378.

23. See, for example, Janet Beizer, "Uncovering *Nana*: The Courtesan's New Clothes," *L'Esprit Créateur* 25.2 (1985) 52–53, and Brooks 18–24.

24. In this same paragraph, Muffat twice refers to Nana as "the beast." This "sinister animal image" (Frye 149), of which the serpent identified with Mélusine is another example, is typical of the demonic mythical element that Frye finds in the "ironic mode."

25. Claude Louis-Combet, *Le Roman de Mélusine* (Paris: Albin Michel, 1986) 105. My analysis of the mirror theme is based for the most part on Louis-Combet's twentieth-century version of *Mélusine*, which the author describes as "pas la transcription moderne d'un texte médiéval, mais l'expression nouvelle et personnelle des hantises qui ont suscité, jadis, l'image de Mélusine et qui nous rendent cette image toujours nécessaire, en sa troublante intimité" (Cover). Louis-Combet's prose brings to life the Mélusine engraved on the cover page of the Old English translation: a mermaid, long hair flowing, holds a comb in one hand and a mirror in the other, her vanity perhaps hinting of potentially destructive wiles. See *Mélusine*, trans. ca. 1500, ed. A.K. Donald, Early English Text Society (1895) (Millwood, NY: Kraus Reprint, 1973). If Louis-Combet dwells longer than Jean d'Arras on the mirror theme, he is nevertheless only highlighting the ambivalent symbolism of the *fountain* in the fourteenth-century novel. For example, Mélusine and Raymondin meet at the "Fontaine de Soif" (Jean d'Arras 24), and it is there that they are married (38); a fountain miraculously springs forth to mark the boundary of Raymondin's lands (34). The fourteenth- and twentieth-century authors are both troubled by the "hantises" incarnate in Mélusine's equivocal nature, illustrating the oft cited words of Lévi-Strauss, for whom a myth is the sum of all its interpretations throughout history: "Il n'existe pas de version 'vraie' dont toutes les autres seraient des copies ou des échos déformés. Toutes les versions appartiennent au mythe." *Anthropologie structurale* (Paris: Plon, 1958) 242.

26. Laurence Harf-Lancner, *Les Fées au moyen âge* (Paris: Honoré Champion, 1984) 174–75.

27. Auguste Dezalay, *L'Opéra des* Rougon-Macquart: *essai de rythmologie romanesque* (Paris: Klincksieck, 1983) 295.

28. Mélusine was a prodigious builder of towns and fortresses. Jean d'Arras recounts how she erected the castle of Lusignan in record time with the help of mysterious workmen who seemed to appear from nowhere: "Ne nulz homs ne savoit dont cilz ouvriers venoient, ne dont ilz estoient. Et en brief temps fu faitte la forteresse, non pas une, mais deux fortes places, avant que on peust venir au dongon. Et sachiez que toutes les trois sont advironnees de fortes tours machicolees, et les voutes des tours tournees a ogives, et les murs haulx et bien crenellez.... Moult fu la forteresce grant et fort a merveilles." Jean d'Arras, *Mélusine* 46.

29. Nicole Belmont, "Les Fées: croyances et légendes populaires en France," *Dictionnaire des mythologies et des religions des sociétés traditionnelles et du monde antique*, ed. Yves Bonnefoy, 1 (Paris: Flammarion, 1981) 402.

30. Zola insists once more on Nana's silent portrayal of Mélusine, whose name, ironically, can mean "musician" or "singer," "la *sirène* révélatrice des harmonies." Eliphas Lévi, *Histoire de la magie* 240, quoted in Suzanne Lamy, *André Breton: hermétisme et poésie dans Arcane* 17 (Montréal: Les P de l'U de Montréal, 1977) 95.

31. See Peter Brooks's aforementioned article for an excellent study of the female nude in nineteenth-century French painting and its relationship to Zola's Nana.

32. Roland Barthes, *Mythologies* (Paris: Seuil, 1957) 148–49.

33. Michel Leiris, *L'Age d'homme* (Paris: Gallimard, 1939) 61.

FREDERICK BROWN

The Master Plan

By the end of 1867, many parvenus felt decidedly old. The Universal Exposition that excited Paris all that year was in fact the last hurrah of a despotism weakened by political strife and economic disorder. Although gold flowed into the Banque de France, showing France's favorable balance of trade, there it accumulated as erstwhile borrowers became tightfisted observers, alert to what Napoleon III himself admitted were "black specks on the horizon." On the horizon loomed Prussia, which had made Europe tremble in 1866 by crushing Austria at the battle of Sadowa, and the sense of manifest destiny her victories brought home contrasted with the pall that hung over the Tuileries. "I hear from other persons besides Lord Cowley that the emperor is very much out of spirits," reported the British ambassador, Lord Lyons, in 1868. "It is even asserted that he is weary of the whole thing, disappointed at the contrast between the brilliancy at the beginning of his reign and the present gloom—and inclined, if it were possible, to retire into private life. This is no doubt a great exaggeration, but if he is really feeling unequal to governing with energy, the dynasty and the country are in great danger." Napoleon's poor health alarmed the financial community even more than his desperate improvisations. Stock prices climbed when he appeared on horseback and fell when a bout of illness conjured up the frightful image of Eugénie trying to govern France as

From *Zola,: A Life*. © 1995 by Frederick Brown.

regent. There was no market for long-term investment in a short-lived regime.

Napoleonic pillars collapsed one after another. First to fall was the Crédit Mobilier, half of whose capital disappeared overnight with the failure in 1866 of a Marseille real estate operation. The Banque de France would not shore it up, and patrician financiers led by Rothschild, who regarded Jacob and Isaac Pereire as reckless adventurers, delivered the coup de grâce, knocking down prices on the Bourse until a share of stock in Crédit Mobilier became a worthless memento. The next to topple was Baron Haussmann. In an exposé entitled *Les Comptes fantastiques d'Haussmann*, Jules Ferry, the future prime minister, laid bare an illicit scheme through which Haussmann had raised funds above and beyond what the legislature had sanctioned for his gigantic project.[1] Debate raged, Napoleon III made concessions enlarging the scope of parliamentary privilege, and Haussmann, whom Adolphe Thiers dubbed "vice-emperor," left office. Thus did the work of rebuilding Paris grind to a virtual halt, with disastrous consequences for some 100,000 people whose livelihood hinged on this enterprise.

Every morsel of freedom thrown to one class or another whetted its appetite for more, and the Empire fell not all at once but concession by concession as even formerly staunch Bonapartists rallied around Dame Liberty. When trade unions became legal in 1864, Louis Napoleon found soon enough that in attempting to buy quiescence he had licensed revolt. Strikes broke out, and strikes bred violence which profited the radical doctrine of ideologues like Auguste Blanqui. No less fruitless was Louis Napoleon's attempt to mollify a contentious legislature. In 1867 he made the government answerable for policy through the mechanism of interrogation or "interpellation," whereupon deputies, unmuzzled but not yet unleashed, bayed in chorus against a despot whose will remained law; forgetting—if they were old enough to remember—how easily France had traduced republican institutions fifteen years earlier.

The chorus of protest was amplified by the press, which spoke uninhibitedly after May 11, 1868, when a law went into effect permitting any Frenchman who had attained his majority and enjoyed his civil rights to publish a newspaper "without prior authorization." The law also reduced the stamp tax levied on papers read for political content, and forbade the much feared admonitions by which Napoleon had made independent-minded publishers heel. To be sure, such publishers would go on paying a steep price. Fines and prison sentences meted out as late as 1870 in courts of summary jurisdiction (*tribunaux correctionnels*) indicate how reluctant officialdom was to surrender its teeth. But criticism grew louder all the same. Hardly a week passed that did not see one or two new journals materialize, and by October 1868 the interior ministry counted ninety-seven in Paris alone, most of them anti-Bonapartist. "What we have is an unprecedented burgeoning of newspapers," observed a journalist who apparently came of age after 1848, which had been equally fecund. "They are cramped for space in kiosks, and newspaper dealers, positively overwhelmed; don't know where to tuck the latest arrivals. Nowadays producing a paper is quite fashionable and one must be dead broke not to join the celebration. Fifty years hence every Frenchman will have a paper on his conscience." Among the dozen or so that survived their first temper tantrum, several established themselves as influential transmitters of republican opinion and gathered strength during the final days of Napoleon's empire.

This storm of print promised relief for drought-stricken journalists all over France. Even before May 11, however, Zola's future brightened somewhat thanks to a gentleman two years older than he named Théodore Duret, whom he met through Manet. Duret hailed from Saintes, near La Rochelle. Born to wealth, he had entertained political ambitions until the elections of 1863, when he ran last against Napoleon's candidate. Prevented from descending upon the capital as a liberal legislator, he traveled around the world as the representative of a cognac distillery and came home laden with Oriental objets d'art. Art rather than cognac was what impelled him to tour Iberia in 1865, where he made Manet's acquaintance. A year later he left Saintes for Paris, which captivated the aesthete but also reawakened the liberal. This tall, aristocratic young man, who looks Grecoesque in a portrait done by Manet, immediately cast his net wide. While frequenting the Café Guerbois, where he earned hospitality with a book sympathetic to Batignolles painters (*Les Peintres français en 1867*), he acquired friends among left-wing newspapermen, one of whom, Mille-Noé, founded *Le Globe* in January 1868. Duret became art critic for this daily, whose first issue announced that it was "the organ of democracy and the partisan of all freedoms." Zola, riding in on Duret's coattails, reviewed books and plays.

That he needed anybody's sponsorship is one measure of the ambiguous position he occupied vis-à-vis militant republicans. Whereas the latter held creative work accountable to political dogma, Zola viewed art and politics as inherently separate realms. "Proudhon would make me a citizen, I would make him an artist, [for] in my view art is a negation of society, an affirmation of the individual outside all rules and social imperatives," he had written at twenty-five, stating a belief that was to be reiterated time and again. As repugnant as he found the moral elevation that critics like Ulbach required of art, the conformity they expected of artists repelled him even more. Though he hated social injustice, he sided not with the crowd but with men who rose above it, who suffered its taunts or quickened its pulse. An engineer striking water from rocks, an artist braving convention, a visionary entrepreneur, a scientist plumbing unexplored depths, a Balzac measuring himself against Dante: these were his heroes, and for such heroism the sententious world of republican discourse had no room. What made him feel all the more dubious about that world was his own pessimism. Convinced that civilized man harbors an incorrigible savage screaming to be let out, he, like Taine, could travel only so far with idealists willfully ignorant of the part played in human affairs by *la bête humaine*.

Nothing daunted, Zola spoke his mind at *Le Globe* and reviewed works that lent themselves to a defense of naturalism or to an attack on religious superstition. "*Eugène Bastin* is not a novel ... but a minute study of real life," he wrote in February. "The author has understood that greater moral rigor and livelier interest attaches to the true than to the fanciful. He took any old subject, a commonplace story, and studied human beings in their daily routine, in the facts of their existence, which could be your existence or mine." After an evening of bromidic theater, he called for the playwright who would someday "dramatize life in its reality, with virtues and vices we encounter on the street." Almost every other review made this same point, advocating now the legitimation of banal events, now the demystification of supernatural phenomena. "Supernatural," for example, was *Les Trésors du château de Crevecoeur, épisode de l'affaire Frigard*, a book that recounted some rural hocus-pocus involving a peasant girl subject to divinatory trances. "Poor mankind, dreaming wide awake and soaring into madness on the wings of passion!" cried Zola. "Free minds have but one consolation, that being to ferret out the truth, to discover what lies behind the ecstasies of Saint Theresa and Léonie the somnambulist." These two names would, no doubt, have put readers in mind of a third, Bernadette Soubirous, whose vision at Lourdes ten years earlier had become grist for the anticlerical mill.

But *Le Globe* provided only temporary shelter. One month after Mille-Noé set it up the paper folded, and Zola, wondering if his vagrancy would ever end, once again went in search of regular employment. Not until spring did he find any. "I've saved the best for last," he informed Marius Roux on April 17. "[Adolphe Belot] has just started a cheap daily, *L'Evénement illustré*, under Adrien Marx's direction!!! They've offered me the Salon, which I took for want of something better. When you return I'll introduce you to Marx, and perhaps he'll let you write a column about Paris." This assignment, which generated seven articles, presented the piquant challenge of having to flatter his own image, with all due modesty. "Yesterday a friend asked me if I would comment on [Manet's portrait of me at the Salon]," he wrote. "'Why not?' I answered. 'I'd like ten columns to repeat aloud what I thought in silence as I watched Edouard Manet during our sittings wrestle tenaciously with nature. Do you take me for a vain sort who delights in lecturing on his physiognomy? Yes, I shall discuss this portrait, and wags who make the most of it are simply imbeciles.'"

Scattered through the horde of indistinguishable genre scenes were more paintings by habitués of the Guerbois than had been the case in 1866, although they were usually "skyed," or hung high above eye level. Also present was a large sculpture by Philippe Solari, *Nègre endormi*, and Zola lavished praise on his old friend. "I find in Philippe Solari one of our few modern sculptors.... He has put behind him the dream of absolute beauty, he does not carve idols for a religion (that disappeared with the ancient Greeks). Beauty to him is the living expression of nature, the individual interpretation of the human body." With phrases flowing so effortlessly from his pen, he might have found a way of devoting some to another childhood friend. But nowhere in the review is mention made of Cézanne, whom the jury had rejected that year.

Meanwhile, Duret had remained on the alert for an opportunity to stake his claim in Paris's ebullient newspaper world. Opportunity knocked soon after the demise of *Le Globe* when he connected with Eugène Pelletan and André Lavertujon, two seasoned dissenters who were keen on founding a paper to boost the republican cause, as well as their own candidacies, in elections scheduled for 1869. By mid-April word of this project reached Zola. "Yesterday I saw Duret at Manet's," he wrote to Roux. "The venture is limping along. I think Pelletan may be as inept as Mille-Noé in business matters. No one is sure when *La Tribune* will appear, or whether it will appear at all." Roux, who had contributed several articles to *Le Globe* and thus knew Mille-Noé, responded in language that crudely expressed his low opinion of politicians on the left. "You think Pelletan has about as much brawn as [the flaccid] Mille-Noé? I believe democracy most definitely cannot be put right. Democracy is not strong. If it is, it is strong like a cheese that stinks but lacks consistency."[2]

Whatever Zola's qualms may have been, the new paper promised to give him more leeway than the unserious *Evénement illustré*. In any event he needed money, and need made Pelletan and company look more attractive with every passing day. As prospects of *La Tribune* materializing improved, Zola rose to the occasion. He badgered Pelletan through Duret until the future editor-in-chief granted him an interview. "I saw Pelletan this morning, and here is how our conversation went," he reported to Duret on May 8. "I'll do a causerie for *La Tribune*, a weekly chronicle about theaters, books, literary events.... We didn't discuss salary. I hope you'll be present when that issue is raised.... Also, please see to it, I implore you, that they hire neither an art critic, nor a bibliographer, nor any other editor who might tread on my turf." Two weeks later he prodded Duret to settle the matter. "Has the salary question been thrashed out? It's a matter of grave importance. I miss working for a daily, which allowed me to earn what I need and live peacefully in an honorable family. I'm sick of *la petite presse* [popular journalism] with its more or less sleazy machinations. It diminishes people and kills them."

Duret let him know that his salary would be 4,000 francs per annum, but the situation remained unclear even after *La Tribune* had published its first issue. "I must apprise you of my conversation with M. Lavertujon," Zola wrote Duret on June 19.

> He seems quite well disposed but couldn't give me any assurances. In short, he doesn't think I can write an article every week because commitments have been made to too many people.... I pleaded my cause by emphasizing Pelletan's promise and, *above all*, pointing out that a "causerie" is a chronicle that must absolutely appear in every issue. But what seemed to affect him most was my saying that I needed the work badly, with a mother to support and nothing to rely upon save my pen ... I told him furthermore how weary I am of popular journalism, how ardently I want safe haven at an upright and serious newspaper. "If *La Tribune* offered me 500 francs a month," I said, "I'd devote myself to it religiously."

In October, after producing a dozen causeries lauded by Pelletan, Zola was still apprehensive, and when Pelletan invited another literary journalist to write something for *La Tribune*, he assumed the worst. "I've learned that we shall soon be fellow collaborators at *La Tribune* and I'm delighted to see you enter a house where I am already settled," he warned Jules Claretie. "But rumor has it that you will share my task and write two of the four causeries I give the paper each month. As you know, I'm a poor devil. May I implore you—you on whom fortune smiles and who place articles just about everywhere—to leave intact my sole resource?" Claretie reassured him that the chronicle was not at stake and that he would have turned it down had it been offered. "I thank you for confiding in me, though I'm a bit peeved that you believed me capable of making cider from my neighbor's apples."

Zola's fear was not without a basis in reality. Pelletan had given him carte blanche only after overcoming doubts and overruling colleagues who thought the young man politically suspect. Thus in May, Duret had urged Zola to be "extra prudent" during negotiations. "You are under siege and attacked all around, so you'd better behave yourself. Everybody including some big names, some very big names indeed, will want to take your place. The first volleys have already been fired. What provokes such rage against you is the fact that you're not a democrat and certain democrats here fancy that they alone should write for it, even the literary articles." This antagonism persisted. Zola dared not lower his guard or speak his mind except in the company of literati like Jules and Edmond de Goncourt, and to them he spoke his mind rancorously at their first encounter in December 1868. "[I] would like to launch something big and not do these ignoble, infamous articles I must turn out for *La Tribune*, amidst people whose idiotic opinions I am compelled to share," they quote him as saying. "The truth of the matter is that this government with its indifference, its unawareness of talent and of everything that's being produced under its nose, thrusts us in our poverty upon opposition journals, which are the only ones prepared to offer us a livelihood!"

Eager to impress these supercilious novelists of whom he made so much and who in turn made so little of others, Zola may have thought it best to picture himself a journalist *malgré lui*. But his sixty-odd causeries, even when they invoke 1793, were not mere exercises in ideological ventriloquism. The voice that derided institutions, policies, and people week after week was unmistakably his own. Indeed, it became increasingly his, for he emerged from this ordeal broader in outlook and laden with enough subject matter to construct the fictional edifice already taking shape in his mind. What he wrote as *La Tribune*'s mordant chronicler foreshadows *Les Rougon-Macquart*.

Along with Dumas *fils* and the Goncourts, Zola waxed apocalyptic on the topic of degeneracy. His causeries abound in lurid anecdotes that demonstrate how France had become a nation devoid of pride, where men of high estate groveled before women of low repute. Obsessed by *la bête humaine*, he saw it consuming patrimonies, loosening family ties, tearing moral fabric, cheapening life altogether. His *bête* held sway over the moribund Empire like a nihilistic force that clouded memory and induced those born with noble patents or expectations of wealth to forget the past or bankrupt the future. "Ah! how many sinister dreams unfold in secret, how many men there are who cast off their black habit as if it were a mere costume, roll on the carpet like a dog, and beg for punishment!" he cried, with an image that was to become a major dramatic moment in *Nana*.

The quake of '89 followed hard on the scandals of the Regency and of Louis XV. I don't know what will follow our own age. I simply note that gentlemen send horses worth 25,000 francs a pair to trollops and fetch besotted women at the jailhouse. A kind of nervous erethism is unhinging our gilded youth. Aristocrats and scions live in lamebrained mirth. They applaud the cheap tunes ground out by Messieurs Offenbach and Hervé, they exalt wretched tightrope dancers cavorting on the legitimate stage. Their mistresses are street urchins who drag them down to their level of language and feeling.

This lament recurs throughout, and often, as here, in tandem with a diatribe against Offenbach, whose comic operas were all the rage. *"La Belle Hélène* amounts to nothing more than a grimace of convulsive gaiety, a display of gutter wit and gestures," he fumed when word reached France that *La Grande Duchesse de Gérolstein* had played to enthusiastic audiences in London. "The day some woman conceives the brilliant idea of running around a stage naked on all fours and acting the part of a stray bitch, that will be the day Paris cheers itself sick."

To ridicule the beau monde for worshipping base idols was also to condemn it for shunning spectacles of everyday life in the lower depths. The same people who lionized Offenbach found naturalism objectionable, and Zola concerned himself as much with their social blindness as with their pornographic voyeurism. "Walk around our working-class slums, strictly incognito," he wrote in a Montesquieu-like letter to Fatouma-Djombé, sultana of Mohéli, who obviously stood for the Empress Eugénie. "There you will see what it behooves a queen to see: lots of poverty, lots of courage, muffled rage against the idle and the wanton. There you will hear the great voice of the populace, growling for justice and bread." By September 1869, when Eugénie went south with her son, opposition to the regime had grown so openly vehement that Zola dared mock her in person. "At Toulon," he wrote, "mother and child were received with open arms. Among the first to greet the travelers were a dozen convicts, who broke their ban on this special occasion.... My only regret is that the empress did not feel compelled to have her son visit the casemates of Fort Lamalgue. Being a strong-minded woman who likes strong-armed tactics, she would, I'm sure, have enjoyed seeing the gloomy dungeon where her spouse had insurgents locked up in December 1851." Another blind eye belonged to Baron Haussmann, the architect of a capital from which thousands of workers had been driven by demolition crews and developers building flats they couldn't afford. "I know M.

Haussmann doesn't like popular festivals. He has forbidden almost all those that once took place in the communes annexed to Paris [eight years ago, including Montmartre]. He relentlessly harasses street peddlers. In his dreams, he must see Paris as a gigantic chessboard, with geometrically perfect lines."

For his weekly prosecution of officialdom, Zola subpoenaed not only proscribed images but censored words. Censorship was, to be sure, no longer the weapon it had been during the "preliberal" Empire of the 1850s, when criticism of Napoleon's regime, however meek, prompted draconian reprisals from above, and when an obscenity charge awaited the author who led his reader astray. Not since Baudelaire and Flaubert stood trial for "*outrage aux bonnes moeurs*" in 1857 had the imperial prosecutor hauled up any writers of note. But many noted writers, Victor Hugo above all, still lived in exile, and the regime still employed a censor to guard its shrunken sphere of influence. "On some Wednesday morning, gain admittance if you can to the office where the censor works," Zola advised the aforementioned sultana of Mohéli. "Take a seat and listen. It's pure vaudeville. These gentlemen believe that there's a revolution taking place in the street. They subject thought to close inspection, sniffing every word for a scent of gunpowder, searching every phrase for a concealed bomb. They end up moving commas around and congratulating themselves on having saved the Empire."

Books were also scrutinized by a *commission de colportage*, whose purview encompassed bookstalls at railway stations and lending libraries as well as the countryside. A book could not be sold in such establishments or hawked from town to town unless it bore a prefectural stamp, and the commission furnished syllabi of approved works. This system having come under attack in parliament, Zola joined the fray with an epistolary tirade against mind control written on August 9, one month after *Thérèse Raquin* was judged immoral. The commission suppressed every plot that called traditional authority into question, and Zola cited as evidence a censored but otherwise undistinguished novel, *Madame Freinex*, whose titular heroine rebuffs her unscrupulous, politically ambitious husband. "I think I know what troubled you," he taunted.

> The author defends woman's freedom of conscience. You underlined the sentence in which Juliette tells her husband that she "has no master." However legitimate this declaration of freedom coming from the mouth of a woman whom a knave wishes to manipulate, it must have struck you as monstrous. Ah, pious young men that you are, you'll always remain true to your

catechism! ... I've said it before, you understand morality only at the most pedestrian level; the morality that transcends purely social duties and stands on truth and absolute justice escapes you and frightens you.

Framing an indictment of censorship around this example was especially meaningful in 1868, when *vielle France* felt threatened by measures that gave women greater intellectual scope. Louis Napoleon's courageous minister of public instruction, Victor Duruy, had just opened public secondary school courses to both sexes, and the Church, including even liberal clergy, protested vehemently. Conservatives and progressives alike viewed woman's mind as the field of Armageddon from which France would emerge Catholic or secular. "The Church intends to possess woman, and for that reason democracy must make it loosen its grip," Jules Ferry told an audience at the Sorbonne in May 1870. "Democracy must decide under pain of death whether woman will belong to Science or to the Church."

Another conflict in which Zola expressed republican sentiment was the one that marshaled pacifists favoring accommodation with Bismarck against nationalists spoiling for glory in a war with Prussia. Since Austria's defeat at Sadowa in 1866, every turn of events had brought Prussia nearer to the brink of war with France. Racked by disease, Louis Napoleon may have been unprepared to join battle, but he found himself caught between an iron chancellor in Germany who thwarted his diplomatic maneuvers and a military establishment at home that wanted a casus belli. Private life offered him no respite from this dilemma. While the emperor grew more indecisive, the empress, whose conviction it was that her son would never rule if her husband did not campaign, grew more belligerent. Sir Charles Oman described how matters stood in remembering a ceremony he witnessed as a child on holiday in France. "The Prince Imperial, then a boy of twelve, was a cadet, and was to drill a company of other cadets of his own age on the gravel in front of the Palace," he wrote in *Things I Have Seen*.

> On a bench overlooking the gravel sat a very tired old gentleman, rather hunched together, and looking decidedly ill. I do not think I should have recognized him but for his spiky moustache. He was anything but terrifying in a tall hat and a rather loosely fitting frock coat ... Behind him stood the Empress Eugénie, a splendid figure, straight as a dart, and to my young eyes the most beautiful thing that I had ever seen ... wearing a zebra-striped black and white silk dress, with very full skirts, and a black and white

bonnet. But it was the way she wore her clothes, and not the silks themselves, that impressed the beholder, young or old.... The Empress was a commanding figure, and dominated the whole group on the terrace—the Emperor, huddled in his seat, was a very minor show. She appeared extremely satisfied and self-confident as she watched the little manoeuvres below. Her son, the Prince Imperial, ... drilled his little flock with complete success and not a single hitch or hesitation. His mother beamed down upon him. The boys marched off, and the spectators broke up after indulging in a little *Vive l'Empereur*!

Perhaps Louis Napoleon entertained strong suspicions that his army, compared with King Wilhelm's well-oiled and proven machine, loomed no larger than this diminutive band. An attempt at reform had produced a reserve, or *garde mobile*, preposterously unfit for battle. The general staff lacked cohesion. The legislature had cut war appropriations. But among patriots, a mystical belief in the Napoleonic legend and exorbitant faith in the new chassepot rifle outweighed evidence that counseled against force of arms. As such evidence mounted, war fever spread, until it seemed to young Charles Oman at least that France was one large parade ground. "In France there seemed to be bands and banners or military display almost every day ... congresses of *Orphéonistes* with gorgeous lyres on their standards, or of *Pompiers* with magnificent brass helmets," he observed. "The soldier was everywhere, very conspicuous because of his various multicoloured and sometimes fantastic uniform ... the trooper of the Cent Gardes—the hundred horsemen—in the brightest sky-blue, with cuirass and steel helmet ... the bearskins of the grenadiers of the Imperial Guard ... the white breeches and black gaiters of the original *grognards* of Napoleon I ... the Zouaves of the Guard with their floppy tasselled headgear and immense baggy breeches, with yellow lace upon their absurdly small cut-away jackets."

Zola regularly interrupted the extravaganza to prophesy that unless France sobered up, this parti-colored cast of actors would soon be indistinguishable skeletons dancing a *danse macabre*. On All Souls' Day 1868 he mourned compatriots who had fallen in battle throughout Europe and pictured an old lady bereft of son or husband scanning the horizon for Sebastopol. The fallen were evoked again in July 1869, when workers began sprucing up the Champs-Elysées with oriflammes to celebrate the hundredth anniversary of Napoleon I's birth. "The administration should assemble not the quick but the dead," he proclaimed. "It should sound the call to arms all over Europe, in Italy, in Spain, in Austria, in Russia. And from all these battlefields, hordes would rise. Ah, what a festive gathering it would make, a gathering of the butchered. Paris would be too small. Never would an emperor have had before his arch of triumph so populous a nation." On the eve of Sedan, it must have seemed much longer than ten years since the battle of Magenta and the ode he had written then enjoining Frenchmen to "go fight where once your fathers fought so nobly." At nineteen he had identified himself as a "student of rhetoric from the Lycée Saint-Louis." Now he vilified a government that got young men drunk on fine phrases before sending them east to die.

Zola did not stay put very long on the rue Moncey. In April 1868 he moved nearer Clichy, having found, behind the apartment building at 23, rue Truffaut, a dollhouse-like pavilion that afforded him protection from the hubbub of a street crowded with shops and alive with women who gathered every day in the washhouse at number 26. A year later, when his newspaper articles were producing a comfortable income, he moved around the corner to a more "bourgeois" street, the rue de la Condamine, and rented another dollhouse, this one larger than the first but still so diminutive that its grandest room could not accommodate both a dinner table and an upright piano until a niche was hollowed out for the latter. Here he settled with his women, enjoying calm at the edge of pandemonium. There was a garden to putter in, and soon a big Newfoundland named Bertrand to receive the affection he lavished on dogs (dogs and other pets would follow Zola throughout his life). There were also friends constantly arriving from Aix to make it all feel even more provincial. "He had me talk at length about myself, my plans, about that Provence he still cherished after eleven years, a faint scent of which entered the house with me, no doubt," wrote Paul Alexis, who left Aix for Paris in 1869 and eventually became Zola's most intimate friend.

> More stay-at-home then than now, with fewer acquaintances and above all less money to spend ransacking antique and curio stores, not rich enough to afford a summer holiday outside Paris, he found a hygienic distraction in this little garden, which took the place of a café, a club, a country house, a chalet at Trouville. I can still see him in a sweater and an old pair of soil-stained pants, shod in big, fur-lined shoes.

Alexis would have known how his compatriot's love of Provence verged on blind hatred if he read *Le Mémorial d'Aix*, where in August 1868 Zola vituperated against the city that never gave François Zola his due. This jeremiad began obliquely enough, with an article deploring the misbehavior of some students who had offended two young ladies by singing ribald verse beneath their balcony and whose trial led to skirmishes on the Cours Mirabeau. "Such scandalous conduct could only have taken place at Aix, a barbarous town," he declared in *L'Evénement illustré*. "Where else but among stupid, churlish people would respectable women ... unfortunate enough to be rich and beautiful arouse the jealousy of the entire feminine public and find themselves harassed by young men obeying nasty insinuations.... Times have changed since Aix fostered the first Courts of Love!"

His shaft hit the mark, and friends told him that indignant aldermen were bent on making him apologize. Before they could do so, however, he shifted ground to the real issue, which was one of name and fame. "My father, a civil engineer, died in 1847 after devoting his last years to a canal project that improved Aix's sanitation and fertilized the drought-stricken countryside," he wrote in *L'Evénement illustré* on July 28. "True to form, Aix has striven to forget the very name of someone who compromised his fortune and health on its behalf. I spent fifteen years there, my entire youth, and of its thirty thousand inhabitants, I can count three at most who haven't stoned me." He had been through the city a year before and found nothing graven on walls or published in papers to suggest that Aixois kept alive the memory of "their benefactor."

Le Mémorial dismissed the charge outright, but Zola attacked with redoubled fury, availing himself of an offer from Léopold Arnaud to bruit his case in *Le Messager de Provence*. Each side wrote ornately vicious letters, one longer than the next, until *Le Mémorial* announced that further debate would be pointless. After releasing a Parthian shot, on September 14 Zola turned to Aix's municipal council and, in the name of a grateful population, demanded "honorific recompense" for François Zola. "Deliver the letter and plead the cause, should it be necessary," he ordered Marius Roux, who, like Cézanne, shuttled between Aix and Paris. "It would be best if the mayor read it in your presence. Be sure to say that I couldn't indicate the exact nature of the recompense, but that naming a street after him seems appropriate. Go so far as to help him choose the street, if possible. I'm asking Arnaud to launch a campaign." When his request was heard six weeks later, the municipal council honored it with such alacrity that one member proposed commissioning a bust. They decided, instead, to rename Boulevard du Chemin-Neuf "Boulevard Zola" and notified Zola *fils* straightway. Soon afterward, Roux, Valabrègue, and other brethren from Aix gathered around the victors for a celebratory dinner in Les Batignolles. Emilie, now forty-nine, had at last won some measure of justice.

Zola did not let matters rest there. A letter sent to Marius Roux on December 4 reflects the ease with which he glided between opportunism and piety:

> I ask you first to find out why I haven't yet received a copy of the municipal council's minutes. Kindly see the mayor and tell him that I await them with rightful impatience. I thank you for worrying about the sale of my volumes in Aix. When you return and give me precise information, I shall know what to do. While you're at it, see if there might not be some way of slipping into *Le Mémorial* the review of *Madeleine Férat* [his latest novel]. Have I vexed Remondet to the point of not being able to count on his paper for publicity?

To make hometown notables honor Zola father and son remained his fixed goal. Belittling Aix only conferred on it the stature it had had for him during childhood, when names were won or lost down south rather than up north. He stoked his rage like a sacred fire and thus kept alive that youth who regularly climbed Les Infernets seeking the vantage point of his father's monument to lord it over those responsible for his mother's social disgrace. Whichever height he occupied in life, he always wanted Aix below.

Something of the same rage that inspired diatribes against *Le Mémorial* found expression in *Madeleine Férat*, a novel published serially as *La Honte* between September 2 and October 20, 1868. The story had been with him since 1865, when he wrote a three-act play entitled *Madeleine*, of which nothing came. Now, salvaging the framework, he improvised yet another vehicle for ideas that lent scientific credence to his private demonology.

Like Thérèse Raquin, Madeleine Férat, the daughter of a sixteen-year-old orphan and a self-made man of forty, is doomed *ab origine*. Her mother dies in childbirth and six years later her father, after suffering financial reverses, sails for America, never to reappear. Madeleine grows up with no one whom she can call family except her neglectful guardian, Lobrichon. The latter takes her home from boarding school when she turns fifteen, having conceived matrimonial designs upon the nubile redhead. He waits four years, then lecherously declares himself. Madeleine flees, wanders through Paris, and is offered shelter in the Latin Quarter by a young doctor, Jacques Berthier, to whom she makes love out of gratitude. They remain together several months until the army drafts him for service in the Far East; footloose womanizer that he is, he departs as if sprung from prison, leaving Madeleine mysteriously tethered to the relationship. "She never loved him deep down; rather, she received his imprint, she felt herself becoming him, she understood that he had taken complete possession of her flesh and her mind. She could never forget him."

No sooner does Jacques embark than Madeleine meets young Guillaume de Viargue, whose story is as fraught with Gothic incident as hers is with genetic hobgoblins. Zola conjures up a Norman castle, a reclusive father immersed in chemical experiments, a devoutly Calvinist housekeeper of great age named Geneviève. Fathered by Viargue senior on an adulterous bourgeoise, Guillaume was raised lovelessly between religion, which taught him to regard himself as the "child of sin," and science, which ignored him altogether. At school, where children mocked "the bastard," only one boy showed him kindness, and, despite their differences of nature and temperament, the two became fast friends. They had since gone separate ways. Always yearning for the perfect union, Guillaume drapes his fantasy on Madeleine as soon as chance throws them together; the strangers find refuge from history in a town house Guillaume acquires. "The lovers could imagine that the past had died.... Madeleine thought she had been born the day before." This beatific state is ruined when Madeleine discovers among Guillaume's effects a photograph of Jacques, who turns out to be that childhood soul mate. Not even the news that Jacques has perished at sea, which breaks immediately afterward, can assuage her. Dead or alive, he lives on, like a devil impossible to exorcise. "She rediscovered him there, in her breast."

Five years later, the strangers are still together, having meanwhile married, begotten a daughter, and inherited the ancestral château. More Calvinist than ever, Geneviève, now a hundred years old, recites stories about destruction visited on lubricious women by "God the Father" as she challenges Madeleine for Guillaume's soul. But otherwise the couple feels safe. "The young woman luxuriated in the emptiness all around her; it seemed to isolate her more completely, to cushion her against wounds from the outside."

The implausibilities continue. While off attending to business, Guillaume encounters Jacques himself, who has not drowned after all, and joyously informs Madeleine that this long-lost brother, home from Cochin China, will join them for a night. Madeleine avoids her Nemesis but reveals the terrible truth to Guillaume, awakening his own worst fears. "The idea of having shared her with another, of having come second, was something he couldn't tolerate.... His wife's former liaison with the man he had considered a god during his youth seemed to him one of those abominations that confound human reason. He saw it as incestuous, as sacrilegious." A recovery from beyond the grave thus results in a fundamental loss, and Guillaume suddenly observes that his daughter resembles Jacques rather than himself. With no inner space they can call their own, he and Madeleine become fugitives shuttling between town and country but condemned to meet their master everywhere. In due course the tale comes full round. Madeleine finds her way to Jacques, yields her body somnambulistically, then learns that her child died at the moment of transgression. This preternatural coincidence tolls a denouement. "One after another all places had become uninhabitable," and Madeleine swallows poison concocted by M. Viargue years before. Stark raving mad, Guillaume dances around her corpse as Geneviève drily mutters: "God the Father did not pardon!"

Madeleine Férat was obviously patterned after *Thérèse Raquin*, with greater emphasis on the motif of "impregnation." Again there is a triangle involving a woman and two temperamentally antithetical lovers. Husband and wife are again effeminate and mannish. And again a ghost rises from the deep to destroy a haunted couple. Just as Camille's mother triumphs at the end of *Thérèse Raquin*, so in *Madeleine Férat* it is Guillaume's surrogate mother, Geneviève, who witnesses the final scene, interpreting what happens as condign punishment for original sin or innate lewdness. Each novel dramatizes the guilt that cannot plead extenuating circumstances to a rational jury. Though fathers are conspicuously absent from both, the fatherless inhabit a moral universe ruled by a patriarch vengeful in his justice, who manifests himself through widowed crones.

With all its melodramatic flummery and physiological humbug, *Madeleine Férat* translates the horror Zola saw in regression to a primitive state. Yearning for adulthood, Madeleine and Guillaume struggle against a force that pulls them backward or downward to where the identities they have acquired and the order they have built come undone. Once Jacques ruins their hermetic Eden by introducing consciousness of the past, they fall from grace. Ejected from themselves, the lawfully wed couple become partners in betrayal. "Guillaume's marriage proposal caused her singular revulsion, [for] it seemed to Madeleine that he was asking something impossible of her, that she was not self-possessed but the possession of another man," writes Zola. Such revulsion might appear excessive if the adulterous act were not experienced on some level as incestuous, and we have seen how incest eventually speaks its name. Bearing the "imprint" of the man who protected Guillaume in loco parentis, Madeleine plays Jocasta to her husband's Oedipus.

Their imbroglio is amplified and parodied in another triangular drama, which they observe unfolding next door under the nose of an old aristocrat named Rieux, whose wife, Hélène, has attached herself, after numerous liaisons, to a vulgar opportunist half her age named Tiburce Rouillard. Where Madeleine and Guillaume suffer for sins they didn't commit, Hélène and Tiburce fornicate without scruple, the one governed by lust, the other by ambition. Where history weighs upon Zola's guilt-ridden protagonists, his guiltless couple are savages unconscious of the past, trampling underfoot class distinctions and generational barriers as they dance naked before the aristocratic Rieux, who regards them scornfully. "Long contemplation of his wife had persuaded him that humans are mean, stupid marionettes. When he searched the wrinkled doll, he discovered, beneath her coquettish mask, infamies and fatuities that led him to consider her a beast good for whipping. Instead of whipping her, he amused himself by studying and despising her." An aristocrat marooned among Second Empire déclassés, a naturalist observing "the human beast" in its mindless progress toward self-degradation, and a puppeteer jerking lost souls, Rieux is, above all, one more avatar of the wrathful father exacting vengeance on the incestuous. This he does when at length Tiburce turns against Hélène. Rieux's final testament stipulates that the rapacious young man shall inherit his entire fortune, provided he marry the woman whom he now brutalizes. "My child, I have come to regard you as my son, I wish to assure your happiness," he says, and with these dying words arranges an infernal troth.

Although *Madeleine Férat* ran uncensored in *L'Evénement illustré*, shortly before its publication in book form authorities told its editor-in-chief, Edouard Bauer, that unless certain passages expounding the impregnation theory were cut from the book, he might be subject to prosecution. Distraught, Bauer informed Lacroix, the book publisher, and he, in turn, exerted pressure on Zola, who would not yield. "Let's reason this out, I beg of you," he answered.

> What has been authorized on the street cannot be banished from the bookstore…. It seems the imperial prosecutor warned [Bauer] that although allowances had been made for him, with his powerful connections, it is unlikely that any would be made for me, an editor at *La Tribune*. There you have preventive censorship plain and simple, and instead of wanting me to purge my work, you should be helping me upbraid the public prosecutor…. I will therefore not approve the cuts you specify. For me it's a matter of law. Self-respect requires me to go forward and face this danger with which I'm threatened. If necessary, I shall relate the story out loud.

After an interview with the prosecutor, Zola devoted a long article to his predicament in *La Tribune*, invoking not only legal precedent but scientific authority. "The few lines they would expurgate contain the book's central thesis, which I took from Michelet and Dr. [Prosper] Lucas," he explained. "I dramatized it austerely and with conviction; good morals are not endangered by a medical study that serves, as I see it, a high human purpose." While the censor presumably saw in "impregnation" a physiological alibi for infidelity, Zola argued that if anything it bolstered the sacredness of marriage. "This study tends to accept the marriage bond as eternal from the physiological viewpoint. Religion and morality tell man: 'You will live with one woman'; and science says in turn: 'Your first wife will be your eternal wife.'" Calvinist in his depiction of woman struggling vainly against a cynical nature, Zola in his self-defense contrived to appear more Catholic than the pope.

He contrived as well to appear more beleaguered than he really was, or so said Lacroix in conversation many years later. The publisher and his author apparently manufactured publicity by staging quarrels and keeping literary chroniclers informed. Along with a legal writ that enjoined Lacroix to publish *Madeleine Férat*, Zola served him gossip for newspaper distribution. "Attached you will find the note that was supposed to run in *Le Figaro*. I find it so complete, so felicitous, that I cannot resolve to file it. Try then, for the love of God, to get it published somewhere. Feyrnet is back, I think. He could plant it in *Le Temps*. If he refuses, look elsewhere." When *Madeleine Férat* finally appeared, Zola referred to such gossip as evidence of literary martyrdom and sought help for this waif disinherited by its publisher. "I don't know if you still review books at *L'Artiste*, but I would greatly appreciate your inserting several lines about the attached volume," he entreated in a typical note. "The imperial prosecutor threatened its life before it was born, as you undoubtedly know from the newspapers. I hope that its misadventures will engage your sympathy."

In the end, the most sympathetic response may have come from Edouard Manet, to whom the novel was dedicated. "My dear friend," he wrote, "I am immersed in *Madeleine Férat* and don't want to wait until the end before sending you my compliments. Your portrait of the redhead makes me jealous, and for the love scenes you find expressions the mere reading of which would deflower a virgin." Otherwise, *Madeleine Férat* received a quiet burial. Obituaries noted either its harsh treatment of women or its abuse of the bourgeoisie.

SOON AFTER *Madeleine Férat* appeared, Jules and Edmond de Goncourt first met Zola, and the figure they evoke in their journal leaps straight out of the novel. Powerful yet frail, burly but with finely chiseled features and waxen skin, he looked to them a dissipated intellectual "made in the mold of his characters, who, physically and emotionally, combine male and female." Never having seen him at table, where he thrived, or having been entertained *chez lui* by his latest pet, a short-tailed monkey named Rhunka, they describe their "admirer and student" as neurasthenic. "The dominant side, the sickly, ailing, ultra-nervous side, suggests someone afflicted with heart disease. An elusive being, deep, paradoxical in sum; pained, anxious, troubled, doubt-ridden." Doubt-ridden he certainly was, and inclined, moreover, to make himself an object of pity by dwelling on the financial obligations that bound him to Grub Street. But hand in hand with the childlike supplicant who invited help from prestigious elders went the gladiator fierce in his hunger for a success even greater than theirs. "Now and again recriminations, in which he told us repeatedly that he was only twenty-eight, sounded a note of bitter resolve and violent energy," they observed. Modest enterprises failed to excite him. He saw his future writ large, and on this occasion, with *Madeleine Férat* behind him, spoke about a ten-volume novel entitled *L'Histoire d'une famille*. He could accomplish it by the time he was thirty-four, he assured the skeptical brothers, if some publisher paid him thirty thousand francs over six years, or enough to live comfortably.

Thus did Zola announce a program destined to occupy him much longer than six years and to engender twenty volumes rather than ten. *L'Histoire d'une famille* was already in preparation when he visited the Goncourts. Mindful of Taine's dictum that no great novelist lacks a philosophy or system, he began acquiring one, and labored through recondite material at the Bibliothèque Impériale. Such treatises as *Leçons de physiologie* by Claude Bernard, *Traité des dégénérescences physiques, intellectuelles et morales de l'espèce humaine* by Bénédicte-August Morel, *Physiologie des passions* by Letourneau, and *De l'identité de l'état de rêve et de la folie* by Moreau de Tours figure prominently in the syllabus he assigned himself in 1868. But his chief inspiration came from the enormous work on which he had relied for *Madeleine Férat*, Dr. Prosper Lucas's *Traité philosophique et physiologique de l'hérédité naturelle*. "No need to indicate here all the works on physiology I consulted," he wrote years later. "I need cite only Dr. Lucas's *L'Hérédité naturelle*, where those who wonder about it can find the physiological system that helped me elaborate the genealogical tree of the Rougon-Macquart." Like a schoolboy given some monstrous *pensum*, he filled sixty pages with notes summarizing arguments, cataloguing hereditary permutations, citing examples, drawing social maps, and at last listing novels to be written.

It made no difference to him that savants considered *L'Hérédité naturelle* more fanciful than factual. This hodgepodge suggested a conceptual framework for *L'Histoire d'une famille* and at the same time bestowed scientific legitimacy on the creative enterprise by showing "how in procreation as in creation life obeys the laws of invention and imitation, which in procreation become the laws of innateness and heredity."[3] Science was what would distinguish his saga from Balzac's, he told himself in a brief memorandum entitled "Differences between Balzac and me":

> My work will be less social than scientific. Through 3,000 characters Balzac wants to write the history of manners; he bases this history on religion and royalty. His entire science resides in statements that there are lawyers, idlers, etc., as there are dogs, wolves, etc. In short, his work wants to be the mirror of contemporary society.

L'Histoire d'une famille, he continued, would be more limited in scope:

> I don't want to portray contemporary society but a single family and dramatize the interplay of race and milieu. *If I accept a historical frame, it is only in order to have a milieu that reacts* [emphasis Zola's]; professions being milieux as much as places of residence. It is especially important that I remain a naturalist, a physiologist. Rather than principles (royalty, Catholicism), I shall have laws (heredity, innateness). I don't want to be a politician, a philosopher or moralist, to imitate Balzac in telling men how to manage their affairs. It will suffice to be a scientist, to describe what is by searching for what lies underneath. No conclusion, moreover. A simple exposé of the facts of a family showing the inner mechanism that makes it run. I even admit the exception.
>
> My characters need not return in particular novels.
>
> Balzac says that he wants to depict men, women, and things. I, on the other hand, combine men and women while acknowledging natural differences, and I subject both to things.

What he envisaged, then, was a drama unfolding through successive generations, in which every conflict would have innateness warring against heredity, or the self challenging the demon within for possession of characters who, like Madeleine Férat, struggle to escape a native milieu, a tainted past, a script visited on them at birth. Whereas Balzac's personae reappear as live actors, his would carry ghosts. Whereas time in *La Comédie humaine* nurtures the dream of transcendence, in *L'Histoire d'une famille* it would conceal the threat of regression, with physiology operating like an idée fixe impervious to events. And finally, whereas Balzac intrudes upon his own stage, he, Zola, would play the impersonal voyeur.

L'Histoire d'une famille housed Zola's particular lares and penates, but it was also styled for family men who felt threatened from below or from outside. Just as evolutionary theory degraded mankind in general by linking it to bestial origins, so revolutionary doctrine raised the specter of a primitive horde subverting the middle class. One historian notes that this siege mentality gripped the Parisian bourgeoisie, who, "to disavow whatever elements of the primitive or the irrational survived in the civilization of their age," sought to "block from mind the provinces and rural life." While custodians of aesthetic order held proto-Impressionists responsible for corrupting morals, moralists held "provincials" or "foreigners" responsible for transforming a once virtuous capital into an Impressionist canvas. The villain was anyone who blurred social boundary lines, who skewed proportions, who celebrated fugitiveness, who glided through France as an epiphenomenon of the general havoc spread by railroads.

Many conservatives came to regard railroads as the preeminent instrument of an erotic force that would, unless stringent measures were taken, destroy the French family and substitute for France itself a mongrel pornocracy governed by queens all in the image of Manet's *Olympia*. "The railroads, exercising a bizarre influence on the intellectual as well as the economic state of society, pour into Paris every day a mobile but tightly packed mass of bustling provincials whose literary culture is, to say the least, slapdash and vagrant," wrote J. J. Weiss in *Theater and Manners*, referring to the exodus from rural France that saw Paris's population treble between 1830 and 1880. Dumas *fils* arraigned the railroad network in *Francillon*, where one character blames society's ills on "the invasion of women from abroad, the glorification of courtesans, the daily trainload of exotic mores that enter the city on every line, hastening local degenerations," and he reiterated this diagnosis in his preface to *La Dame aux camélias*:

> Railroads were created. The first rapid fortunes made by the first speculators seized upon pleasure, instantaneous love being one of the first needs ... The new transportation facilities brought to Paris a host of rich young people from the provinces and from abroad. The newly enriched, most of whom had risen from the lowest classes, did not fear to compromise themselves with such

and such a girl who had won herself a name at the Bal Mabille or the Château des Fleurs. It was necessary to provide for the sensual appetites of a progressing population, as well as for its physical nourishment.

"Invasion" often recurs in baleful prophecies inspired by women traveling unwed from the depths of society to the heights. "[The whore] has invaded society and knows it," wrote the Goncourts. "Nowadays she dictates manners, she muddies opinion, she nibbles iced chestnuts in the loge next to your wife, she has her own theater (Les Bouffes) and a world of her own—the Stock Exchange.... These are abnormal times. With its heart and mind so violently turned upside down ... society cannot but explode."

If hereditary doubleness was to constitute the inner drama of *L'Histoire d'une famille*, its backdrop would be a world illustrating the confusion between high and low or the destructive survival of the primitive in modern man. "Characteristic of the modern movement is the ... democratic thrust, the collapse of hierarchical order (whence the familiarity between fathers and sons, the mingling and shoulder-rubbing of different types)," Zola noted. "These are troubled times. It is the trouble of our times I portray. Take note: the greatness of the effort that propels the modern world forward I don't deny. I don't deny that we can come more or less close to freedom, to justice. But my belief tells me that men will always be men, animals good or bad as circumstances dictate." Using images then in fashion, he noted further that his family (whom he gave various hyphenated names before Rougon-Macquart) would end up a victim of speed, "unhinged" by its own frantic movement upward. "It will burn like matter devouring itself, it will exhaust itself in little more than a generation because it will have lived too fast."

No doubt Zola observed the motto he was later to engrave above his desk: *Nulla dies sine linea* ("No day without a sentence"), for at the beginning of 1869 a first volume had already been plotted chapter by chapter and nine more outlined, complete with characters forming a mature genealogical tree. Each novel would investigate some particular milieu, he explained in his proposal to Albert Lacroix, and one such would be the licentious Boulevard:

A novel whose milieu is café society and whose heroine is Louise Duval, daughter of the working-class couple. Offspring of both the Goiraud [Rougon] and the Bergasse [Macquart], one branch hungry for pleasure, the other eaten up by vice and poverty, she is at once a social misfit and a fungus harmful to society. Besides the hereditary effects, there is the fatal influence of the contemporary world. Louise is what is known as a "high-flyer." Picture of the world in which such doxies live. Poignant drama of a woman doomed by her appetite for luxury and facile satisfaction.

We shall see how *Nana* sprang from this seed twelve years later. But so did every other seed eventually bear fruit. *La Curée, La Faute de l'abbé Mouret, Son Excellence Eugène Rougon, L'Assommoir, L'Oeuvre, L'Argent, La Débâcle*—the first published in 1872, the last in 1892—were all conceived together in 1869.

Lacroix plumped for *L'Histoire d'une famille*, which soon became *Les Rougon-Macquart: l'histoire naturelle et sociale d'une famille sous le Second Empire*, and drew up a contract as original as the project itself. Expecting two novels a year, he offered in return five hundred francs a month, with the understanding that this stipend represented an advance against money earned from serialized publication. If income from feuilletons did not equal his investment, the difference would be obtained from book sales. Only after Lacroix had collected three thousand francs for each novel would the author collect royalties, and royalties meant eight sous, or somewhat less than half a franc, per copy sold.

As usual with Zola, necessity mothered invention. His causeries had been suspended after February 18, 1869, when *La Tribune* gave every line of type over to electoral issues, producing consternation in the Zola household. The causeries resumed on July 18 and Zola continued writing them throughout the year, but this weekly assignment, which someone else might have considered occupation enough, did not impede the progress of *Les Rougon-Macquart*. By September 1870 a first volume, entitled *La Fortune des Rougon*, had been sold to *Le Siècle*, where for months it waited its turn behind other feuilletons. The following spring, Zola, even before he finished *La Fortune*, set to work on the sketch of a second volume.

What leisure he had was enjoyed with friends on the rue de la Condamine or at the Café Guerbois, with family at Bennecourt, and with all comers at Manet's studio. Gingerly, however, he came to venture further afield and to reconnoiter circles dominated in person or in absentia by important literary figures.

There were people clustered around the playwright Paul Meurice, for example, the high priest of Hugo worship (he had once edited Hugo's *L'Evénement*). Looking distinctly ecclesiastical, Meurice held services every Monday evening, and in November 1868, after Zola had praised his work in *La Tribune*, he had sent the benevolent critic an invitation. "I would like to make your acquaintance. Now and again our mutual friend, Manet, spends Monday evenings with us; it would be nice if you accompanied him one day." Zola had attended more than one such soirée when word got out that Meurice and company were launching a newspaper with proceeds from Victor Hugo's latest novel, *L'Homme qui rit*. It was during the hiatus in Zola's employment at *La Tribune* and he lost no time jumping aboard. "I've heard much talk about *Le Rappel* recently and am told that you need chroniclers," he wrote Meurice. "If you haven't yet filled your quota, please keep me in mind. I'm behind you all the way. Perhaps you will want to consider at some point a novel in the series I discussed with you. I know that right now you have masterpieces on your plate." *Le Rappel* carried seven articles by Zola between May 1869 and May 1870, which is to say that Meurice welcomed him, but tentatively. While Zola's polemical verve commanded respect, his somber estimate of human nature vexed liberals who took their cues, literary and otherwise, from Victor Hugo. At *Le Rappel* as at *La Tribune*, *Thérèse Raquin* won no applause, and in due course relations became unpleasant. An encomium to Balzac on the occasion of Michel Lévy's publishing *La Comédie humaine* turned out to be his valedictory.

Altogether different were relations with Jules and Edmond de Goncourt, who, in one of the stranger literary partnerships of the nineteenth century, produced books that combined a mannered refinement of style and a passion for documentary rectitude. While writing at length about Fragonard and Watteau (in *L'Art du dix-huitième siècle*), they studied Paris's lower depths and declared in the preface to their novel *Germinie Lacerteux* that an age of universal suffrage could hardly continue to keep common people under a "literary interdict," or deem their obscure miseries unworthy of high fiction. Although it created nothing like the furor of *Madame Bovary*, this novel about the double life of a seemingly chaste maidservant figured importantly in the development of literary realism during the 1860s.

Zola had wooed the brothers before he met them and afterward proved even more assiduous in devising opportunities to promote their work.[4] "I have a request to make of you," he wrote on January 9, 1869. "Since January I have been contributing bibliographical articles to *Le Gaulois* and specialize in forthcoming books.[5] I should like to whisper something about your *Madame Gervaisais*, on condition that this indiscretion profit you ... What must I reveal? In what way would you have me be indiscreet?" Gratitude was not the strong suit of such misanthropic peacocks as the Goncourts (least of all during this period, when syphilis had already gone some way toward undermining Jules in body and mind), but Zola's courtship, which they regarded as some small compensation for the neglect lavished upon them by a vulgar world, earned him invitations to the villa they had recently purchased near the Bois de Boulogne, in Auteuil.

It also earned him an introduction to Gustave Flaubert, whom he found disappointing at first. "I arrived with a preconceived Flaubert, a Flaubert whose works had made him the pioneer of our century, the painter and philosopher of our modern world," he remembered after Flaubert's death.

> I imagined him beating a new path, founding a regular state in the province conquered by romanticism, striding energetically and confidently toward the future. What I found instead ... was a great strapping devil, a paradoxical spirit, an impenitent romantic who knocked me silly for hours with a barrage of stupefying theories. I'd go home sick, fagged out, dazed, telling myself that the man was not equal to the writer. I've since changed my mind, I've savored a temperament full of contradictions ... and would not see my Flaubert altered a jot. But the first impression was nonetheless rude.

Zola met these writers of another generation just as their lives had started unraveling. They and their literary kinfolk were no longer numerous enough to surround a table at the restaurant Magny, where in 1862 Sainte-Beuve had assembled them for what became a ritual dinner. Sainte-Beuve died in 1869. In 1869 death also claimed Flaubert's lifelong friend, Louis Bouilhet. Then, on June 20, 1870, Edmond de Goncourt lost Jules after watching him rave through the tertiary stage of syphilis. Zola stumbled upon a wake and found himself clasped to the bosom of mourners shaken by intimations of their own mortality. When fear subsided there would be time enough for Oedipal conflict. But in 1869–70, before they really knew one another, bereavement fostered closeness between arriviste and arrivés.

There were those in whose opinion Zola had already arrived. A steward to great men, he himself figured as a great man to certain compatriots and particularly to his newest friend, Paul Alexis. Seven years younger, Alexis first heard about Zola from Antony Valabrègue, his chum in the same schoolyard where Zola had once consorted with Cézanne. The exploits of this alumnus loomed large at the Collège Bourbon, and when *Les Contes à Ninon* appeared Alexis read it under cover, like a cult book. Bowing to parental pressure, he grudgingly studied law. He even finished law school, but a sense of literary vocation had meanwhile affirmed itself. Influenced by Marius Roux (who published some of his verse in *Le Figaro*, misrepresenting it as Baudelaire's) and at one remove by Zola, Alexis felt increasingly *dépaysé*. "The melancholy of [Aix's] promenades on Sunday brought tears to my eyes. Indifferent to stately old town houses blackened with age, to the hush of streets where grass sprouted between paving stones, I'd sometimes daydream, like Madame Bovary, before this word PARIS printed on the label of pomade jars." He concluded that poverty in the capital would suit him better than prosperity in the subprefecture, and after bootless appeals to his father, a rich notary, fled Aix with two hundred francs borrowed from Valabrègue. Valabrègue, who set Alexis up on the rue Cardinal-Lemoine in the Latin Quarter, lost no time shepherding him across Paris for an introduction to Zola, every detail of which remained graven in his mind. "Around September 15, 1869, at 8 p.m., I and my hometown friend, the poet Antony Valabrègue, boarded the top deck of an 'Odéon-Batignolles-Clichy' omnibus," he wrote.

> Having arrived in Paris several days earlier to "do" literature, but still quite young and with some verse in the style of Baudelaire as my only baggage, I was about to meet that Emile Zola whom I had never seen but whom I had heard much talk about since my fourteenth year.... We clambered down on reaching avenue de Clichy. A few steps beyond "the Fork" and we stood before 14, rue de la Condamine. My heart began pounding. The first words out of Zola's mouth were: "Ah! there you are, Alexis! I was expecting you." I felt that our initial handshake sealed a pact, that I had just yielded all my affection and could count on the staunch friendship of a kind of older brother.

Time proved him right. He would thenceforth serve Zola unwaveringly and be served in return.

One of the first services this "older brother" asked him to perform did him honor, for on May 31, 1870, along with Paul Cézanne, Marius Roux, and Philippe Solari, Alexis bore witness to Zola's marriage in the town hall of Les Batignolles. Why Zola made an official commitment just then is not known, but some reasons seem obvious. After five years of cohabitation, Alexandrine must have thought it high time that she enjoy as much respectability as the dowager queen of the ménage.[6] Her lover had turned thirty on April 2 and stood to earn a predictable income from novel writing. No doubt Zola wanted to get his house put in order for the immense enterprise he was undertaking.

Marriage may also have offered them security against the grim prospect of war. Since September 1868, when Queen Isabella of Spain fell from power, relations between France and Prussia had seriously deteriorated as both sought to have a friendly candidate chosen for the Spanish throne. Bismarck backed Leopold von Hohenzollern, though he knew that Louis Napoleon would not countenance a Hapsburg on his Pyrenean flank. No less dogged was France's parliament, where talk of French honor rose above disclosures of imperial skulduggery. To Louis Napoleon's tacit chagrin, each side wanted a casus belli and, with patriotic rhetoric fanning indignation throughout the land, republicans stood alone in denouncing this savage conspiracy. Zola made his voice heard as one such republican. Two years earlier he could not have imagined himself Louis Ulbach's bedfellow, but bedfellows they became when Ulbach founded *La Cloche* in December 1869; given free rein, Zola took up where he had left off at the now defunct *Tribune*. Twenty-two articles spaced over seven months were so many philippics against the Napoleonic regime, and its bloodthirstiness inspired the most eloquent of them. A law muzzling the press for reasons of national security did nothing to quiet Zola. "Remember, France has sown the world with far-flung cemeteries," he wrote on July 25, six days after the outbreak of war.

> From China to Mexico, from the snows of Russia to the sands of Egypt, there isn't an acre under the sun that doesn't cradle some slaughtered Frenchman. Silent and forsaken cemeteries that slumber in the lush peace of the countryside. Most of them, nearly all, lie outside some desolate hamlet whose crumbling walls hold memories of terror. Waterloo was but a farm, Magenta had scarcely fifty houses. A tornado swept through these wee settlements, and their syllables, innocent the day before, acquired an odor of blood and powder such that humanity will forever shiver when pronouncing them.

Another article, in which he suggested that Napoleon III was France's true enemy, moved authorities to charge him with "inciting hatred and scorn of the government and provoking disobedience of the laws." National calamity invalidated the writ: just before his court appearance, Prussia won decisive victories on the Rhine. One month later there would be no empire to answer to.

As a widow's only son, and nearsighted into the bargain, Zola was doubly exempt from military service. But supporting his kin became problematical in a city under martial law. *Le Siècle* had already suspended publication of *La Fortune des Rougon* when on August 18 Ulbach shut down *La Cloche* for the interim. "With this frightful war, my pen falls from my hand. I'm like a soul in Purgatory. I roam the street," Zola lamented to Edmond de Goncourt. "An excursion to Auteuil would cheer up this poor devil of an unemployed novelist." On September 4, two days after Louis Napoleon passed into German captivity at Sedan, where he had watched General von Moltke's cannon pulverize General MacMahon's mousetrapped army, republican deputies formed a Government of National Defense. The Empire thus fell, and Zola decided to leave Paris, into which provisions for a siege were flowing, along with thousands of refugees terrified of the German onslaught. "If I left Paris I promised to let you know about it," he wrote Goncourt on September 7. "My wife is so frightened that I must take her away. I'll accompany her but if possible shall return in a few days to man my post. What an appalling business, this war!" If the bravado of his fellow journalists did not inspire him to join the Francs-tireurs-de-la-Presse (such private volunteer militia sprang up all over Paris), he felt required at least to make some excuse, it seems.

Two days after Victor Hugo's triumphant return from exile, Zola headed south with Emilie, Alexandrine, and dog Bertrand. He did not return until March 14, 1871.

Notes

1. The title of Ferry's exposé was inspired by *Les Contes fantastiques d'Hoffmann*.
2. Zola and Roux would later break over the Dreyfus Affair when Roux was working for a fiercely anti-Dreyfusard newspaper, *Le Petit Journal*.
3. In Lucas, *innéité*—translated here as "innateness"—signifies that which is the individual's own, apart from what is inherited.
4. Of their inseparability Jules wrote in 1866: "We are now like women who live together and whose states of health become confused with each other, who menstruate at the same time; we get migraine headaches on the same day."
5. Zola contributed to this mildly liberal paper until October 1869, when the editor asked him to take no notice of "irreligious" books.
6. In a book on Zola's early career, Colette Becker points out that the Civil Code then in effect required a son to obtain parental consent to marry until the age of thirty. Her surmise is that Zola married Alexandrine two months after his thirtieth birthday because Emilie Zola's consent had not previously been forthcoming.

ENDNOTES

(page numbers refer to the Farrar Straus Giroux edition)

170. "I hear from other persons besides Lord Cowley": Thompson, *Louis Napoleon*, p. 277

171. "any Frenchman": Claude Bellanger, ed., *Histoire générale de la presse française*, Paris, Presses Universitaires de France, 1969, II, p. 346

171. "What we have is an unprecedented": Henri Mitterand, *Zola journaliste*, Paris, Armand Colin, 1962, p. 86

173. "*Eugène Bastin* is not a novel": O.C., X, p. 735

173. "Poor mankind, dreaming wide awake": Ibid., p. 726

173. "I've saved the best for last": CORR., II, p. 118

173. "Yesterday a friend asked me": O.C., XII, p. 862

174 . "I find in Philippe Solari": Ibid., p. 887

174. "Yesterday I saw Duret at Manet's": CORR., II, p. 118 (April 17, 1868)

174. "You think Pelletan": Thomson, "Une correspondance inédite, vingt-sept lettres de Marius Roux à Emile Zola," p. 362

174. "I saw Pelletan this morning": CORR., II, p. 122

175. "Has the salary question": Ibid., p. 124

175 . "I must apprise you of my conversation": Ibid., p. 129

175. "I've learned that we shall soon": Ibid., p. 158 (October 7, 1868)

175. "I thank you for confiding in me": Ibid., p. 159

175–76. "You are under siege": Ibid., 126 (May 21, 1868)

176. "[I] would like to launch something big": Goncourt, *Journal*, II, p. 475 (December 14, 1868)

176. "Ah! how many sinister dreams": O.C., XIII, p. 207

177. "*La Belle Hélène* amounts to nothing": Ibid., p. 117

177. "Walk around our working-class slums": Ibid., p. 132

177. "At Toulon mother and child": Ibid., p. 249

177. "I know M. Haussmann": Ibid., pp. 196–97

178. "On some Wednesday morning": Ibid., p. 131

178. "I think I know what troubled you": Ibid., X, p. 758

179. "The Church intends to possess woman": Françoise Mayeur, *L'Education des filles en France au XIXe siècle*, Paris, Hachette, 1979, p. 140

179. "The Prince Imperial, then a boy of twelve": Thompson, *Louis Napoleon*, pp. 291–92

180. "In France there seemed to be bands and banners": Ibid., p. 291

180. "The administration should assemble": O.C., XIII, p. 234

181. "He had me talk at length about myself": Alexis, *Emile Zola*, p. 91

181. "More stay-at-home then than now": Ibid., p. 175

181. "Such scandalous conduct": Robert, "Une polémique entre Zola et *Le Mémorial d'Aix*," p. 6

181. "My father, a civil engineer": Ibid., p. 7

182. "Deliver the letter and plead the cause": CORR., II, p. 152

182. "I ask you first to find out": Ibid., p. 171

183. "She never loved him deep down": O.C., I, p. 715

183. "The lovers could imagine": Ibid., p. 734

184. "She rediscovered him there": Ibid., p. 740

184. "The young woman luxuriated": Ibid., p. 763

184. "The idea of having shared her": Ibid., p. 801

184. "God the Father did not pardon": Ibid., p. 896

185. "Guillaume's marriage": Ibid., p. 760

185. "Long contemplation of his wife": Ibid., p. 769

185. "My child, I have come to regard you": Ibid., p. 878

186. "Let's reason this out": CORR., II, p. 165 (November 14, 1868)

186. "The few lines they would expurgate": O.C., X, pp. 768–69

186. "Attached you will find the note": CORR., II, p. 169 (November 26, 1868)

187. "I don't know if you still review": Ibid., p. 175 (December 7, 1868)

187. "My dear friend, I am immersed": *Manet*, exhibition catalogue, p. 522

187. "made in the mold of his characters": Goncourt, *Journal*, II, p. 475 (December 14, 1868)

187. "Now and again recriminations": Ibid.

188. "No need to indicate here": RM, II, p. 800

188. "how in procreation as in creation": Ibid., V, p. 1697

188. "My work will be less social than scientific": Ibid., pp. 1736–37

189. "block from mind the provinces": Daumard, *Les Bourgeois de Paris*, p. 326

189. "The railroads, exercising a bizarre influence": Maurice Descotes, *Le Public de théâtre et son histoire*, Paris, Presses Universitaires de France, 1964, p. 311

190. "the invasion of women from abroad": Ibid.

190. "Railroads were created. The first rapid fortunes": Alexandre Dumas *fils*, *Théâtre complet*, Paris, Michel Lévy, 1896, I, p. 26

190. "[The whore] has invaded society": Goncourt, *Journal*, I, p. 312 (January 18, 1857)

190. "Characteristic of the modern movement": RM, V, pp. 1738–39

190. "It will burn like matter": Ibid., p. 1741

191. "A novel whose milieu": Ibid., p. 1775

192. "I would like to make your acquaintance": CORR., II, p. 168

192. "I've heard much talk about": Ibid., p. 197 (March 24, 1869)

193. "I have a request to make of you": CORR., II, p. 187

193. "I arrived with a preconceived Flaubert": O.C., XI, p. 135

193. "We are now like women": Goncourt, *Journal*, II, p. 308 (December 20, 1866)

194. "The melancholy of [Aix's] promenades": *"Naturalisme pas mort." Lettres inédites de Paul Alexis à Emile Zola*, edited by B. H. Bakker, Toronto, University of Toronto Press, 1971, p. 3

194. "Around September 15, 1869, at 8 p.m.": Alexis, *Emile Zola*, pp. 90–91

195. "Remember, France has sown the world": O.C., XIII, p. 303

196. "With this frightful war": CORR., II, pp. 223–24

196. "If I left Paris I promised": Ibid., p. 225

HOLLIE MARKLAND HARDER

The Woman Beneath: The femme de marbre in Zola's La Faute de l'abbé Mouret

The first time that Albine brings Serge, the village priest, into the overgrown *parterre* in Emile Zola's *La Faute de l'abbé Mouret*, she directs his attention away from the overabundant plant life that dominates the garden where she grew up and leads him instead toward a cool, dank grotto. Peering through an opening in the rocks, Albine and Serge see a statue in the shape of a woman that has been interred there for nearly a century. Albine then leads Serge away from the grotto and into the ebullient flora and foliage of the sunny *parterre*, and the image of the marble figure slips from their minds. Although described in sensuous detail, as we shall see, this statue seems to have no further significance in the novel: the discovery of the marble sculpture neither contributes to the progression of the novel's plot nor figures in the story. Throughout the rest of the novel, the statue remains in the grotto, hidden beneath the events that take place in the Paradou.

Unlike Albine, who at the end of the novel recalls to Serge the existence of the marble statue, critics of *La Faute* have largely forgotten or ignored the buried marble figure. Indeed much of the criticism on this work has focused on the biblical story of Adam and Eve that serves to structure Zola's novel, leaving little or no room for inquiries about a statue that seems to have no equivalent in Genesis.[1] Critical descriptions of the Paradou, as well as studies of women in *La Faute* and explorations that trace the theme

From *Nineteenth-Century French Studies* 24, nos. 3–4 (1996 Spring–Summer). © 1996 by The University of Nebraska Press.

of the subterranean throughout Zola's novels, ignore the marble figure.[2] This omission is curious given that certain sculpted forms in *La Faute*— including representations of Christ, the Virgin Mary, and the earth goddess Cybèle—play a prominent role in critical interpretations of this novel.[3] Moreover, the statues of the Virgin Mary and Cybèle incarnate opposite poles of the dichotomous image of woman in *La Faute* that critics have underscored more generally in their discussions of Zola's portrayal of female characters.[4] These statues represent a fundamental dualism that figures into critical explications of this novel, a dichotomy that is not limited to sculpted forms, but, as Mieke Bal points out, extends also to Albine and Désirée, Serge's feebleminded sister.[5] In a sense, even those critics who try to escape binarism end up rearticulating this division.[6]

If the sculpture of Cybèle and the statue of the Virgin Mary are worthy of remark, representing two extremes, why does the marble statue escape critical scrutiny? Has this sculpture been ignored because it does not fit into the binary structure of analysis that critics have created? How might the critical unearthing of the marble statue change the way in which we read *La Faute de l'abbé Mouret*? With these questions in mind, the logical point of departure for analysis of the statue is the single passage in the novel that describes the *femme de marbre*, a text that addresses the apparent dichotomy in Zola's portrayal of women (and men, for that matter) and the problems that such binarism creates. Although part of this discussion will center on the statue's physical appearance and its resemblance to other women in the novel, we will see that Zola does not limit feminine traits to female characters nor masculine traits to male characters: *La Faute* calls into question the difference between the cultural ideology of gender and the notion of biological sex. We will discover how and why Serge refuses to acknowledge the possibility of ambiguity between types of women (the virgin and the sensual woman) and how he does not accept the idea of ambiguity between the sexes. Finally we will see that the end of the novel signals a rejection of Serge's return to an either/or categorization of the sexes and instead appeals for still another way of perceiving masculinity and femininity.

Serge Mouret, the priest of Plassans in *La Faute de l'abbé Mouret*, finds himself in the Paradou in the first place when the village doctor takes him there to recuperate from a bout with fever and delirium. In the Paradou, Serge completely forgets his position as priest while convalescing under the care of Albine, a young woman who is as untamed as the garden's untended acres. Once Serge gains strength, he and Albine begin to explore the Paradou, a vast section of land that was once the site of a superb chateau and immense gardens decorated with fountains and statues. Albine leads Serge through the riotous vegetation that has taken over the grounds, directing him first to the buried marble statue, and eventually to an enormous tree under which Serge and Albine consummate their love. Soon afterwards, Serge catches a glimpse of his village through a hole in the wall that surrounds the Paradou, and he immediately recalls his obligations to the Church and the vow of chastity that he has broken. Serge returns to Plassans to resume his duties as priest, but Albine persuades him to go once more to the Paradou. Despite the sensuality of Albine and the garden, Serge remains untouched by both, and he again returns to the village, leaving Albine alone in the Paradou, where she commits suicide by suffocating herself with flowers. The novel concludes with Serge as the village priest officiating at Albine's burial.

The pivotal moment with respect to the *femme de marbre* occurs at the beginning of the novel when Albine and Serge venture into the *parterre* together for the first time and find the opening of a grotto obscured by thick vegetation:

> Au fond d'un bouquet de peupliers et de saules une rocaille se creusait, effondrée, des blocs de rochers tombés dans une vasque, des filets d'eau coulant à travers les pierres. La grotte disparaissait sous l'assaut des feuillages. En bas, des rangées de roses trémières semblaient barrer l'entrée d'une grille de fleurs rouges, jaunes, mauves, blanches dont les bâtons se noyaient dans des orties colossales, d'un vert de bronze, suant tranquillement les brûlures de leur poison. (1346)

The narrator continues this overtly sexual description of the exterior of the grotto, detailing the plants' resemblance to the perfumed "chevelure" of a "fille géante ... dans un spasme de passion" and the way in which "d'autres plantes, plus frêles, s'enlaçaient encore à celles-ci, les liaient davantage, les tissaient d'une trame odorante" (1346–47).[7]

Several elements in the couple's approach to the grotto warrant closer examination. Perhaps most significant is the fact that the image of the grotto immediately suggests a connection to the notion of the grotesque. The term dates back to Renaissance Italy when decorative shapes were found in the excavated ruins of villas and baths. These designs, which fill space without focusing on a single subject, are situated by Geoffrey Galt Harpham in "a margin between art and something 'outside of' or 'beyond' art" (xxii). As Eva Kuryluk recalls, these ruins were incorrectly thought to be artificial grottoes designed for Diana and her nymphs, and this misinterpretation, which

Kuryluk deems "truly Freudian," has come to define the realm of the grotesque as "meaning anything coming from or belonging to the cave" and to associate women with images of the subterranean (11–12). Following closely the works of Mikhail Bakhtin and Wolfgang Kayser, Kuryluk recognizes that the grotesque represents a tradition in opposition to the dominant, official culture.[8] Furthermore, the polarities that structure the grotesque give shape to the image of the cave and serve as a basis for the way that woman is depicted. For example, caves offer the promise of protection but threaten imprisonment, a perception that, as Kuryluk avers, corresponds to the notion of woman who both nourishes and imprisons the embryo. Because of connections between the womb and the cave, "all closed spaces tend to be perceived as female and are associated with both protection and threat" (Kuryluk 19–21).

The notion of the grotesque serves to illustrate how the movement between two extremes inherent in the image of the cave can also occur in the categorization of women as chaste or erotic beings. In Zola's depiction of the grotto where the marble statue is buried, the flowers imitate this oscillation between two extremes: they are plant and human, pure and sensual, obstruction and signpost, protection and poison, and it is precisely oppositions such as these embedded in the imagery of the grotto that are incorporated into the description of the marble statue. For example, the marble figure occupies both a horizontal and a vertical space. Inside the grotto, the marble statue lies outstretched on its back, and this horizontal position contrasts directly with the upright pose that the statue originally occupied in the Paradou. In the cave, the sculpture is at once a vertical statue and a reclining figure. This type of contrast also is evident in the statue's face, which a steady stream of water has worn away. No longer does the face illustrate the figure's individual identity; instead it is a featureless slab of smooth white stone. Additional oppositions emerge through Serge's perspective:

> Alors, lui voulut voir à son tour. Il se haussa à l'aide des poignets. Une haleine fraîche le frappa aux joues. Au milieu des joncs et des lentilles d'eau, dans le rayon de jour glissant du trou, la femme l'était sur l'échine, nue jusqu'à la ceinture, avec une draperie qui lui cachait les cuisses. C'était quelque noyée de cent ans, le lent suicide d'un marbre que des peines avaient laissé choir au fond de cette source. La nappe claire qui coulait sur elle avait fait de sa face une pierre lisse, une blancheur sans visage, tandis que ses deux seins, comme soulevés hors de l'eau par un effort de la

nuque, restaient intacts, vivants encore, gonflés d'une volupté ancienne.

Contradictions appear initially in language that characterizes the statue as being both dead and alive. The sculpted figure is presented as a "noyée" who has committed suicide, yet she possesses "deux seins ... intacts, *vivants encore*" (my emphasis). Moreover, Serge affirms that the marble statue seems alive to him when, climbing down from the cave's opening, he says to Albine, "Elle n'est pas morte, va!" The narrator's consistent references to the statue as a *femme de marbre* serve to personify the marble figure. Like Pygmalion, the narrator frees this body of stone to react as though it were a living human being despite the apparent "suicide": when Serge looks into the grotto, he feels a rush of air meet his face as though the marble statue were breathing. In keeping with this oscillation between opposites, the marble statue is at once naked and veiled. The figure is described as "nue jusqu'à la ceinture"; it is partially covered (but also partially uncovered) by a stream of water, a "nappe claire," that is at once concealing and transparent; and finally the marble figure is clothed by "une draperie qui lui cachait les cuisses" (1347).

A more profound type of contradiction characterizes the marble statue. Although the statue displays traits that are diametrical opposites, the marble sculpture also brings together traits from the statuette of the Virgin Mary and the sculpture of Cybèle, two figures that have been labeled as opposites. Critics have already noted some connections that exist between Albine and the Virgin Mary, and between Serge's sister Désirée and Cybèle, but the marble statue shares certain characteristics that go beyond a physical resemblance to both the sculpture of Cybèle (and therefore Désirée) and the statuette of the Virgin Mary (and so Albine).[9]

The marble statue's similarity to Cybèle and Désirée is suggested by the narrator, who describes all three figures while they are lying in an outstretched position.[10] All assume a horizontal, sexually provocative posture, but the narrator deemphasizes the sculpted figures' role as erotic, passionate beings and stresses their place as procreators, a role illustrated by the animals that flank Désirée and by the vegetation that surrounds Cybèle.[11] The statue's location in the Paradou serves to associate the notions of plant and animal fertility as well: underground, the marble figure occupies the space where plants germinate and where, symbolically, animals conceive. In addition, these three figures all function in the world of the subterranean. In antiquity, the disciples of Cybèle celebrated her cult in "antres et cavernes."[12] Similarly, Désirée spends most of her time in the "basse-cour," an appellation that evokes the lower end of the hierarchy to which this area, as well as grottoes, belong (1264). The narrator indicates that "elle s'enterra là," in the barnyard, an image that mirrors the placement of the marble statue buried under the Paradou.

Although situated above ground, the Virgin Mary and Albine also share certain affinities with the *femme de marbre*. All three are associated with the color white, which is perhaps paradoxical, given that white traditionally symbolizes sexual purity and that the marble statue, the Virgin Mary, and Albine also find themselves cast in the mold of the sinner/seductress.[13] Furthermore, in the case of all three women, water serves as the means to silence them: a stream from an underground spring in the Paradou drowns the marble statue; similarly, Albine commits suicide by suffocation, "se noyant" in the perfume of the Paradou's flowers (1516); and during one of Serge's reveries in front of the Virgin Mary, he calls her "une fontaine que le saint Esprit avait scellée" (1289).[14] Finally, the tantalizing image of the swelled breast connects the marble figure, Albine, and the Virgin Mary, and underscores both chastity and sexuality.[15] The same object, however, also serves to link the marble statue, Désirée, and Cybèle, symbolizing a reproductive function and a sexual presence. Like the image of the breast, the figure of the marble statue as a whole is ambiguous, and this indefiniteness allows the statue to be simultaneously a representation of chastity, procreation, and sexuality.

If the body of the marble statue physically unites these pairs into one, the face, which is a featureless slab of stone, makes any connection between these pairs nearly impossible. Freudian psychology may help to explain how this disparity between the statue's body and the head creates and justifies the figure's missing face. According to Freud's theory of condensation in dreams, two images can merge "so that certain features common to both are emphasized" while "those which fail to fit in with one another cancel one another out and are indistinct in the picture" (293). This account explains why physical characteristics shared by Désirée and Cybèle and by Albine and the Virgin Mary emerge distinctly in the body of the marble statue, and why the statue's face, which is composed of individual traits not shared by all of these women, consequently appears as a featureless blur. The face of the marble statue is not exclusively that of Désirée or Cybèle, nor that of Albine or the Virgin Mary, nor is it a merging of the four. The face of the marble statue, that is to say, its identity as a woman, lies somewhere outside of this duality, beyond a blending of two different types of women; its identity is something that is not visible but that is perceptibly other. The marble statue, then, bridges the gap that critics have created between two types of women and suggests a third way of categorizing female characters in *La Faute* according to criteria that lie beyond the realm of the body.

The description of the marble statue reveals a similar movement of opposites coming together to form a third element. Throughout most of the passage, rhetorical devices immobilize the marble figure, as, for example, in the use of past participles to deprive the statue of nearly all possibility of action. The figure does not fall or drown in the active voice; instead it is cast as a fallen woman ("tombée") and as a drowned woman ("une noyée"), and the imperfect tense ("elle était sur l'échine") petrifies the statue more effectively than its body of stone. Despite such quiescence, the marble figure does manage to make one gesture: its breasts, "soulevés hors de l'eau par un effort de la nuque ... gonflés d'une ancienne volupté," express intense sexual pleasure. Ironically, this gesture, the statue's only movement, is played out in the passive voice. But the passive phrasing of the description reverses itself when we understand that the figure's own sexual pleasure causes the nape of the neck to arch and the breasts to rise. Because the statue acts upon itself, it is neither purely passive nor exclusively active, but rather it lies outside of this polarity.

From the description in the novel, the reader cannot determine the nature of the statue's pleasure, which signals a type of sexual ambiguity that Sarah Kofman calls woman's bisexuality, the notion that woman is both masculine and feminine, active and passive (*Enigma* 148–58).[16] Because the source of the statue's pleasure cannot be defined as strictly masculine or feminine, Kofman would label it as both. However, this "bisexuality" does not clarify the issue of gender identity since both men and women can take pleasure in a masculine and in a feminine fashion. Moreover, if the marble statue represents the merging of the genders as Kofman suggests, then it is neither masculine nor feminine. Instead the statue becomes androgynous and unisexual, and the idea of gender is abolished. Perhaps most importantly we should remember that in Kofman's interpretation, the combination of masculine and feminine qualities ultimately does not dispense with the fundamental dichotomy of castration that divides men from women. As far as the statue is concerned, the mode of sexual pleasure, which is Freud's means of identifying gender, remains indefinite (much like the statue's blurred face), and the distinction between the notion of masculine and feminine is still undefinable. Clearly, then, the presence of the marble statue in *La Faute de l'abbé Mouret* not only collapses the dichotomous image of the chaste woman versus the erotic woman, it also forces a reconsideration of how gender itself is determined.

In order to understand more fully the marble statue's place in the configuration of the female characters of *La Faute*, we have to return to the

description of Albine and Serge approaching the grotto. Their discovery of
the statue is not by chance: Albine directs Serge to the corner of the garden
that conceals it. In doing so, however, she assumes a curiously reluctant
attitude, as though she does not have the mental or physical stamina to
complete her trip: "C'était Albine qui conduisait Serge, bien qu'elle parut se
livrer à lui, faible, soutenue à son épaule" (1346).

Because Albine leads Serge directly to the statue, she must have learned
previously about its existence. Yet the novel does not explain how or from
whom Albine comes to know about it. She could not have discovered the
statue during her explorations of the Paradou because she says that never
before this outing with Serge has she dared to brave "tout ce noir" that the
grotto contains (1347). Yet her hesitancy during this trip to the grotto shows
that she is reluctant to pursue her curiosity with Serge. Albine therefore
knows about something that is concealed (the grotto and what it may
represent—possibly the secret of the nature of feminine sexuality), and yet
she appears not to know. In this sense, Albine is a Freudian "criminal"
because she fails to tell Serge the "truth" about her sexuality. As Kofman
might put it, Albine "knows her own [sexual] secret, knows the solution to
the riddle and is determined not to share it" (*Enigma* 66). Albine's ability to
perceive the nature of her own sexuality without the help of a man, and her
disinclination to reveal the secret of her sexuality to Serge, label her as what
Kofman designates in Freudian terms a narcissistic woman:

> What makes woman enigmatic here is no longer some "inborn
> deficiency," some sort of lack, but on the contrary her narcissistic
> self-sufficiency and her indifference; it is no longer the woman
> who envies the man his penis, it is he who envies her for her
> unassailable libidinal position, whereas he himself ... has been
> impoverished, has been emptied of this original narcissism in
> favor of the love object. (*Enigma* 52)

The narcissistic woman that Albine would represent in this
interpretation is one of three types of women that Kofman isolates in Freud's
essays. The "first woman" is the hysteric, the woman who does not know the
secret of her sexuality and who consents to accept the notion of female
castration (*Enigma* 66–67).[17] The "second woman" is represented by both
Freud's mother, who imparts knowledge of death and sexual difference, and
therefore truth, and also by the narcissistic woman, who, like Albine, knows
the truth but declines to divulge it. The "third woman" incarnates neither
sexual lies nor truth because she refuses to recognize the basis upon which

these distinctions are made; the "third woman" rejects and refuses to acknowledge the division of sexual difference. As Elizabeth L. Berg remarks:

> It is not that there is no sexual difference for the affirmative [third] woman; rather sexual difference is seen as undecidable, producing an irresolvable oscillation between masculine and feminine. The affirmative woman is the female equivalent of the fetishist, who affirms both of two contradictory statements.... Like the fetishist, who posits the possibility of the phallic mother, the affirmative woman paradoxically affirms her femininity while refusing to be castrated. (19)

In this interpretation, the third woman would be analogous to the marble statue in *La Faute*. The veil that hides the marble figure's genitals renders the statue's gender "undecidable," but Berg limits it unnecessarily to two options: a Freudian state of castration (called feminine) or non-castration (called masculine). Like Kofman's analysis, Berg's theory remains within the duality of Freud's castration theory and thereby affirms it. The statue's sex organs, which continue to determine gender according to Berg, are hidden by the "draperie" just as the marble statue's face, which determines her individual identity as a woman, is covered by the "nappe claire" of flowing water. If the statue's blurred, indistinct face suggests an identity beyond that of *either* a chaste woman *or* an erotic woman, perhaps the statue's indistinct sex may allude to the possibility of a gender beyond *either* castration *or* non-castration.

In fact, just as Albine and the statue call into question the notion of feminine gender, the similarities between Serge and the marble figure force us to reconsider his role as a masculine figure. In dreams that haunt him shortly after his arrival at the Paradou but before he sees or learns about the marble figure, he occupies the place of the buried statue:

> C'était étrange avant d'être né, on rêve de naître ... J'étais enterré quelque part. J'avais froid. J'entendais s'agiter au-dessus de moi la vie du dehors. Mais je me bouchais les oreilles, désespéré, habitué à mon trou de ténèbres, y goûtant des joies terribles, ne cherchant même plus à me dégager du tas de terre qui pesait sur ma poitrine ... Où étais-je donc? Qui donc m'a mis enfin à la lumière?....
> (1343–44)

Visualizing himself in the underground position of the statue, Serge, like the marble figure, subverts the accepted division between genders. Similar to the marble statue, he experiences ambiguous pleasure while he is underground. Moreover, the narrator focuses on Serge's "poitrine" (as opposed to his *torse*), a word that in this novel is highly charged with feminine qualities.

As Serge concludes the narration of his dream, he continues to see himself in the place of the statue:

> C'est toi, nest-ce pas, qui m'a tiré! de la terre? Je devais être sous le jardin.... J'attendais, vois-tu, depuis longtemps. Mais je n'espérais pas que tu te donnerais à moi sans ton voile, avec tes cheveux dénoués, tes cheveux redoutables qui sont devenus si doux. (1343–44)

Yet, at the end of this conversation, Serge reassumes a more traditional masculine role. Despite the fact that at this point in the novel the two have not yet begun a sexual relationship, Serge claims to have seen Albine without her "voile," implying a certain intimate knowledge of women that explains their difference from men. He also alludes to her "cheveux redoutables," an image that evokes the Medusa's head of snakes. The figure of the Medusa, which joins the phallus to the female body, incarnates sexual ambiguity and links this state of undecidedness to the threat of castration and petrification, an idea to which we will return. But Serge transforms Albine's hair into a comforting fetish that allows him to deny (and confirm) female castration. Above all, it enables him to imagine that her body is nothing more than an altered version of his own. Although the novel itself suggests that the notion of feminine gender lies beyond the question of castration, Serge clings to this dichotomy, but ultimately, as we will see, he is the one who proves it false.

Serge's gender again seems problematical in his spiritual rapport with the Virgin Mary and God. In his hallucinatory relationship with the Virgin during the first half of the novel, he plays an overtly masculine role. His reveries depict the Virgin Mary as "un sanctuaire" and a "bel intérieur"—in other words, as a grotto—that Serge "habitait" (1289). This daydream of the male phallus inside the female cave clearly prefigures the image of the statue inside the cave in the Paradou. By the end of *La Faute*, the same interior image of femininity describes Serge himself: he is "une maison vide" where God "pouvait habiter" (1510). Moreover, Serge's name itself betrays a similar type of slippage between two opposites. The common noun *le serge* denotes a type of thick cloth, thereby recalling the domain of weaving and cloth-making that Freud reserves for women. *Le serge* is distinguished from other cloth by its oblique ribbing that causes it to have a "right" side and a "wrong" side. In *La Faute*, Serge has two "sides" (one masculine and one feminine), which, like those of a piece of cloth, cannot be separated. Like the marble statue, Serge cannot be reduced to an either/or duality; both sides are needed to form the fabric of his identity.

Serge constructs rigid categories that differentiate between types of women and distinguish the sexes, but, as we have seen, these divisions begin to break down as soon as they appear in the novel. The sensual woman (represented by Cybèle and Désirée) and the chaste woman (designated by the Virgin Mary and Albine) do not form a dichotomy but rather have in common a number of traits and characteristics: In addition to the qualities that have already been enumerated here, Cybèle, Désirée, the Virgin Mary, and Albine all are sexually attractive to Serge. Although he tries to maintain and strengthen the differences that separate the Virgin and Désirée from Cybèle and Albine, these women inevitably reveal similar erotic traits and elict from Serge pronounced sexual desire. His sexual attraction to these women (or statues, as the case may be) effectively abolishes the virginity/sensuality division that Serge had sought to maintain, and it illustrates Janet L. Beizer's notion of "a dual movement" in *La Faute* in which there is "a perpetual straining toward difference ... accompanied, or threatened, by a collapse into sameness."[18]

The lack of differentiation between these women summons up for Serge strong feelings of malaise and revulsion and underscores the danger that he feels in the presence of Cybèle, Désirée, Albine, and the Virgin Mary.[19] They pose a threat that undermines what Kofman calls the male "économie sexuelle," a system in which men scorn certain sexual, sensual women but admire and adore those women that they imagine as sexually pure (*Respect* 15). Kofman claims that men struggle to maintain this system in order to protect themselves from having sexual relations with the mother (*Respect* 16). In order to prevent his own confusion, Serge seeks to reinstate the division between the two types of women, but his method is extreme. He distances himself from their inherent threat by expelling them from his intimate sphere: he never reenters Désirée's barnyard; he rejects the cult of Mary, which had been the foundation of his faith; and he buries Albine.

Similar to the way in which the separation of the chaste woman and the erotic woman breaks down in *La Faute de l'abbé Mouret*, the division between genders also collapses due to the feminine and masculine qualities that both Serge and the marble statue exhibit. Serge, however, cannot tolerate this type of gender blending. Soon after his discovery of the marble statue in the Paradou, he stands at the opening of the grotto and expresses worry about what the statue represents: "Ca noun avait laissé un souci. Il faut voir partout [dans le Paradou]. Peut-être serons-nous tranquilles après" (1385).[20] In the scene that follows, Serge and Albine make love for the first time, permitting Serge to chase away his feelings of gender ambiguity and reestablish gender divisions (in an effort to be "tranquille" once again). Serge never attempts to unearth the statue, leaving it buried and silent in the Paradou, perhaps in order to make sure that the "souci" that the marble statue represents does not resurface. At the end of the novel, he continues to fight to maintain separation between genders by aligning himself with the cult of Christ: "il avait quitté Marie pour Jésus, sacrifiant son coeur, afin de vaincre sa chair, rêvant de mettre de la virilité dans sa foi" (1479).

The story of Albine and Serge alludes to the events that unfold in Genesis 2–3, but it does not duplicate them. Like their biblical predecessors, Albine and Serge are brought together in a garden by a third party—Doctor Pascal—whose name alludes to his quasi-divine role. In the Paradou, Albine and Serge enjoy a brief period of physical and spiritual unity, which disappears once Serge realizes that he has broken his vows. Unlike Adam and Eve, however, Serge and Albine do not transgress the laws of God but rather the laws of the Church, and after his disobedience, it is Serge, not God, who banishes himself from the garden. In Zola's novel, the division of the sexes results from human actions rather than from divine decree.

Despite Serge's attempts to reinstate difference between types of women and between genders, in the end he maneuvers a return to sameness in *La Faute*. On account of him, the other characters suffer a similar fate of isolation or death. Because of his rejection, Albine surrenders to the Paradou's flowers, which engulf and suffocate her. After the death of Albine, the only person besides Serge who knows of the statue's existence, the figure falls into oblivion. The lusty figure of Cybèle disappears from the Plassans countryside, replaced in Serge's eye by the sterile, dry, and half-dead landscape of the cemetery where Albine is buried: "Dans le champ *vide*, le soleil *dormait*, sur les herbes *sèches*" (1522; my emphasis). Désirée resumes her place in the barnyard, this time playing the role of the executioner: "Personne comme elle ne tranchait la tête d'une oie d'un seul coup de hachette ou n'ouvrait le gosier d'une poule avec une paire de ciseaux" (1520). Even the figure of the Virgin Mary disappears from Serge's concept of the Church: "d'un effort suprême, il chassait la femme de la religion, il se réfugiait dans Jésus" (1480). Abandoned by Serge, the Paradou is no longer a place of fecundity and love; instead it becomes a cemetery. Albine dies there, and so does the marble statue, as well as, in a figurative sense, a fundamental part of Serge; Albine's uncle Jeanbernat wants to bury her in the Paradou, and he himself wants to be interred there in the manure pile behind the lettuce patch (1255).

Serge, like the others, succumbs to this destiny of isolation and death. Once he returns to Plassans after his brief interlude with Albine in the Paradou, he is repeatedly described as being made of stone, which connects him to "la pierre blanche" and "le marbre" that mark the grave of Caffin, who preceded Serge as priest (1526). Serge's last name Mouret (suggesting *mourait*) underscores his fate: as a result of his celibacy, which is portrayed as a type of castration imposed by the Church, he dies figuratively by petrification. Serge recalls having experienced in the seminary "cette robe glacée qui lui faisait un corps de pierre" (1504), and in the church after his return from the Paradou, he appears as a castrated body of stone:

> Sa face nue ressemblait à celle d'un saint de pierre que ne troublait aucune chaleur venue des entrailles. Sa soutane tombait à plis droits, pareille à un suaire noir, sans rien laisser deviner de son corps.... Maintenant, au milieu de ses cheveux coupés, elle apercevait une tache blême, la tonsure qui l'inquiétait comme un mal inconnu, quelque plate mauvaise grandie là pour manger la mémoire des jours heureux. (1464)

Even when Serge returns briefly to the Paradou, he remains immovable and stone-like: "Tout à l'heure, en venant, jai cru qu'on me j'était sur les épaules une robe glacée, qui se collait à ma peau, et qui, de la tête aux pieds, me faisait un corps de pierre ..." (1504).

Serge's symbolic neutering here takes the form of a dress, which seems to correspond to Freud's depiction of woman as a castrated man. But instead, what dominates is his lack of sexuality. At this moment in the novel, Serge is not masculine or feminine; he has forfeited his gender. Whereas the marble statue displays her indiscernable gender beneath the Paradou, Serge, who is above ground, tries to hide completely his indistinct gender by denying his sexuality. To Serge, admitting his ambiguity means accepting the Medusa's punishment of castration and petrification, in other words, death.

In *La Faute*, then, Serge seems to come full circle. As a celibate village priest, he suffers from nervous delirium and is taken to recuperate with Albine in the Paradou. In this Provençal paradise, the healing that takes place is not only physical: the notion of the chaste woman begins to merge with an image of the erotic woman, and the dichotomy of castration that separates men from women starts to close. With Albine, Serge discovers the *femme de marbre* and his own sexuality. Eventually, Serge remembers his past as a priest and in the end, decides to return to his duties in the village, effectively ending and reversing the healing process that had taken place in the garden.

Finally Serge decides to rededicate himself once and for all to the Church, thereby rejecting his sexual life with Albine as well as the ambiguous sexuality of the marble statue. At the end of *La Faute*, Serge tries to reestablish his binary view of the sensual woman and the virginal woman, and he exiles all the women to whom he had been close because he can no longer tolerate the union of these two female types. Likewise, in the realm of sexuality, Serge attempts to reinstate the dichotomy of the castrated woman versus the uncastrated man. Instead, he proves this dichotomy to be false: Serge's symbolic castration does not turn him into a woman; it renders him asexual.

However, the end of the novel does not reflect Serge's resolution. *La Faute* concludes with the burial of Albine, which is interrupted by the announcement of the birth of a calf. Such an ending could illustrate Désirée's maxim, "Un s'en va, un autre arrive!" (1521), and the continuous cycle of life and death. But the emptiness that characterizes the novel's end shows that Zola does not accept the simplistic dualism in the notion that the birth of a calf is an even exchange for the death and suffering that has taken place in the environs of Plassans. Perhaps this ending signals that one part of Serge has died and another has come to take its place.

In any case, the end of the novel demonstrates Zola's ultimate rejection of Serge's categorization of women as either chaste or erotic and his insistence upon the notion of castration as a valid means to distinguish the sexes. As we have seen, Serge's loss of virility does not turn him into a woman; it renders him sexless. From his experience, we can see that to rely solely on visual perception in determining gender is to trap the marble statue (and Serge) within the binarism of Freud's castration theory. Although Berg's notion of a "third woman" allows for oscillation between these poles, it remains within an either/or framework. In trying to determine the gender of the marble statue, then, perhaps we should not limit our concerns to what lies beneath the figure's sculpted veil. This kind of inquiry may be the wrong one to pursue, since focusing on the statue's genitals reduces the notion of gender to something that is perceptible to the eye. Even though the marble statue displays both masculine and feminine characteristics in *La Faute de l'abbé Mouret*, its sex remains hidden, thereby suggesting that the notion of gender may be something that lies outside of the realm of the visible sex organ.

By rejecting the idea that woman is nothing more than a castrated man, the novel makes room for another way of perceiving female gender, whereby the marble statue represents the nonphallic woman whose identity is not based on a comparison with man.[21] If this is the case, the key to her gender lies not behind the veil but rather inside the body, beneath the surface, and therefore it is invisible and irrefutably other.[22] Nevertheless, the distinction between man and woman cannot be reduced to yet another binary division such as interiority versus exteriority; like women, men possess internal sex organs that are not visible. Despite the fact that the statue remains hidden, the figure, which represents the resolution of feminine gender identity, continues to exist in the grotto beneath the grounds of the Paradou. The image of the buried marble statue—the woman beneath—appears to be a metaphor for the elusive gender identity of woman, which lies beyond the realm of the visible. Just as the notion of the grotesque is situated "between art and something 'outside of' or 'beyond' art" (Harpham xxii), the *femme de marbre* in the grotto represents a concept of femininity that lies somewhere outside or beyond the traditional notion of gender.

NOTES

1. See Janet L. Beizer, who presents a summary of how similar processes of comparing Genesis to *La Faute* have failed to create a consensus among critics as to how to interpret Zola's novel, and who demonstrates structural patterns of difference and similarity that occur in Genesis and *La Faute*; and Mieke Bal, whose analysis of *La Faute* uncovers Zola's criticism of Genesis and of the culture that this biblical text has engendered.

2. For example, Bettina L. Knapp's description of the Paradou outlines the rise of Serge's affection for Albine, but she omits the episode in which Albine and Serge venture into the garden together for the first time as a couple and discover the marble statue (113). Likewise, during his examination of "fatal streams" in Zola, Winston Hewitt disregards the underground stream in the grotto that drowned the marble woman (122–27). Moreover, in his discussion of the theme of concealment in Zola's work, Hewitt ignores the existence of the grotto. Jean Borie does not mention the marble woman or explore the implications of her presence in the Paradou (225–36). Similarly, Auguste Dezalay affirms the existence of "le lien entre la description du souterrain et la référence à une activité mentale obscure et cachée" (118), but for none of Zola's works does he present a psychological analysis of the theme of the subterranean. In Chantal Bertrand-Jennings's intricate description of the Paradou, she correctly underscores that in the garden there is evidence of "la vie sous ses diverses formes du mineral, du végétal, de l'animal et de l'human (sic)" ("Zola ou l'envers de la science" 95). However, she does not mention the presence of the marble (mineral) woman in the Paradou.

3. F.W.J. Hemmings mentions the statuettes of the Virgin Mary and Christ that populate Serge's church, and he alludes to Zola's comparison of the landscape to the lusty figure of Cybèle. Hemmings also reaffirms that Albine and Serge are not alone in the Paradou, but instead of recognizing the marble woman, he asserts that "the Garden is truly a third person, ever-present and everywhere present" (*Emile Zola* 86).

4. Bertrand-Jennings emphasizes "la dissociation manéchéiste du sensible et du sensuel" that occurs in Zola's characterizations of women in all but the last volumes of the *Rougon-Macquart* series. She links this division to Zola's separation between the soul or spirit and the body, between good and evil, and between idealized platonic love and frenetic physical love (*L'Eros et la femme* 26). For her part, Naomi Schor urges a "recognition of the contradictions, the split within Zola's female characters" when interpreting "the condition of woman in Zola" (17).

5. Bal isolates two types of women in Serge's life—Albine and Désirée—and traces their development and signals their moment of bifurcation: "Désirée restera jusqu'au bout la fille rétardee—mais au corps adulte—tandis que Albine progresse, apprend, grandit" (161). Although a full-fledged woman, Désirée (like the Virgin Mary) will never use the sexuality with which she is endowed. Albine, however, will.

6. In Borie's discussion of "figures féminines" in Zola's work, he points out that not two but three types of women surround Serge in *La Faute*: Albine, the Virgin Mary and Serge's sister, Désirée. In his study of these three women, Borie compares them to the three caskets in Freud's 1913 analysis of *The Merchant of Venice* in which "le héros doit choisir entre trois femmes: la mère elle-même, la jeune fille désirée mais inconsciemment choisie en tant que substitut pour la mère, et la mère tellurique qui finalement le recevra dans son sein, c'est-à-dire la mort" (229). I would suggest that the three types of women that Borie distinguishes based on Freud may represent instead a restatement of the mother/lover binarism. Borie correctly differentiates between "la mère elle—même"—the pure, untouchable woman—and the others. However in Zola's work where the sexual woman personifies the material world and its inevitable decline into death, "la mère tellurique ... c'est-à-dire la mort" and "la jeune fille désirée" collapse into one figure.

7. In Freud's lecture "Femininity," he equates weaving with pubic hair. Freud attributes the invention of weaving to woman's effort to "imitate" nature's covering for the female genitals in order to hide the "deficient" female sex organ (cited in Kofman, *Enigma* 49).

8. In *Rabelais and His World*, Mikhail Bakhtin finds the roots of the grotesque in the phenomenon of the carnival and in the efforts of the participants to ridicule and turn topsy-turvy the banal events of everyday life. In *The Grotesque in Art and Literature*, Wolfgang Kayser focuses on the psychoanalytical element of the grotesque, underscoring the part that the unconscious and insanity play in the formation of the grotesque.

9. A.A. Greaves illustrates similarities In the sexual images used to describe Albine and the Virgin Mary and underscores the physical resemblance between these two women. Roger Ripoll equates both Désirée and Cybèle with the "divinisation de la Terre-Mère" (18).

10. The marble statue lies "sur l'échine," and in the sculpture of Cybèle that embellishes the entrance to the village, she is "allongée sur des gerbes" (1261). In a second depiction of Cybèle, which serves as a metaphor for the Plassans countryside, the narrator again casts this earth goddess as an erotic reclining figure: "La nuit, cette campagne ardente prenait un étrange vautrement de passion.... On eut dit quelque forte Cybèle tombée sur l'échine, la gorge en avant, et rêvant encore de fécondation"

(1308). In one of the narrators most detailed descriptions of Désirée, she mirrors the reclining image of Cybèle and prefigures the elements of the marble statue: Désirée is both dressed and uncovered; she has a well-defined bosom, and she has a noticeable breathing pattern (1261).

11. Désirée and Cybèle are carefully described so as to represent the opposite of the promiscuous Artauds, the inhabitants of Plassans who reproduce like plants ("ainsi qu'une des végétations noueuses de la vallée" [1231]) and like animals ("Les Artauds … forniquaient aver la terre, selon le mot de Frère Archangias" [12401). Furthermore, Frère Archangias, a teacher at the Plassans church school and a self-appointed surveillant of the villagers' morals, condemns the illegitimate procreation of the Artauds, which takes place in the wheat fields: "Depuis quinze ans, je n'en at pas connu une [des Artauds] qui ne soit allée dans les blés avant de passer à l'église" (1238). Associated with Désirée and Cybèle, animals and wheat are natural products of the fertile earth. However these same objects represent promiscuity and damnation for the Artauds. The manipulation of these symbols betrays the narrator's attempt to depict Cybèle and Désirée exclusively as instruments of procreation and not as sexual objects.

12. "Cybèle," *Grand Dictionnaire Universel du XIXe siècle*, 1982 ed.

13. The marble statue is a "femme de marbre tombée" and a "marbre que les peines avaient dù laisser choir" (1347); her fate appears to be a punishment imposed upon her because of her sins as a morally corrupt, fallen woman, a perception that recapitulates and perpetuates the image of Eve. The Virgin Mary is cast as a seductress during one of Serge's hallucinatory reveries in front of the statuette. The narrator's reference to the "lèvres peintes" on the statuette of the Virgin Mary (1222) recalls the biblical figure of Jezebel, whose painted face is an infamous sign of the seductive power of female sexuality (Warner 232). Albine also earns the title of sinner—the only sinner—in the Paradou. Her physical beauty incarnates seduction and transgression: "Toujours la faute était là; la nudité *d'Albine*, éclatante comme un soleil, éclairait les verdures du Paradou" (1478; my emphasis).

14. The image of a sealed fountain is found in Song of Solomon 4.12: "Tu es un jardin fermé, ma soeur, ma fiancée, / Une source fermée, une fontaine scellée" (Warner 62–63).

15. Mary's virgin breast full of milk (1289) links her to the image of the marble statue whose swelled breasts protrude from the stream in the cave. Albine's breasts entice Serge at the end of the novel when she goes to beckon Serge back to the Paradou (1465).

16. This analysis is based on the activities of heterosexual men and women. Theoretically homosexual men share with women the capacity to experience pleasure in modes that are traditionally labeled as masculine (penile) and feminine (anal).

17. The designations "first," "second," and "third woman" appear in Elizabeth L. Berg's article, "The Third Woman."

18. Beizer underscores the differences that Zola seeks to establish between the Artaud clan and the Rougon-Macquart family, and eventually between the Artauds and Zola's own family (190).

19. For example, Serge characterizes his sister Désirée as a "chère innocente" who appears to possess "la pureté de ces pauvres d'esprit auxquels l'Evangile accorde le royaume des cieux" (1233), and yet seeing her, Serge cannot squelch his feelings: "Cependant, elle l'*inquiétait* depuis quelque temps: elle devenait trop forte, trop saine: elle sentait trop la vie" (1233; my emphasis). The Plassans countryside unnerves Serge when he finds it transformed into the voluptuous, reclining figure of Cybèle: "Jamais, comme à cette heure de nuit, la campagne ne l'*avait inquiété*, aver sa poitrine géante, ses ombres molles, ses luisants de peau ambrée, toute cette nudité de déesse, à peine cachée sous la mousseline argentée de la lune" (1308; my emphasis). Serge's visions of the Virgin Mary as a sexually mature woman give him "des troubles étranges" and link her to the prodigious reproduction of the Artauds: "La maternité de Marie, toute glorieuse et pure qu'elle se révélât, cette taille ronde de femme faite, cet enfant nu sur ses bras l'*inquiétaient*, lui semblaient continuer au ciel la poussée débordante de génération au milieu de laquelle il marchait depuis ce matin" (1295; my emphasis). The first time that Serge sees Albine in the Paradou (before his delirium), he is "pris dans [le] rire [d'Albine], comme dans une oncle sonore qui résonnait partout contre sa chair; il la respirait, il l'entendait vibrer en lui. Oui, tout son *mal* venait de ce rire qu'il avait bu" (1310; my emphasis).

20. At no place in the novel does the marble statue make Albine anxious. On the contrary, the statue is a source of happiness for Albine, a memory that she evokes while trying to persuade Serge to return to the Paradou with her (354).

21. Dorothy Kelly discusses the notion of woman's nonphallic nature in her article on Balzac's "Le Chef d'oeuvre inconnu" (178).

22. In *Speculum of the Other Woman*, Luce Irigaray introduces the notion that" a 'nothing to be seen,' a something not subject to the rule of visibility or of specula(riza)tion, might yet have some reality" and could be responsible for the difference between man and woman (50).

WORKS CITED

Bakhtin, Mikhail. *Rabelais and His World.* Trans. Helene Iswolsky. Cambridge: MIT P, 1968.

Bal, Mieke. "Quelle est La Faute de l'abbé Mouret?" *Australian Journal of French Studies* 23 (1986): 149–168.

Belzer, Janet L. "This Is Not a Source Study: Zola, Genesis, and *La Faute de l'abbé Mouret*." *Nineteenth-Century French Studies* 18 (1989–90): 186–195.

Berg, Elizabeth L. "The Third Woman." *Diacritics* 12 (1982): 11–20.

Bertrand-Jennings, Chantal. "Zola ou l'envers de la science: *De La Faute de l'abbé Mouret* au *Docteur Pascal*." *Nineteenth-Century French Studies* 9 (1980–81): 93–107.

———. *L'Eros et la femme chez Zola: De la chute au paradis retrouvé.* Paris: Klincksieck, 1977.

Borie, Jean. *Zola et les mythes ou de la nausée au salut*. Paris: Seuil, 1971.

"Cybèle." *Grand Dictionnaire Universel du XIXe siècle*. 1874: 1982 ed.

Dezalay, Auguste. "Le Thème du souterrain chez Zola." *Europe* 468–469 (1968): 110–122.

Freud, Sigmund. *The Interpretation of Dreams*. Trans. James Strachey. London: Hogarth P, 1960. Vol. 4 of *The Standard Edition of the Complete Psychological Works of Sigmund Freud*. 24 vols. 1953–74.

Greaves, A. A. "A Question of Life or Death: A Comparison of *Le Rêve* and *La Faute de l'abbé Mouret.*" *Nottingham French Studies* 19 (1980): 16–24.

Harpham, Geoffrey Galt. *On the Grotesque: Strategies of Contradiction in Art and Literature*. Princeton: Princeton UP, 1982.

Hemmings, F. W. J. *Emile Zola*. London: Oxford UP, 1953.

Hewitt, Winston. *Through Those Living Pillars: Man and Nature in the Works of Emile Zola*. The Hague: Mouton, 1974.

Irigaray, Luce. *Speculum of the Other Woman*. Trans. Gillian C. Gill. Ithaca: Cornell UP, 1985.

Kayser, Wolfgang Johannes. *The Grotesque in Art and Literature*. Trans. Ulrich Weisstein. New York: Morningside, 1981.

Kelly, Dorothy. *Fictional Genders: Role and Representation in Nineteenth-Century French Narrative*. Lincoln: U of Nebraska P, 1989.

Knapp, Bettina L. *Emile Zola*. New York: Frederick Ungar, 1980.

Kofman, Sarah. *The Enigma of Woman: Woman in Freud's Writings*. Trans. Catherine Porter. Ithaca: Cornell UP, 1985.

———. *Le Respect des femmes*. Paris: Editions Galilée, 1982.

Kuryluk, Eva. *Salome and Judas in the Cave of Sex: The Grotesque: Origins, Iconography, Techniques*. Evanston: Northwestern UP, 1987.

Ripoll, Roger. "Le symbolisme végétal dans *La Faute de l'abbé Mouret*: reminiscences et obsessions." *Les Cahiers naturalistes* 12–31 (1966): 11–22.

Schor, Naomi. "Mothers Day: Zola's Women." *Diacritics* 5 (1975): 11–17.

Warner, Marina. *Alone of All Her Sex: The Myth and Cult of the Virgin Mary*. New York: Alfred A. Knopf, 1976.

Zola, Emile. *La Faute de l'abbé Mouret*. Vol. 1 of *Les Rougon-Macquart*. Bibliothèque de la Pléiade. Paris: Gallimard, 1960–67. 5 vols.

P. M. WETHERILL

Flaubert, Zola, Proust and Paris:
An Evolving City in a Shifting Text

Although I do not mention Balzac in my title, his presence may be felt in much of what I have to say. Since Guichardet's exhaustive study appeared,[1] it has been difficult not to see him as the starting point from which to follow the narrative development of the city at least as far as *A la recherche du temps perdu*. I have not drawn a great deal on Guichardet, however, for she is especially interested in *La Comédie humaine* as a fascinating encyclopaedia of information about the city (and as an excuse for giving more). In the paper which follows, I wish rather to explore ways in which city and narrative interact, the one determining our perception of the other. I am anxious to keep my approach relatively simple and compact: this is why I have restricted my comments to the second half of the nineteenth century and to the Paris of everyday experience as it shapes the narrative process—and as it is shaped by it. Hence the absence of Fourier's, Rimbaud's and Baudelaire's fantasies from my explorations.

There is no simple interrelationship between narrative and the city: narrative does not develop in some magical and recognisable way which we can understand by looking at how the quartier Saint-Georges gives way to Haussmann's façades, or the way Baltard's *pavillons*, in mid century, introduce spacious steel and glass structures.[2] The Eiffel tower is not a category out of *Figures III*, any more than the white frontage of Louis-Philippe's Paris, as it

From *Forum for Modern Language Studies* 32, no. 3 (July 1996). © 1996 by Oxford University Press.

is superseded by the golden stone of Napoleon III. If, as Ragon says, "l'architecture 'de tradition' [...] s'est mise, avant de mourir, a recapituler tous les styles",[3] such serious rehearsal is distinct from what post-modernism was to get up to, whereas Realist and even modernist narrative shows no similar diversity, playful or otherwise. Nineteenth-century Realist narrative is unique and new—Musset's complaint: "Nous avons de tous les styles sauf du nôtre",[4] which becomes less valid after his death, is only ever applicable to bricks and mortar.

The relationship between urban space and narrative line is complex and dangerously theoretical. At most, we can say that perception, as it develops in its interaction with the city (amongst other things), triggers ways of telling which offer new strings and nebulae of event, representing the city in turn as a shifting space where things happen. At the same time as this diachronic interplay, Haussmann's factual architecture and Zola's non-metaphoric urban narrative are simultaneous and reciprocal products of the same mentality—just as *art nouveau* at the turn of the century is tuned to the essentially metaphoric needs of *A la recherche du temps perdu* (see I: 835, 838).[5] Narrative manipulates urban space to its own ends—and is manipulated by it. If the Paris of *L'Éducation sentimentale* is largely pre-Haussmann (with the exception of the last brief chapters), the mentality behind its composition, its linear movement, its changes of site and its significant removals belongs very much to the city whose first significant stage was being completed whilst Flaubert was writing.

Frédéric Moreau takes Rosanette from the rue de Provence, via the Palais Royal where they dine, through the rue Duphot and the Bd des Capucines and the rue Caumartin to the rue Tronchet, where Frédéric will desecrate the room he has prepared for Mme Arnoux....

The city, with its *noyaux* and its *catalyses*, its *opposants* and its *adjuvants*, becomes an emblem for the narrative processes it contains—just as narrative is the expression of urban space.

The mental construct of the city may therefore be seen as a product of the narrative which produces it—and vice versa. Narrative both explains and determines. This is not a direct precisely definable causal relationship, but rather one of fuzzy, evolving perception. In one sense, my argument has to do with the way in which different types of narrative analysis cease to be valid beyond a given historical point. Genette's study of narrative discourse, pioneering work though it may be, ceases to be unambiguously useful when we reach Proust, the author on whom it is centred. Narrative is not merely the manipulation of a diegesis: in post-realist forms of urban perception, it may also be the kind of lexical interplay which has Swann eating in a restaurant, *La Pérouse*, which has the same name as the street where Odette lives. Similarly Marcel on his frequent pilgrimages to Swann's house: "à propos de n'importe quoi, je disais le nom de cette rue"—narrative deploys from a *nom de pays* and sets off the physical movement, the "pèlerinage jusque devant la maison de Swann" (GF 560).

This development covers a period in which the city itself, once Haussmann has had his wicked way with it, has barely changed. The Paris of Zola's narratives[6] is physically the Paris of Proust's.

Sociologically, of course, this is less true. Population shifts, creating new districts of opulence and poverty, the slow demise of mythic places of display (the Palais Royal, the Grands Boulevards) and the rise of others (the Bois de Boulogne). The drift in narrative process from Flaubert and Zola to Proust goes much deeper than this, however: Paris ceases to be the *ville-parcours* which Haussmann had created and becomes the *ville-îlot* we find in Proust.

The narrative process is clearly addressed here. There is nothing more banal than to say that Haussmann's Paris is a space of circulation and destination: "C'est la rue qui domine et non pas l'habitat, qui semble devenir secondaire".[7]

Unlike Rambuteau's Paris, with its intimate spaces, its narrow clogged thoroughfares and the brief stretches of its passages (Choiseul, Vivienne, Panoramas), Haussmann creates extensive movement through the city's central zone, making it a place of distant spatial goals and culminating points. The city's straight lines and wide arterial boulevards impose this and answer to this need, just as movement beyond (into and out of that space) is made easy and encouraged by railway stations which are the city's explicit exit points. This is the perfect site and expression of Realist narrative which stresses similar patterns of metonymic continuity and contiguity, logical linearity, communication and causality. It is the site of Zola's *débandades* which so significantly come at the beginning of his novels: the sweeping outward movement from the Gare-Saint-Lazare in *La Bête humaine*, the floods of workers going into Paris in *L'Assommoir*, the *noce* walking down the rue du Faubourg-Poissonnière to the Louvre and Lantier's interminable walk at the outset of *L'Oeuvre*. Even works like *Pot-Bouille*, centred on the house in the rue de Choiseul, or *L'Assommoir* itself, with the essential axis of its tenement building, are rigorously turned outward to the street, connections between buildings, and movement from place to place. *Pot-Bouille* is specifically constructed round the new Paris: the new house is next to the rue du Quatre-Septembre (as it would be called after 1870) whose *percement* is specifically alluded to in the novel's opening pages.

And of course it is the place of arrival and departure: in *Pot-Bouille*'s opening, arrival is precisely and topographically sketched. *La Bête humaine*'s first pages describe the place and activity of the gare Saint-Lazare; Gervaise has just come to town.

Haussmann's buildings set up centrifugal and centripetal movement which goes well beyond their walls, for Foucault has encouraged us to see Haussmann's Paris as a place of supervision and control[8] with its military and police barracks, its hospitals (Lariboisière is being built at the beginning of *L'Assommoir*), and its open spaces newly designed and built. It is a space of cause and effect, classification and categories which give further precise significance to the *ville parcours*. Destinations are not uncertain, for social classes are increasingly associated with particular parts of the town: Gervaise lives in Rochechouart and Rosanette in the rue de Provence—they could not really live anywhere else.

In the second part of the period, such classification gives way to the metaphoricisation of urban space. If the Verdurins live appropriately enough near the rue Saint-Honoré, Swann is characterised by his double eccentricity: he lives on the as yet unfashionable Ile Saint-Louis. Which means that he does not live where he belongs: he lives at the other end of Paris, in strategic opposition to Odette[9] and to his own drably unoriginal future home—with the *relais* of the restaurant La Pérouse in the middle. Lines of action and event follow this emblematic axis and Proust strengthens this opposition and declassification in the Cahiers. Swann's original residence is "près du Jardin des Plantes", which is more respectable—as is his house as it is originally described in the *cahiers*: "Une ravissante petite maison où étaient logés dans les étages qu'il n'occupait pas lui-même ses tableaux et ses collections de botanique" (Tadié I: 670)—a far cry from the house of Proust's final version: "Un vieil hôtel où il entassait ses collections" (GF 110).

Swann is thus eccentric in many ways. His activity is in large measure secret—he is the secret double of Marcel whose social image is a distortion of his real self. Personality is anything but turned out towards the street. Even when it is, street and public place are anything but destination and *parcours*. They are areas of concentration, centripetal sites of social reinforcement and ritual, which allow Mme Cottard in her precise uniform to make her tournées, seen by Swann's telescopic gaze:

> de la plateforme [d'autobus] il la suivit de ses yeux attendris, qui
> enfilait la rue Bonaparte, l'aigrette haute, d'une main relevant sa
> jupe, l'autre tenant son en-tout-cas et son porte-carte dont elle

laissait voir le chifre, laissant baller devant elle son manchon. (GF 515)

Especially, Proust's streets offer closely enclosed and delimited scenes of display, as Odette well knows and Proust strongly emphasises:

> les endroits chics, que veux-tu que je to dise moi, par exemple, le dimanche matin, Avenue de l'Impératrice, à cinq heures le tour du Lac, le jeudi l'Éden Théâtre, le vendredi l'Hippodrome, les bals. (GF 365).

> son regard devenait sérieux, inquiet et volontaire, si elle avait peur de manquer la fête des fleurs ou simplement l'heure du thé, avec muffins et toasts, au "Thé de la rue Royale". (GF 368)

Again this is very different from the display-processions of *L'Éducation sentimentale* or *La Curée*, for Proust's characters occupation of the town is ironically placed on the same level as their ritualised and chic use of its resources, obsessively returning to the same point, recurrent, never linear: "Elle n'avait pas pris tons les fruits au même endroit, mais les raisins chez Crapote dont c'est la spécialité, les fraises chez Jauret, les poires chez Chevet, où elles étaient plus belles, etc." (GF 439). This pattern, with similar irony, equates Swann's search for Odette (GF 348–52) with the purchase of fruit from Fauchon—except that Odette doesn't seem to be where she should be: "Elle n'était pas chez Prévost [...] Il poussa jusqu'à la Maison Dorée, entra deux fois chez Tortoni et, sans l'avoir vue davantage, venait de ressortir du Cafe Anglais [...]" (GF 349–52).

All this implies a specific movement through and narrative use of marked and meaningful urban space which is in strong contrast to Flaubert's characters, who always live where they belong. Their display is not emblematic and circular but metonymic and linear, with inevitable results in enplotment: when Arnoux drops art and takes up pots, Flaubert's narrative takes him from the Boulevard Bonne-Nouvelle to the rue de Paradis; Frédéric's own move to the rue Rumford places him firmly in the Dambreuse camp—and the emphatic marking-out of a zone of significant metonymic occupation clearly organises the opening narrative of *Le ventre de Paris* and *L'Argent* as characters repeatedly move backwards and forwards through the space of the markets and the Bourse.

Topography means something on a broader social or even political plane. So the rue Duphot, where Marcel vainly and ludicrously looks out for a glimpse of Swann on his visits to the dentist, is a very different street from the one of the same name which brings Frédéric and Rosanette close to involvement in the 1848 Revolution:

> Par la rue Duphot ils atteignirent les boulevards [...] La foule était trop compacte, le retour direct impossible; et ils entraient dans la rue Caumartin, quand, tout a coup, éclata derrière eux un bruit pareil au craquement d'une immense piece de soie qu'on déchire. C'était la fusillade du boulevard des Capucines. (p. 284)

In contrast, Proust's Paris is one of emblematic interrelationship, superposition, simultaneity and echo. Different events may go on in the same space. Swann's relationship with Odette runs parallel to the affair he is having with a working girl:

> La petite ouvrière l'attendait près de chez lui, à un coin de rue que son cocher Roger connaissait, elle montait à côte de Swann et restait dans ses bras jusqu'au moment où la voiture l'arrêtait devant chez les Verdurin. (GF 337)

The topographical linkage is quite explicit. Multiple events make double use of urban space. Grouping replaces sequence, the sense of physical obstacle and distance has disappeared; for a time at least, there is no sense of forward narrative thrust. The contrast with earlier writing is significant. Frédéric's double affair with Mme Dambreuse and Rosanette might appear similar, but in addition to the bedroom-farce dimension of Flaubert's narrative and the fact that events are continuing to take place, Proust's overlapping narrative and *parallel* topography are quite lacking.

Narrative, throughout the period I am looking at, is clearly centred on topography. Marcel uses maps as much as Flaubert or Zola: "J'avais toujours à portée de ma main un plan de Paris, qui parce qu'on pouvait y distinguer la rue où habitait M. et Mme Swann, me semblait contenir un trésor" (GF 556). The obsession is the same as Félicité's, but it is even more firmly based on the nature of maps and topographical reality. As much, in fact, as Flaubert's writing or Zola's researches. The difference, of course, is not that Proust's Paris is an invented place, but that the topographical preoccupation is displaced onto the characters. It is a place of fantasy, a mental state devoid of the documentary and didactic function it has in earlier writing.[10] Its function is purely narrative: "Pendant que je montais l'avenue des Champs-Elysées, Gilberte était venue par la rue Boissy d'Anglas" (GF 548). The two avenues exist, but they are significant solely because of their implied separation: they are two distinct ways of getting to the same point. So it is logical that the precision of Proust's references should vary widely according to their function. Paris in Proust is frequently a place of fantasy representation, a bolster to dreaming. Much more than a marker of the categorical divisions of Paris, precision, when it comes, needs to be set against the vagueness of so many other references: we know where Swann, Odette and Marcel's uncle live,[11] but we do not know exactly where Swann removes to or where Marcel himself lives, and it only much later that we are given the Verdurins' first address.[12] Paris is shown in varying precision, with some narrative sequences spatially and temporally clear whilst others are much more uncertain: when Swann leaves the Verdurin house/flat in search of Odette on the Boulevards, we have no idea of the distance covered or the route taken.[13]

This is quite different in turn from Combray, whose narrative moves along and is justified by precisely mapped topography. The walks along the Vivonne, Tante Léonie's observance of passers-by, follow narrative avenues whose spatial constraints are clearly defined. But of course, *Combray* is significant only in relation to *Un amour de Swann*—and vice versa. The interpenetration of the two brings their contrasting topography and their conflicting narrative process into close conflict: Marcel's Parisian encounter with la Dame en rose is recounted from within the space of Combray (GF 173 ff.) ...

Such minglings are far removed from the clear division of Frédéric's existence in (or Emma's fantasies on) Paris and their life at Nogent and Yonville. The stability of these oppositions is very different from the still dubious district where Odette lives, with its modern hôtels particuliers and "quelque sinistre échoppe, témoignage historique et reste sordide du temps où ces quartiers étaient encore mal famés" (GF 339).

Flaubert's world is different from the late nineteenth-century Proustian world which could tolerate the ultimate social confusion: "le premier salon du faubourg Saint-Germain" (l'hôtel de Guermantes [II: 28]) is on the right bank.

Urban space is blurred and internalised; it is no longer an identifiable frame for the definition of character and the determination of event. States of mind and forms of action are no longer so precisely referenced—or rather, they are referenced by the variable, mental space which configures urban space: the distance from the Quai d'Orleans to the rue La Pérouse is considerably less important than it is for Zola's characters as they move through the city.

Nothing is more clearly emblematic of this blurring than Proust's fog-bound Paris (II: 397), which produces the same effect on the landscape of narrative as sleep at the beginning of *Combray*. Topography is cut through with many strange contradictions: "le vide de ces courtes rues [...] la neige [...] le négligé de la saison, le voisinage de la nature, donnaient quelque chose de plus mysterieux a la chaleur, aux fleurs qu'il avait trouvees en entrant" (GF 339).

The disappearance of Paris altogether conflicts with such an extreme level of interaction: "mes regards—que les objets de ma chambre de Paris ne génaient pas plus que ne faisaient mes propres prunelles, car ils n'étaient que les annexes de mes organes, un agrandissment de moi-même" (I: 667). Internal and external perception merge, movement through Paris is movement through oneself.

In spite of superficial similarities, such fluctuating definitions are quite different from events in Flaubert or Zola. When Dambreuse/D'Ambreuse switches from noble Faubourg to rue d'Anjou and Chaussée d'Antin, he shows a logical manipulation of the city as significant space. His move has explicit meaning within the objective classificatory context of Paris and the broad, recurrent social narrative of a mid-nineteenth-century career: like his change of name, it marks Dambreuse's deliberate break with the idle aristocracy and his choice of active bourgeois capitalism, which his ventures into property, mining and railways bear out.

Proust's Paris is a place, not just of time, but of time in narrative: it is the place which leads Marcel to remembrance, but this is specifically the place recalled by voluntary *not* involuntary memory. Unlike Combray, saturated with history, it is the *present* place out of time itself where the memory of Balbec returns to Marcel when he buys a sprig of apple blossom "dans le mois de mai de l'année suivante" (I: 707). It is also the place where the loss of time takes on the appearance of the city itself, strengthening a point I have already made: "les maisons, les routes, les avenues sont fugitives, hélas, comme les années" (GF 5'73). It is the place which leads Odette, in her mute dialogue with admirers, to recall and project many encounters:

> aux lèvres un sourire ambigu où je ne voyais que la bienveillance d'une Majeste et où il y avait surtout la provocation de la cocotte [...] Ce sourire en realite disait aux uns: "Je me rappelle très bien, c'était exquis!"; à d'autres: "Comme j'aurais aimé! ç'a été la mauvaise chance!" (GF 563–4)

And for Swann too, it is the place of forward projection and uncertain invented events as he thinks of Odette's future absence: "(Swann) avait le loisir plusieurs mois à l'avance d'en dissoudre l'idée amère dans le Temps à venir qu'il portait en lui par anticipation [...] avenir intérieur" (GF 491). But of course, Proust's prolepses, like the place of meditation, are blocked off— the run-through of Flaubert's or Zola's narratives, in a city which has a map, gives way to the circular walks in *Combray*, claustrophobic obsession and room-locked fantasy which excludes the street sensed beyond the curtain and all the outlets it might offer, in favour of "le spectacle total de l'été". Proust's "real" streets offer frustration and separation, and the emotions born of this privation. Swann searches for Odette who has been swallowed up by the City.[14]

Paris has been a hiding place and an obstacle at least since Adeline and her children searched for Hulot's love nest. Swann looking for Odette on the Boulevards is a familiar event. There is a close parallel (at least diegetically) with Frédéric Moreau's search for Arnoux via Regimbart at the beginning of the second part of *L'Éducation sentimentale*. However, Odette *invites* Swann to look for her (GF 348)—she creates a *ville-puzzle* which Swann is expected to explore and solve. This is one of the few *parcours* in the novel, and it is full of a hidden, meaningless topography: Prévost, Maison dorée, Tortoni and so on. Only one reference is to a permanent, recognisable site: the boulevard des Italiens—but this is not enough to articulate the scene. The significance of place and movement is lost: place reference in Proust's narrative is nothing more (especially for late twentieth-century readers) than a reference which has lost topographical specificity, even if the general significance of these pleasure palaces is retained. In contrast, for Frédéric Moreau, Tortoni and the Maison dorée are specific sites for erotic and political fiasco.

Swann eventually finds Odette, but apart from the fact that he is on the Boulevards, this is pure chance: "il venait de ressortir du Café Anglais [...] pour rejoindre sa voiture au coin du boulevard des Italiens, quand il heurta une personne qui venait en sens contraire: c'était Odette" (GF 352). Her reappearance in this disarticulated space is as aleatory and mysterious as her disappearance—and of course, Odette hadn't been at Prévost's at all: "je n'y étais pas allée le soir où je t'ai dit que j'en sortais quand to m'avais cherchée chez Prévost" (GF 508)—she hadn't even been with Forcheville... Paris is the place of the double, lying manipulation of space. The narrative sequence of its streets holds the potential for illogical but highly consequential changes of character: "Dans cette même voiture qui l'emmenait chez Prévost, il n'était plus le même [...] un être nouveau était avec lui" (GF 349)—and fusions of personality and the world at large which are very close to the work's beginning: "comme un fiévreux [...] des rêvasseries qu'il ruminait sans se distinguer d'elles" (GF 348–9). It is also in constant danger of bringing up other, irrelevant (and therefore diversive, obstructive) forms of discourse, as when we learn that Swann's search is carried out with the help of his coachman, described as "le doge Lorédan de Rizzo".

Frédéric's search for Regimbart and Arnoux reveals an urban space which figures frustration in very differing ways. This is a city of multiple disappearances: Arnoux, Hussonnet, Pellerin, Regimbart are no longer to be found and grotesque obstacles continually get in the way: "Il crut même apercevoir au loin [le] chapeau [de Regimbart]; un corbillard et des voitures de deuil s'interposèrent. L'embarras passé, la vision avait disparu" (p. 106). And Frédéric is (so to speak) taken for a ride by the waiter. And yet, Flaubert's narrative stresses the city's ready meaningfulness and, all in all, the logic of what Frédéric is doing.

This contrasts with Swann's attitude: "[...] il avait couru Paris non parce qu'il croyait possible de la rejoindre mais parce qu'il lui était trop cruel d'y renoncer" (GF 352).

Given Frédéric's problem, there is little else he could do, and what he is doing stands a fair chance of succeeding, as is borne out by what happens— and of course Regimbart and Arnoux are not trying to stay out of sight. There is total topographic accuracy and an exhaustive (if hysterical) reasonableness in Frédéric's course from the rue de Fleurus to the rue du Faubourg-Poissonnière to the Prefecture de police to the quartier des Beaux-Arts(?) to the rue Notre-Dame des Victoires and the Place Gaillon, from the Bourse to the Madeleine to the Gymnase to the rue des Francs-Bourgeois-Saint-Michel, and in the deluge of cafe names which mark his progress (pp. 107–8). Paris is a space where, with application, problems can be solved.

And once he finds out where the Arnoux now live, his journey from Regimbart's café to the rue Poissonnière has a surrealistic smoothness about it: "Frédéric alla de l'estaminet chez Arnoux, comme soulevé par un vent tiède et avec l'aisance extraordinaire que l'on éprouve dans les songes" (p. 109).

As we see, in Flaubert as in Proust, the consistency of the town can change. It can be the logical if lunatic arena Frédéric demonstrates it to be here, as he criss-crosses its surface, using it as a fund of clues for his problem. Or it can be a source of endless chance encounters, the perfect arena for *noyaux* and *catalyses* which send the narrative off in unexpected directions. And yet, in Flaubert there is no loss of linearity. Even chance event leads to subsequent event, and not, as is so often true of Proust, expansion which shifts the text's central preoccupation.

The way Paris functions as narrative space in Flaubert, Zola and Proust points to conflicting perspectives of reality and myth—which terms relate rather to the vision of the writers themselves than to any objective criteria.

In contrast to Balbec, Combray, Venice, Florence, Proust's Paris is largely devoid of resonance. Its early protagonists, Legrandin, the Verdurins, Norpois and Cottard confirm it to be the scene of cliché and tired formula. There, language destroys *Combray*'s complex substance, sense and experience. It is the place of daily banalities where Marcel records such nuggets as: "le lundi où la blanchisseuse devait rapporter le gilet blanc que j'avais couvert d'encre" (GF 533). It is the place of habit, the dulling of response and discovery. *Noms de pays: le nom* points obstinately outwards away from Paris—giving full value to "ces lieux merveilleux que sont les Bares" (I: 645) and to the need to "rendre la difference entre le depart et l'arrivée non pas aussi insensible mais aussi profonde qu'on peut [...] la ressentir dans sa totalité, intacte" (I: 644).

The rejection of Paris (returns to Paris are much more discreet) and the documented search for mythic places beyond contrasts with the whole romantic-realist mentality which both re-creates the cities of the past (Viollet-le-Duc) and turns Zola's and Flaubert's Paris into an unreal city then to be experienced—places of contemplation and triumphant penetration, constantly left and returned to,[15] setting up a characteristic narrative of convergence, as when Frédéric or Emma (who has to make do with Rouen) see the city from outside, and then move through it to their supposed destination:

> Puis d'un seul coup d'oeil, la ville apparaissait. (Seuil I: 662)

> On monta une rue; tout à coup il aperçut le dôme du Pantheon.
>   La plaine, bouleversée, semblait de vagues ruines. (p. 104)

Such panoramas are absent from *A la recherche du temps perdu*. And yet it would be simplistic to suggest that Flaubert's Paris is a less mythic place than Proust's.

Myth is strongly present in the motifs of Swann searching for Odette as if she were some Eurydice—the motif of fog and its associations with "un compagnon de voyage rencontré dans quelque plage située aux confins du monde battue des vents ou ensevelie dans les brumes" (Tadié II: 699, cf. 100 and 1678 ff.)—which for once clearly breaks down the distinction between Paris and Balbec (and Doncières).

The Bois de Boulogne is similarly transformed into "un lieu factice, et dans le sens zoologique ou mythologique du mot, un Jardin" (GF 566). It is Proust's *approach* to myth which is different: Balzac's, Flaubert's and Zola's earlier mythology is based on a fantasy of Paris and contrastive narrative irony which sets spectacle against personal experience. Thus Frédéric witnessing the return from the Bois de Boulogne:

> Des femmes nonchalamment assises dans des calèches [...] défilaient près de lui [...] la Seine verdâtre dans toute son étendue se déchirait en moires d'argent contre les piles de ponts.
>   Il alla dîner, moyennant quarante trois sols le cachet, dans un restaurant, rue de la Harpe. (pp. 23–4)

More significantly still, the earlier writers set the prospect of Paris against the contradiction of subsequent narrative: Emma Bovary's mythic Parisian dreamings conflict with the actual experience she finds in Rouen, and determine the course of narrated event; Lucien de Rubempré's dreamings, like those of his Flaubertian take-off, Frédéric Moreau, are the motor behind the move to Paris and the stage-by-stage confrontation of its mythic space, its concrete networks and its subsequent let-down—both conform to the sequence we find in *L'Éducation sentimentale*:

> Mais il n'existait au monde qu'un seul endroit pour [...] faire valoir [les secrètes opulences de son esprit]: Paris! car, dans ses idées, l'art, la science et l'amour (ces trois faces de Dieu comme eût dit Pellerin) dépendaient exclusivement de la capitale. (p. 91)

> et cette contemplation était si profonde que les objets extérieurs avaient disparu. (p. 103)

> De hautes portes, comme il y en a dans les fermes, laissaient voir par leurs battants entr'ouverts, l'intérieur d'ignobles cours pleines d'immondices. (p. 104)

More explicitly, Gervaise's realisations crush the value of any supposed earlier aspirations.

These antitheses differ from those much less clearly narrated oppositions which set the reality of the Verdurin salon against the mythology of the Bois de Boulogne—and there is certainly no clear chronological relationship between the two.

If what I have said so far shows the general drift of my argument, it does of course offer a gaping omission, for I barely mention *La Curée*. Of all the novels of the nineteenth century, this is of course the one which most systematically explores the shaping of Paris into the communicative, narrative network of which I have made so much play. Saccard's Rastignac-like vision from the Butte Montmartre in the second chapter echoes a great deal of what I have been saying: "le second réseau trouera la ville de toutes parts pour rattacher les faubourgs au premier réseau [...] une entaille [...] une autre entaille [...] des entailles partout [...]" (*Rougon-Macquart*, Pléiade I: 389) This project and its underlying meaning define the motifs of the novel's first one and a half chapters: the *parcours* of the opening, an elegant possession of the city's broad avenues contrasting with the flashback in the following chapter. This analepsis is remarkable not merely for what it tells us about the reconstruction of Paris, but also for the Balzacian fiction contained in this documentary: the account of Saccard's arrival in Paris, the political origins of his power, his early dealings, the situations and the group of characters he works through remind one more of *La Comédie humaine* than of *Rougon-Macquart*. Saccard's haphazard movement about the city is more reminiscent of Lucien de Rubempré's early explorations than of *Le ventre de Paris* or *L'Argent*. The *errance* described through the pre-Haussmann city is a prelude to the destruction and conquest which clearly map out the city's new space and the transformed narrative which will occupy it. Such a novel is clearly relevant to my thesis, but its historical, centripetal aspect is one which needs separate detailed treatment. Rather than build my argument around one text I have preferred to look at a development over a series of works, leaving the other perspective, perhaps, for later.[16]

NOTES

1. *Balzac archéologue de Paris*, Paris: SEDES, 1984.

2. M. Ragon, *Histoire de l'architecture*, Paris: Seuil, 1986, vol. I, pp. 240ff.

3. Ragon, op. cit., p. 181.

4. Ragon, op. cit., p. 179.

5. References to *A la recherche du temps perdu* quote Clarac's Pléiade edition by volume and page. Tadié's later Pléiade edition is indicated specifically. References to *Du côté de chez Swann* are to the Garnier-Flammarion edition (GF). References to *L'Education sentimentale* concern the Classiques Garnier edition of 1984.

6. Like the Paris Frédéric and Mme Arnoux go out into at the end of *L'Education sentimentale*....

7. M. Ragon, op. cit., p. 137.

8. See Ragon op. cit., pp. 180–1.

9. Odette's own address is much more ambiguous than that of Rosanette or Nana. See GF 339, quoted below.

10. One exception is Emma Bovary's fantasies (Seuil I: 594) which take inspiration from a map of Paris. However, her dreaming is made up of a sequence of explicitly classified localities and forms of behaviour.

11. Respectively Quai d'Orleans, rue Lapérouse and rue de Bellechasse.

12. III: 285: rue Montalivet.

13. Cf. I: 682: "la distance qu'il fallait franchir [pour aller diner]—peu distincte dans la nuit noire de celle qui séparait leurs domiciles parisiens du café Anglais on de la Tour d'Argent."

14. Indeed, Swann himself is swallowed up and imprisoned by the city: "quitter Paris pendant qu'Odette y était et même quand elle était absente [...] c'était pour lui un projet si cruel qu'il ne se sentait capable d'y penser sans cesse que parce qu'il se sentait résolu à ne l'exécuter jamais" (GF 489).

15. A step forward from Parisian experience in Balzac: Lucien comes to Paris and leaves once. Flaubert makes the strategic choice of a town which is near to Paris—he also has a developing railway system to rely on. There's a paper to do (if it hasn't already been done) on the link between narrative and transport systems.

16. An earlier version of this text was the basis for a paper which I gave in May 1992, at a conference on the city organised by the University of Sussex. See my Proust, "Du côté de chez Swann", University of Glasgow French and German Publications, 1992, the bibliography of which is relevant to this article. Links with and variations on the arguments outlined here will be found, inter alia, in: W. Benjamin, Das Passagenwerk, in Gesammelte Schriften, Frankfurt/Main: Suhrkamp, 1977, vol. V, 2; (see too V, 1); M.-A. Caws (ed.), City Images, New York: Gordon and Breach, 1992; G. Duby (ed.), Histoire de la France urbaine, Paris: Seuil, 1988, vols. IV and V; J. Gaillard, Paris la ville, Paris: Champion, 1977; C. Harvey, Consciousness and the Urban Experience, Oxford: Blackwell, 1985, and The Condition of Post-Modernism, Oxford: Blackwell, 1989; S. Kern, The Culture of Time and Space, 1880–1918, Princeton University Press, 1983; D. J. Olsen, The City as a Work of Art, Yale University Press, 1986; L. A. Pimentel, Metaphoric Narrative in "A la Recherche du Temps perdu", University of Toronto Press, 1990; C. Prendergast, Paris in the Nineteenth Century, Oxford: Blackwell, 1992; B. Pyke, The Image of the City in Modern Literature, Princeton University Press, 1981; R. Williams, The Country and the City, Oxford University Press, 1973. I have not been able to profit from Shinichi Saiki's very rich Paris dans le roman de Proust, Paris: SEDES, 1996.

NICHOLAS RENNIE

Benjamin and Zola: Narrative, the Individual, and Crowds in an Age of Mass Production

According to Walter Benjamin, nothing is more properly ["befugter"] the subject of nineteenth-century literature than the crowds that populate the modern urban landscape (1.618).[1] As he points out, the age of mass production (*Massenproduktion*) is accompanied by the emergence of an equally new phenomenon—the crowd, or *Masse*[2]—and the difficulty of representing, or at least evoking, this amorphous entity quickly becomes an aesthetic problem for literature and the visual arts. Benjamin cites Hugo and Engels, as well as E.T.A. Hoffmann, Poe, and in particular Baudelaire, in whose verses, he argues, the crowd is constantly present, if unnamed.[3] He also refers to the development of impressionist painting, which marks an important step in the adaptation of the human eye to scenes of flowing multitudes.[4]

It is intriguing, however, that in his literary wanderings through the topography of nineteenth-century Paris Benjamin should have almost nothing to say about Émile Zola, an especially prolific describer of this environment and one of the great virtuosi of modern crowd depiction. Already Henry James had called attention to Zola's ability to "make his characters swarm,"[5] arguing that it was both the "fortune" and "doom" of the *Rougon-Macquart* cycle to "deal with things almost always in gregarious form, to be a picture of numbers, of classes, crowds, confusions, movements,

From *Comparative Literature Studies* 33, no. 4 (1996). © 1996 by The Pennsylvania State University.

industries.... (James 513). More recently, Henri Mitterand has argued that Zola was "le premier romancier ... à faire de la foule un personnage en soi" ["the first novelist to make of the crowd a character in itself'] and Naomi Schor has written a book on *Zola's Crowds* in which she calls attention to the author's increasing preoccupation, in the course of his novelistic enterprise, with the "technical difficulties" of depicting the human masses that populate his novels.[6] Yet Benjamin does not speak of Zola's throngs, nor do his sparse references to the novelist say much about the relationship between Zola's interest and his own in the culture of Second Empire France.[7] I am, moreover, unaware of critical literature that compares Benjamin's and Zola's work in any detail.[8]

It is not the primary aim of this essay to attempt to decide the motives for Benjamin's reticence, though the following analysis may offer clues. Rather, I shall concentrate on Zola's 1883 novel *Au Bonheur des Dames* [*The Ladies' Paradise*] and on the texts resulting from Benjamin's *Passagen-Werk* [*Arcades Project*] (1927–1940)[9] to describe some of the differences betwen the two writers in their representation of crowds. I shall focus in particular on basic dissimilarities in their formal approach and theoretical conclusions. Of particular importance in this context will be Benjamin's understanding of the myth of eternal recurrence.[10]

I

Arriving for the first time in Paris, the heroine of Zola's *Au Bonheur des Dames* stops in awe before a storefront: "C'était ... un magasin de nouveautés dont les étalages éclataient en notes vives, dans la douce et pâle journée d'octobre" ["It was a fancy goods store whose displays burst colorfully in the soft, pale October light"] (389).[11] Having come to Paris in the hope of being engaged as a shop assistant by her uncle, Denise Baudu will instead be drawn into the service of the burgeoning department store (or, in Henry James' words, "colossal modern shop"[12]) that first attracts her attention and which, from the beginning, manifests itself as the novel's central protagonist. Ultimately, at the end of her trials and after a detailed account of the mechanisms of the *grand magasin* and of the consequences its development has in revolutionizing retail business,[13] Denise will agree to marry Octave Mouret, the store's organizing genius. She will thus reign "toute-puissante" ["all powerful"] (803) over the machinery of the store and the displays that had lured her at the start. At the opening of the novel, however, Denise is still mesmerized by the sumptuous display of fabrics, and the narrator's gaze joins her own in enumerating the articles that make up the array: "des pièces de lainage et de draperie, mérinos, cheviottes, molletons ..." ["articles of wool and cloth, merinos, cheviots, flannels ... "] (390). The *étalage* has an overwhelming effect in its endlessness, the observer's gaze is lost in an infinite regression: "C'était un développement qui lui semblait sans fin, dans la fuite de la perspective, avec les étalages du rez-de-chaussée et les glaces sans tain de l'entrésol ..." ["It was a seemingly endless progression, extending to the vanishing point, with the ground-floor displays and the plate-glass of the mezzanine ... "] (390).

In its fascination with this *mise en abîme*, Zola's description bears a curious resemblance to the endless array of things that clutter the landscape of nineteenth-century capitalism in Benjamin's writing. A passage at the beginning of the exposé *Paris, die Hauptstadt des XIX. Jahrhunderts* [*Paris, Capital of the 19th Century*], echoes Denise's arrival at the threshold of modern mass production with a quotation from Balzac: "Es war die Zeit, in der Balzac schreiben konnte: 'Le grand poeme de l'étalage chante ses strophes de couleurs depuis la Madeleine jusqu'à la porte Saint-Denis'" ["It was the age in which Balzac could write: 'The great poem of displays sings its strophes of color from the Madeleine to the Porte Saint-Denis'"] (5, 84). Benjamin engages in a monumental inventory of artifacts left behind by an epoch, reminiscent of how Octave and his staff exhaustively list the articles in their store. In an introduction added to his own French translation of this exposé, Benjamin speaks of the sense of "dizziness" [*vertige*] that attends what he characterizes as a nineteenth-century conception of history:

un point de vue qui compose le cours du monde d'une série illimitée de faits figés sous forme de choses. Le résidu caractéristique de cette conception est ce qu'on a appelé 'L'Histoire de la Civilisation', qui fait l'inventaire des formes de vie et des creations de l'humanité point par point.

[a point of view that constructs the course of world events as an unlimited series of facts frozen in the forms of things. The characteristic residue of this conception is what has been termed 'The History of Civilization,' which conducts an inventory of the forms of life and of humanity's creations point by point.] (5.60)

Benjamin obsessively revisits the images that constitute this "phantasmagoria," entering a world of "mysterious affinities": "Palme and Staubwedel,

Föhnapparat und die Venus von Milo, Prothese und Briefsteller ..." ["Palm tree and duster, hair-drier and the Venus of Milo, prosthesis and letter-writer's guide ..."] (5.1045). Such objects reappear frequently, acquiring the status of leitmotivs both in the course of Benjamin's revisions of his text, and within individual drafts of his notes.[14]

As in *Au Bonheur des Dames*, where the narrator's gaze is continually drawn back to the vivid "symphonies d'étalages" (469) and the "gigantesque étalage" (761) of Octave's flourishing store, Benjamin returns with insistence to the étalage of objects in a somber landscape of decay. In his early notes he observes that the spatial equivalent of eternal recurrence is *Superposition* (5.1023), stressing that the principle of montage informs his own textual procedure (5.1030)[15] and indicating that his work incorporates and is motivated by this structure of infinite repetition. Endless repetition or reflection also prefigures death, however: "Blicken zwei Spiegel einander an, so spielt der Satan seinen liebsten Trick und öffnet hier ... die Perspektive ins Unendliche" ["Where two mirrors face each other, Satan plays his favorite trick and opens ... a perspective into endlessness"] (5.667).

Susan Buck-Morss notes that the "[s]atanic qualities of death and eternal recurrence coalesce around [the] commodity world as fashion" (Buck-Morss, *Dialects of Seeing* 239). More generally, satanic repetition is, for Benjamin, characteristic of a world structured by mass production: "das Immerwiedergleiche erscheint sinnfallig in der Massenproduktion zum ersten Mal" ["the always-the-same first manifests itself in an obvious manner in the age of mass production"] (1.680). As Howard Stern has pointed out, Benjamin alludes to the possibility of "Motive der Rettung" ["themes of salvation"] (1.677) within such repetition.[16] Nonetheless, the obsessive return of themes and objects in Benjamin's work reflects a serious predicament—that of the modern consciousness struggling to assimilate the infinite:

> Die Neurose produziert den Massenartikel in der psychischen Ökonomie. Er hat dort die Form der Zwangsvorstellung. Sie erscheint im Haushalte des Neurotikers in ungezählten Exemplaren als die immer gleiche.
>
> [Neurosis generates articles of mass production in the economy of the psyche. There they take the form of obsessions, which appear in the neurotic consciousness in countless exemplars as always the same.] (1.662–63)

Compulsive repetition informs the individual's perspective of the things that surround him. The private *Bürger* is not simply surrounded by things, but defined by them. Appropriated by modern systems of production, he sells his soul to the "devil" of infinite regression. The words Benjamin quotes from Léon Deubel are emblematic: "Je crois ... à mon âme: la Chose" ["I believe ... in my soul: the Thing"] (5.53). The individual's "soul," his individuality, is negated by the infinitely reproducible object. For Benjamin, the bourgeois subject struggles in vain to leave traces of a particular self in the things that crowd in on him: "Es ist als habe es [das Bürgertum] seine Ehre darein gesetzt, die Spur, wenn schon nicht seiner Erdentage so doch seiner Gebrauchsartikel and Requisiten in Äonen nicht untergehen zu lassen" ("It is as though the bourgeoisie had made it a point of honor to preserve for aeons the trace of its commodities and accoutrements, if not that of its 'earthly days'"] (1.548). The reference to Faust's last words[17] rings in hollow mockery of the bourgeoisie's attempt to preserve the illusion of the individual's immortality. Throughout Benjamin's work, humanity leaves its traces only as in a vast archaeological site, or more frequently as in a geological site strewn with the remnants of prehistoric life. Thus, the "interiors" of the nineteenth century—apartments and rooms, but also the myriad cases, covers, boxes and containers of all sorts made to house the appurtenances of an epoch—are found vacant like abandoned cocoons, shells and the dry, hollow bodies of insects (5.1035; 5.286).[18]

The landscape of scattered things reflects the particular only by repeating it; the individual is replaced by the crowd, the *amorphe Masse* (1.619) that reappears throughout Benjamin's work as an entity without defining qualities beyond that of its very endlessness. An individual passing through the modern city and its crowds experiences a sequence of "shocks" comparable to those felt by a worker on a production line (or by the viewer of a film) (1.630–31); among the flow of pedestrians, the *flaneur* is himself like an item for sale amid a swirl of shoppers (1.557–58). The multitudes of faces repeat themselves ad infinitum, without a sign of recognition to animate them. Benjamin's crowded passages, spaces that are neither fully interior nor properly exterior, thus appear eerily empty, like scenes in the photographs of Eugène Atget.[19] If the crowd remains unnamed and undescribed in Baudelaire's verses (1.621–22), the same is true in Benjamin: traces of the crowd abound, but the crowd itself is never named as a presence. Its components are alienated and reified to the extent that their presence must remain implicit in the description of things.

II

The principle of repetition that informs Benjamin's depictions of the landscape of modernity precludes their achieving a sense of closure. The *étalage*—or "spreading out"—of objects in the modern urban environment leads to a dispersal of human experience, and the narrative genre that conforms to and expresses this experience, writes Benjamin, is the fragment or the anecdote (5.273).[20] The consciousness dispossessed of a coherent body of experience, however, reacts in defense, attempting to restore unity to its world. This is the predicament of the bourgeois Faust, who struggles in vain to assimilate his own experiences, striving heroically to impose on them a compelling form. Benjamin ascribes to the realist enterprise a similar effort to overcome the force of repetition that is implicit in modern production and commodity exchange. A fragment in "Zentralpark" begins:

> Der Jugendstil ist als der zweite Versuch der Kunst, sich mit der Technik auseinanderzusetzen, darzustellen. Der erste war der Realismus. Diesem lag das Problem mehr oder minder im Bewußtsein der Künstler vor, die durch die neuen Verfahrungsweisen der Reproduktionstechnik beunruhigt waren.

> [Art nouveau must be represented as art's second attempt to come to terms with technology. The first was realism. For realism the problem existed, more or less, in the minds of artists who were alarmed by new processes in the technology of reproduction.] (1.660)

This observation is followed by a parenthetical reference to Benjamin's notes for his work on mechanical reproduction, and almost immediately precedes his comment that the notion of eternal recurrence expresses a kind of neurosis that mass production has generated.

If we turn now to the *étalage* of commodities in *Au Bonheur des Dames*, the question arises as to the effect of repetition in Zola's novel. At the start, Denise, who later will herself be reduced to the function of a mannequin (497), gazes at the headless dummies in the window of the Bonheur:

> ... la tête absente était remplacée par une grande étiquette, piquée avec une épingle dans le molleton rouge du col; tandis que les glaces, aux deux côtés de la vitrine, par un jeu calculé, les

reflétaient et les multipliaient sans fin, peuplaient la rue de ces belles femmes à vendre, et portant des prix en gros chiffres, à la place des têtes.

[... the missing head was replaced by a large card stuck with a pin to the red swanskin fabric of the neck; meanwhile the mirrors that were artfully placed at the two sides of the window reflected and multiplied the figures endlessly, populating the street with these beautiful women for sale, who bore prices in large numerals in place of their heads.] (392)

The decapitated figures are multiplied and reflected into the street that they thereby come to "populate." The women clients lured into the Bonheur will likewise "lose their heads," in Rachel Bowlby's words,[21] succumbing to the "névrose nouvelle" ["new neurosis"] (632) of shopping (and shoplifting) and duplicating the effect of so many commodified bodies filling streets and interiors alike.[22] Threatening to turn individual characters into virtual images endlessly reproduced, however, the mechanism of the department store also threatens to destabilize the narrative in which it assumes the central role. If the novel begins as the story of specific, identifiable characters, what happens to its narrative unity when these characters are overtaken by a machinery whose purpose is the generation of masses— masses of clients, sellers, and items for sale? Referring to Benjamin's psychology of mass production one can rephrase the question: does the *mise en abîme* of commodified bodies and things inspire in the narrator a kind of "neurosis," motivating him compulsively to impose narrative coherence on a world that defies unity? Or do he and his characters in some way succeed in arresting what Benjamin—quoting the professional revolutionary Auguste Blanqui—terms a "retour éternel des choses" (5.75)?

III

The novel foregrounds the correspondence between the flow of commodities and crowds. When Denise comes to the Bonheur to seek employment, she at first gazes in bewilderment not at the displays of clothing and fabrics, but at the similarly endless stream of personnel who hurry through the entrance to their work: "La plupart filaient seuls et s'engouffraient au fond du magasin, sans adresser ni une parole ni même un regard à leurs collègues, qui allongeaient le pas autour d'eux ..." ["Most filed in alone, swallowed up in the inner recesses of the shop without so much as a word or glance for the colleagues who hurried beside them ... "] (416). The description recalls a passage that Benjamin cites from Engels, in which Engels records his impression of the crowds in London: "... sie [rennen] an einander vorüber, als ob sie gar Nichts gemein, gar Nichts mit einander zu thun hätten ... and dock fällt es Keinem ein, die Andern auch nur eines Blickes zu würdigen" ["... they run past each other as though they had nothing at all in common, nothing at all to do with one another ... yet it occurs to no one even to bestow a glance on the others"] (1.620).

The scene is repeated and intensified later on in the novel as crowds of shoppers surge into the store, forming eddies around the counters that are covered with articles for sale, and ultimately becoming indistinguish able from the parti-colored heaps of cloth. From the start, the same violence characterizes the explosion of colors in Octave's displays and the onslaught of shoppers who press towards them with voluptuous delight. This is evident in the vocabulary of these passages: the narrator speaks of the "bousculade de la vente," ["jostle and shove of the sale"] of the "débâcle de toile" ["surging turmoil of fabrics"] (432) and an "incendie d'étoffes" ["blaze of cloths"] (434) intended to "blind" the clients, of the "écrasement" ["crush"] (433) that Octave expects on the first of three great sale days. If Octave is ruthless in his "exploitation de la femme" ["exploitation of Woman"] (461), his talent for manipulating his clientele is merely an extension of his genius for arranging the objects in his displays.[23] This violence awakens the desire of the shoppers and forges a radical identification of purchaser with product. Octave's clients are stunned by an array of silks in which they seem to find their own reflections:

> Des femmes, pâles de désirs, se penchaient comme pour se voir. Toutes, en face de cette cataracte lâchée, restaient debout, avec la peur sourde d'être prises dans le débordement d'un pareil luxe et avec l'irrésistible envie de s'y jeter et de s'y perdre.

> [Some women, pale with desire, bent forward as if to see themselves. All of them, faced with this unimpeded cataract, remained standing, in mute terror of being swept along by such luxury, and at the same time drawn irresistibly to abandon themselves to it.] (487)

A simple equation results between client, sales-clerk, and commodity. As Octave explains to the Baron Hartmann (458), the *grand magasin* flourishes by virtue of a high turnover, the sale of large bulks of commodities and the rapid renewal of capital. The principle of high turnover simultaneously dictates the hiring and firing of shop-assistants; in unfavorable seasons scores of them are "swept away" (*balayé[s]*, 539), like the discarded cloths that clutter the store at the end of a sale. The same process provides for the brisk and continual circulation of buyers among the articles for purchase. Octave constructs his displays in the knowledge that his dizzying montage of fabrics will be mirrored by a vertiginous repetition of the client: Paris itself is "une immensité qui toujours fournirait des acheteuses" ["an immensity that would always furnish shoppers"] (492).

IV

Zola's novel highlights the immediate relationship between mass production, which reveals itself in a vast *étalage* of commodities, and the production of crowds. People and things are perpetually thrown together. At the same time, however, Zola refuses to abandon his narrative to this reckless promiscuity. New and exhilarating, the flawless operation of the machinery of commodity exchange constitutes an irrepressible life-force. The titular hero of Zola's novel, the Bonheur ultimately ensures the salvation of those individuals who have the wits to join its forces.

In Zola's *magasin de nouveautés*, the marketing of "the new" is, as Bowlby indicates, a value in itself: "the unifying criterion for its merchandise [is] newness, fashionability" (67). In Benjamin, by contrast, there is no hope of salvation implicit in the "newness" of commodification. The pain of alienation is eclipsed by the anguished realization that individuals are unable to perceive their reification, the negation of their individuality. By its very repetition, the *Chockerlebnis* that informs Benjamin's modernity dulls individuals' awareness of the forces that destroy them. Thus, Benjamin emphasizes that precisely what is perceived as "new" becomes a mere repetition of a newness that is always the same: "Das, was 'immer wieder dasselbe' ist, ist nicht das Geschehen sondern das Neue an ihm, der Chock, mit dem es betrifft" ["What is 'always the same' is not the event, but what is new about the event, the shock with which it hits home"] (5.1038).

In *Au Bonheur des Dames*, instead, repetition implies a seemingly endless heightening of desire. For Benjamin the forced departure of the prostitutes who had worked there marks the gradual demise of the urban passages (5.1028); in Zola's novel, which bears the subtitle "Eros 1883," the boundless seduction of society still appears to be gaining momentum. At the first sale, Mme Desforges is enchanted by the erotic power of Octave's "salon oriental," exclaiming: "N'est-ce pas, un vrai harem?" ["A real harem, isn't it?"] (499). This erotic energy fuels the machinery of Octave's store, replenishing itself perpetually by drawing shoppers from the entire city—and eventually from the whole continent. Its public is as yet innocent, responding in naive excitement to every new surprise that Octave prepares. Immediate gratification has not yet led to indifference and disaffection. The tone is set at the very beginning: Denise blushes at the start of the novel as she passes one of Octave's displays, in every sense a virgin as she arrives in Paris for the first time.

While the unrestrained desire of Zola's shoppers can produce a turbulent confusion of people and things that dehumanizes the clientele, the passions aroused by the Bonheur—ranging from the voluptuous submission of rapt shoppers to the bitter hatred of bankrupt competitors—nonetheless seem to remain a repository of individuality. Two opposing movements consequently establish a chiastic structure within the novel. On the one hand, the story describes the dramatic expansion of Octave's enterprise. At the start the department store is still hemmed in by the buildings of medieval Paris and its clientele is limited. By the end of the spectacular third sale, the Bonheur has grown to become "un vaste développement d'architecture polychrome" ["a vast development of polychrome architecture"] (761), the store and its surroundings are choked by a crowd of "près de cent mille clientes" ["nearly one hundred thousand clients"] (765), and revenues reach staggering proportions: "Enfin, c'était le million, le million ramassé en un jour, le chiffre dont Octave avait longtemps rêvé!" ["At last, it was the million, the million collected in a single day, the sum of which Octave had long dreamt!"] (800).

On the other hand this expansion is accompanied by a sharp focusing of the narrator's perspective. At the beginning Denise stands timidly before the store as a faceless crowd of shop-assistants presses its way through the doors. After this no other crowd in the novel achieves a comparable degree of anonymity. Denise is still hesitating on the sidewalk when a sympathetic soul—Henri Deloche—appears, and shortly afterwards her gaze singles out the figure of Octave, to whom the reader is immediately introduced (417). From this point to the end of the story, the sense of infinite regression inspired by the bustling crowd is invariably mitigated by signs of recognition. Even when Zola describes the unprecedented throngs of shoppers that fill the Bonheur at its third sale, it is only a matter of moments before the depiction of the "fleuve humain" ["human river"] narrows abruptly to foreground a select number of characters—what Schor defines as a *bande*—with whom we are already acquainted. In this scene, Mme de Boves, her daughter Blanche and Mme Guibal have themselves only exchanged a few words when they recognize another friend—Henriette Desforges—among the crowd of women (765–66). By the closing lines of *Au Bonheur des Dames* the crowd—James' "sounding chorus"—has receded fully into the background; as Denise and Octave embrace in his office beneath the portrait of Octave's deceased wife—and the store's former owner, Mme Hédouin, we only just overhear "l'acclamation lointaine d'une foule" ["the distant acclamation of the crowd"] (803).

Zola cannot do away with his characters, letting them dissolve in the multitude like Baudelaire's *passante*. To do so would be to destroy the underpinnings of a narrative that interweaves individual fates and ends with the union of its hero and heroine. A principle of repetition derived from the structure of commodity exchange is evident in *Au Bonheur des Dames*, but it is subordinated to a unified structure of narration rather than appearing in the narrative's dissolution. The principal figures in the novel never succumb to the estrangement that afflicts the individual in Baudelaire's or Benjamin's crowds. In what would otherwise be a nameless flow of pedestrians, the characters in Zola who bear names act as reliable points of reference. According to Benjamin, Poe had seized the experience of the modern crowd in his "Mystery of Marie Roget," in which the detective seeks to reconstruct the victim's route in a city through which she has passed unrecognized and without leaving a trace; Benjamin concludes: "Der ursprüngliche gesellschaftliche Inhalt der Detektivgeschichte ist die Verwischung der Spuren des Einzelnen in der Großstadtmenge" ["The original social content of the detective story is the erasure of the individual's tracks in the urban crowd"] (1.546). In Zola, however, this "erasure" never occurs. Indeed, a small group of characters consistently reappears from the crowd; no individual is ever "lost" for more than a moment. Thus, it is only a matter of time before Octave's detective Jouve succeeds in tracing and arresting a shoplifter, and we are aware that it is Mme de Boves even before she is caught (791). Similarly, it is no surprise when we find that the man hit by an omnibus on the crowded Place Gaillon (M. Robineau) also belongs to this inner circle of familiar figures (412).

As Schor argues, such a group of figures (or *bande*) constitutes a central device in Zola's depiction of crowds in the *Rougon-Macquart*. The *bande* exercizes an essential mediating role as "un ensemble de personnages secondaires qui se situe à mi-chemin entre l'individu et la foule" ["a group of secondary characters located halfway between the individual and the crowd"].[24] As a model of the crowd, it represents an anonymous swarm of people by illustrating its constituent types. The members of this group have a synecdocal function, each representing a specific social sector. In *Au Bonheur*, which Schor describes as an important "transitional novel" for Zola's representation of crowds,[25] this group is made up chiefly of those who attend the salon of Mme Desforges, Octave's mistress: Mme Marty is the "indescriminate shopper," Mme Guibal the "platonic shopper," and Mme de Boves becomes the "frustrated shopper" (Schor, *Zola's Crowds* 156–57). For Schor, it is largely this device that makes Zola a master of crowd depiction (Schor, "Individu et foule chez Zola" 27). However, this foregrounding of individuals whose personalities develop with the story necessarily compromises the effect of the crowd as an anonymous force. The narrator-sociologist refuses to pair the "satanic" reflection of the infinite in mass production with a limitless repetition in the structure of the crowd. Baudelaire writes that "[l]e plaisir d'être dans les foules est une expression mystèrieuse de la jouissance de la multiplication du nombre" ["[t]he pleasure of being in crowds is a mysterious expression of delight in the multiplication of number"].[26] Though it fascinates him, Zola senses the possibility of such multiplication as a threat. Baudelaire speaks of the artist-flaneur's joy in immersing himself "dans le nombre, dans l'ondoyant, dans le mouvement, dans le fugitif et l'infini" ["in the multitude, in the rising swell, in movement, in the ephemeral and infinite"].[27] Zola's Octave at one point similarly plunges into the crowd, "en pleine foule, ... pris lui-même du besoin physique de ce bain du succès" ["into the thick of the crowd, ... himself seized by a physical need for this bath of success"] (492), but he soon enough emerges to reassert his control over the shoppers. Denise, for her part, ultimately overcomes a system of exchange of people and objects that has threatened to crush her since her arrival in Paris. She is in the end victorious, and in her victory she affirms as a motor for social and economic progress the enterprise over which she gains command. She affirms it as a "mécanisme" (727), but as one that promises to bring improvement to individual lives. The Bonheur becomes a *phalanstère* (799), the "Maschinerie aus Menschen" ["machinery of human beings"] that Benjamin describes as Fourier's "utopia" of a classless society (5.47). As Michel Serres has shown, Zola's department store operates as a destructive, all-consuming engine. Paradoxically, however, this same engine submits in the end to human control.[28]

V

Benjamin describes realism as the response of artists alarmed by the possibilities of mechanical reproduction. Accordingly, the realist work—and by extension, I would argue, the naturalist text—attempts to cope with modern systems of production not by affirming them, but by trying to suppress them. The attempt to "arrest" the cyclic momentum of production, later redoubled in the *Jugendstil* period (1.660), itself leads to a form of psychological "mass production," the generation of images that recur compulsively (*Zwangsvorstellungen* [1.662–63]). With regard to Zola's novel, these observations help us to see how in the same passages in which he describes the "fleuve humain," Zola finds it necessary to defend himself from what Benjamin calls "die Perspektive ins Unendliche" (5.667) that threatens to annul the particular—the individual—within his work.

This reaction takes two forms. On the one hand, the narrative consciousness generates the recurrence of figures and themes in an effort to establish these as points of reference. If repetition threatens to divest the individual of all particularity (the individual client becomes one of myriad shoppers and commodities), the recurrence of the same character may lend him or her a certain stability as a presence within the story. Zola repeatedly draws individuals out of the multitude, effectively disturbing the repetition of figures and faces that constitutes the crowd itself and subjecting the crowd to an individual's control. In this way, both Denise and Octave are selected from the blurred crowds of Parisians in the first two chapters, and by the end the once daunting engine of modern production has submitted to their command. As they exert their power over the store and the masses that fuel its operation, so too does the narrator, by extension, struggle to contain the forces of entropy that threaten his narrative. Like Wordsworth, Zola is compelled to respond in some way to the "unmanageable sight"[29] of the urban masses; neither he nor Octave, his double as crowd-manager, can abandon themselves completely to the unorganized movement of the throng.[30] These recurring moments in which the narrator counteracts the dizzying effect of crowd scenes by focusing on members of the *bande* are comparable to the moments of "blockage"—self-loss followed by confirmation of the self's unity—that Neil Hertz has identified in literature of the sublime.[31]

On the other hand, we also find the narrator simply surrendering to images that return to him obsessively, as in a dream. He becomes like Denise's uncle Baudu, who is unable to turn his mind from the *grand magasin* that will swallow up his business and his family: "Mais là, de nouveau, il revint au Bonheur des Dames; tout l'y ramenait, c'était une obsession maladive" ["But there, once again, he came back to the Bonheur des Dames; everything led him back to this, it was an unhealthy obsession"] (591). This recurrent gaze bespeaks a pain that is always the same. The "progress" represented by the Bonheur's expansion is accompanied by devastation—the destruction of entire quarters of Paris under the auspices of Haussmann (Baron "Hartmann"), the bankruptcy of small businesses unable to compete with Octave's enterprise, and the disintegration of the family torn by the exigencies and temptations of the Bonheur: "tout craquait, la famille n'existait plus ..." ["everything was disintegrating, the family no longer existed"] (600). The *Zwangsvorstellung* is the symptom of a crisis, the reflex of a consciousness trying helplessly to catch up with the forces of mass production, and simultaneously a sign that it may only be possible to experience history as repetition of the same—as the impossibility of history or as "post-history."[32] At the same time that Zola appears rigorously to deny the centrifugal effect of modernity on the individual consciousness, his text points to the appropriation of the individual by systems of production and exchange that are beyond his control. This is perhaps best illustrated by the theme of the Bonheur's sales, a theme that likewise finds an analogy in Benjamin's texts. For Benjamin the notion of eternal recurrence is closely linked to Blanqui's last work, *L'Éternité par les astres* (1871). Benjamin sees Blanqui's avowal of the impossibility of change within the infinitely repeated series of events that form history as a frightening recantation. With it, Blanqui does not repudiate his belief that the existing social structure is false, but that it can be altered. His acknowledgment of the "eternal recurrence" of the status quo is both an absolute concession and a curse hurled at the bourgeoisie: "Blanqui unterwirft sich der bürgerlichen Gesellschaft. Aber es ist ein Kniefall von solcher Gewalt, daß ihr Thron darüber ins Wanken kommt" ["Blanqui surrenders to bourgeois society. But he capitulates to it with such violence that its throne rocks"] (5.168). Zola's socialism is clearly of a different stamp from either Blanqui's or Benjamin's. Yet in the three grand *mises en vente* that revolutionize the Paris of his novel—by dramatizing both the changes that have occurred in mass production and marketing, and the unprecedented mass mobilization of consumers—it is perhaps possible to read a note of the same irony that underlies Blanqui's work. The ever greater *étalages* with which Octave channels and obstructs the passage of his bourgeois clientele during his three sales recall the barricades erected in Paris in 1830, 1848, and 1871. And after each "revolution" the bourgeois social and economic order emerges with renewed vigor.[33]

Au Bonheur des Dames preserves its narrative unity. We are allowed glimpses of a world that threatens the integrity of individual consciousness, but the novel does not end with the disappearance of the individual and the dispersal of the unified narrative voice that speaks on the individual's behalf. On the contrary, Zola adopts novelistic patterns of *Bildung* and quest to affirm the ultimate victory and integrity of his protagonists. Zola struggles to contain the forces of endlessness and repetition that threaten both his characters and the structure of his own narrative, and in so doing he erects a defense against an opposing style of narration, one that Benjamin names in speaking of the "street rebellion of the anecdote" ("Straßenaufstand der Anekdote" [5.77]). However, this affirmative drive is itself perhaps also indicative of a particularly modern fear: that in an age of mass production "individuality" may have been reduced to a mere trope that repeats itself endlessly.

NOTES

1. References indicate volume and page number in: Walter Benjamin, *Gesammelte Schriften*, Rolf Tiedemann and Hermann Schweppenhäuser, eds., 7 vols. (Frankfurt: Suhrkamp, 1982).

2. "Die Entstehung der Masse ist ... gleichzeitig mit der der Massenproduktion" (1.668). In "Über einige Motive bei Baudelaire" Benjamin makes it clear that the *Masse* is not made up of a specific social class: "Von keiner Klasse, von keinem irgendwie strukturierten Kollektivum kann die Rede sein. Es handelt sich um nichts anderes als um die amorphe Menge der Passanten, um Straßienpublikum" (1.618).

3. "Die Masse ist Baudelaire derart innerlich, daß man ihre Schilderung bei ihm vergebens sucht" (1.621). On the following page we read: "Keine Wendung, kein Wort macht in dem Sonett 'A une passante' die Menge namhaft."

4. "Vielleicht hat der tagliche Anblick einer bewegten Menge einmal ein Schauspiel dargestellt, dem sick das Auge erst adaptieren muße.... Das Verfahren der impression istischen Malerei, das Bild im Tumult der Farbflecken einzuheimsen, ware dann ein Reflex von Erfahrungen, die dem Auge eines Großstadters geläufig geworden sind. Ein Bild wie Monets Kathedrale von Chartres, die gleichsam ein Ameisenhaufen aus Steinen ist, würde diese Annahme illustrieren können." (1.628).

5. Henry James, "Emile Zola," *Documents of Modern Literary Realism*, ed. George J. Becker (Princeton: Princeton UP, 1963) 518.

6. Henri Mitterand, *Zola: L'histoire et la fiction* (Paris: Presses Universitaires de France, 1990) 8; Naomi Schor, *Zola's Crowds* (Baltimore: Johns Hopkins UP, 1978) 154. See also Schor's "Individu et foule chez Zola: structures de médiation," *Les Cahiers naturalistes* 56 (1982): 26–33. Except where otherwise indicated, all translations are my own.

7. In the *Passagen-Werk*, Benjamin notes that Zola's *Thérèse Raquin* depicts the passages of Paris in the period of their demise (5.269–70, 1046). The observation is retained in abbreviated form in the exposé *Paris, die Hauptstadt des XIX. Jahrhunderts* (5.47). In "Zum gegenwärtigen gesellschaftlichen Standort des französischen Schrifts tellers," Benjamin praises Zola for having adopted an exemplary critical stance in his descriptions of France in the 1860's (2.786–88). Possibly implying reservations with

regard to Zola's work, however, a passage in Benjamin's review of Döblin's *Berlin Alexanderplatz* warns against a strain of *Hintertreppennaturalismus* that Benjamin finds in some contemporary literature (3.234). Benjamin may have felt some of the same ambivalence that Lukács expresses when he says that "Zola's subjectively most sincere and courageous criticism of society is locked into the magical circle of progressive bourgeois narrow-mindedness." George Lukács, "The Zola Centenary," trans. Edith Bone, *Critical Essays on Emile Zola*, ed. David Baguley (Boston: G. K. Hall, 1986) 82.

8. In her own work on the representation of crowds, Schor refers to Benjamin neither in *Zola's Crowds*, nor in "Individu et foule chez Zola." In his article "Zola and the Counter Revolution: *Au Bonheur des Dames*," *Australian Journal of French Studies* 30 (1993): 233–40, Brian Nelson includes in a note a general reference to Benjamin's *Passagen-Werk*, without, however, elaborating on the relationship between this text and Zola's novel (Nelson 234). Nor have I found detailed references to Benjamin in any major studies of Zola's work. Similarly, monographs on Benjamin tend to say little about Zola. In *The Dialectics of Seeing: Walter Benjamin and the Arcades Project* (Cambridge: MIT P, 1989), Susan Buck-Morss includes only passing references to Zola, as do the contributors to the large volume entitled *Walter Benjamin et Paris: Colloque international 27–29 juin 1983*, ed. Heinz Wismann (Éditions du Cerf, 1986). The same is true of Karlheinz Stierle's *Der Mythos von Paris: Zeichen und Bewußtsein der Stadt* (Munich: Carl Hanser, 1993), a study that models itself to a significant extent on the *Passagen-Werk*. Schor herself scarcely mentions Zola in "*Cartes Postales*: Representing Paris 1900," *Critical Inquiry* 18 (1992): 188–244, an article in which she discusses Benjamin's work at some length.

9. I refer here not just to the material collected under the heading *Passagen-Werk* in volume 5 of the Suhrkamp edition of Benjamin's works, but also to *Charles Baudelaire. Ein Lyriker im Zeitalter des Hochkapitalismus*, which, as the editors of Benjamin's *Schriften* note (1.1064–66), is closely related to this larger project. My title also alludes to the close affinity, noted by Buck-Morss, between the *Passagen-Werk* and Benjamin's essay on "Das Kunstwerk im Zeitalter seiner technischen Reproduzierbarkeit." See Buck-Morss, "Benjamin's *Passagen-Werk*: Redeeming Mass Culture for the Revolution," *New German Critique: An Interdisciplinary Journal of German Studies* 29 (1983): 212.

10. For the sake of brevity, I shall avoid comparing Benjamin's concept of eternal recurrence to that of Nietzsche, whom Benjamin cites frequently. Of particular importance, in this context, is section D of the *Passagen-Werk*, entitled "Die Langeweile, ewige Wiederkehr" (5.156–78). Related passages include the following: 1.657, 673; 5.424–5, 455, 691.

11. Page numbers refer to *Émile Zola, Les Rougon-Macquart: Histoire naturelle et sociale d'une famille sous le Second Empire*, Armand Lanoux and Henri Mitterand, eds., 4 vols. (Paris: Gallimard, 1964) vol. 3.

12. James 519. As Mitterand observes in his notes to the novel (1672–76), *Au Bonheur des Dames* is set in the period 1864–69, but Zola compresses into this time some fifty years of development in the retailing business. Thus, the eponymous store can begin as a *magasin de nouveautés* and evolve quickly into a *grand magasin*.

13. Kristin Ross writes that *Au Bonheur des Dames* is "the only late nineteenth century French novel to treat in detail the social environment surrounding the emergence of the modern commercial techniques of retailing and advertising pioneered, above all, by France during the Second Empire (1851–1870)." Introduction to Émile Zola, *The Ladies' Paradise*, trans. Henry Vizetelly (Berkeley: U of California P, 1992) 6. For a history of the development of the department store, see Michael B. Miller, *The Bon Marché: Bourgeois Culture and the Department Store, 1869–1920* (Princeton: Princeton UP, 1981); of particular relevance here is section one, entitled "Revolution in Retailing." For the earlier history of the arcades, see Johann Friedrich Geist's monumental *Arcades: The History of a Building Type*, trans. Jane O. Newman and John H. Smith (Cambridge MA: MIT P, 1983).

14. The texts collected under the title *Über Haschisch* profile a mode of consciousness that registers such forms of repetition with particular clarity: "Es ist höchst eigentümlich, daß die Phantasie dem Raucher Objekte ... gern serienweise vorstellt. Die endlosen Reihen, in denen da vor ihm immer wieder die gleichen Utensilien, Tierchen oder Pflanzenformen auftauchen, stellen gewissetmaßen ungestalte, kaum geformte Entwürfe eines primitiven Ornaments dar." Walter Benjamin, *Über Haschisch: Novellistisches, Berichte, Materialien*, ed. Tillman Rexroth, introd. Hermann Schweppenhäuser (Frankfurt: Suhrkamp, 1972) 57–58. For a valuable, concise analysis of the figures of repetition and discontinuity and the function of "ornament" particularly in these texts, but elsewhere in Benjamin's writing as well, see Howard Stern, *Gegenbild, Reihenfolge, Sprung: An Essay on Related Figures of Argument in Walter Benjamin*, ed. Volkmar Sander, New York University Ottendorfer Set. 15 (Bern: Peter Lang, 1982).

15. Peter Demetz highlights Benjamin's "topographical consciousness," in which "space rules over time." Peter Demetz, introduction, *Illuminations*, by Walter Benjamin (New York: Harcourt Brace Jovanovich, 1978) 17.

16. Stern 77. I quote Stern's translation of Benjamin's phrase.

17. "Zum Augenblicke dürft' ich sagen: / Verweile dock, du bist so schön! / Es kann die Spur von meinen Erdetagen / Nicht in Äonen untergehn.— / Im Vorgefühl...." Johann Wolfgang Goethe, *Faust* (ll. 11581–85), vol. 3 of *Goethes Werke*, ed. Erich Trunz, 14th ed., 14 vols. (Munich: C.H. Beck, 1991) 348.

18. In his introduction to *Über Haschisch* (22), Hermann Schweppenhäuser identifies such enclosure and encasing as a metaphor for the "commodity character" [*Warencharakter*] of objects. For a critique of this analysis, see Stern 15–6.

19. For Benjamin's discussion of the emptiness in Atget's photographs, see his "Kleine Geschichte der Photographie" (2.379).

20. In *Einbahnstraße*, Benjamin will argue that books are "eine veraltete Vermittlung zwischen zwei verschiedenen Kartothekssystemen," superfluous texts interposed between the notes of authors and the notes compiled by readers (4.103). Citing this passage with reference to the incomplete *Passagen-Werk*, Buck-Morss writes: "Had [Benjamin] lived, the notes would not have become superfluous by entering into a closed and finished text.... The *Passagen-Werk* is as it would have been...." "The Flaneur, the Sandwichman and the Whore: The Politics of Loitering," *New German Critique: An Interdisciplinary Journal of German Studies 39* (1986): 99.

The same could not be asserted of Zola's notes, or *Carnets d'enquêtes*, which are organized toward the fulfilment of a novelistic, narrative project.

21. "Like these models of what they desire or desire to be, the women who stare in wonder have lost their heads. Wanting to make themselves one with the mindless, topless image, they are objectified—and objectify themselves—into mere bodies, potential bearers of clothes." Rachel Bowlby, *Just Looking: Consumer Culture in Dreiser, Gissing and Zola* (New York: Methuen, 1985) 73.

22. As in Benjamin, the boundaries between outside and inside are often elided in Zola. At one point we read of Octave: "S'il en avait découvert le moyen, il aurait fait passer la rue au travers de sa maison" (614). A later passage depicts the store's lingerie departments as an intimate boudoir and, at the same time, as "une alcôve publiquement ouverte" (781). For discussion of such openings of enclosures see "Maisons" in Jean Borie, *Zola et les mythes: ou de la nausée au salut* (Paris: Éditions du Seuil, 1971) 125–252; and Peter Brooks, *Body Work: Objects of Desire in Modern Narrative* (Cambridge MA: Harvard UP, 1993) 153.

23. Michel Serres notes that Octave is "surtout topologue"—a master in spatial relations and in the organization of people and objects in space. *Feux et signaux de brume* (Paris: Bernard Grasset, 1975) 283.

24. Schor, "Individu et foule chez Zola" 29.

25. Schor (*Zola's Crowds* 154) takes the phrase from F.W.J. Hemmings, who does not use it to refer directly to Zola's representation of crowds. See Hemmings, *Émile Zola* (Oxford: Clarendon P, 1966) 147.

26. Charles Baudelaire, *Oeuvres complètes*, ed. Claude Pichois, 2 vols. (Paris: Gallimard, 1975–76) 1.649.

27. Baudelaire 2.691. See also section XII of *Le Spleen de Paris*, entitled "Les Foules": "Il n'est pas donné à chacun de prendre un bain de multitude: jouir de la foule est un art..." (1.291).

28. Serres 282. Robert J. Niess observes that Zola "always tends to see machines in human ... terms." "Zola's *Au Bonheur den Dames*: The Making of a Symbol," *Symbolism and Modern Literature: Studies in Honor of Wallace Fowlie*, ed. Marcel Tetel (Durham: Duke UP, 1978) 137.

29. From Book 7 ("Residence in London") of *The Prelude* (l. 732).

30. Schor points out that in Zola, "les chefs [sont] ceux qui ont ou briguent le pouvoir sur la foule; hors de la médiation, pourrait-on dire, point de pouvoir." "Individu et foule chez Zola," 30. This comment serves to highlight the function of narrative itself, in Zola, as an acquisition of power over the crowds that are its subject.

31. See Neil Hertz, "The Notion of Blockage in the Literature of the Sublime," *Romanticism*, ed. Cynthia Chase (London: Longman, 1993) 78–97. (I am grateful to Emily Sun for having pointed out the relevance of this text to my argument.) See also Stierle's *Der Mythos von Paris*, where the "unreadability" of the modern urban landscape (and its crowds) is a principal theme. According to Stierle, the narrator of Poe's "The Man of the Crowd" escapes self-loss by an act of repression, rendering the eponymous subject of the story "unreadable" precisely in order to deny what is uncannily familiar in the person of this stranger. As Stierle argues, both readability

and unreadability may thus be "strategies" by which a narrator retains a measure of stability in the movement of the crowd (Stierle 615). If this is true, the strategy of control adopted by Zola's narrator is the opposite of Poe's.

32. James L. Rolleston argues that for Benjamin "the key truth of the 'age of history' is the impossibility of history, the perpetual replaying of the same scenario of power, exploitation, and the illusion of change. This truth is expressed in the myth of eternal recurrence...." "The Politics of Quotation: Walter Benjamin's Arcades Project," *PMLA* 104 (1989): 18. The term *post-histoire*, which Arnold Gehlen associates with the work of Antoine Augustin Cournot, appears in Gehlen's "Die Säkularisierung den Fortschritts," *Einblicke*, ed. Karl-Siegbert Rehberg, 7 vols. (Vittorio Klostermann: Frankfurt, 1978) 7.403–12; see also Gianni Vattimo, "The Structure of Artistic Revolutions," *The End of Modernity: Nihilism and Hermeneutics in Postmodern Culture*, trans. and introd. Jon R. Snyder (Baltimore: Johns Hopkins UP, 1988) 91–109. With regard to Zola, Guy Robert points to the theme of recurrence in his work that is at odds with any notion of change or progress: "... la vision de l'univers qui s'impose à Zola est trop profondément épique pour qu'elle n'implique pas, plus ou moins claire à la conscience du poke, la nécessité de voir se répéter jusqu'aux confins du temps des situations et des actes simples et signifiants." *'La Terre' d'Emile Zola* (Paris: Société d'Édition les Belles Lettres, 1952) 385–86.

33. A note in the *Passagen-Werk* includes the observation that in French, the word "Revolution" [sic] camt to include the meaning "clearance sale" (5.1000). Buck-Morss calls attention to this passage in "Benjamin's *Passagen-Werk*" 231.

MARIE-SOPHIE ARMSTRONG

The Opening Chapter of La fortune des Rougon, or the Darker Side of Zolian Writing

Although Zola viewed the opening chapter of *La fortune des Rougon* (1871) as "un pur tableau pittoresque qui ouvre l'oeuvre,"[1] it is legitimate to question the value of this characterization. As Henri Mitterand has noted, the first pages of *La fortune* are not simply the opening pages of the novel, they are the opening pages of the whole twenty-volume series, and their content "peut être lu comme le récit fondateur de l'ensemble du cycle" (1980:173). When Zola embarked on the writing of *La fortune* in 1869, he was turning in to publisher Lacroix the outline of what was to be "[un] grand roman de moeurs et d'analyse humaine, en dix épisodes" (Dossier 1755). The value of this information is paramount to our understanding of *La fortune*, for it allows us to consider the novel not so much as the first of the building blocks upon which the rest of the series was to be erected, but rather as the "tip of the iceberg," the only visible portion of the series informed by the yet invisible mass of *Les Rougon-Macquart*. Such a perspective on the novel encourages the view that the first pages of the series are crucial in the revelation of the formidable literary venture at hand.[2]

Henri Mitterand has hinted at the self-reflexive nature of the opening chapter of *La fortune des Rougon* in two ways. He has recognized in the pear trees that grow out of the rich soil of the Saint-Mittre cemetery, the opening space of the series: "[la] première image de l'Arbre généalogique, dessiné en

From *Dalhousie French Studies* 44 (Fall 1998). © 1998 by Dalhousie University.

tête d'*Une page d'amour* et du *Docteur Pascal*" (1980:174), and he has wondered whether the young Silvère, the first character of the *Rougon-Macquart* series, whom we first see in the former cemetery, might not be a representative of Zola within the fiction: "ne dirait-on pas que le narrateur vient se confondre lui-même avec son personnage? En tête des *Rougon-Macquart*, l'homme qui erre parmi les monuments d'une société disparue, qui la tire du sommeil pour lui rendre son identité et lui révéler le sens de son histoire, n'est-ce pas une figure du romancier?" (1980:181).[3]

The examination of the space and of the actors of the first chapter along such lines is indeed worthwhile. Remarkable in the context of our reading is the fact that the "aire" Saint-Mittre, the contemporary avatar of the former cemetery, and the stage for the first half of the chapter, has been turned into "un chantier de bois."[4] In 1869 the word "chantier" would have indeed had a literary resonance for Zola, for not only was *La fortune* "sur le chantier," as Zola's friend Paul Alexis reports after visiting the novelist in September 1869, but so were *Les Rougon-Macquart* (Zola 1960:I:1536). The description of the sawmill which occupies the worksite reinforces the hypothesis of a symbolic equivalence between the "aire Saint-Mittre" and the space of Zolian writing:

> Une scierie, qui débite dans un coin les poutres du chantier, grince, servant de basse sourde et continue aux voix aigres. Cette scierie est toute primitive: la pièce de bois est posée sur deux tréteaux élevés, et deux scieurs de long, l'un en haut, monté sur la poutre même, l'autre en bas, aveuglé par la sciure qui tombe, impriment à une large et forte lame de scie un continuel mouvement de va-et-vient. Pendant des heures, ces hommes se plient, pareils à des pantins articulés, avec une régularité et sécheresse de machine. (8)

While the "continuel mouvement de va-et-vient" of the saws attests to the daily repetition in which the writer engages ("Nulla dies sine linea" was Zola's motto) and evokes the very motion of the quill on the page (a notion reinforced by the verb "imprime"), "la basse sourde et continue" of the *scierie* might well index the quiet but constant underground dimension of the writing of the *série*. It follows that "[les] deux scieurs de long [qui] [...] se plient" for hours might well be viewed as a first, plural representation of Zola the writer applying himself ("se pliant") to a rigid writing schedule. The mention of the "*R-é-G-ularité* et sécheresse de *MA*chine" would present us with the rational, scientific dimension of Zola's project, the phrase also constituting a phonetic reminder that Zola, as the Goncourts have commented, viewed the "*R-ou-G-on-MAcquart*" as "[une] grande *MA*chine" (Armand Lamoux in 1960:I:x).

The second portion of the description of the "chantier" further supports this interpretation:

> Le bois qu'ils [les scieurs] débitent est rangé, le long de is murailie du fond, par tas hauts de deux ou trots mètres, et méthodiquement construits, planche à planche, en forme de cube parfait. Ces sortes de meules carrées [...] sont un des charmes de faire Saint-Mittre. (8)

In the "bois débité" and accumulated on the worksite one may well detect Zola's concern, at the onset of the series, with his novelistic output (his "débit"). Moreover, when one recalls the care with which the novelist gathered his documentation for each work—one thinks of the *Ébauches* with their outlines, lists of possible names for characters and places, etc.—it is legitimate to recognize in the "tas [...] méthodiquement constructs planche à planche" a figuration of Zola's works, methodically constructed, put together, so to speak, "pas à pas," "page à page."

Sketched in the daytime description of the "aire" Saint-Mittre, the representation of the *Rougon-Macquart* project becomes further elaborated in the nighttime depiction of the worksite. Let us consider the spectacle confronting the young Silvère who has come to the former cemetery to await his beloved, Miette:

> Serrant l'arme contre sa poitrine, il [Silvère] scruta attentivement du regard les carrés de ténèbres que les tas de planches jetaient au fond du terrain. Il y avait là comme un damier blanc et noir de lumière et d'ombre, aux cases nettement couples. Au milieu de faire, sur un morceau du sol gris et nu, les tréteaux des scieurs de long se dessinaient, allongés, étroits, bizarres, pareils à une monstrueuse figure géométrique tracée à l'encre sur du papier. Le reste du chantier, le parquet de poutres, n'était qu'un vaste lit où la clarté dormait, à peine striée de minces raies noires par les lignes d'ombres qui coulaient le long des gros madriers. (10)

References to writing have become more explicit: in the "morceau du sol gris" upon which the horses of the millworkers "se dessin[ent]" as if "tracé[s] à l'encre sur du papier" as well as in the "clarté [...] à peine striée de minces raies noires," one recognizes both the representation of the page barely covered, and, by metonymy, that of the work yet in its early stages. The structured aspect of the *Rougon-Macquart* series previously identified in the daytime description now reappears with more insistence. The "cases nettement coupées" formed by the planks recall Zola's wish to fit, to place ("caser") a specific topic in each of the novels of the *Rougon-Macquart* series—"Un roman sur les prêtres," "Un roman militaire," "Un roman sur l'art," "Un roman sur les grandes démolitions de Paris" etc. (1960:V:1735), so that one might say of Zola what he himself says of Flaubert: "Dés lors, il établissait des cases, et la chasse aux documents commençait avec le plus d'ordre possible" (1966:XI:147). The space of the chessboard ("damier") provides in fact a powerful analogue for other aspects of Zola's writing. It exemplifies the binary structure which the novelist intended for his work, the *alternance* of black and white constituting a reminder that for Zola "l'élément femme [doit être] pondéré avec l'élément homme. Le *noir* pondéré avec le *blanc*, la *province* avec Paris" (1960:V:1741; Zola's emphasis).

But if the nocturnal representation of the space of writing further underlines the rational dimension of Zolian writing identified in the daytime description, i.e., the desire for order and balance displayed in the *Documents et plans préparatoires*, it also brings out a darker dimension of writing not acknowledged by Zola at the onset of the *Rougon-Macquart* project. Sitting "au milieu de faire," the "monstrueuse figure géométrique tracée il l'encre sur du papier" (10) not only suggests the "teratological" content central to Zola's work (the many images of the monster which appear under one form or another in the *Rougon-Vacquart*); it points more generally to the somber, unconscious dimension inherent in Zolian writing, a dimension already implicit in the "noeuds monstrueux" (6) of the "genealogical" pear trees.

In view of the metaphorical significance attributed to the space of the "aire" Saint-Mittre, one can easily infer the nature of the part which Silvère, the first character in the *Rougon-Macquart* series, is to play in the scenario of writing. Recalling, through his "maigreur de chevalier errant" (11), "la silhouette sèche du cieur de long monté sur sa poutre" (9)—a figure whose scriptural dimension has been previously established—, the young man acts indeed, as suggested by Mitterand, as the first representative of Zola in the series.[5] In accordance with the romantic topos of the "poète élu," Silvère is progressively drawn out of the darkness by a celestial force—"Il s'était placé dans un coin noir; mais, peu à leu, la lune qui montait le gagna, et sa tête se trouva en pleine clarté" (11)—and anointed to a scriptural mission, becoming a Messiah of writing: "Lorsque la remie sonna à l'horloge voisine, il fut tiré en sursaut de sa rêverie. En se voyant danc de lumière, il regarda devant lui avec inquiétude" (12). Not surprisingly, it is after the symbolic confrontation of Silvère/poet with his scriptural project at to the "aire" Saint-Mittre that Miette, Silvère's beloved, appears.[6] First presented as "une voix légère comme un souffle, basse et haletante" (13), she is, in this Musset-like "nuit de decembre" (the plot of *La fortune* begins on the eve of December 2) no other than the muse, the incarnation of inspiration.[7]

In light of this reading of both the space and the characters of the first chapter of *La fortune*, one suspects that the plot making up the second half of the chapter, namely the powerful advance of the "colonne des Républicains" witnessed by Silvère and Miette, may well be linked to Zola's scriptural enterprise. The discovery of a number of parallels between Miette/muse and the column of marchers encourages such a hypothesis. Thus, Miette's voice, "légère comme un *souffle*," is now amplified in the "étranges *souffles* d'ouragan cadencés et rythmiques" (26) rising from the army. Similarly, the military dimension of the young girl's hair—her "cheveux *superbes*," "d'un *noir* d'encre," "plantés rudes et droits sur le front," "*mass[és]* derrière sa tête" (15), evoke a "casque vivant" (15)—has been converted in the "élan *superbe*" of the "*masses noires*" (27), "compacte[s], solide[s]" (28) of the column of "insurgés." One notes, moreover, that a similar water imagery informs both descriptions. The "vague jaillissante" of Miette's hair "[qui] *coulaient* le long de son crane et de sa nuque, pareils à une mer crepue, pleine de bouillonnements et de caprices" (15), has now become the "torrent [...] [de] flots vivants" (27) and the "longue *coulée* grouillante et mugissante" (28) of the army of Republicans.

As the last "character" to appear in the initial chapter of *La fortune*, the army of insurgents may be read as the gigantic, phantasmic version of inspiration and writing more modestly incarnated in Miette, and may be seen to actualize the energy of *Les Rougon-Macquart*. The *Documents et plans préparatoires* to the series give credence to this interpretation.[8] The confrontation of the depiction of the crowd of marchers with the "Notes sur la marche générale de l'oeuvre" is particularly revealing as it shows that the characteristics of the "colonne," i.e., its energy, compactness, passion, determination, echo the qualities of writing which Zola valued when he was laying the groundwork for *Les Rougon-Macquart*. Thus, "l'élan superbe, irrésistible" (27) of the three thousand men "unis et *emportés* d'un bloc par un vent de colère" (28) and the "étranges *souffles* d'ouragan cadencés et rythmiques" (26) materialize in the fiction "le *souffle de passion*" which, according to Zola, "anim[e] le tout, courant d'un bout à l'autre de l'oeuvre" (1960:V:1743), Zola's emphasis) and for which he feels a strong necessity: "garder dans mes livres un *souffle* un et fort qui, s'élevant de la première page, *emporte* le lecteur jusqu'à la dernière" (1960:V:1742).

Described as "terriblement grandiose" (27), endowed with the "impétuosité vertigineuse de *torrent*" and a "*grondement* continu" (32), the march of the "insurgés" more specifically embodies Zola's perspective on style: "Veiller au style," the novelist insists, "[p]lus d'epithètes. Une carrure magistrale. Mais toujours de la chaleur et de la passion. Un *torrent grondant*, mais large, et d'une marche majestueuse" (1960:V: 1744).

Finally, the army of marchers may be seen to reflect organizational concerns on Zola's part. The initial appearance of the crowd of men as a "*masse* compacte, *solide*, d'une puissance invincible" (28), its distribution into "*masses* noires" (27) materializes "la *construction solide des masses*, des chapitres" envisioned by Zola in the *Documents et plans préparatoires* (1960:V:1743, Zola's emphasis). The very succession of the "masses" formed by the various contingents thus conveys "*la logique, la poussée de ces chapitres*, se succédant comme des blocs superposés, se mordant l'un l'autre" with "chaque chapitre, chaque masse [devant] être comme une force distincte qui pousse au dénouement" (1960:V:1743, Zola's emphasis).[9]

If one considers the metaphorical, scriptural value attributed to the army of "insurgés," it is hardly surprising that the latter should also help translate into fiction the esthetic dimension of Zolian writing. One detects more particularly the relationship of Zolian writing to the literary achievements of the precursors, Balzac and Hugo. While the crowd of 3,000 men making up the army suggests the world of the *Comédie humaine* behind Zola's enterprise—"Balzac à l'aide de 3 000 figures veut faire l'histoire des moeurs," Zola notes in his "Différences entre Balzac et moi" (1960:V:1736)—, the depiction of the nightly march of the "colonne" in the fifth chapter of the novel points more precisely to the presence of Balzac.[10] Thus, the second paragraph of the chapter becomes the fictional modulation of a eulogistic article on Balzac written by Zola in May 1869, at the exact time he was beginning the composition of *La fortune*.[11]

LA FORTUNE DES ROUGON

À gauche, la plaine s'élargit, immense tapis vert, piqué de loin en loin par les taches grises des villages. À droite, la chaîne des Garrigues dresse ses pics désolés, ses champs de pierre, ses *blocs* couleur de rouille, comme roussis par le soleil. Le grand chemin, formant chaussée du côté de la rivière, passe au milieu de rocs *énormes*, entre lesquels se montrent, à chaque pas, des bouts de la vallée. Rien n'est plus sauvage, plus étrangement grandiose, que

cette route taillée dans le flanc même des collines. La nuit
surtout, ces lieux ont une horreur sacrée. Sous la lumière pêle, les
insurgés s'avançaient comme dans une avenue de ville détruite,
ayant aux deux bords des *débris* de temples; la lune faisait de
chaque rocher un fût de *colonne* tronqué, un chapiteau *écroulé*, une
muraille trouée de mystérieux *portiques*. En haut, la masse des
Garrigues dormait, à peine blanchie d'une teinte laiteuse, pareille
à une immense cité cyclopéenne dont les *tours*, les obélisques, les
maisons aux terrasses hautes, auraient caché une moitié du ciel;
et, dans les fonds, du côté de la plaine, se creusait, s'élargissait un
océan de clartés diffuses, une étendue vague, sans bornes, où
flottaient des nappes de brouillard lumineux. La bande
insurrectionnelle aurait pu croire qu'elle suivait une chaussée
gigantesque, un chemin de ronde construct au bord d'une mer
phosphorescence et toumant autour d'une *Babel* inconnue. (162)

C'est comme une tour de *Babel* que la main de l'architecte n'a pas
eu et n'aurait jamais eu le temps de terminer. Des pans de *muraille*
se sont déjà *écroulés* de vétusté, jonchant le sol de leurs *debris*
énormes.

L'ouvrier a employé tous les matériaux qui lui sont tombés
sous la main, le plâtre, la pierre, le ciment, le marbre, jusqu'au
sable et à la boue des fossés. Et, de ses bras rudes, avec ces
matières prises au hasard, il a dressé son édifice, sa tour
gigantesque, sans se soucier de l'harmonie des lignes, des
proportions équilibrées de son oeuvre. [...] Il semble qu'on
l'entend souffler dans son chancier, taillant les *blocs* à grands
coups de marteau, se moquant de la grace et de la finesse des
arêtes, faisant maladroitement saucer des éclats. Il semble qu'on
le voit monter pesamment sur ses échafaudages, magonnant ici
une grande *muraille* nue et rugueuse, alignant plus loin des
colonnades d'une majesté sereine, perçant les *portiques* et les baies à
sa guise, oubliant parfois des tronçons entiers d'escalier, mêlant
avec une inconscience et une énergie aveugles le grandiose et le
vulgaire, le barbare et l'exquis, l'excellent et le pire. (1966:X:924)

In addition to the use of a strikingly similar imagery, one notes a considerable difference in tone between the two texts. It is as if Zola's admiration for Balzac, rekindled by a rereading of *La comédie humaine* in 1869, has given way in the fiction to a sense of awe and oppression.[12] I shall suggest shortly an explanation for the rather puzzling discrepancy in Zola's perception of Balzac.

While wishing his work to be "tout autre chose" than Balzac's—"Je ne veux pas peindre la socidté contemporaine, mais une seule famille, en montrant le jeu de la race modifiée par les milieux (1960:V:1737)—Zola nonetheless considered himself a disciple of "le maître du roman moderne" (1966:XI:157), stating: "On avance dans la voie qu'il a tracée, chaque nouveau venu poussera l'analyse plus loin et élargira la méthode" (1966:XI:58). The novelist's position toward Romanticism and Hugo was significantly different. It was not one of continuation by "improvement," but one of dismissal. If the achievements of Balzac were groundbreaking and worth improving upon, those of Hugo and Romanticism were more superficial. In July 1869, as he was composing *La fortune*, Zola wrote of Romantic poets: "Nos poètes ont de délicieux turlututus dans lesquels ils soufflent d'adorables petites choses. J'admire très volontiers leur orfèvrerie. Mais j'aimerais mieux un maître *bûcheron* dont les puissants coups *de cognée* ébranleraient la *forêt* poétique" (1966:X:883).[13] It is significant that the image of the "master lumberjack" reappears in the first chapter of *La fortune*. Describing to Miette the composition of the first contingent of marchers, Silvère comments: "Les *bûcherons* des *forêts* de la Seille [...]. Sur un signe de leurs chefs, ces hommes iraient jusqu'à Paris, enfonçant les portes des villes à coups *de cognée*, comme ils abattent les vieux chênes-lièges de la montagne" (29). In the context of our "scriptural" reading of the "colonne," it is legitimate to view the first contingent as the embodiment of Zola's aesthetic ambition. This interpretation is all the more plausible as the "chênes-lièges" which the lumberjacks cut down would seem to anticipate the equivalence that Zola was later to establish between the image of the oak tree and Romanticism. In 1878, realizing the difficulty in doing away with Romanticism and the figure of Hugo, the novelist writes: "Il semble impossible que d'ici à longtemps aucune plante nouvelle pousse dans notre sol littéraire, à l'ombre du chêne immense que Victor Hugo a planté. Ce chêne du lyrisme romantique étend ses branches à l'infini" (1966:XII:371). More generally, the use of a military image like that of the column of marchers to express a literary reality is worth noting, for it anticipates the very rhetoric that Zola is later to employ in non-fictional writings. While *Une campagne* and *Nouvelle campagne*, the titles of literary essays written in

1880–81 and 1895–96 for *Le Figaro* are a case in point, the following sentence from *Le roman expérimental*, written ten years after *La fortune*, more readily materializes the symbolic tenor of the column: "Le siècle appartenait aux naturalistes, aux fils directs de Diderot, dont les *bataillons* solides suivaient et allaient fonder un véritable État" (1966:X:1236).[14] Finally, the presence of Zolian aesthetics is also implicit in the powerful flow of the crowd ("le flot hurlant de la foule" [27], "cette longue coulée" [28], "la foule coulait" [32]) which anticipates Zola's depiction of the "mouvement naturaliste" as "le mouvement même de toute la société contemporaine [...] un immense courant qui roule sur le monde, en entraînant chaque chose vers le but commun, avec une force lente et irrésistible" (1066:XII:73). In spite of Zola's desire to sever himself and his literature from Hugo and Romanticism, and in spite of the optimism with which he welcomes his task, it is legitimate to ask to what degree the novelist's ambition is realized.[15] Thus, the liminary chapter of *La fortune* in which we see Zola's ambition to found a new type of literature brought to life, is, ironically (one should say, tragically), grounded in one of the key texts of the precursor: *La legende des siècles*.[16] More precisely, the incipit of *La fortune* is to *Les Rougon-Macquart* what the prologue of *La legende des siècles* is to that work, i.e., the narration of its origins, and it might well be called, like Hugo's prologue, "la vision d'où est sortie ce livre."[17] The following words spoken by the I-narrator of the prologue of *La légende* might indeed be those of Silvère/Zola:

> De l'empreinte profonde et grave qu'a laissée
> Ce chaos de la vie à ma sombre pensée,
> De cette vision du mouvant genre humain,
> Ce livre, où près d'hier on entrevoit demain,
> Est sorti, reflétant de poëme en poëme
> Toute cette clarté vertigineuse et bliéme;
>
> (*Légende* 13)

Just as the texts which make up *La Légende* expound on the major sections and figures of the wall of humanity described in the initial vision by the narrator of the prologue, the twenty volumes of the *Rougon-Macquart* series expound on the content of the vision of the column/work presented in the opening chapter. Like Hugo's book of poems, the *Rougon-Macquart* series is born out of an initial vision which it reflects "de roman en roman," and the resemblances between the two visions are striking. While the military dimension of Hugo's wall—"on eût dit une armée / Pétrifée avec le chef qui la conduit" (*Légende* 8)—receives full-fledged recognition in the military image of the column, Hugo's "mur des siècles," described as a "bloc," "une muraille et [...] une foule" (*Légende* 8), is replicated in the opening pages of *La fortune*, in the "masse compacte, solide" (28) of the column of marchers. Moreover, the vastness and clamor of Hugo's wall, the "bruit de multitude" (*Légende* 8) that rises from the "chaos d'êtres" (*Légende* 9) and "peuple de fantomes" (*Légende* 11) of the prologue, are now echoed in "la grande voix de cette tempête humaine" (27) which in *La fortune* seems to be rising from "un peuple invisible et innombrable" (27). Hugo's "évolutions de groupes monstrueux" (*Légende* 8) have now become "[la] longue coulée grouillante et mugissante, monstrueusement indistincte" (28), and one observes a similar incidence of light on each crowd:

> Parfois l'éclair faisait sur la paroi livide
> Luire des millions defaces tout à coup.
> (*Légende* 8)

Quand les premiers insurgés entrèrent dans ce rayon, ils se trouvèrent subitement éclairés d'une clarté dont les blancheurs aiguës découpaient avec une netteté singuliière les moindres arêtes des visages et des costumes. (28)

The presence of Hugo in *Les origines*, as Zola calls *La fortune* (4), soon generates a high degree of anxiety in the narration. It is interesting that the passage that is most telling in this respect is the passage of the night crossing of the Garrigues countryside by the "insurgés," the very passage in which we have identified the presence of Balzac. While being the rendition into fiction of Zola's May 1869 article on the author of *La comedie humaine*, the depiction of the march through the desolate Provençal landscape simultaneously echoes the fragmented picture of mankind that appears to the I-narrator in Hugo's prologue to *La légende*:

LA FORTUNE DES ROUGON

À gauche, la plaine s'élargit, immense tapis vert, piqué de loin en loin par les taches grises des villages. À droite, la chaîne des Garrigues dresse ses pics désolés, ses champs de pierres, ses blocs couleur de rouille, comme roussis par le soleil. Le grand chemin, formant chaussée du côté de la rivière, passe au milieu de rocs énormes, entre lesquels se montrent, à chaque pas, des bouts de la vallée. Rien n'est plus sauvage, plus étrangement grandiose, que cette route taillée dans le flanc même des collines. La nuit surtout, ces lieux ont une horreur sacrée. Sous la lumière pale, les insurgés s'avançaient comme dans une avenue de ville détruite, ayant aux deux bords des *debris* de *temples*; la lune faisait de chaque rocher un *fût* de colonne *tronqué*, un chapiteau écroulé, une *muraille* trouée de mystèrieux portiques. En haut, la masse des Garrigues dormait, à peine blanchie d'une teinte laiteuse, pareille a une immense cité cyclopéenne dont les *tours*, les obélisques, les maisons aux terrasses hautes, auraient caché une moitié du ciel; et, dans les fonds, du côté de la plaine, se creusait, s'élargissait un océan de *clartés* diffuses, une étendue vague, sans bornes, où flottaient des nappes de *brouillard* lumineux. La bande insurrectionnelle aurait pu croire qu'elle suivait une chaussée gigantesque, un chemin de ronde construct au bord d'une mer phosphorescence et tournant autour d'une *Babel* inconnue. (162)

LA LEGENDE DES SIÈCLES

C'était une *muraille* et c'était une foule [...]. (8)

La pâle vision reparut lézardée,
Comme un *temple* en ruine aux gigantesques *fûts*,
Laissant voir de l'abîme entre ses pans confus. (12)

Au lieu d'un continent, c'était un archipel;
Au lieu d'un univers, c'était un cimetière;
Par places se dressait quelque lugubre pierre,
Quelque pilier debout, ne soutenant plus rien;
Tous les siècles *tronqués* gisaient; plus de lien;
Chaque époque pendait démantelée; aucune
N'était sans déchirure et n'était sans lacune;
Et partout croupissaient sir le passé détruit
Des stagnations d'ombre et des flaques de nuit.
Ce n'était plus, parmi les *brouillards* où l'oeil plonge,
Que le *debris* difforme et chancelant d'un songe. (12–13)

Toute cette *clarté* vertigineuse et blême [...]. (13)
Ce livre, c'est le reste effrayant de *Babel*;
C'est la lugubre Tour des Choses, l'édifice
Du bien, du mal, des pleurs, du deuil, du sacrifice,
Fier jadis, dominant les lointains horizons,
Aujourd'hui n'ayant plus que de hideux tronçons,
Spars, couchés, perdus dans l'obscure vallée. (14)

The discrepancy previously noted between the tone of the article on Balzac and the tone of the fiction can now be explained. Or rather, it can be dismissed. If the passage from *La fortune* bears the marks of both Balzac and Hugo, "the two paternal imagos that presided over his [Zola's] writing destinies" (Schor 1978b:179), one realizes, in view of the organic relationship uniting the first chapter of *La fortune* with *La légende des siècles*, that it is not so much "la grande ombre de Balzac" (Zola 1966:XI:612) as it is the gigantic shadow of Hugo that obscures these lines and, by metonymy, all of Zola's writing. Behind Balzac, whom Zola regarded as "notre véritable pére" (1966:XI:65), stands Hugo the bad father, the ogre. The scene in the Garrigues is steeped in an inhibiting, paralysing aura, with such details as "[l]'horreur sacrée," "la lumière pâle," "[la] cité cyclopéenne" and "[le] fût de colonne tronqué," conjuring up a castration fantasy. With its tone of dread and veneration, as well as its architectural imagery, the passage anticipates Zola's 1877 perspective on his precursor: "Avoir jamais sa taille, c'est un rêve fou [...]. Il serait beau déjà d'avoir les muscles assez forts pour remuer quelques strophes, tandis que lui a bâti des tours cyclopéennes, avec les matériaux inépuisables de ses vers" (1966:XII:301). In light of what precedes, one may suggest that the "monstrueuse figure" (10), which occupies the center of the "aire" Saint-Mittre, the metaphorical worksite of *Les Rougon-Macquart*, may represent the anxiety-provoking literary father, Hugo.[18]

There remains to be examined one aspect of Zolian writing not acknowledged in the *Documents et plans préparatoires* of the series that ties in with Zola's complex perspective on literary property. If we accept the march of the Republicans to be the allegory of the "Notes générales sur la marche de l'oeuvre," special attention must be given to the fact that toward the end of the opening chapter of *La fortune* the progression of the marchers is momentarily stopped. In metaphorical terms this pause would signify that the progress of writing, the motion of *Les Rougon-Macquart* is momentarily jeopardized. The event that takes place during this pause needs to be recalled before a metaphorical interpretation can be proposed. Overcome by feelings of euphoria at the sight of the insurgents, Silvère and Miette join the crowd of Republican marchers. Their joy, however, is short-lived, as one of the insurgents, having recognized Miette, exclaims: "Son père est au bagne, nous ne voulons pas avec nous la fille d'un voleur et d'un assassin" (33). Miette proceeds to defend her father, Chantegreil, against the accusation of theft ("Vous mentez [...] si mon père a tué, il n'a pas volé" [34]) and is spared further shame only by the somewhat miraculous intervention of a man who has known Chantegreil and rehabilitates him in the memory of others: "Le gendarme qu'il a descendu, à la chasse, d'un coup de fusil, devait déjà le tenir lui-même au bout de sa carabine. On se défend, que voulez-vous! Mais Chantegreil était un honnête homme, Chantegreil n'a pas volé" (34). The question of Chantegreil's innocence in matter of theft is far, however, from being settled. We detect the complexity of the issue later in the novel when we discover Miette's perspective on her father's actions: "Alors elle soutenait que son père avait bien fait de tuer le gendarme, que *la terre appartient à tout le monde*, qu'on a le droit de tirer des coups de fusil où l'on veut et quand on veut" (205, my emphasis). The facts can now be reconstructed: Chantegreil is a poacher who has killed a gendarme after the latter has most likely caught him in the act of stealing. Two opposing approaches to the concept of property are here pitted against each other. While to the eyes of society Chantegreil is viewed as a thief, Miette believes her father to be innocent, invoking the concept of collective property in his defense. Her father has not stolen, she argues, he has merely helped himself to what belongs to everyone. It is significant that the way in which Miette defends her father against accusations of theft echoes the manner in which Zola defended himself against the accusations of literary theft, i.e. plagiarism, leveled against him throughout his career. For instance, accused in 1877 of having plagiarized parts of Denis Poulot's *Le sublime* to write *L'assommoir*, Zola argued that he had not stolen but merely borrowed from reality, since *Le sublime* was "un libre de documents."[19]

It is not surprising that Miette's open relationship to nature, which exemplifies her father's perspective on property, anticipates and allegorizes Zola's 1896 view of literary property:

> Miette, avec cette conscience large des femmes, ne se gênait pas pour cueillir une grappe de raisins, une branche d'amandes vertes, aux vignes, aux amandiers, dont les rameaux la fouettaient au passage". (199).

> [...] la propriété d'une oeuvre de littérature ou d'une oeuvre d'art ne sera jamais une propriété comme un champ, un chateau, une

épée ou une bêche. La matérialité, le libre imprimé, la partition gravée, en disparait, et il ne reste que l'idée qui flamboie, la fiction qui ravit, la mélodie qui chante. C'est la fleur sauvage poussée au bord du chemin, l'oiseau libre entendu dans le buisson, que tous les passants se croient en droit de prendre et d'emporter. Est-ce qu'on est un voleur pour ramasser sous le ciel clair des pensées, des images et des sons, qu'un autre avait pris lui-même il la communauté? Ce n'est qu'un échange, au gré du vent et de la rencontre. Les Brands écrivains, les grands artistes seraient indignes d'avoir été élus glorieusement, s'ils ne consentaient à luire pour tout le monde, comme le soleil. (1966:XIV:762–63)

Whereas the Silvère/Miette couple actualizes the open, idealistic, romantic side of Zolian writing presented in the *Documents et plans préparatoires*, the Chantegreil/Miette couple brings to light an unsuspected facet of the novelist and his art. In *Chantegreil*, we have Zola the *"chantre,"* the poacher, who, for the sake of his art, adheres to a distinctively unique, "non-bourgeois" conception of literary property. In turn, Miette embodies a more modern conception of writing—that of a writing which is no longer the product of pure inspiration as it is in the Romantic tradition but rather, a composite product, made of others' writings.

The coexistence of these two conceptions of writing (the Romantic and the Realist) creates, however, a major conflict within Zola. Although one side of the novelist espouses the poacher's cavalier, open attitude towards property, another side of the writer cannot remain totally guilt-free while practicing this brand of writing. When later in the novel Silvère reflects about Miette: "Elle n'avait qu'un défaut. Elle maraudait mais il l'en aurait corrigée," he echoes Zola's more bourgeois stand on literary property expressed in the "Notes préparatoires" to the series: "Dans mon artiste, ou un autre, dire qu'étant enfant, il aimait *voler*; plus tard la raison combat cela" (1960:V:1724). While wishing to be liberated from conventional morals and act as a freethinker, Zola falls prey to society's narrower definition of property, viewing himself the way society views Chantegreil, i.e., as a thief, or, translated into metaphorical terms, as a plagiarist.

Although the artist's theft seems to be dismissed as a bad habit, a "péché de jeunesse" that can be outgrown—in the "Notes préparatoires" the artist only steals "étant enfant," and in the fiction Miette is but a young girl—, Chantegreil's trial proves otherwise. If we recognize a facet of Zola in the poacher Chantegreil, then this trial may be read as Zola's staging, on the threshold of the *Rougon-Macquart* series, of his own trial on the grounds of what he perceives to some degree to be plagiarism. Just as Chantegreil's trial momentarily puts the march of the insurgents in jeopardy, Zola's personal wrestling with literary ethics, symbolized by this trial, has the potential of hindering, even paralyzing "la marche de l'écriture." It is remarkable that the issue is not resolved. Against all logic, Chantegreil's trial is aborted and the poacher is absolved without his guilt ever being proven. Thus, the writing of the series is allowed to proceed without the question of Zola's relationship to literary property ever being clarified. The issue is swept under the carpet, left unresolved, repressed.

Henri Mitterand has insisted on the unique value of the first pages of *La fortune des Rougon*, noting how one finds embedded in them "les liturgies de la mort, les actes du sacrilège, les étapes du châtiment, le mariage de l'amour et de la mort" (1980:176). To this list one may add "les liturgies de l'écriture," for the "pur tableau pittoresque qui ouvre l'oeuvre" is also a visionary "tableau" of the writing enterprise of *Les Rougon-Macquart*. However, the incipit chapter of the series not only modulates into fiction the optimistic, rational discourse of the *Documents et plans préparatoires*, it also highlights areas of darkness and tension central to Zola's writing and not acknowledged in the preparatory work. Thus Zola's writing appears fraught by contradictions, the locus of conflictual perspectives, particularly in the area of influence and literary ethics, as the author, who believes himself free from influence and above conventional literary morals, is awed by the cumbersome figure of Hugo and bogged down by bourgeois morals.[20] In the end the powerful repression of these issues—issues which involve the nature and identity of Zolian writing—is to give in part its dynamics to the *Rougon-Macquart* series.

NOTES

1. Zola 1960:V:1760: in this volume are reproduced the *Documents et plans préparatoires des Rougon-Macquart*; they consist of three sections: the *Documents*, the *Notes générales* (which include the "Differences entre Balzac et moi," the "Notes générales sur la marche de l'oeuvre," and the "Notes générales sur la nature de l'oeuvre"), and the *Plans*. For an extensive discussion of these materials, see Gourdin Servenière's Introduction (Zola 1990:vii–cxx).

2. Schor recognizes the founding role played by the opening chapter of *La fortune* for the rest of the series when, commenting on the tombstone of the former Saint-Mittre cemetery described in the initial chapter, she claims: "it would not be any exaggeration to affirm that all of the Rougon-Macquart rests on this moss-eaten

stone" (1978b:19). See more particularly the first chapter of Schor 1978b, entitled
"The Founding Myth" (especially 3–21), and also Schor 1978a.

3. If one excepts these remarks by Mitterand, readings of the first chapter, and
more generally of the whole novel have not explored the "metatextual" dimension of
La fortune. Among the varied readings which the novel has generated, one would need
to mention, besides Schor's Girardian perspective on *La fortune*, Chaitin's
psychoanalytical analysis which parallels "the search for truth and freedom" in the
novel with "the quest for psychic integration" (158). Becker has considered the novel
in its contemporary setting viewing it as the illustration of the rise to power of a
"classe de petits bourgeois entreprenants et envieux, d'affairistes sans scrupules"
(141). More recently, Cosset has used *La fortune* as "un champ d'investigation
particulièrement adéquat pour observer les méthodes zoliennes et en déduire les
principes généraux mis en oeuvre dans les *Rougon-Macquart* pour faire part au lecteur
des discours et des pensées des personnages" (157).

4. Zola 1960:I:7. All subsequent page references to this edition of *La fortune* will
appear in the text.

5. Silvère is the first of a series of characters who act as author figures in *Les
Rougon-Macquart*. Thus, Lethbridge 1985 views Étienne Lantier in *Germinal* as a
representative of Zola. In reference to *L'assommoir* the same critic reminds us that
"there is widespread critical agreement that the figure of Goujet is implicitly
associated with Zola himself" (1990:133). Exploring the scriptural dimension of *La
bête humaine*, Lethbridge stresses how "the 'mécanicien' offers us the most satisfying
variant of the novelist as craftsman" (1990:135), while Hamon notices how in the
same novel judge "Denizet [...] est bien le lieu d'incarnation d'un vif débat
d'esthétique littéraire" (142), how "[il] possède de nombreux traits, comme dévoyés
par l'excès de psychologie, d'un romancier naturaliste: 'analyse', 'logique', 'vérité'"
(143).

6. Looking at the Miette/Silvère relationship, critics have reflected upon the
theme of unhappy sexuality. Got has shown how "Zola fantasme inconsciemment
l'union charnelle de ses héros, que consciemment il leur refuse" (157), while Belgrand
has demonstrated more generally that "la qualité [des] [...] relations amoureuses [de
Miette et Silvère] [...] révèlent la situation de l'auteur face aux précédents
mouvements littéraires: il n'y a pas rupture mais mutation" (51).

7. Of Romantic artists awaiting inspiration Zola will say in 1877: "ils
l'attendaient comme une maîtresse qui vient ou ne vient pas" (1966:X1:63).

8. For a discussion of the *Documents et plans* of *Les Rougon-Macquart* see more
specifically Mitterand's chapter "La genèse du roman zolien" (1987:37–54).
Mitterand stresses "la prégnance, dans l'*Ébauche*, d'un discours volontariste,
planificateur, et la présence massive, opaque, d'un sujet régisseur et raisonneur" (42).

9. In his discussion of the various types of "élans" present in *Les Rougon-
Macquart*, Dezalay has noticed how in *Germinal* "l'impression de massivité donnée
par les sept grandes parties" of the novel as well as the frequency of the term
"poussée" in numerous sentences of the novel may well transpose into the fiction
Zola's wish for a "construction solide des masses," the importance of "la logique, la
poussée de ces chapitres" (1983:52).

10. The number of characters in *Les Rougon-Macquart* approximates 1,500.

11. According to Paul Alexis, Zola began writing *La fortune* in May 1869; see Zola 1960:V:1536.

12. A new edition of *La comédie humaine* by publisher Michel Lévy had been coming out since the beginning of 1869; see Zola 1960:V:1536.

13. Zola will in fact use this imagery when referring to Romantic style and more particularly Hugo's throughout the 1870's. He will express his desire "[de] porter la hache" "dons ce style si capricieusement ouvragé, si chargé d'ornements de toutes sortes" (1966:XI:247). Also he will claim that "le meilleur service que des amis pieux pourraient lui rendre [à Hugo] après sa mort, ce serait de porter la hache dans son oeuvre si considérable" (1966:XII:324).

14. The sentence appears in a 1879 study entitled "Le naturalisme au théâtre" and integrated in the collection of essays making up *Le roman expérimental*.

15. Zola's indebtedness to Romanticism has been noted by several critics, from Wurmser who recognizes in Zola "le plus romantique des grands romanciers français" (51) to, more recently, Braun who writes that Zola is "l'héritier de la déjà longue et complexe histoire du romantisme européen. Il intègre la dimension symbolique et mythique venant du romantisme" (70).

16. Hugo's imprint upon Zola can in fact be identified throughout *La fortune* (see Armstrong 1996b). More generally, Dezalay has argued that in *Les Rougon-Macquart* Zola "s'est livré longtemps et assidûment à une véritable 'lecture-écriture' de Hugo" (1985:436).

17. One is here reminded of Walker's claim that "[f]or [Zola], as for Hugo, his first great literary hero, poetic creation and world creation were barely distinguishable" (180).

18. The anxiety generated in Zola by Hugo, the figure of the precursor, is also strong in the third novel of the series, *Le ventre de Paris* (see Armstrong 1996a). The issue of Zola's repression of Hugo has also been explored by Zarifopol-Johnston who views *Notre-Dame de Paris* as "*Germinal*'s ghostly intertext" (193) and argues that in *Germinal* "Zola has tried to bury deep from view" (193) Hugo's presence in his work.

19. "Le *sublime* nest pas une oeuvre d'imagination, un roman; c'est un libre de documents dont l'auteur cite des mots entendus et des faits vrais. Lui emprunter quelque chose, c'est l'emprunter à la réalité," writes Zola (1978:II:548). Zola holds on to the same arguments years later in 1896 when he was accused of plagiarizing a work entitled *Le Vatican, les papes, et la civilisation* to write *Rome*. The book is, according to Zola, "une compilation sur le Vatican," "une oeuvre collective" (1966:XIV:797).

20. The issue of Hugo's influence on Zola and that of Zola's perception of himself as plagiarist are in fact closely related. For more on the subject see Armstrong 1997.

REFERENCES

Armstrong, Marie-Sophie. 1996a. "Hugo's 'égouts' and *Le ventre de Paris.*" *French Review* 69.3: 394–408.

———. 1996b. "Une lecture 'Hugo-centrique' de *La fortune des Rougon.*" *Romanic Review* 87.2:271–83.

———. 1997. "Où le petit Zola tire parti de Hugo le Grand, et du dilemne qui en résulte." *French Forum* 22.2:165–80.

Belgrand, Anne. "Le couple Silvère-Miette dans *La fortune des Rougon.*" *Romantisme: revue du dix-neuvième siècle* 18.62 (1988): 51–59.

Becker, Colette. "Les machines à sous de *La fortune des Rougon.*" *Romantisme revue du dix-neuvième siècle* 13.40 (1983): 141–52.

Braun, Martin. "Émile Zola et le romantisme: la mine à travers un symbole de la littérature européenne du XIXe siècle." *Zola sans frontières.* Ed. Auguste Dezalay. Strasbourg: Presses de l'Université de Strasbourg, 1996. 57–72.

Chaitin, Gilbert. "The Voices of the Dead: Love, Death and Politics in Zola's *La fortune des Rougon.*" *Literature and Psychology* 26.3 (1976): 131–44, and 26.4 (1976): 148–58.

Cosset, Evelyne. "La représentation de 'l'acte de parole' des personnages dans *La fortune des Rougon.*" *Les cahiers naturalistes* 65 (1991): 155–68.

Dezalay, Auguste. 1983. *L'opéra des Rougon-Macquart: essai de rythmologie romanesque.* Paris: Klincksieck.

———. 1985. "Lecture du génie, génie de la lecture: *Germinal* et *Les misérables.*" *Revue d'histoire littéraire de la France* 3:435–46.

Got, Olivier. "L'idylle de Miette et de Silvère dans *La fortune des Rougon*: structure d'un mythe." *Les cahiers naturalistes* 46 (1973): 146–64.

Hamon, Philippe. "Le juge Denizet dans *La bête humaine.*" *Mimesis et Semiosis.* Ed. Philippe Hamon and Jean-Pierre Leduc-Adine. Paris: Nathan, 1992. 137–44.

Hugo, Victor. *La légende des siècles.* Ed. Jacques Truchet. Bibliothèque de la Pléiade. Paris: Gallimard, 1950.

Lethbridge, Robert. 1985. "Étienne Lantier 'romancier': genèse et mise en abîme." *Les cahiers naturalistes* 59:43–54.

———. 1990. "Zola and the Limits of Crafts." *Zola and the Craft of Fiction.* Ed. Robert Lethbridge and Terry Keefe. Leicester: Leicester University Press. 133–49.

Mitterand, Henri. 1980. "Une archéologie mentale: *Le roman expérimental* et *La fortune des Rougon.*" *Le discours du roman.* Paris: Presses universitaires de France. 164–85.

———. 1987. *Le regard et le signe.* Paris: Presses universitaires de France.

Schor, Naomi. 1978a. "Mythe des origines, origine des mythes: *La fortune des*

Rougon." *Les cahiers naturalistes* 24.52:124–34.

———. 1978b. *Zola's Crowds*. Baltimore: Johns Hopkins University Press.

Walker, Philip. "Zola: Poet of an Age of World Destruction and Renewal." *Critical Essays on Émile Zola*. Ed. David Baguley. Boston: G. K. Hall, 1986. 172–85.

Wurmser, André. "Ancienne maison Balzac, Zola successeur." *Europe* 30.83–84 (1952): 45–54.

Zarifopol-Johnston, Ilinca. *To Kill a Text: The Dialogic Fiction of Hugo, Dickens, and Zola*. Newark: University of Delaware Press, 1995.

Zola, Émile. 1960. *Les Rougon-Macquart*. Ed. Henri Mitterand. Bibliothèque de la Pléiade. 5 vols. Paris: Gallimard, 1960–67.

———. 1966. *Oeuvres complètes*. Ed. Henri Mitterand. 15 vols. Paris: Cercle du livre précieux, 1966–70.

———. 1978. *Correspondance*. Ed. B. H. Bakker and Colette Becker. 10 vols. Montréal: Presses de l'Université de Montréal, 1978–95.

———. 1990. *La fortune des Rougon*. Ed. Gina Gourdin Servenière. Geneva: Strategic Communications, 1990.

MICHELLE E. BLOOM

"Zola Fantastique": An Analysis of the Story "La mort d'Olivier Bécaille"

Given Zola's longstanding status as the "chef de l'école naturaliste,"[1] the title "Zola fantastique" is an unlikely one. Focusing on Zola as a *conteur* is no less surprising, since his short stories receive little critical attention, and most of that dates back to the 1960s and 1970s. Even in *Zola et les genres*, a recent work (1993), the critic David Baguley relegates the stories to parenthetical status, appropriately at the same time that he acknowledges and responds to the current critical imperative to devote attention to what he calls "textes mineurs de grands écrivains" (23). When Baguley declares, "Mon sujet consiste donc à définir la 'généricité' de certains romans (et contes) de Zola ...," he places Zola's stories in parentheses, both literally and figuratively (1). In tracing the evolution (read: progress, teleology) of Zola's *oeuvre*, Baguley proceeds to include the "contes" as one of the "formes 'adolescentes'" that Zola used in his early days as a writer (2). Indeed, Zola wrote the short stories at the outset of his career and, to his credit, Baguley does devote a chapter to Zola's "contes de fée," but "adolescent forms" is distinctly pejorative, regardless of the quotes the critic places around the adjective. In any event, the aim of my study is not to evaluate the quality of Zola's stories, one way or the other, but to demonstrate their critical interest, which is not necessarily a function of quality.

From *Symposium* 53, no. 2 (Summer 1999). © 1999 by the Helen Dwight Reid Educational Foundation.

A brief review of the criticism that does address Zola's stories will
provide my point of departure and will serve to contextualize my work. I also
aim to demonstrate how my approach calls much deserved attention to the
Zola story "La mort d'Olivier Bécaille" (1879) by treating it as an entity and
in terms of a theme (death) and a closely related genre (the fantastic) rather
than by studying it in relation to Zola's *oeuvre*, be it the Rougon-Macquart or
his other stories.[2] To this end, in the second part of this essay, I will analyze
"La mort d'Olivier Bécaille" as a fantastic tale. This approach will afford a
focus on this short story as a literary text (a linguistic construct) and will
contribute to the view of Zola as a multifaceted figure, who is a "conteur
fantastique" in addition to the "chef du naturalisme." Finally, this type of
analysis will allow for a critical examination of Tzvetan Todorov's overly
rigid definition of the fantastic, as delineated in his seminal study, *Introduction
à la littérature fantastique*.

"Zola conteur": An Overview of the Criticism

The proliferation of French paperback editions of Zola stories in recent
years, which reflects publishers' interest in them, may also anticipate the
appearance of critical attention to the stories in the near future.[3] However,
at this point, most of the little criticism devoted to Zola as a short story
writer dates back decades, as mentioned above, and entails the biographical
and literary historical approaches favored at the time. Accordingly, those
critical essays tend to contribute to our picture of Zola's life and his *oeuvre*
without doing justice to his short stories as literary texts. The biographical
readings of the stories include Roger Ripoll's discussion, in the "Notice" to
the Pléiade edition of Zola's *contes et nouvelles*, of the parallel between the
author's own obsession with death and that of the titular character of "La
mort d'Olivier Bécaille" (1534–1536). At the same time, Ripoll himself
ultimately and aptly rejects the biographical reading when he concludes that
the story is not a "document biographique" (1536).

The literary historical criticism of "Zola conteur," which takes the
more precise form of treating the stories as precursors of the *Rougon-
Macquart*, falls into the trap of subjugating the stories to the novels, seeing
them as a means to an end, worthy of analysis only, or at least primarily,
because of their relationship to the works to which they led. Indeed, much of
the critical attention to "La mort d'Olivier Bécaille" results from and
considers its anticipation of *La joie de vivre*.[4] Although such comparative
studies potentially illuminate story and novel alike, one must be careful not

to treat the former as dependent and secondary works. As Ripoll justly argues, "Il faut ... prendre ces textes [les contes] au sérieux, c'est-à-dire les considérer pour eux-mêmes, et non pas comme des dépendances des Rougon-Macquart. La production de Zola conteur a sa cohérence propre" (xi). However, Ripoll seems to contradict his own claim in the following statement: "Ces récits, si longtemps négligés parce qu'ils s'accordaient mal avec l'image que l'on se faisait de Zola.... Les lire nous amène à lire autrement Les Rougon-Macquart" (xvi). I do not aim to illuminate Zola's novels but instead to call critical attention to one of his stories, "La mort d'Olivier Bécaille," insofar as it sheds light on the "fantastique du dix-neuvième siècle."

A combination of biographical and literary historical approaches treats the stories as "early Zola." Such studies offer a portrait of the hardships of the struggling, up-and-coming writer and at the same time diminish his early writings. Ranging chronologically from Henri d'Almeras's 1901 article "Les débuts inconnus d'Emile Zola" to the above mentioned comments by Baguley, these commentaries tend at worst to write off Zola's early writings and at best to slight them unintentionally, by virtue of considering them and their author "immature."

Of more interest to us here is criticism that compares "Zola conteur" to other short story writers, in particular because these other authors tend to be "maîtres du fantastique," which leads right into the second part of this essay. Interestingly, and not surprisingly, at the same time that "La mort d'Olivier Bécaille" evokes fantastic writers other than Zola, some of the criticism that seems to pair him with more canonical fantastic writers must be read carefully because it does not really do so.[5] For instance, in his 1968 article "Zola conteur," Robert Ricatte points up the difference between Zola and a "pure fantastic" writer, rather than the similarity, when he says: "*Pour une nuit d'amour*—ce conte dont aurait aimé peut-être qu'il fut écrit par Barbey d'Aurévilly plutôt que par Zola" (213).

The title of Baguley's 1967 article, "Maupassant avant la lettre? A Study of the Zola Short Story: 'Les Coquillages de M. Chabre'" couples Zola and Maupassant, and the essay follows suit. However, the object of study is the comic, not the fantastic, which is certainly appropriate given the story in question. Although this comparison does not further my argument about Zola and the fantastic directly, before moving onward it is relevant to point out that Baguley's work on "Les Coquillages de M. Chabre" does well to call attention to yet another side of Zola, beyond "Zola naturaliste" and other than "Zola fantastique": "Zola comique."[6] Unlike Gautier's fantastic, as seen in "Onuphrius," and indeed as opposed to many works in the genre, Zola's fantastic, as exemplified in "La mort d'Olivier Bécaille," lacks humor. As Baguley aptly puts it with reference to these two stories: "Tandis que Gautier se plonge avec légèreté dans une fantaisie littéraire qui tourne parfois au bouffon, Zola prend tout au sérieux" (1966, 125). Consequently, I would argue that "Zola comique" adds yet another dimension to this multifaceted figure.

Criticism that does draw parallels between Zola and nineteenth-century fantastic writers evokes a wide variety of the latter, making a compelling case for "Zola fantastique." In "Les sources d'inspiration de Zola conteur," F. W. J. Hemmings compares the Zola of "Soeur des pauvres" (*Contes à Ninon*) with Nodier (36–37). "La mort d'Olivier Bécaille" is an even more fantastic text than "Soeur des pauvres" by Todorov's definition, which excludes fairy tales, as I will explain later. Studies of "La mort d'Olivier Bécaille" in particular evoke the gamut of well-known nineteenth-century fantastic writers. For instance, in their celebrated *Journal*, the Goncourt brothers describe the short story in terms of the American master of the genre: "La mort d'Olivier Bécaille ... ressemble à une imitation de Poe faite par Henri Monnier" (1027).

In his preface to the 1991 collection of Zola stories, *Pour une nuit d'amour*, Yves le Gars states that, "Comme tous les vrais textes fantastiques, 'La mort d'Olivier Bécaille' tire sa source des obsessions et des cauchemars de l'auteur" (10). If the second clause of this remark leads back to the type of biographical-psychoanalytical reading I would like to avoid, the first part of the sentence more importantly deems the story a "real fantastic text," transcending the critical tendency to brand Zola a "one-hundred percent pure Naturalist"—as if such a label is not mythical—retrospectively, with the benefit of hindsight. Le Gars continues to place "La mort d'Olivier Bécaille" where it belongs, generically, when he comments, "Littérairement parlant, ce texte s'inscrit dans la tradition du conte fantastique du XIXe siècle: on pense à Gautier ... ou au récit de catalepsie qu'on trouve dans *Le Colonel Chabert* de Balzac" (11).

As far as criticism that comments on the affinities of "La mort d'Olivier Bécaille" with other fantastic stories of its time, Baguley's article "Les sources et les fortunes des nouvelles de Zola" (1966) suggests resonances with Poe, Hoffmann, and the Balzac of *Le Colonel Chabert* even before arriving at the above mentioned Gautier of "Onuphrius," on which he focuses. In declaring, "L'aventure de Bécaille est calquée sur celle d'Onuphrius" (125), Baguley insists not on the spirit of the resemblance, but on the letter. By contrast, my interest is in Zola's success in capturing the spirit of the fantastic, as suggested by the notion that "La mort d'Olivier Bécaille" evokes the nineteenth-century names at the core of the genre—not only Poe, Hoffmann, Balzac, and Gautier, but also Barbey, Maupassant, and Nodier.[7] Accordingly, my analysis will not entail a comparison between "La mort d'Olivier Bécaille" and one other fantastic story, although it will include brief comparisons as appropriate. Instead, I will focus on "La mort d'Olivier Bécaille" with reference to Todorov.

"Zola fantastique": An Analysis of "La mort d'Olivier Bécaille"

The beginning of "La mort d'Olivier Bécaille" refers to the end of a life, but it does so in an impossible way: "C'est un samedi, à six heures du matin que je suis mort après trois jours de maladie" (127). In his previously mentioned preface to the 1991 collection *Pour une nuit d'amour*, Le Gars suggests that this opening "illustre parfaitement la nature fictive, pour ne pas dire fantômatique, du 'Je' de l'écriture" (11). More prosaically put, in this impossible and seemingly clear-cut narrative situation, a first-person narrator, Olivier Bécaille of the title, as we later learn, narrates posthumously. By "impossible," I mean, as does Todorov, not possible within the realm of the natural world, according to natural laws. Todorov tends to call this "supernatural," although I prefer not to use that term because it tends to be restrictive due to what it does and does not evoke. In any case, Bécaille reveals the situation to be "less impossible" (and less superatural), as well as more complex than it first appears, when he claims that he never died at all. Rather, ill since he and his wife arrived at the Parisian hotel after their long train ride from the provinces, Bécaille, in a cataleptic state as of six o'clock on the morning of their third day in Paris, is mistaken for dead. As he recounts in the continuation of his opening paragraph:

> Ma pauvre femme fouillait depuis un instant dans la malle, où elle cherchait du linge. Lorsqu'elle s'est relevée et qu'elle m'a vu rigide, les yeux ouverts, sans un souffle, elle est accourue, croyant à un évanouissement, me touchant les mains, se penchant sur mon visage. Puis, la terreur l'a prise; et, affolée elle a bégayé, en éclatant en larmes: Mon Dieu! Mon Dieu! Il est mort! (127)

Bécaille's wife Marguerite's diagnosis is confirmed first by her neighbor, Madame Gabin, then by a doctor. If this seems hard to believe, it is nothing compared to what follows: Bécaille is buried alive, then escapes from his coffin. I will return to these events in more detail, but for the moment, the important point is that although Bécaille provides an explanation for this sequence of events in the form of catalepsy, this explanation, to which I will also return, is tenuous enough, and the series of events is improbable enough, that the story remains fantastic.

I will proceed to consider Zola's representation of his narrator's ambiguous position between life and death in light of Todorov's definition of the fantastic, the central element of which is ambiguity. Although the story does not adhere strictly to Todorov's definition of the fantastic, it is a fantastic story by virtue of its representation of the liminal space between life and death. Thus it calls into question the rigidity of Todorov's definition, the core of which is the following:

> D'abord, il faut que le texte oblige le lecteur à considérer le monde des personnages comme un monde de personnes vivantes et à hésiter entre une explication naturelle et une explication surnaturelle des événements évoqués. Ensuite, cette hésitation peut être ressentie également par un personnage ... Enfin il importe que le lecteur adopte une certaine attitude à l'égard du texte: il refusera aussi bien l'interprétation allégorique que l'interprétation "poétique." Ces trois exigences n'ont pas une valeur égale. La première et la troisiéme constituent véritablement le genre; la seconde peut ne pas être satisfaite. (37–38)

In summary, then, Todorov requires the hesitation of the reader, which he defines elsewhere as the implicit reader, rather than the actual reader, or as he puts it, "non tel ou tel lecteur particulier réel, mais une 'fonction' de lecteur, implicite au texte" (36). The hesitation of a character is optional. However, Todorov also demands a non-allegorical, apoetic reading of the text, which means that fairy tales are necessarily and unfortunately excluded from the genre, instead classified as the "merveilleux" (59). He defines the fantastic in relation to the "réel" and the "imaginaire" (29). Generically, his fantastic is sandwiched by what he calls the "étrange" (the uncanny) and the "merveilleux" (the marvelous), which correspond, respectively, with the "réel" and the "imaginaire." If the reader's hesitation is resolved and the supernatural explained by the rational, the text becomes merely "étrange." On the contrary, if the hesitation is resolved in favor of the supernatural, the story is labeled "merveilleux."

In the case of "La mort d'Olivier Bécaille," there are two possible explanations for the self-proclaimed posthumous narration. The first, catalepsy, is defined by the *Trésor de la langue française* as the suppression of all reflexes for locomotion, reduction of sensitivity, and the contraction of muscles. Catalepsy, a condition that occurs in hypnosis and in schizophrenia, entails a "waxy rigidity of the muscles so that the patient tends to remain in any position in which he is placed," according to *Dorland's Illustrated Medical Dictionary*.[8] As it turns out, and in short, following Bécaille's opening statement, he recounts that, unable to move or speak, he was mistaken for dead and buried alive but that he emerged from this state, escaped from the coffin, and "came back to life." He characterizes his former condition as "léthargie" (137), "lassitude" (143), and "syncope" (148, 149) and recounts, for instance, that he could not feel the sensation of his neighbor's finger on his eyelid (134). He himself proposes the explanation most widely accepted by critics when he says, "Il devait s'agir d'un de ces cas de catalepsie dont j'avais entendu parler.... Evidemment c'était une crise de cette nature qui me tenait rigide, comme mort, et qui trompait tout le monde autour de moi" (136). I would argue that an uncritical acceptance of catalepsy as the explanation for Bécaille's narrative oversimplifies a problematic and ambiguous fiction.

According to Todorov's definition, catalepsy could swing "La mort d'Olivier Bécaille" into the genre that he calls the "étrange," since reason explains a supernatural event. Bécaille is not narrating posthumously, nor has he died and come back to life, literally. Rather, he was never dead. However, Todorov's "merveilleux scientifique" provides another way of classifying the story. In this subgenre, "le surnaturel est expliqué d'une manière rationnelle mais à partir de lois que la science contemporaine ne reconnaît pas" (62). He gives the example of magnetism in the stories of Poe, Hoffmann, and Maupassant: "Le magnétisme explique 'scientifiquement' des événements surnaturels, seulement le magnétisme lui-même relève du surnaturel" (62). The case of catalepsy differs somewhat from that of magnetism because it is not "supernatural." On the contrary, catalepsy continues to be recognized medically today, if not widely so, even by medical doctors and medical reference books such as Dorland's. However, Zola's fictionalization of this scientific phenomenon distorts it or, put otherwise, renders it fantastic. As opposed to Bécaille, who becomes immobile while sleeping, a person in a cataleptic state tends to be frozen in motion, as seen in the images of Charcot's cataleptic hysteric patients reproduced in figures 82–92 in Didi-Huberman's *Invention de l'hystérie*. As suggested by the Dorland's definition mentioned above, a cataleptic patient normally changes position, albeit passively, when put in another position by someone else. Although this does not happen to Bécaille, who is presumed dead immediately, a faithful narrative portrait of catalepsy, depicting it over time rather than capturing it in a moment in a photographic fashion, would involve touching a person frozen in mid-action. This would stimulate a change of position and would thus not entail taking the person for dead. Further, a cataleptic continues to have vital signs, so in an accurate portrayal, these would be measured. One appropriately ambiguous point in "La mort d'Olivier Bécaille" is whether or not such a step was taken, a question Bécaille himself asks without answering (definitively): "M'avait-il [le "médecin des morts"] touché la main? Avait-il posé la sienne sur mon coeur? Je ne saurais le dire" (138). However, it is likely, at least in Bécaille's estimation, that the doctor did not take such steps: "Il me sembla qu'il s'était simplement penché d'un air indifférent" (138). Of course, the goal here is not to assess Zola's faithful representation of reality, in and of itself. To state a significant tautology, fiction, even Realism, is fiction, not reality. At the same time, this issue does have bearing on the assessment of the story as fantastic. Although Zola's catalepsy is inspired by the late-nineteenth-century conception of this scientific phenomenon, his fictional version of it deviates not only from our understanding of catalepsy enriched by a century of scientific knowledge, but also from the condition as it was construed in his time. What is significant about this is that the scenario Zola creates is highly improbable according to the laws of the natural world, yet takes place in the context of such a "real world," and thus qualifies as fantastic.

However, in Todorovian terms, the story goes beyond the fantastic, in one direction or the other. "La mort d'Olivier Bécaille" becomes "étrange" if catalepsy is accepted as a rational explanation. Yet in light of Zola's fictionalization of this phenomenon, the story could certainly go the other way, into the "merveilleux," or more specifically the "merveilleux scientifique" (62).

According to a less rigid and less schematic conception of the fantastic, "La mort d'Olivier Bécaille" is quite a fantastic text, generically speaking. And such a conception of the fantastic is appropriate, given that the interest of both the genre and the story in question lies in the transgression of boundaries (between self and other, life and death, reality and illusion or dream, for instance), not in the absence or presence of the supernatural per se. If "La mort d'Olivier Bécaille" is arguably fantastic in Todorov's terms, his requirement for the uncertainty about the supernatural in a fantastic text excludes from the genre not only fairy tales, but also a story such as Villiers de l'Isle-Adam's *histoire insolite* "Les Phantasmes de M. Redoux" (1888). As I show in a different article, Villiers's titular character, a Frenchman, spends the night in Madame Tussaud's wax museum and hallucinates about Louis

XVI's decapitation, putting himself in the monarch's place both physically (he ensconces himself on the guillotine and is subsequently trapped in it) and psychologically (he fears his own decapitation). "Les Phantasmes de M. Redoux" would not qualify as fantastic according to Todorov's definition, because any question about the supernatural is answered. Not only do Redoux's proclivity toward "phantasmomanie" and his inebriation provide rational explanations for his hallucinations, but we also find out, when he does, from the museum guard, that the blade of the guillotine that he perceived as a threat to his life had been absent all along, as it had been removed for sharpening. Whereas Todorov would likely argue that Villiers's story is "étrange,"[9] I propose that Redoux's vividly imagined reenactment of the execution of Louis XVI, stimulated by the fantastic space of the wax museum, makes it fantastic, taken broadly. I would suggest that we want to take the term loosely, because what is interesting about "M. Redoux" coincides with what is fruitful about the study of the fantastic: the exploration and definition of self, the relationship between life and death, limits and transgressing them. My contention with the exclusion of "M. Redoux" from the fantastic due to the rational explanations for the events in the wax museum resonates with Deborah Harter's primary criticism of Todorov in *Bodies in Pieces* on the grounds that he eliminates from the genre tales in which madness "explains away" the supernatural.

What makes "La mort d'Olivier Bécaille" both fantastic and important is its investigation and representation of the liminal space between life and death along with the related ambiguity of self-definition. Even in retrospect, as Bécaille narrates, he seems uncertain of his previous state. He asks repeatedly whether he was really dead ("Etait-ce donc la mort?" 127; "Etait-ce bien la mort?" 128). Retrospectively, he wavers in identifying this state, first affirming without qualification, "je venais de mourir" (131) but then contradicting this assertion with, "ce n'était pas la mort sans doute" (132). The "sans doute" ironically does cast doubt on the statement, which nevertheless introduces the strong possibility, though not the certainty, of negating the initial affirmation ("je venais de mourir"). Finally, when the doctor who comes to declare him dead says a lamp is not necessary (since he is obviously dead), Bécaille exclaims in his narrative what he was ostensibly unable to articulate in his cataleptic state: "je n'étais pas mort! j'aurais voulu crier que je n'étais pas mort!" (138). We must keep in mind that Bécaille's uncertainty satisfies the second of Todorov's three criteria, a character's hesitation, but that this is an optional condition for the Todorovian fantastic.

It is the (implicit) reader who must be uncertain as to whether Bécaille's experience is supernatural or not in order for the story to qualify as fantastic according to Todorov. Indeed, it is highly improbable, though not impossible, that someone could be mistaken for dead over a protracted period of time and could escape from literally "six feet under."[10] Yet these improbable events have ostensibly taken place in "the real world."

Of course, this leads us to question the reliability of the narrator, something we should always do in reading a first-person narrative (see Todorov 88, 89). Are we uncertain that these events could have happened in the "natural world," or are we uncertain whether they occurred at all? Although Olivier Bécaille does not declare or deny his madness in the way Poe's first-person narrators do,[11] we have reason to wonder whether the whole story is not a figment of the character's overactive, neurotic imagination. Without doing a psychoanalytic reading of "La mort d'Olivier Bécaille," I can say without hesitation that the story reflects the morbid and sexual anxieties of the narrator,[12] so much so that the account seems to owe to his imagination rather than to his experience. The narrator's own admission that he is predisposed by nature to "inventions horribles" (146) and his repeated remarks that he became crazy ("je sentais des bouffées de folie monter à mon crâne," 149; "ce fut à ce moment que je devins fou," 150) encourage skepticism about his story.

It is possible, albeit ambiguous and unprovable, that Bécaille's self-declared obsession with death and his feelings of inadequacy with regard to his wife stimulate his invention of the events. He acknowledges a longstanding obsession about death: "Tout petit, j'avais déjà peur de mourir" (128). He admits that, "En grandissant, j'avais gardé cette idée fixe" (128). He speaks of his "anxiété," his fear of sleep because of its resemblance to death. Regarding sexuality, he admits his inadequacy in his relationship with Marguerite when he calls himself "chétif" and excuses her finding a new lover after his alleged death on the grounds that he had never been her lover, but rather a brother (157). It is not necessary to invoke Freudian psychology to support the view that the fear that one's loved one may find someone else, and someone more suitable, is a common insecurity, and has been no doubt since people have populated the world. Accordingly, such insecurities frequently lead people to imagine the realization of such scenarios, be it through reflections, dreams/nightmares, narratives, or a combination of them. In the case of the character Olivier Bécaille, narrative is the overarching mode of expression, through which he represents thoughts and dreams.

In conjunction with his obsessions and anxieties, Olivier Bécaille's acknowledgment of his uncertainty as narrator calls his reliability into question. After the doctor declares him dead, Bécaille experiences agony "comme un rêve horrible, ou mes sensations étaient si singulières, si troublées, qu'il me serait difficile de les noter exactement" (139). Once in the coffin, his ideas "perdaient de leur netteté, tout roulait en moi dans une fumée noire" (143). He says that as of the moment he is transported out of the hotel room, his "souvenirs sont très vagues" (145). He acknowledges lack of clarity, confusion, to the extent that one wonders not only how "accurately" he is recounting what happened, but also if he is sane, and if the events he is narrating have happened at all.

Whether the character Olivier Bécaille was truly buried alive or simply imagined the events and narrated the story is indeterminate and immaterial. The story is fantastic whether the events happened or not. Indeed, what is important is Olivier Bécaille's active mental life, his imagination and his perceptions. In this sense, this Zola character resembles the first-person narrator of Maupassant's story "Le Horla." The fantastic ambiguity of that Maupassant tale lies in whether the "Horla" of the title, a vampiristic "être invisible" (203), is a supernatural being or a figment of the narrator's imagination, a self-projection, as its name suggests semantically: "hors-là." Maupassant's failure to resolve this issue makes "Le Horla" the prototype of the Todorovian fantastic.[13] The first-person narrator's philosophical questions about perception lead to his "interrogation of self" in the form of his implicit posing of the questions, Who am I? Where do the boundaries between myself and the other lie? The second question might be seen as a euphemism for the question he explicitly poses repeatedly: "Am I crazy?" ("suis-je fou?"). This inquiry into self parallels Olivier Bécaille's less explicit self-questioning about his ontological status, which we might reduce to the question "am I/was I dead?" This question encompasses other questions that Bécaille poses regarding the body and the soul, self-consciousness and perception, in life and in death. His reflections about body and soul ("Etait-ce mon âme qui s'attardait ainsi dans mon crâne, avant de prendre son vol?" 128) and about being and nothingness ("La mort n'était donc pas le néant, puisque j'entendais et je raisonnais," 131–32) are existential ones par excellence.

My insistence on such concerns in "Olivier Bécaille" raises the question of the distinction between a fantastic tale of this sort and an existentialist work.[14] The perhaps unsatisfying and contradictory answer is that the differences matter less than the similarities. The reason this is perhaps contradictory is that I have emphasized the importance of considering "La mort d'Olivier Bécaille" a fantastic tale, and now I am saying that generic distinctions do not matter. I think both are true. It is important to consider the story fantastic because it broadens our conceptions of the fantastic and of Zola. On the one hand, "fantastic" is merely a label like any other, and thus reductive and arbitrary. On the other hand, such labels are necessary linguistic constructs, and classification allows us to perceive and organize the world, as Nietzsche suggests with respect to language in "On Truth and Lying in the Extramoral Sense" and as Todorov, resonating with Nietzsche, himself aptly says of genres in his opening: "Il ne peut donc pas être question de 'rejeter la notion du genre' [...]: un tel rejet impliquerait le renoncement au langage et ne saurait, par définition, être formulé" (11–12).

Studying the fantastic depends on a system of classification no more than studying Zola's *oeuvre* does. The notion that Zola expresses such a universal theme as death in a fantastic text no less than in his naturalist fiction does not reduce him to a monolithic figure. Rather, a study of "La mort d'Olivier Bécaille" helps to debunk the myth of the pure father of Naturalism and confirms our picture of Zola as a multifaceted figure. The story also contributes to our conception of the hybridity of the fantastic and its wide-ranging appeal to authors, whether or not they are known for their work in this genre.

Without judging Zola's stories one way or the other, I would propose that the fantastic provides the ideal forum for representing anxieties about fundamental issues such as death and sexuality exactly because narrators and characters are not grounded in reality, but are carried away by their imaginations.[15] Baguley concludes the chapter on fairy tales in *Zola et les genres* by describing the author's movement away from stories toward novels in the following terms: "Le jeune Zola ... tourne le dos au passé, se convertit de l'esthétique du désir à l'esthétique de l'imitation d'un monde qu'il ne s'agit plus de fuir mais de conquérir" (160). I would argue that, regardless of Zola's path, the fantastic, by representing the integration of imaginary elements into a (fictionalized) real world, allows author and reader both to escape from reality and to face it head-on, simultaneously, in Janus-like fashion. Indeed, no less than the Rougon-Macquart, fantastic tales including "La mort d'Olivier Bécaille" provide insight into both the imagination and the reality of late-nineteenth-century France.

Notes

1. In his essay "Le naturalisme," Zola himself rejects the role of the father of Naturalism, ceding the place to Balzac (104–05).

2. "La Mort d'Olivier Bécaille" first appeared in *Le Messager de l'Europe* in March 1879. It was published shortly thereafter in *Le Voltaire* (April 30–May 5 of the same year) (Satiat 25).

3. The proliferation of inexpensive, short paperbacks in France may help account for the recent publication of several editions of Zola stories. "La mort d'Olivier Bécaille," for instance, can be found not only in the Pléiade edition of Zola's *contes et nouvelles*, but also in a Librio edition, or coupled with *Le monstre aux mille sourires* (Alfil), no less than in GF Flammarion's *Naïs Micoulin et autres nouvelles*.

4. See Baguley 1966, footnote 16 for references to articles considering "La mort d'Olivier Bécaille" as a precursor of *La joie de vivre*.

5. The phrase "canonical fantastic" is perhaps an oxymoron, given the marginalization of the genre. In his foreword to Richard Howard's translation of Todorov's work, Robert Scholes puts this idea more eloquently and more delicately when he calls the fantastic "one of the humbler literatures" (viii).

6. Although I do critique Baguley's introductory remarks subjugating Zola's short stories to his novels, I also agree with Charles Elkabas, who in his *NCFS* review of Zola *et les genres* lauds the Zola critic for extending our reading of Zola beyond generic boundaries.

7. Note that Poe is the only non-French author in this list of nineteenth-century "conteurs fantastiques." However, like E. T. A. Hoffmann, Poe was "adopted" by the French, and certainly more highly esteemed by them than by his official compatriots, undoubtedly in large part due to Baudelaire's translations of his works.

8. Since my project is literary rather than scientific, I will not engage in an in-depth study of the phenomenon of catalepsy. However, interested readers might refer to Didi-Huberman's remarks on catalepsy within the specific context of the Salpêtrière and with respect to nineteenth-century female hysterics. The parameters of Didi-Huberman's study do not correspond precisely enough with the fictional context of "La mort d'Olivier Bécaille" or with the gender of the titular character to justify further commentary here. For more medically oriented nineteenth-century works on catalepsy, see Dionis and Petitin.

9. Todorov does nuance his categories by introducing the "fantastique-merveilleux" (the "fantastic-marvelous"), which is situated between the two genres that make up its name, as well as the "fantastique-étrange" (the "fantastic-uncanny"), in which the uncertainty of the fantastic is resolved, and in favor of the uncanny rather than the marvelous. Todorov might apply this second compromise subgenre to a tale such as "Les phantasmes de M. Redoux," except that he would probably contend that the events in the wax museum never even engage the supernatural.

10. Zola takes the expression "six feet under" literally when he has the buried Bécaille ask himself: "N'avais-je pas entendu dire qu'a Paris on enterrait à six pieds de profondeur?" (149).

11. Among the Poe stories that feature first-person narrators who convey their madness in part by denying it are "The Black Cat" and "The Tell-Tale Heart."

12. Note that I am commenting on the morbid and sexual anxieties of the *narrator*, without making any claims about those of the *author*, because the latter falls outside of my domain.

13. Todorov calls "Le Horla" one of Maupassant's best fantastic tales (91).

14. To explore the convergence of the fantastic and Existentialism further, it would be interesting to examine Sartre's essay "Aminadab ou du fantastique considéré comme un langage" (*Situations I*) as well as his film script, *Les jeux sont fairs*. Although Sartre himself called the latter "tout le contraire d'une pièce existentialiste" (in an interview published in *Le Figaro*, as cited by Keefe 84) because of its determinism, I find that Existential concerns commingle with the fantastic in this text.

15. This contention is consistent with Todorov's argument that "la psychanalyse a remplacé (et par là même a rendu inutile) ta littérature fantastique" (169).

WORKS CITED

D'Almeras, Henri. "Les débuts inconnus d'Emile Zola." *La Revue* 37 (1901): 614–18.

Baguley, David. "Les sources et la fortune des nouvelles de Zola." *Les Cahiers naturalistes.* (32) 1966: 118–32.

———. "Maupassant avant la lettre? A study of the Zola short story: 'Les Coquillages de M. Chabre'." *Nottingham French Studies* 6.2 (October 1967): 77–86.

———. *Zola et les genres.* University of Glasgow French and German Publications, 1993.

Bloom, Michelle. "Staging the Execution of Louis XVI at Madame Tussaud's: Villiers de l'Isle-Adam's 'Les Phantasmes de M. Redoux'." *Symposium* 49.3 (Fall 1995): 190–203.

"Catalepsie." *Trésor de la Langue Française.* Paris: CNRS, 1971–94.

"Catalepsy." *The Dorland's Illustrated Medical Dictionary.* 25th Ed. Philadelphia: Saunders, 1974.

Didi-Huberman, Georges. *Invention de l'hystérie. Charcot et l'iconographie photographique de la Salpêtrière.* Paris: Macula, 1982.

Dionis, Pierre. *Dissertation sur la mort subite et sur la catalepsie; avec la relation de plusieurs personnes qui ont été attaquées.* 2nd Ed. Paris: Laurent d'Houry, 1718.

Elkabas, Charles. Review of *Zola et les genres. NCFS* 23.1–2 (Fall–Winter 1994–95): 275–76.

Goncourt, Edmond et Jules de. *Journal, Memoires de la vie littéraire II, 1866–86.* Bouquin, Robert Laffont, 1956. Letter of Friday, November 16, 1927.

Harter, Deborah A. *Bodies in Pieces: Fantastic Narrative and the Poetics of the Fragment.* Stanford, CA: Stanford UP, 1996.

Hemmings, F. W. J. "Les sources d'inspiration de Zola conteur." *Les Cahiers naturalistes* 9.23–25 (1963): 29–114.

Le Gars, Yves. "Avant-Propos." *Pour une nuit d'amour.* Aix-en-Provence: Alinea, 1991. 7–11.

Maupassant, Guy de. "Les Horlas," Arles: Actes Sud, 1995.

Nietzsche. "On Truth and Lying in the Extramoral Sense." *The Portable Nietzsche*. Ed. and trans. Walter Kaufmann. New York: Penguin, 1982. 42–47.

Petetin, Jacques-Henri-Désiré. *Mémoires sur la découverte des phénomènes que présentent la catalepsie et le somnambulisme*. Nendeln/Liechtenstein: Kraus Reprint, 1978.

Ricatte, Robert. "Zola conteur." *Europe* 468–469 (April–May 1968): 209–17.

Ripoll, Roger. "Préface" and "Notice." *Emile Zola: Contes et nouvelles*. Paris: Gallimard, Pléiade, 1976. ix–xvii, 1527–1543.

Sartre, Jean-Paul. Interview with Paul Carrière. *Le Figaro* 29 April 1947. Cited by Terry Keefe, "Sartre's *L'Existentialisme est un humanisme*." *Critical Essays on Jean-Paul Sartre*. Ed. Robert Wilcocks. Boston, MA: G. K. Hall, 1988.

Satiat, Nadine. Introduction. *Naïs Micoulin et autres nouvelles*. Paris: Flammarion, 1997. 7–55.

Scholes, Robert. Foreword. *The Fantastic: A Structural Approach to a Literary Genre*. By Tzvetan Todorov. Trans. Richard Howard. Ithaca, NY: Cornell UP, 1975. v–xi.

Todorov, Tzvetan. *Introduction à la littérature fantastique*. Paris: Seuil, 1970.

Villiers de l'Isle-Adam. "Les Phantasmes de M. Redoux." *Clair Lenoir et autres contes insolites*. Paris: Flammarion, 1984. 167–74.

Zola, Emile. "La mort d'Olivier Bécaille." *Naïs Micoulin et autres nouvelles*. Paris: Flammarion, 1997. 127–57.

———. "Le naturalisme." *Collection des oeuvres complètes: Emile Zola. Oeuvres critiques*, vol. 46, *Une campagne* (1880–1881). Eugène Fasquelle, no date. 101–18.

ANTHONY SAVILE

Naturalism and the Aesthetic

In the educated speech of today the term 'aesthetic' occurs in two distinct contexts. First, people use it to designate a set of artistic concerns and stylistic choices that dominate the production of a period or the work of particular artists. Thus we speak of the aesthetic of the Counter-Reformation or the High Renaissance, or of the aesthetic common to the Pre-Raphaelite painters. In a quite different context the expressions 'aesthetic' or 'aesthetical' are used to speak about a range of philosophical preoccupations arising out of our thought and talk about the arts and about those natural objects and artefacts that engage our sensibilities and taste beyond the arts. As it happens, the topic of naturalism is liable to turn up quite freely in either context, and while the main subject of this essay is naturalism in its more narrowly philosophical usage, just because the more familiar use of the term is in connection with a specific literary programme or a specifically artistic effect, that is, within aesthetic preoccupations of the first kind, it will be sensible to say something about those before turning to strictly philosophical material. At the very end I shall make a remark or two relating these different sorts of naturalism to one another.

From *The British Journal of Aesthetics* 40, no. 1 (January 2000). © 2000 by Oxford University Press.

I. Naturalism as a Literary Programme

It is sometimes said that naturalism in literature is no more than an extension or exaggeration of realism, or that it is nothing other than the transposition to literature of what realism is in art. But in the literary productions of the mid- and late-nineteenth century both sorts of narrative writing are found and there are differences between them that need to be marked even if critical practice has not always kept them apart. I start with the project of realism in art which arose as a choice of subject matter in French painting in the 1850s and 1860s that set itself firmly against the dominant romanticism of the day. The favoured subject matter of romantic painting from the Revolution of 1789 on had been classical allegory, heroic battle-scenes, and mythical or historical set pieces. All these topics lent themselves readily to studio production, they privileged fancy and imagination, and they laid heavy stress on compositional values. In consequence, they tended to detach themselves from the living model and were at most only minimally concerned with the detail of how such subjects and scenes might have appeared to the eye.

Setting himself against the romanticism of his day Gustave Courbet, the original 'realist' (but sometimes spoken of as a 'thoroughgoing naturalist'),[1] and those artists coming immediately after him concentrated on rendering mundane subjects from everyday life and in particular sought to capture the visible character of the natural world and contemporary society. For example, Courbet accentuated the fleshly nature of his model: her thick limbs and perspiring wrists were in marked contrast to presentations of stylized elegance that expressed an earlier feminine ideal. While Courbet painted in his studio and from memory of scenes beyond it, his successors, Jean-François Millet and Théodore Rousseau, pursued their realistic concerns out of doors, away from the studio. Scenes from peasant country life in the plain around Barbizon were recorded *in situ* by Millet, and Rousseau is remembered for detailed studies in the nearby Fontainebleau forest. Later, intense preoccupation with visual appearance and the rendering of atmosphere marked the work of the Impressionists, still working to a recognizably 'realist' agenda. When the term 'naturalism' does occur in discussion of nineteenth-century post-romantic French painting, it does so very largely as a synonym for realism of the kind described.

If realism originated with painting shortly before the mid-nineteenth century, it was soon enough transposed to literature, a transposition partly effected by Champfleury's literary manifesto *Le Réalisme*, which appeared in 1857. Just as Courbet had announced his intention of staying with everyday scenes of modern and vulgar life, so the realist novel strove to capture the detail of life as lived, and chose for its settings humdrum milieux in which there was little place for moral idealization, far-fetched plot, and implausible interventions of destiny. The psychology of character that was adopted tended to reflect common positivistic assumptions that people were motivated by self-interest and were largely the playthings of social forces beyond their control. The successful realist novel would then display the workings of such character and circumstance in the determination of plot, even to the abandonment of plot should that interfere too much with the lifelike documentation of events.[2]

The philosophical backdrop to nineteenth-century aesthetic thought in France was supplied by the positivism first of Comte and then of Taine. However, the most notable influence in marking the difference between literary realism of the kind outlined and the succeeding naturalism was provided by the experimental physiologist Claude Bernard through his celebrated *Introduction a l'étude de la médecine expérimentale* (1865), a work which Zola took as his guide in articulating his own naturalistic programme in a series of columns written for *Le Messager de l'Europe* in 1879 and entitled 'Le Roman Expérimental' and 'Le Naturalisme au Théâtre'.

In essence, what Zola sought to do was to extend to the novel the gains he saw that had begun to be won in the natural sciences through their application of experimental methods. As he said in 1880,

> If the experimental novelist is still groping his way in total darkness and in the most complex of sciences, that does not prevent that science from existing. It is undeniable that the naturalistic novel, as we understand it today, is a true experiment that the novelist is performing upon mankind, aided in that by observation.[3]

Just as Bernard had taught his medical colleagues to progress beyond the rough and ready methods of prevalent clinical practice (the 'empirisme' he so detested) by the systematic testing of hypotheses under experimental conditions, so Zola proclaimed the power of the novel to show how men's passions and spiritual lives are likewise governed by strict laws and how those laws are liable to work out in particular circumstances. 'Our role as intelligent beings', he wrote, 'is to penetrate the working of things, to penetrate the "how", to become superior to them and reduce them to obedient cogs.'

In the light of this, the distinction between the realistic and the naturalistic novel can be drawn in terms of the distinction so important to

Bernard and Zola between observation and experiment. As Bernard put it 'in the philosophical sense of the terms, observation displays and experiment *instructs*'.[4] For Zola, the realist tends to amass detail, he is a slave to his material, and is as inert a recorder as the camera. The naturalist, by contrast, instructs his readers by the controlled observations that his imagination allows him to construct. His intuition leads him to test a general empirical hypothesis (an 'idée expérimentale') by seeing whether it rings true in the invented circumstances of his novel.

Zola's own words express this as well as any:

> Just see what clarity emerges when one puts oneself in the position of applying experimental method to the novel, with all the scientific rigour that the subject allows today. A stupid reproach that is made to us, to us naturalistic novelists, is that we are simply trying to be photographers. In vain do we proclaim that we accept individual temperament and personal expression, they still go on replying with imbecile arguments about the need to organize the story to create a genuine work of art. Well, once you apply the experimental method to the novel the whole dispute evaporates. The idea of experiment itself brings the notion of modification with it. We take facts as our starting point; they are the inevitable basis, but to display the mechanism that drives those facts, we have to create and direct the phenomena—that is our inventive share in the business, the genius in the work. Thus I recognize here and now that we have to modify nature, but without departing from nature, when we use the experimental method in our works. If we bear in mind the teaching 'Observation displays, experiment instructs' we can claim for our books that they do indeed teach that fine experimental lesson.[5]

What does not emerge from this passage, but which the desire to assimilate the novel to the procedures of the natural sciences makes plain, is that the driving force behind the programme is the dream of amelioration of our state through the control that such understanding that the novelist provides puts in our hands. If the dream of the scientist is to make himself master of life in order to direct it, then so too is it the dream of the experimental novelist.

> Our goal is theirs; we too want to be the masters of phenomena, of the personal and intellectual elements of things, in order to

control them. We are, in a word, experimental moralists, showing by experiment how a passion operates in a given social setting. Come the day when we understand the mechanism of this passion we shall be able to treat it, to minimize it or at least to render it as harmless as may be. And that is the practical utility and moral goal of our naturalistic books, which conduct experiments upon mankind, which take apart and then rebuild the human machine to show how it operates under the influence of different environments. In due course, when we are sure of the laws, if we want to produce a better state of society all that will have to be done will be to apply them to the individual person and to their social milieu.[6]

Now, setting aside all consideration of whether Zola's own novels actually conform to his programme (or whether other writers than Zola worked to his programme in anything like a plausible manner) we can ask whether there are insuperable obstacles to its success. Is the programme a coherent one? Certainly, Zola's ideas quickly came in for scathing criticism, famously at the hands of Brunetière in *Le Roman Réaliste en 1875*, though it is not always clear to what extent the attack is aimed at the novels for failing to implement the programme or at the programme itself. My remarks here concern the latter alone. If the naturalistic programme suffers from philosophical weaknesses, the result will be that no novel can succeed *as* a naturalistic novel, but that will not imply that there are no successful naturalistic novels, only that what accounts for their success cannot be their faithful execution of the programme their authors espoused.

We have seen Zola himself rebutting two objections that he often encountered. But objections of a different order may seem more damaging. First, it may be said that the scientistic programme that marks naturalism wherever it is found can only escape criticism if it can live up to the goal it sets itself, the discovery or revelation of those deterministic laws that govern the workings of the human machine (be that social or private). It is a commonplace reflection of our own day that it can hardly behove the novelist to make such discoveries since there are no such discoveries to be made, nor could there be. Briefly put, the reason for this lies in the fact that any generalizations governing human behaviour—be it in the large or in the small—can scarcely be anything other than generalizations of people's behaviour in recurrent kinds of circumstance as issuing from their perceptions, their desires, and their beliefs. Yet there could be no substantive lawlike statements applying to such material, because we can see quite clearly that the addition of further desires and beliefs to a tentatively identified mental set that might initially be thought to support such a generalization will ensure that it breaks down. In general, if I expect it to rain I will stay at home; but if I expect it to rain but I also believe that my getting wet will improve my health, then I may very well go out. The generality that people stay indoors when it rains comes nowhere near the status of a law. More lifelike examples will always encounter the same obstacle.

In all fairness this observation is better directed against the prevalent positivist desire to extend the reach of the hard sciences to psychology and sociology than against the literary programme even though it is a consequence of the criticism that that programme would need to be adjusted to be capable of successful execution. But since the social sciences have been able to temper their goals, there is no reason why the novelist may not follow suit, abandon his quest for laws and concern himself instead with interesting high-level generalizations and other modes of behavioural explanation than the nomological-deductive one that nineteenth-century French theory found so seductive.

A second hesitation one might have is that it is central to Zola's conception of the novel that we can regard it as a controlled experiment; indeed he thinks of it very much as an experiment that confirms a certain hypothesis (as Bernard's experiment on blood flow to and from the liver to confirm his hypothesis that the liver was the organ responsible for the production of blood sugar). Following this model, the novelist tells a convincing story about individuals and perhaps describes them as reacting in such and such ways to their environment. We may say to ourselves as we read: 'in those circumstances they could hardly have done anything else'. But whereas in the laboratory the controlled experiment confronts a hypothesis by observations that are (ideally) made independently of belief in the truth of the hypothesis—the idea being to let brute nature have her own independent say—in the case of the novel the outcome of the 'controlled experiment' is determined by what the author takes to be plausible, and the trouble is that what he takes to be plausible is not unconnected with his faith in the hypothesis that he would like to be testing.

To this again the naturalist is not entirely without reply, though whether it goes far enough is questionable. This takes the form of saying that the idea of observations that allow nature to speak for herself is a myth: what nature says has to be interpreted and can only be interpreted in the light of beliefs that the interpreter himself endorses. So there is no stepping outside the circle of our judgements of plausibility, no access to a natural world that is brutely given as the objection supposes there to be. Nevertheless, the critic will continue, even if we make some concession to this response, it will still be true that the worker in the field, unlike the novelist, can repeat his experiments and can draw on agreements with others about how we should interpret observations. The novelist's controlled experiment is controlled only by his own sense of plausibility, and that deprives him of the crucial distinction between observation that merely appears to indicate this, that, or the other, and one that does indeed have that sense.

At this point the naturalistic novelist must obviously concede that at best his stories be thought of as probative thought-experiments. Testing them on the ground is not his business, and however pertinent the reminder about the mythical nature of the factually given might be, that cannot erase the distinction between a genuine experiment and a merely imagined one. Here I think we come upon a more substantial objection to the project than before. A thought-experiment may test (usually to refute, but not always) a general hypothesis. Now just as an observation in the void has no scientific significance, so in the absence of a hypothesis the mere unfolding of a chain of events cannot aid us to 'act on the world and arrive at a better social state'. True, the novelist may well get us to say that in such circumstances as the author depicts these people's lives could not have run differently, but the success of the naturalistic programme would depend on our being able to see the events of the plot as confirming (or, perhaps, even simply illustrating) a general truth, and one that the author envisages us as finding confirmed by the verisimilitude of his tale. Yet all we can do is to say something such as that in circumstances *like* these, people *relevantly like* these will suffer in such and such ways, and that is not a hypothesis that is confirmed (or disconfirmed) by the events of the plot at all. But without a definite hypothesis what might be offered as a striking thought-experiment has no force as such. The claim it might have to approximate to experimental science is spurious. But as I said before, this defect in the programme, while it may prevent any novel from being successful as a naturalistic novel, does not give the critic any weapon against the artistic success of the novels that the naturalists wrote.

II. Naturalism in Philosophical Aesthetics

Moving away from naturalism as a literary and aesthetic programme and turning towards the topic in its application to philosophical aesthetics, I should first say something about the metaphysical concerns out of which it arises. Although philosophical naturalism is a specifically nineteenth-century phenomenon, its leading concerns found expression in modern philosophy in the mid-seventeenth century. First and foremost was the desire to recognize only existences that could be situated in the natural world. Hence any claims to existence on the part of supernatural beings, God, angels, or whatever could only be taken seriously if they were handled as part of the world in space and time. A prime example of this reorientation is Spinoza's identification of God with Nature, the one extended substance that does and must exist. Another is Hume's rather later treatment of miracles as natural events for which we offer unsatisfactory explanations.[7] (Spinoza too, we may recall, had no room for non-natural explanation.[8])

Another leading concern to which nineteenth-century thought lent its peculiar twist was the conviction that anything that exists must be transparent to the intellect. Again Spinoza provides the lead here, since the essence of substance (that is, the natural world) coincides with what the intellect perceives, and modes falling under each essential attribute inherit this transparency. Similarly, on this side of the Channel Hume thought that when we see aright the structure of existence in terms of impressions and ideas, there is no room for real existences that escape our cognitive powers since the very notion of an impression and an idea is introduced in terms of what we experience. We are just constantly misled into construing things in ways that defy this evident truth.

The twist that the nineteenth century lent to these concerns, very largely on account of the positivism developed in the 1830s and later, first by Comte and then by Taine, already seen to be formative of the literary programmes sketched above, came with its equation of what is accessible to the intellect with what is accessible to the intellect in a systematic fashion, namely with what can be brought within the ambit of the natural sciences with their emphasis on the objectivity and the mathematizability of what they study and its conformity to strict laws.[9] Seen from the naturalistic point of view there were many claimants to reality whose passage at the gates was held up for entry not because they brought with them an odour of the supernatural, but because it was unclear how they might be accommodated by the natural sciences, or because the ways in which it was envisaged that they might be so accommodated turned out to be unsatisfactory when exposed to searching and disinterested scrutiny.

The example that first comes to mind here is the mind itself. Not far behind in these stakes are claims of ethics and aesthetics to be concerned not with real self-standing entities, but with real enough features or properties of things and events. Their possession by objects, by people, and by their deeds have usually been thought to be what will legitimate our unreflective assumptions that ethical and aesthetical evaluations as good or beautiful, or more specifically decadent or diverting, made of particular subjects in particular circumstances, are apt to be true (or false) and should not be dismissed as having no determinate purchase on the world at all. The naturalists' problem was to show how such assumptions could be sustained.

The ethical and the aesthetical cases go hand in hand here—recall Wittgenstein's dictum that 'Ethik und Aesthetik sind Eins' (*Tractatus* 6.421)—nevertheless my discussion will be cast solely in terms of aesthetic material, even though as far as I am aware no serious effort has ever been made to bring it firmly within the naturalistic fold, whereas by contrast nineteenth-century utilitarianism and its twentieth-century offspring, welfare economics, have tried to find more than merely metaphorical substance in Taine's observation that 'vice and virtue are natural products just like vitriol and sugar'.[10]

As it happens the two classic philosophical texts of aesthetic theory, Hume's essay 'Of the Standard of Taste' and Kant's *Critique of Judgement*, are both centrally concerned with the legitimacy of the assumption that naturalism hopes to make good. The standards they took to apply for aesthetic assertions to count as truth-apt were less well-defined than the nineteenth-century naturalism supposed them to be, but even so to connect naturalistic thinking with critical and aesthetic discourse it is indispensable to see how the debate stood in the light of their work. Even if the outcome is not very clear, the lie of the land that others have to encounter will be apparent.

Common to Hume and to Kant is their determination not to dismiss as illusory the appearance of correctness in the best judgements of good critics, and for both thinkers the tacit assumption was that the notion of correctness in question is that of truth. Further, neither of them believed there was any reason to suppose that truth in these matters will be secured by taking the speaker who finds a rose beautiful to be saying something merely about himself and true or false simply on account of his being appropriately affected. Both of them struggle to locate something that both preserves our sense of truth and goes further than that.

One idea that Kant may have believed he found in Hume—I do not say it is there in Hume to be found—is suggested by a passage of Hume's essay in which he compares the beauty of a poem to the leather and iron resting at the bottom of a barrel of wine and which together account for the leathery and metallic taste that experts detect. The analogy in the offing might be that in like fashion the sensitive critic is responsive to certain features of a poem such as its phonetic pattern (perhaps suitably allied to its content, though Hume makes no suggestion about the detail) which calls forth the response that beautiful poems leave in our mind. Now Kant may have taken Hume to have been proposing a reduction of the beautiful to some such pattern, and since that would be a fully naturalistic move it needs discussion independently of whether or not the thought was in fact one that crossed Hume's mind.[11]

The immediate appeal of the suggestion is that it declines to identify aesthetic qualities with sentiments in the way that a number of earlier British figures of the eighteenth century had found appealing. (I have in mind particularly Shaftesbury, Burke, and Karnes.) In this way it would avoid Reid's objection that

> the excellence [in a musical air] is not in me: it is in the music. But the pleasure it gives is not in the music; it is in me. Perhaps I cannot say why it is in a tune that pleases my ear, as I cannot say what it is in a sapid body which pleases my palate, and I call it a delicious taste; and there is a quality in the tune that pleases my taste, and I call it a fine of excellent air.[12]

Moreover, seen from the naturalistic point of view it would have the further advantage, which Reid admits to not knowing how to secure, of saying exactly what it is in the sapid body that pleases the taste and by extension what it is in the music that is beautiful and pleases the ear.

Whatever its merit, though, the suggestion is not acceptable, and it came in for strong criticism from Kant in §§34, 44, 57 of the *Critique*. As he put it, 'the judgement of taste (i.e. the judgement that something is beautiful) is not an objective cognitive judgement. It does not bring the object judged under a determinate concept' (*CJ* §57). As I interpret him, Kant is pointing out that to say that something is beautiful is to convey no information of a specific kind about the object as it is in its own right; we do not know anything at all about how it is going to appear; all the judgement commits us to is that it is appropriate for anyone to respond to it with pleasure for some *indeterminate* reason (*ibid.*).

The naturalist intent on doing his best for the position Kant was attacking could well say that his criticism is only likely to move us if we neglect to pay attention to the distinction that neither Kant nor Hume were sensitive to between the sense and the reference of the predicate expressions in our aesthetic judgements. So while it may indeed be correct that a judgement that something is beautiful does not tell us what the beautiful object is like, it will nonetheless be true that beautiful objects have that particular objective property that good judges are generally sensitive to and which, Kant's criticism notwithstanding, find their place in what Hume calls 'general principles of beauty' ('Standard', para. 16). Thinking of Hume in this light, we could envisage him agreeing with Kant in that there is no concept we might substitute in our aesthetic statements for 'is beautiful' *salvo sensu*, but saying that leaves it an entirely open matter whether there is not some concept that we could substitute for it *salva veritate*. And that, the naturalist who finds the present suggestion congenial will say, is all he needs to withstand Kant's criticism and to mark his disagreement as it needs to be marked.

With hindsight, however, it is possible to see in Kant's text a rebuttal of this last move. For he observes that 'there is no objective principle of taste possible', namely 'a principle under the condition of which we could subsume the concept of an object and then infer, by means of a syllogism, that the object is beautiful' (*CJ* §34). So his thought would be that no matter what specification of objective 'general principle' you like, taken as the reference of the aesthetic predicate '... is beautiful', there is no reason to think that it would go hand in hand with what the sense of the predicate commits us to (namely, as Kant sees it, the response of pleasure in sensitive viewers or readers). In words from a later century, for Kant it would always be an open question whether what was conformable to the principle was indeed beautiful. G. E. Moore summed it up in a rare remark of an aesthetic nature:

> It will never be true to say: this object owes its beauty *solely* to the presence of this characteristic, nor yet that: wherever this characteristic is present the objects are beautiful because they have certain characteristics, in the sense that they would not be beautiful unless they had them.[13]

Yet there is something too dogmatic about this way of putting it. The point needs strengthening if it is to carry conviction, and one appealing way to do that would be to point out that the claim that Kant's Hume would be defending and Kant himself denying is that there are identities between what is beautiful and determinate objective features of things that are beautiful. Then the Kantian could pursue his argument and observe that since identities are necessarily true if they are true at all, there would be *necessary* substitutivity *salva veritate* between the term designating the 'general principle' and the aesthetic term under scrutiny. *That* there is absolutely no reason to believe. One could always envisage going round the corner and coming across something that one found made oneself and others respond in ways so compelling that we could not be persuaded to withdraw the appellation 'beautiful' from it (or 'dumpy', 'dainty', 'disgusting', 'lurid', 'gaudy', and so on—we are not concerned simply with the beautiful here) even though that new-found object showed very little conformity to the general principle that we are imagining to be under discussion and patently lacked whatever objective character is being supposed to bind its compliants together.

As I have presented it, this is a point well made against the idea that Kant may have thought was Hume's. Whether or not it counts against the real Hume is another matter, but certainly it looks good enough against the naturalism of the late nineteenth century, since the mathematizable and systematizable features of things in terms of which those thinkers and their successors sought to count as the real qualities that the world contains would all fall within the scope of the argument. It is certainly a powerful one, and we need to be persuaded of its power before moving on.

It cannot be attacked, I think, for changing the subject, as would be the case if the imagined introduction of failures of identity had stemmed from supposing ourselves to be significantly differently constituted than in fact we now are. Compare here the failure of attempts to block the identification of colour with the actual constitution of light-reflecting bodies by an argument along the line that if our eyes were structured other than as they are, very different bodies might well appear to us just as red things do now, and so be properly adjudged red. The failure there consists in forgetting that we must explain 'red' in terms of what appears red to human beings *constituted as we actually are* and to consider other constitutions than ours or variations of our own has no bearing on what makes something red. But in the argument under consideration I was explicitly holding our constitution fixed and supposing that it is evidently on the cards that we should come across new and unexpected sorts of things quite unlike others we know that we find it compelling to recognize as beautiful.

Of course, once we descend to more specific aesthetic predicates like 'dumpy' or 'dainty' it might seem less easy to be taken by surprise than in the case of 'beautiful', but we need to remember that the surprise in question (as far as the naturalistic moral is concerned) is about the specific physical embodiment of the dainty or the dumpy, and maybe it is not too hard to see *that* being variable without impugning the dumpy nature of the things in question.

At this point someone enamoured of the naturalistic stance might perhaps wonder whether I am not conflating epistemic and metaphysical possibilities. The fact that for all we know any identity of reference we consider may break down does not imply that *when the right naturalistic reference is found* that it too could break down. Such a person may allow that we are ignorant in these aesthetic cases, and others like them, of the true naturalistic reference of the terms in point but insist that that does not undermine his position. The projection of our ignorance onto the objects themselves is quite illegitimate.

I do not accept that this is what is going on here, so I feel untouched by this reflection, which would be telling indeed if it were based on a truth. To make it look thoroughly unattractive all that is needed is to remind the naturalist at this point that identity claims can be challenged in two directions. So far what I have done is to suggest that for any objective and physical nature a claim of identity between it and a given aesthetic property of an object will fail because it is possible that the aesthetic property be maintained while the physical property is not. But, one could as easily challenge it the other way round by saying that any given physical property that suits the naturalistically inclined metaphysician might be realized without the aesthetic property that seems most clearly allied with it being present. There is something absolutely right about Kant's saying that the test of the presence of the aesthetic property has to be people's responses, yet we might very well find things physically similar to those we think of as (say) dumpy, but because of the function they have for us, or their known history, we refuse to find dumpy—they are perhaps menacingly squat, not really dumpy at all. So one could conclude that what aesthetic properties one attributes to things depends on a host of cultural and psychological factors that may vary while their naturalistically favoured features (those that in the given case allow them to be recruited to systematic natural science) are held stable.

As yet I have done no more than explore the naturalistic proposal from the side of the object. But the version of it I have in effect rejected is not the one Hume is usually seen as endorsing, and despite the appeal of Reid's observation we may reflect that when it has been pushed to do so, philosophy has not been reluctant to discern a different structure to things than that which our unexamined ways of speaking suggest. In the aesthetic domain, philosophy often has felt so pushed. So, pressed by his metaphysical imperatives, the naturalist may admit that he has to move in a different direction, failing which he will conclude that aesthetic (and, let us not forget, ethical) features of things only appear to belong in the world, not that they have a sure place there. To save us from that sorry conclusion he will say we should turn attention away from the object and concentrate on the subject instead, a figure who has hitherto been kept firmly in the background.

The move is well attested in the history of the subject, as is evident from the account Moore gives of 'nature' in *Principia Ethica*. 'By nature then I do mean ... that which is the subject matter of the natural sciences, *and also of psychology*.'[14] The surprise that inclusion of psychology in this formulation is likely to induce in the reader should disappear when we reflect that on naturalistic assumptions subjects' psychological states have a real claim to be part of the world either because they fall under strict laws (of psychology yet to be discovered)[15] or because they must ultimately be reducible to appropriately amenable physical properties of the subjects whose states they are. On this assumption, when it comes to making cognitive sense of ethical claims, it is clearly the psychological states of the subjects that matter and not those of the world that is responsible for those states. Certainly this is how things have seemed to English theorists of the mid-nineteenth century and beyond whose ethics was conducted in terms of the computations of Bentham's felicific calculus or its descendants.[16]

In the aesthetic arena the naturalist might well find encouragement here in Hume's and in Kant's insistence on the importance of the subjective aspect of the matter. Let us suppose that he takes as canonical Kant's explanation of the beautiful at *CJ* §9 (*ad finem*) as 'that which pleases universally without a concept'. Then he might say if we are to acknowledge the beautiful and other aesthetic characteristics of things as having any real purchase on the world, given the admitted impossibility of reducing them to such physical states of the objects as would satisfy naturalistic requirements, there is no alternative but to identify the truly beautiful in terms of the responses that the contemplation of objects is liable to produce, the delight, pleasure, or enthusiastic engagement that people take in them. In the formula just quoted Kant puts his finger on this in just the right way, stressing the psychological responses that lend a reality to a beauty we tend to project upon the objects of our gaze while at the same time pointing out how unrevealing of the object itself such assertions are. If that is how the beautiful is to be treated, so too must we treat the rest of the aesthetic panoply. Thus the naturalist may reason.

In 'A Sensible Subjectivism?' David Wiggins points out how very unattractive this position is when taken *au pied de la lettre*. If we were to abstract entirely from the objects of our attention as the Kantian picture suggests, we should be forgetting that our responses, of pleasure, of distaste, of amusement, of curiosity, and so on, are themselves intentional in nature. They are directed at specific properties of objects, and we need to make this quite explicit because it is only in terms of the objects and their properties that we manage to differentiate between one response and another at any but the crudest experiential level. However, so far as our aesthetic responses go, the properties that are in question, to which we need to be able to allude in specifying those responses at a degree of resolution that differentiates usefully between one and another, are precisely those aesthetic properties that the naturalist is now hoping to explicate in terms of our psychological states. Curiously enough, his enthusiasm for the psychological leads to a diminution of its richness; as we focus on it to the exclusion of all else, so it fades away.

Nor should we forget that there are all sorts of reasons why any independently detectable response can be evoked. We do not, for instance, only laugh at the comic but sometimes also at the embarrassing or the shocking; it is not only the obscene that provokes disgust. Again it is by reference to the nature of the objects closely described that we shall distinguish between the genuinely comic and the merely risible, the obscene and the revolting, and so on.

Thirdly, the psychological move neglects one feature of Kant's explication that has so far been passed over, namely his recognition of the exemplary and normative nature of our pleasure in the beautiful—normative in the sense that it makes our pleasure a response that the object merits (in a phrase of John McDowell's). This should make us reflect that when we look at our responses of delight to things of beauty that we encounter and ask what would make it true that our response is a merited response, there is simply no point in looking further inwards to explain that. Our only hope is to look more closely at the nature of the object that elicits that response. So the naturalist's attempt to account for the reality of the aesthetic (or for that matter the ethical) in terms of psychology alone, as he conceives of it, and setting the objects themselves to one side, is doomed to failure.

III. NATURALISM WITHOUT SCIENTISM?

Where does this leave us? I have taken naturalism to be a thesis both about particulars and about their properties. Nothing said in the previous sections has impugned the thought that particulars that have an aesthetic character are items in the world subject to the laws of physics. (Neither have I suggested that all works of art are physical objects. Works of music and poetry, for example, are surely not.) The naturalism I have found unacceptable is one that sees the real features that things have either being such as can be directly subsumed under terms that work hard in the theories of natural science or else are reducible to such terms. In full generality naturalism is a false doctrine, because the aesthetical (and ethical) properties of things and events (works of art and their performances, natural objects, and artefacts on the one hand, men and their deeds on the other) are neither directly subsumed by science nor are reducible to the terms of science, and this is true whether we seek a naturalistic basis of the aesthetic either in the objects that give rise to our responses or to the subjects whose responses those objects evoke. There may indeed be a raft of other properties that admit of naturalistic treatment, but those of ethics and aesthetics are not among them.

Despite the initial positive thrust of his doctrine the naturalist will fear at this point that we are obliged to write off such characteristics of things as not having a genuine existence in the world as some sort of delusive projection of human fancy. However, his reason for thinking that this is forced on us is so far founded only on his commitment to the scientism of the late nineteenth century. What would really be needed to get us to this sorry point would be the conviction that there is no other way to handle aesthetic (and ethical) terms that would enable us to make true statements with their help. It is far from clear that this cannot be done.

Let us go back to the point where we left the discussion between Hume and Kant. First, the moral Hume invites us to draw from the example about the metallic-tasting wine would be badly put by identifying aesthetic qualities with those mathematizable objective features of things responsible for the experience that gives rise to our judgements. Hume himself would very likely concur. In the ninth paragraph of his essay he says that

> to check the sallies of the imagination, and to reduce every expression to geometrical truth and exactness, would be the most contrary to the laws of criticism (because it would produce a work, which by universal experience has been found the most insipid and disagreeable).

This rejected view is sometimes encapsulated in the seventeenth-century denial that beauty and the rest are 'real' properties of objects, where this usage (found originally in Galileo's talk of 'primi e reali accidenti') associates what is real with what Locke later identified as the primary qualities. This reminder of a past way of talking immediately alerts one to the alternative of considering aesthetic properties as somewhat akin to the secondary qualities, ones which are not 'really' in the object in the seventeenth-century way of talking, that is they are not non-relative properties of objects, but whose possession by the object is real enough in our modern sense of that term, that is they are properties the possession of which, although not specifiable except in relation to our ways of picking them out in our experience, does permit us to say truly that that jam is sweet, this smoke is acrid, and that sheet of paper pale grey.

In §57 of the *Critique* Kant comes down in favour of treating beauty not as a determinate concept (one governed by strict objective criteria of application). He does, however, allow that the judgement of taste must be based on *some* concept (or property), since otherwise he thinks it would not enjoy the universal validity that it does. So he infers that we must have to do with an *indeterminate* concept instead. Unfortunately, he then goes on to identify the indeterminate concept with the supersensible substrate of phenomena, but this mishap very probably stemmed from his looking for something in itself indeterminate for the indeterminate concept to refer to. What he failed to appreciate was that a concept that is indeterminate need not refer to a thing (or property) that is indeterminate at all, but only that it should be indeterminate what thing or property it refers to. Correcting for this mistake, Kant could well have said that a beautiful object is one that has *some* feature or other that produces the universal response of pleasure, and that at least comes discernibly close to a secondary quality account of the matter.

Without endorsing the secondary quality model in the version Locke gave of it at *Essay* II.viii.10 (where the redness of an object is identified with the object's liability to produce the experience of red) we can acknowledge that for present purposes it is highly suggestive. (i) It does not identify the quality with the ground of the liability—the initial naturalistic suggestion mooted and rejected in the last section; (ii) it points to the need to account for the truth of assertions like 'x is red' by introducing properties that can only be adequately and informatively described in terms of our experience (here the appearance of red); (iii) the experience that we allude to in describing them itself makes reference to that very property (namely the property red); and (iv) it makes no pretence of offering a reduction of the secondary qualities naturalistically to the primary ones and yet at the same time declines to dispute their right to a place in the world.[17]

What is remarkable and suggestive here is that in the case of Lockean secondary qualities it is the experiential response that serves to specify the property in question, people's sensitivities, that is, and there is no way in which closer specification could be achieved in terms of some more 'objective' measure. The naturalists' mistake was to think that the only properties the world could contain were those that permitted of 'objectivization'. But here we see that we are dealing with properties that of their very nature cannot be objectivized. To embark on such a course merely changes the subject. And we may reflect that just as the nature of the objective features of the world are liable to be more precisely picked out with the advance of the sciences, so the boundaries of the subjective features of things will be fixed by the limits of our capacities to come to experience things in discriminating ways.

Is this a result that the naturalist could live with? Not, of course, as long as he insists on the scientism he inherited from the nineteenth century. But otherwise why not? The pursuit of a secondary quality analogy gives us a way of offering a viable philosophical account of how sentences attributing aesthetic properties to things could be true. It conforms perfectly happily to two leading concerns of philosophical naturalism I pointed to at the start of the last section: in the aesthetic arena it does not find itself endorsing the existence of supernatural beings and properties, nor does it endorse existences other than those we find cognitively accessible. All that has given way is the over-restrictive view of how far cognition can extend and what the appropriate rules of proof should be. As Hume himself pertinently observed (in a slightly different context): 'theories of abstract philosophy, systems of profound theology have prevailed during one age: in a successive period they have been universally exploded' ('Standard', para. 26).

The only other remark that I have to make is this: the rehabilitated naturalist of the earlier style may still feel he needs greater assurance than has been forthcoming that those aesthetic properties whose patents of existence I have sought to ratify have not been left too thoroughly mysterious to clear even the first hurdle. It may seem as if refusing to identify aesthetic properties other than in terms of what refined human responses can be brought to recognize implies they have been exiled from the natural world altogether. But this would be mistaken. If we think of the dumpy and the dainty, it is evident that these complex (though perfectly familiar) properties are not identical with any purely physical properties of things, but they could not be possessed by the teapot and the teaspoons but for the physical constitution that they have. Being dumpy is not possible without a physical constitution of the right sort, and a truly dumpy object's ceasing to be dumpy is a change that comes about in a physical object only if the appropriate physical changes befall it. In cases such as these the aesthetic features of my tea service supervene on the objective nature of its elements without being identical with any of them. That is one major way they have their place in the world of physical objects without mystery.[18]

But surely, mystery there still is, the naturalist will retort. For to take the secondary quality analogy seriously and to say, as I have, that the responses by which we mark out the secondary qualities have to be identified in terms of the properties to which they are responses, abounds with mystery the moment it is recalled that in the secondary quality case, as Locke envisages, the properties in question were nothing other than the liability the object has to elicit such responses. Transferring that model to the aesthetic domain will not do at all, and if nothing more can be said, then the threatened negative conclusion we have envisaged looms over us.

That may indeed be right. But there is light at the end of the tunnel, I think, if only we emend Locke's original dispositional account of the secondary qualities. Pale grey is the property of paper that we see, the acridity the property of the smoke we smell, and sweetness the property of the jam we taste. None of these are simply dispositions to evoke such sensible experiences, for the dispositions are not things we see, smell, and taste. True, pale grey things do have this disposition, just as they have the particular light reflecting texture that they do, but neither is identical with the secondary property. That, the property of being red, is different from both but superveniently dependent upon them. It is not a mystery because we detect it in perception, can distinguish it from other such properties, and tie it down to the physical world in these ways.[19] If we can say that about the secondary qualities a similar reflection becomes available when we move to their close cousins in the aesthetic or ethical arena.[20]

IV. LITERARY NATURALISM REFORMED?

At the start I said that the naturalistic literary programme and naturalistically pursued philosophical aesthetics have close links. It has become apparent that they were both bound to come to grief and that the source of their grief is the same, to wit an over-hasty commitment to a scientism fostered by the spectacular successes of the natural sciences in the late nineteenth century. The response I have suggested in the philosophical domain, in the domain of philosophical aesthetics, has sought to preserve the central tenets of an earlier, more relaxed naturalism by shedding the scientistic burden. That might at least raise the question whether a humanized literary programme too might not have been envisagable that was recognizably 'naturalistic' but undeformed by the scientistic obsessions that in fact drove it. If so, I submit, it would have had room for these two features and still not lend itself to assimilation with the realism from which it sought to distinguish itself. First, it could sensibly explore not so much *the* (supposedly uniform) workings of human society and its individual members' lives, as construct its plots around various really possible ways in which social and personal pressures can bear upon the lives that they affect. Second, rather than think of his scenarios as testing general hypotheses with a view to discovering or illustrating how things regularly work, the reformed naturalist could envisage his work as helping us to find out what to make of the situations he imagines in humane and affective terms. Thereby he may contribute to the development of our capacities for reflective response to situations outside the novel. Not so much discovery of how the world works as discovery of what we may make of its multifarious possible workings. To do something to realize that possibility is surely to play a part in ameliorating our human lot, not as he originally envisaged, by enabling us to change it through theoretical understanding, but more by showing us how to understand it in humane terms, and thus making it more our own. Perhaps some of the success of the novels of that naturalist *par excellence*, Zola, derives less from their proximity to the naturalistic programme as he expounded it than from their conformity to these more attainable and more humane goals.

NOTES

1. See L. Hourtique, *Histoire Générale de L'Art (France)* (Paris, 1911), pp. 398–399; also Elie Faure, *Histoire de L'Art (L Art Moderne)* (Paris, 1948), pp. 253–254.

2. See the Goncourts' demand that 'today's novel be constructed from documents recounted or taken from life, just as history is constructed from written documents' (*Journal*, 24 October 1864).

3. E. Zola, *Le Roman expérimental* (Garnier-Flammarion, Paris, 1970, pp. 64–65 (my translation).

4. C. Bernard, *Introduction à l'étude de la médecine expérimentale* (Garnier-Flammarion, Paris, 1966), p. 33 (my translation).

5. Zola, *Le Roman Expérimental*, pp. 65–66.

6. *Ibid.*, p. 77.

7. '... the knavery and folly of men are such common phenomena that I should rather believe the most extraordinary events to arise from their concurrence than admit so signal a violation of the laws of nature', in 'Of Miracles' in *Essays, Literary, Moral and Political* (London, George Routledge & Sons, n.d.), p. 557.

8. See *Ethics*, I, Appendix.

9. It would be a mistake to think that this ideal was a novel one in the nineteenth century. An historian of ideas would certainly point to the influence of Descartes in the background here, reminding us in particular how French conceptions of scientific method were imbued with Cartesian Rules of Method. The difference between Descartes and his nineteenth-century disciples is that they were genuinely successful in the systematization of science, whereas for him it was a distant dream.

10. Zola uses this axiom from Taine's *Histoire der la Littérature Anglaise* as his epigraph to the second edition of *Thérèse Raquin*. It should remind us that the naturalists' aspirations were fundamentally positive, not negative. They thought that through naturalistic reduction they had a way of according their proper existential status to features of our world that would otherwise be all too tenuous. The negative aspect only begins to appear when the real difficulties of carrying through such reductions come to be recognized while the metaphysical impetus to naturalism is maintained.

11. Taking rather more care, one should say that the beauty in the verse must be supposed to be akin to the microstructure of the wine occasioned by the immersion of the leather and iron in it, for it is that physical character of the liquid that the naturalist will see the taste reducing to, if anything. *En passant*, I remark that it is not clear that Kant ever read this essay of Hume's, even though we know he did read others. So perhaps his attack on the possibility of an objective standard of taste at *Critique of Judgement* §34 is not occasioned by this passage at all.

12. Cited approvingly in D. Wiggins, 'A Sensible Subjectivism?', at footnote 15, Essay V of *Needs, Values, Truth* (Blackwell, Oxford, 1986), p. 195, an essay to which I am heavily indebted in sections II and III.

13. G.E. Moore, *Principia Ethica* (Cambridge: Cambridge U.P., 1903), §121.

14. *Ibid.*, my emphasis.

15. The novelty of the science of psychology is frequently called in aid as a reassurance that the laws that elude the searcher are waiting to be found. Above we saw Zola doing just this as early as 1880.

16. Against this background we can see Nietzsche's jibe in *Götzendämmerung* ('Sprüche und Pfeile' §6) that 'man does not strive for happiness: only the English do that' as an early repudiation of ethical naturalism.

17. True, sometimes Locke does equate the quality with the experience of the quality, as when he says that objects have no colour in the dark (see *Essay* II.viii,18,19), but this is quite inconsistent with his theoretical stance on the matter at *Essay* II.viii.10. He himself insists on the distinction between qualities and ideas of qualities, and this inconsistency simply runs the two together (in just the way that Berkeley took to be mandatory and with such disastrous results).

18. It is tempting to see just such a suggestion in the offing in Moore's remark at *Principia Ethica* §121 quoted in the body of the text above.

19. The suggestion is worked out in some detail in Colin McGinn, 'Colours, Another Look', *Journal of Philosophy* (1996).

20. Close cousins and no more, if only for the reason that the aesthetic properties of things we are sensitive to are normative in a way the familiar secondary qualities are not. See J.H. McDowell, 'Values and Secondary Qualities', in Ted Honderich (ed.), *Morality and Objectivity* (London: Routledge, 1985), reviving the Kantian insight of *Critique of Judgement* §§18 and 19.

HENRI MITTERAND

Zola, "ce rêveur définitif"

"Ce rêveur définitif" is a definition of the poet by Benjamin Péret. We are only now beginning to read Zola with this key. It is extremely difficult and time-consuming to dismantle the mannequin left by traditional criticism and schoolteaching stereotypes in place of the true profile of the author of the *Rougon-Macquart*. This is not, however, due to a lack of serious analytical work. For more than half a century a dynamic revisionist process has been underway, developing against Zola's own convictions, and revealing a remarkable pilgrim of the imaginary, as well as a virtuoso of narrative composition, in the shadow of the so-called "naturalist". However, we still hear the same ignorant and lazy refrain that identifies Zola crudely with realism and its naturalist variant: a realism that copies the real, the realism of superficial social observation, crude psychology, outmoded narrative techniques, and a naive progressive ideology.... We must, then, keep returning to the workbench. We must affirm again and again the usefulness of modern critical inquiry to our knowledge of a novelistic *oeuvre* that was as much inspired and artistic as an observation of mentalities and behaviour.

COMMUNICATING VESSELS

The study of Zola's figural language is an important, indeed essential, strand

From the *Australian Journal of French Studies* 38, no. 3 (September–December 2001). Translated by Fiona Neilson. © 2001 by Monash University.

of this modern revision. It has shown, sometimes brilliantly, that *mimesis*, the representation of the forms and phenomena of the real, is rarely conceived of by Zola in its pure state: it quickly turns into expression by analogy, which substitutes for the object of reference a figure that is to some degree comparable.[1] Beyond that, it identifies profiles and mythical motifs that form the deep foundations of the metaphorical and symbolic representations of the surface.[2] Each commentator has worked according to his own interests and intuitions: one on the symbolic images of Paris—Paris-building site, Paris-cauldron, Paris-prey, Paris-brothel, etc.; another on the theriomorphic animation of the machine—the still of *L'Assommoir*, sweating with poisoned alcohol, the Voreux of *Germinal*; another on the ubiquity of images of expansion and regression; another on the dynamic of energy sources in the *Rougon-Macquart*—blood, sap, sweat, alcohol, money, sperm; yet another on the founding myths of the Rougon-Macquart family.[3] In this way a network of connections has come slowly to light, a network that comes more from the work of the imagination, feeding on the treasure of earlier fictions, than from an ethnographic naturalism. *Le Ventre de Paris* is simultaneously a description of the Halles, the biology of an anthropomorphic city, and the story of the eternal struggle between the Fat and the Thin.

It is this power, this continual productivity of the image and concretions of images interconnected by a constant play of sequences and links, that gives Zola a special, eminent place in post-Balzacian realism, and that makes a sort of sur-naturalism out of his fictional (rather than his theoretical) naturalism, once one has a good grasp of all the elements. It is a sur-naturalism allied with symbolism, in some ways a precursor of Art nouveau ... and perhaps of surrealism, if we consider Breton's avowal: "Je n'ai jamais éprouvé le plaisir intellectuel que sur le plan analogique".[4]

Digging even deeper, however, than the anchor-point of the work in the history of facts and ideas, and beyond its metaphorical fabric and mythical investment, we can see a world of prototypical figures emerge, foreign or antecedent to the taking over of being by rationality, morality and discourse: the tall shadows bringing, in their primitive state, desire, delirium, violence, murder, as well as festivities and carnival—or heroic youthfulness. For example, those that engender Étienne Lantier, crushing Laval's head with a rock to possess Catherine for himself, in his rival's very blood—or inversely, in *La Fortune des Rougon*, Miette dying enveloped in the folds of the red flag. Romantic visions à la Delacroix, or à la Hugo, but also, coming from even more distant sources, intuition of a prodigious human naturality, sometimes tragic and terrifying, sometimes Dionysian and carnavalesque, that of the titanic struggle between the life instinct and the death instinct: on the one hand, the bulimic rumblings of the Halles, or the wild gallops of sex (in *Nana* and *Pot-Bouille*), or the bacchic trances of the fair; on the other, the criminal mutual destruction of enemy brothers (*La Fortune des Rougon*), the glimmers of incest of *La Curée*, or the suicidal fury of the mine's damned against the unknown god of capital. The Aeschylian birth, according to Nietzsche, of tragedy. Everywhere the same machinery of desire and murder, the same cruelty of man, of gods, or of History, the same chaos. Until the moment when a young hero, himself torn by an inner struggle between instinct and reason, succeeds in shaping out of this chaos "a dialectical optimism", according to another saying from Nietzsche: of a kind more Apollonian than Dionysian.

If we take into account the excess and the vividness of these visions' sudden appearance, we also arrive by this route at the frontiers of a surrealism. Even if we admit that they are heavily ballasted with mythological and literary reminiscences, their abundance and the density of their interconnections give them an absolute singularity in the literature of the century. Discarding academic proprieties and positivist wisdom, in which, nonetheless, he had total confidence, Zola returns to and regenerates the "first art" of narrative. It is in this that he is modern as well as paradoxical. "Admirables jardins des croyances absurdes, des pressentiments, des obsessions et des délires. Là prennent figure des dieux inconnus et changeants", will write Aragon in *Le Paysan de Paris*.[5]

SLIDING AND PRECIPITOUS EVENTS

We must certainly be wary of trying to find in Zola a fully-fledged surrealist *avant la lettre*. These anachronisms would be both facile and fragile. For their part, the pontiffs of surrealism would never allow it. Deterred from a more than cursory reading of the *Rougon-Macquart* by his disdain for fiction, and also probably by the discourse on "naturalism" of the time, André Breton did not bother to take a closer look. Aragon, carried away by his devotion to the principles of socialist realism, restricted himself to a few generalities—sometimes benevolent, sometimes aloof, but in any case traditional—on Zola's contribution to social history. The author of the *Rougon-Macquart* was traversing his so-called "purgatory" period during the 1920s—although still hailed by some important voices: Gide, Mauriac, Céline, Cocteau.

And yet ... Listen to Cocteau, who sometimes situates himself on the margins of surrealism:

Comme j'aimerais plaider la cause de Zola et mettre sur la table des juges de quoi les confondre et les convaincre que ce grand réaliste était un grand polite.

Comme j'aimerais plaider la cause du réalisme véritable et dire: "Le réalisme consiste à peindre avec exactitude les objets d'un monde propre à l'artiste et sans le moindre rapport avec ce qu'on a coutume de prendre pour la realité".

Aussitôt on verrait sortir des coulisses d'un théâtre qu'on accuse d'être une sorte de transcendance du *Grand-guignol* un cortège de scènes si singulières, si hautes, si nobles, si émouvantes, que j'arrive mal à comprendre que leur merveille ne guérisse pas les aveugles et ne les oblige pas à reconnaître leur erreur.

Quoi, c'est de ce grossier Zola, de ce bloc de tourbe, de ce monstre obscur, ennemi de toute grâce, que sortent les chevaux blancs de la mine, la locomotive morte sous la neige, l'enfant qui saigne sur les images d'Epinal, l'ivrogne qui flambe, mille et mille exemples d'un lyrisme savant analogue au lyrisme naïf de *Fantômas* lequel enchantait Guillaume Apollinaire, et dont j'estime qu'il doit toujours nous servir de guide.[6]

What is it that attracts Cocteau in Zola's writing? Not the analogies integrated into the discourse of representation, but phenomena grasped as they are and immediately perceived as just as strange as fascinating—prior to any metaphorical textualization. The dead locomotive beneath the snow: we think of Magritte. A child who bleeds to death on images of Epinal: we might think of Balthus. The reader will find all the symbols he wants. But fundamentally, we only find a frozen gaze, fixed, hallucinated, before an illogical spectacle of the real. It is therefore not enough to record the procession of metaphors, symbols and myths. If their importance is now obvious to us, they are not the sole constitutive factors of the Zolian *insolite*. Paradoxically, perhaps, a return to the real, to the natural, is essential; an opposite way to that of analogic discourse, turning its back on metaphorization to return to things as they appear to the errant novelist in search of describable realities, but in the face of which he loses himself in stunned contemplation, and which release an immediate eruption of the imaginary in the real, by a sort of sudden release of the gaze.

Zola, in the spring of 1872, strolls through the Halles in search of atmospheric effects for *Le Ventre de Paris*. Here is a general view, used as a simile:

Un aspect des Halles, vues de biais, de la rue Montmartre: une grande arcade d'une avenue, haute, béante, puis des pavillons de biais, avec leurs deux étages de toits, leurs persiennes, leurs entassements bizarres, qui ressemblent à des terrasses suspendues, à des architectures hindoues, à des couloirs aériens, à des ponts volants jetés sur le vide.

C'est d'une légèreté et d'un caprice fantastiques. C'est babylonien.[7]

But here is the close-up of a hairdresser's window:

Rue Saint-Honoré. Le coiffeur marchand de cheveux. Cheveux dans des boîtes en has (chignons, nattes, anglaises), pendant en haut (queues, nattes, cache-peigne, frisons). Tours, etc. De toutes les couleurs, noirs, gris, blancs, rouges, blonds, châtains, et de toutes les nuances. En has têtes d'homme et de femme en cire coupée, avec des cravates de velours rouge (sanglant). Une tête d'homme avec la barbe et les moustaches, mi-blanche et mi-noire, alterné. La femme en buste qui tourne, écharpe plissée de satin, avec une bouche en cuivre dans le creux des seins. La bouche souriante, les yeux clairs, les cils plantés raides et trop longs. Les cheveux sont étiquetés. (p. 362)

And this singular silhouette:

Un marchand de mort aux rats, avec des rats pendus à une croix, et une boite de bois sur le flanc. (p. [369])

In contrast to the first sketch, here we have two examples of what one could perhaps call the tendentious conversion of naturalism to surrealism. Fifty years later, Aragon will also stop in front of another hairdresser's window, the one in the *Passage de l'Opéra*, and will dream at length of this marvel: the blond hair of feminine wigs.[8] Two "Paris peasants": Zola and Aragon. For both of them daily life is bizarre; it contains encounters that destabilize rational thought and replace it, without a transition, with the work of dreams. Before it becomes part of discourse, the transfiguration is an affair of the gaze and of mental process: of *clairvoyance*. As in a mirage, the heads of mannequins in the shop-window of the Halles, with their red ties, change into real human heads, decapitated heads. The revolving bust of a woman smiles like a real woman. How bizarre: her hair has a price-tag. She is for sale. The passer-by knows that all this is but a simulacrum, an artificial fusion of the inert and the animate, but it has slid in an instant into a puddle of unnerving strangeness: one of these "sliding events" [*faits-glissades*] that André Breton will evoke magisterially in *Nadja*.

This example alone, taken from the preparatory notes for *Le Ventre de Paris*, leads one to avoid any confusion between the surnaturalism of Zola's thought and metaphorical and mythical language and the other phenomenon, nearer the surrealist imaginary, that often characterizes his perception of the objective world: the instantaneous, automatic substitution of the banal, recognizable as such (the wigs), with a vision from elsewhere (the bloody head): sometimes from culture, sometimes from the unconscious, sometimes from both simultaneously. There is much to say, no doubt, about the fantasy of the decapitated heads.

Once again, this is not about making Zola a fully-fledged surrealist *avant la lettre*, but simply to state that the naturalism he conceived, and with which he is credited in the critical and pedagogical vulgate, is bursting at the seams in his fiction, and first of all in the preparatory notes for his novels. Or else—and this comes to the same thing—that he pushes it to its extreme limits in order to discover the underside, the margins, the unreason, even the magic spells, of the natural. We simply have to escape from the positivism that has nurtured his theses, and to read him in the light of later discoveries that he partly anticipates in another sphere of his activity; to adjust our sights, to read his novels not only for the robustness of their information on daily life, and on the modes of existence and thought of a past age, but with a searching and focused vision. We can then discern very different reliefs, which seem to have been born from a collision between the use of observation—its rules infinitely repeated—and his disturbed systems of perception, feeling and imagination.

I have referred, in connection with *Le Ventre de Paris*, to *Le Paysan de Paris* and *Nadja*. Strange Paris, mysterious Paris, magical Paris, an inexhaustible store of wonders and of attacks on logic and the accepted order of things. If you reread certain pages of *La Curée, Son Excellence Eugène Rougon* and *Une page d'amour*, you will discover a grand dreamer of the strangeness of the city. From the window of the Café Riche's private room, where she is going to give herself to her son-in-law Maxime Rougon, Renée notices a hatter's slogan that she does not understand, amongst the advertisements on a kiosk, "sur un carreau, dans un cadre jaune et vert, une tête de diable ricanant, les cheveux hérissés [...]".[9] The devil on the boulevards. An image simply seen, without commentary or rhetorical translation. Not an explicit symbol, but only an icon, set down incongruously in the middle of Paris. No one notices it, nor stops to look at it: a banal advertising object. Nothing: but the spectacle of this nothing, which chills Renée with fright, making her clairvoyant for an instant, achieves this time the dimension not of the "sliding event" but rather the "precipitous event" [*fait-precipice*], that which according to Breton is accompanied

> de la sensation très nette que pour nous quelque chose de grave, d'essentiel, en depend, jusqu'à l'absence complete de paix avec nous-mêmes que nous valent certains enchaînements, certains concours de circonstances qui passent de loin notre entendement, et n'admettent notre retour à une activité raisonnée que si, dans la plupart des cas, nous en appelons à l'instinct de conservation.[10]

Not a "figure", in the tropological sense of the term, but rather a marker, a warning effect. The devil of the boulevard is not there for purposes of comparison, nor as meaningful in himself. Perhaps he indexes the presence of evil at the heart of Parisian pleasures? But no one would know how to read him as such, not even Renée, whom he has hypnotized. At most, he forewarns of a destiny: damnation. But he has appeared in any case as a random object: as a "planned accident", or as a magical apparition, before the eyes of the young woman, the only one to notice it.

In *Son Excellence Eugène Rougon*, it is the icon of a grey overcoat, slogan-sign of a tailor that, placed at the top of a building on the Ile Saint-Louis, lets itself be seen by the procession that accompanies the Prince Imperial to the Hôtel de Ville, the day of his baptism. Nothing can be more inappropriate, more derisory, but also more questioning than this flying of a fake bourgeois coat above the imperial pomp. Again, an ironic coincidence, and probably more than that: a warning, in the form of a mark of common rank or vulgarity placed on an immaculate protocol, and announcing other upsets. And what if this ready-made grey coat of modern advertising reminded Napoléon le Petit, although without malice, of the one that Napoléon le Grand used to wear? These apparently gratuitous encounters, which reveal less despicable ones later, are the "farces" of coincidence. What Aragon called "the metaphysics of the concrete" and Engels, long before him, called "the form of manifestation of necessity" ...

The inventory of these humorous aspects of things, relayed by the novelist's humour, remains to be made. They are sometimes born from Zola's stupefied or amused fixation before a fantasy of the real—he probably *saw* the hatter's devil and the tailor's aerial coat, as he saw the hairdresser's severed heads—and at other times from an imagined variation of the model. Let us stop once more on the tombstone of the disused Plassans cemetery, in *La Fortune des Rougon*, then next to the trunk and fishing rod of the Rambaud household in the last pages of *Une Page d'amour*. On the rudimentary level of the symbolic, the tomb is a metonymic image of death. But chance had it that, on the first eve of the armed resistance of the Var Republicans in the *coup d'état* of December 1851, recounted in *La Fortune des Rougon*, the two young people who will be its heroes, Miette and Silvère, come to sit down, to enact their chaste love, on a tombstone bearing the first name of a young girl who has been sleeping there since time immemorial: Marie. "Ci-gist... Marie... morte..." (II, p. 31). Miette is the Provençal diminutive of Marie. If Breton's Nadja had passed by, quite obviously she would have read the future of these two adolescents in this "petrifying coincidence": it is on this tomb that a policeman will smash Silvère's head open during the bloody week in December, assassinated to open the road to fortune for the Rougons. Right from the start, the stone was coded. Breton speaks, for his part, of "life's cryptograms" ...[11]

The failed act also has something cryptographic about it. Zola had this intuition long before Freud. At the end of *Une Page d'amour*, when Hélène Mouret, deprived of love by sickness and her daughter's death, has consented to marry an old family friend, the two spouses walk through the snow-covered Passy cemetery, where the young Jeanne lies at rest, before leaving Paris forever; and it is at this moment that Hélène suddenly realizes that she has forgotten her husband's fishing-rods. She does not know, either, if she has "bien fermé la grosse malle"—the trunk of memories, which would only seek to escape. And her husband suddenly raises his voice: "Je suis sûr que tu as oublié les cannes à pêche!—Oh! absolument, cria-t-elle, surprise et fâchée de son manque de memoire. Nous aurions dû les prendre hier" (II, p. 1092). The fishing-rods—a substitute for what is only too obvious—in the midst of icy graves. This association, perhaps a last-minute "automatic" discovery, or a deliberately humorous allusion, says a lot about the young woman's unconscious and desperate disgust for the frustrations that await her.[12]

LIBERTINAGE

Sex, castration, death. For Zola, and later for the surrealists, woman is the figure of modern beauty: Thérèse, Madeleine, Miette, Renée, Albine, Gervaise, Hélène, Nana, and their sisters to come. All desirable, all irradiated by eros. But also all destroyed by it, in one way or another. *Les Rougon-*

Macquart, from *La Fortune des Rougon* to *Le Docteur Pascal*, exude an obsession with the feminine, its mysteries and fatalities. All the disguises, all the perversions and all the misfortunes of desire. Zola negotiates as best he can the cant and the censorship that informed representations of sex. He is shrewd because he knows the limits imposed by the dominant morality, all the while mocking them, and he will not condemn himself to publishing clandestinely. Nonetheless he breaks with academic convention to a degree hitherto unseen in literature, by making his work a long history of sexual initiation and carnal love. The women he portrays all obey the pleasure principle in the way they lead their existence. It is a form of liberation of the novel, and also a form of construction of a new morality. Perhaps the morality of *l'amour fou*. And an experience of the dangerous game of taboos: Miette, the virgin of the Republic; Renée, in love with her son-in-law; Albine, in the arms of a priest himself seized by desire; Clotilde, who gives herself to Dr Pascal, her uncle. These variations do not happen without interrogations or doubts. But is it done differently in Ernst, Dali and Picasso? It is the internal contradiction of his endless battle with the Church's discourse: a touch of original sin remains in the wild passions of these young women, and death, at the end of the road, often appears as the punishment of a sin. There is no happy love and there is no innocent love.

There is no more remarkable staging of these interactions between nature and the law than *La Faute de l'abbé Mouret*. Overall, the imagery of this novel, with its vegetable decorations, its woman-flower, its androgynous, momentarily devirilized priest-ephebe, seems closer to the *fin-de-siècle* aesthetic, part-Pre-Raphaelite, part-art nouveau, than the "surrealist revolution". The Paradou more closely resembles the oneiric universe of the *douanier* Rousseau than those of Tanguy or Delvaux, especially since its timeless chateau and labyrinthine garden, inhabited only by two young people unknown to the world, naturally lends itself to all sorts of transgressions. In any case, the main theme and principal episodes of this novel turn their back on vague *fin-de-siècle* ideals by the audacity of their *libertinage*, in every sense of the term: philosophical and carnal. If we are to give any meaning to the notion of naturalism, it is to this work that it is most applicable, even though it hardly bears the traces of social documentation, and even less of a preoccupation with the sordid. Because *La Faute de l'abbé Mouret* affirms and illustrates the victory of *nature* over dogma. A new earthly paradise will not cease communicating its animal instincts to a modern Adam and Eve, as new, virginal and preserved from all inhibitory discourse as on the first day of creation. The author of *La Faute* could have written these lines from *L'Amour fou*:

[...] j'entends justifier et préconciser toujours plus électivement le comportement lyrique tel qu'il s'impose à tout être, ne serait-ce qu'une heure durant l'amour et tel qu'a tenté de le systèmatiser, à toutes fins de divination possible, le surréalisme.[13]

This hour of love costs dearly. Serge Mouret will return to his first castration and Albine will let herself die of despair on a bed of roses whose perfume poisons her. The solitary chateau will transform itself into a mausoleum, sanctioning "le double jeu de l'amour et de la mort".[14] The image of the dead Albine rejoins that of the "femme de marbre tombée de tout son long dans l'eau qui coule" (I, p. 1347), a fountain statue that fascinated Serge during their wanderings through the Paradou:

C'était quelque noyée de cent ans, le lent suicide d'un marbre que des peines avaient du laisser choir au fond de cette source. La nappe claire qui coulait sur elle avait fait de sa face une pierre lisse, une blancheur sans visage, tandis que ses deux seins, soulevés hors de l'eau par un effort de la nuque, restaient intacts, vivants encore, gonflés d'une volupté ancienne. (loc. cit.)

Another Ophelia. They are startling reflections of the *Rougon-Macquart* in the depths of their textual waters, and in their prose-poem inflections.[15]

CADAVRES EXQUIS

I am torn between two fears: that of excessively underlining the points of convergence, and that of neglecting many examples that support a deviant reading of Zola. Actually, the theoretical and programmatic intentions of the author of *Le Roman expérimental* are not themselves immune to surprising changes of direction. The imaginary hides beneath the thesis. How can we coherently define an experimental novelist, who practises the same manipulations on live subjects as the biologist? One step further, and we would put him on the side of Raymond Roussel rather than on that of Claude Bernard... Brunetière and Céard would object to Zola that none of this is serious. But what if it was the most serious and most poetic trait of Zola, this aptitude to invent situations in which human experience is pushed to its most extreme limits? Like that of Serge Mouret and Albine, or again like that of Angélique in *Le Rêve*, so possessed by the stories of the *Légende dorée* that she dies.

So that when Zola, very early in his career, in 1868, discovers the *Traite de l'Hérédité naturelle* by Doctor Lucas,[16] he reads it deliberately as a dreamer, as an *illuminé*. What he is delighted to find in it, is less a scientific investigation than a treatise of tragic invention, an encyclopedia of virtual characters and situations illustrating the fatalities of heredity: a veritable dictionary of the novelistic imaginary, just as much as, and more than, a treatise on life sciences. Or an extraordinary theatre, manipulated by Lucas with a puppeteer's pleasure, with inspired discoveries that would have delighted Soupault, Crevel or Vaché: "A Rome les plus belles courtisanes sortent du peuple"; "Il y avait un religieux qui avait un si bon nez qu'il distinguait a l'odeur des femmes chastes ou non"; "Hommes qui ont du tigre et de la brute dans le sang, innocemment coupables". These are Lucas's phrases, not Boccaccio's. With the same excitement, Zola discovers in *L'Hérédité naturelle* the combinatory model used by Lucas to construct his classification of the mechanisms of heredity, based on a limited number of variables: props (the father, the mother), traits/characteristics (physical, mental), factors, modes, circumstances. A finite series of elements that engenders an infinity of combinations. He dazes himself with all this, and from Lucas's painstakingly categorized combinations he derives his own list of possible novelistic hypotheses, a litany of possible hereditary configurations, in which a sort of precursor of the associative game of "exquisite cadavers" or automatic writing can be found:

> [...]
> Hérédité d'un vieux male et d'une jeune femelle.
> Hérédité du facteur au moment du colt.
> Hérédité d'un mauvais accouplement d'age, de tempérament.
> Hérédité du type le plus ardent, le plus stable, le plus ancien.
> Hérédité dans une province (en Normandie, un normand)
> [...]
> Etc., etc.[17]

The scientific reference has served only as a launchpad into fiction. We can see light shadows, not even at the sketch stage, and which will only come into existence eight, ten or fifteen years later, flit past in this litany: Gervaise, Nana, Cécile Grégoire, etc. Along with them go many other virtual figures that will never be born and will remain aborted phantoms, hidden in the secret dreams of their begetter. An infinity of seeds has thus been put in place between the author of *L'Hérédité naturelle* and the future inventor of *L'Histoire naturelle et sociale d'une famille*. Only a few dozen will emerge into the open air of the scenario and writing—and of posterity. The creative intelligence also resides in the choice that actualizes the possible ones. But how can we speak of "naturalism" when only images from a magic lantern scroll across the screen?

NATURALISM AND REVOLUTION

Here we are in the engine-room of the *Rougon-Macquart*. But the machine will only really get going by adding a second motor: the climate provided by the political battle of the last three years of the Second Empire, which will correct and counterbalance the Lucas-effect and ballast Zola's novelistic project with history and polemic. Here, perhaps, is the last "factor"—to speak like Dr Lucas—in the more or less distant resemblance between Zola and the surrealists.

The word *revolution* occupies a central place in surrealist discourse. It is not the most common word in Zola's discourse, but in terms of *revolt*, the author of *Germinal* and *J'accuse* has nothing to envy the authors of *La Revolution surréaliste*. It is not only a question of feelings, but also of attitudes and languages, up to and including the artists' demand for independence with regard to revolutionary disciplines. The 1930 divorce between Breton, who brutally repudiated the notion of commitment, and Aragon, who committed himself to the Communist Party for the rest of his life, might recall the divergence between Zola, a critical but non-militant observer, and Vallès, who committed himself to the Commune and returned from exile in 1880 to make "the cry of the people" heard.[18] When Breton declared that "le seul devoir du poète, de l'artiste, est d'opposer un non irréductible a toutes formules disciplinaires", he was only repeating remarks often made by Zola.

The essential point, however, is not the resolute refusal to enlist people to his cause, the affirmation of the superiority of art over politicians' politicking, as we say today. It is, rather, the same feeling of disgust, the same degree of furor and disdain in the face of injustice, oppression and conformity. From 1868, Zola enters into battle with the Establishment, and he will never make peace. Conservatives and conformists of all persuasions respond with gusto, and continue moreover to do so in an underhand manner. *J'accuse* is no less provocative or incendiary than "*Front rouge*".... And again, the surrealists were thirty-year-olds when they launched their fiery attacks, whereas Zola took aim at decorated kepis and ministerial top hats at an age when, usually, serenity has succeeded indignation. Zola never knew Jarry; but have we paid enough attention to the fact that *J'Accuse* was contemporaneous with *Ubu-Roi*? Jarry's play provoked laughter, whereas Zola's pamphlet provoked fear, because he used it to appeal directly to public opinion, removing parliamentary and judicial filters with a stroke of the pen, and giving all the weight of his literary and moral stature, all the force of his style, to his indictment. A fierce, devastating eloquence. No circumscribed agitation, but a decisive subversion of institutional complacency and hypocrisy at the most appropriate moment. The most revolutionary action of the century, said Jules Guesde afterwards. Perhaps also the most surrealist gesture, if one of the criteria of surrealist activity is to do what no one has dared do until now, entirely disrespecting all codes of political and social good behaviour in order to "make things change".

Moreover, this was not Zola's first attempt. His whole career, in his fiction as well as in his essays and pamphlets, was punctuated by attacks on the bourgeoisie. *La Fortune des Rougon, La Curée, Une Page d'amour, Pot-Bouille, Germinal, L'Oeuvre, Paris*. The last line of *Le Ventre de Paris* is: "Quels gredins que les honnêtes gens!" (I, p. 895). Zola lived like a bourgeois and thought like an anarchist, never tamed. We need to read carefully the closing sentences of his novels: this is where the provocative or menacing formulae, the notes of black humour or disillusionment, and sometimes revolutionary prophecies, appear. The final sentence of *Germinal*[19] bears an extraordinary resemblance to the vision of André Breton, perceiving the factories of the northern suburbs of Paris from the heights of Montmartre in the early morning: "Vers la péripherie les usines, premières a tressaillir, s'illuminent de la conscience grandissante des travailleurs."

"La Republique sera naturaliste ou ne sera pas." People have mocked this declaration, which is admittedly somewhat extravagant. Yet did it not spring from the same presupposition that equated revolution and surrealism? As René Crevel wrote: "Toute poésie est une révolution en ce qu'elle brise les chaînes qui attachent l'homme au rocher conventionnel."[20] Let us reverse the facts: every revolution, every republic, can only survive and stay true to its founding principle—the spirit of freedom—if it breaks the chains of conformity. This is the essence of the debate in 1880 between the author of *L'Assommoir* and republican censorship.

The campaign for Manet in 1866. The attacks on the Empire in 1870. The assault on Moral Order in 1873. The scandal of *L'Assommoir* in 1877. The provocation of *Nana* in 1880. The warning of *Germinal* in 1885: "Hâtez-vous d'être justes, sinon la terre s'ouvrira." The Five against *La Terre* in 1887. The pillorying of the generals of 1870 in *La Debâcle* in 1892. The frontal attack on state power in 1898. And I could go on. Zola never stopped being subversive, unsociable in fact, and a danger to the established order.

He was the most liberal of men in regard to all the powers that demand respect and obedience. Thus the least "reasonable". This does not, of course, bestow on him a certificate of pre-surrealism, but at least these ruptures with the Establishment show that he assigned himself, early in his career and definitively so, a political, moral and aesthetic role as guard, critic and voice of reply,[21] as most surrealists will do later. He exercised this role relentlessly in the registers of both narrative fiction and polemical essay. And in both he did so as a poet, if we admit, like Paul Eluard—who retraces here, without thinking, the programme of the Rougon-Macquart—that "la poésie véritable est incluse dans tout ce qui ne conforme pas à cette morale qui, pour maintenir son ordre, son prestige, ne sait construire que des banques, des casernes, des prisons, des églises, des bordels".[22]

*   *   *   *

Paul Valéry made fun of those novels that open with a sentence of this sort: "La marquise sortit à cinq heures." He was in fact referring to the entire novel genre with this sarcasm. André Breton echoed him:

> Le procès de l'attitude réaliste demande à être instruit, [...] C'est elle qui engendre aujourd'hui ces livres ridicules, [...] On ne m'épargne aucune des hesitations du personnage: sera-t-il blond, comment s'appellera-t-il, irons-nous le prendre en été? Autant de questions résolues une fois pour toutes au petit bonheur.[23]

Marcel Duchamp, contemplating the Mona Lisa, a portrait of the sort of young woman often found in paintings and novels—and not necessarily of the marquise genre—was content to add this iconoclastic subtitle: *LHOOQ*. This alphabetical pun would suit Zola's principal female characters perfectly... And that changes everything. This takes us well beyond Valéry's marquise and Breton's blond young man. The caricature is not where we would expect it.

Breton reproaches novels for their "style d'information pure et simple", their stereotypes, their "superpositions d'images de catalogue", their "cartes postales", "l'intraitable manie qui consiste à ramener l'inconnu au connu".[24] He does not condemn prose narrative, but he admits it only as the vector of accident, of mystery, of the marvellous, linked directly to illuminations that have escaped from the unconscious. In the literary domain, only the marvellous is capable of fertilizing "des oeuvres ressortissant à un genre inférieur tel que le roman et d'une façon générale tout ce qui participe de l'anecdote".[25] Let us pass over the "inferior genre" and "the anecdotal", which are rather summary terms. Two remarks in conclusion: it is surprising that the author of the *Manifeste* did not recognize the *mirabilia* of *La Bête humaine* (in the etymological sense of the term, itself etymon of marvel: that of which contemplation stupefies); conversely, an attentive reading of the *admirable* surrealist texts, poetry, stories and mixed manifestos, provides probably the best introduction there is to Zola's peaceful, or violent, follies.[26]

NOTES

* The French version of this text appeared in *Mélusine*, XXI, 2001, pp. 133–147.

1. For example, the Halles compared to the belly of Paris.

2. "Des mythes nouveaux naissent sous chacun de nos pas" (Louis Aragon, *Le Paysan de Paris*, Paris, Gallimard, 1926, p. 13).

3. See the work of Jacques Noiray, Auguste Dezalay, Jean Borie, Roger Ripoll, Guy Robert, Michel Serres, Maarten van Buuren, etc.

4. André Breton, *Signe ascendant*, Paris, Gallimard, 1949, p. 7.

5. P. 13.

6. Jean Cocteau, "Zola le poète", *Les Cahiers naturalistes*, no 11, 1958, pp. 442–443. See also one of the rare articles devoted to the "surrealizing" aspects of Zola: J. H. Matthews, "Zola et les surréalistes", *Les Cahiers naturalistes*, no 24–25, 1963, pp. 99–107.

7. See Henri Mitterand, ed., *Émile Zola: Carnets d'enquêtes. Une ethnographie inédite de la France*, Paris, Plon, 1987, p. 349.

8. Aragon, *Le Paysan de Paris*: "Je me suis souvent arrêté au seuil de ces boutiques interdites aux hommes et j'ai vu se dérouler leurs cheveux dans leurs grottes." (p. 48)

9. All quotations from the *Rougon-Macquart* are taken from the edition directed by Armand Lanoux, Paris, Gallimard, Bibliothèque de la Pléiade, 1960–1967, 5 vols, and will be given parenthetically in the text. See *La Curée*, I, p. 450.

10. André Breton, *Nadja*, in *Oeuvres complètes*, ed. Marguérite Bonnet, Paris, Gallimard, Bibliothèque de la Pléiade, 1988–1999, 3 vols, see I, p. 652.

11. Nadja: "Il se peut que la vie demande à être déchiffrée comme un cryptogramme" (I, p. 716).

12. Everything is frozen at the end of this novel, like Hélène's bare feet on her wedding night with Rambaud: "Ils s'étaient mariés en noir. Le soir des noces, lui aussi avait baisé ses pieds nus, ses beaux pieds de statue qui redevenaient de marbre" (II, p. 1089).

13. In *Oeuvres complètes*, II, p. 722.

14. Louis Aragon, *Le Paysan de Paris*, p. 42. See also Robert Desnos: "Je n'imagine pas d'amour sans que le goût de la mort, dépourvue d'ailleurs de toute sentimentalité et de toute tristesse, y soit mêlé." (quoted by Gérard Durozoi and Bernard Lecherbonnier, *Le Surréalisme: theories, themes, techniques*, Paris, Larousse, 1972, p. 175).

15. André Breton, *Poisson soluble* in *Oeuvres complètes*, I, p. 349: "Le fantôme a environ deux cents ans, il parle encore un peu français. Mais dans sa chair transparente se conjuguent la rosée du soir et la sueur des astres." Woman, suicide, the past, water, translucent whiteness... Albine means "white one" [la blanche]. See again, in *Le Paysan de Paris*: "[...] la même blancheur déi-fiée depuis les temps qu'on l'adorait dans les suburbes romaines préside toujours au double jeu de l'amour et de la mort, [...]" (p. 42).

16. Dr Prosper Lucas, *Traité philosophique et physiologique de l'Hérédité naturelle, dans les états de santé et de maladie du système nerveux* [...], Paris, J.-B. Baillière, 1847–1850, 2 vols.

17. The game of associations gets even freer and more open when Zola leaves in search of the tide of a work in progress, for example, *L'Oeuvre* or *La Bête humaine*.

18. In contrast to Breton and Aragon, the relationship between Zola and Vallès did not stop being one of solidarity and friendship.

19. "Des hommes poussaient, une armée noire, vengeresse, qui germait lentement dans les sillons, grandissant pour les récoltes du siècle futur, et dont la germination allait faire bientôt éclater la terre" (III, p. 1591).

20. Quoted by Gérard Durozoi and Bernard Lecherbonnier, op. cit., p. 231.

21. *Contre-attaque* is the name of a revolutionary theoretical group put together by the surrealists and Georges Bataille in 1935.

22. Quoted by Durozoi and Lecherbonnier, op. cit., p. 231.

23. André Breton, *Manifeste du surréalisme*, 1924, in *Oeuvres complètes*, I, pp. 313–314.

24. Ibid., I, pp. 314–315.

25. Ibid., I, p. 320.

26. As does the definition Julien Gracq gave to the surrealist *oeuvre*, which maintains "à leur point extrême de tension les deux attitudes simultanées, que ne cesse d'appeler ce monde fascinant et invivable où nous sommes: l'éblouissement et la fureur" (quoted by Durozoi and Lecherbonnier, op. cit., p. 87).

Chronology

<table>
<tr><td>1840</td><td>Emile-Edouard-Charles-Antoine Zola is born in Paris on April 2 to Francesco Zola and Emilie Aubert. His father, Francesco, began his career as a soldier, but his real interests were mathematics and engineering. After the 1830 Revolution, Francesco took up permanent residence in France. Zola's mother was the daughter of a French glazier and occasional house painter.</td></tr>
<tr><td>1843</td><td>Francesco moves to Provençal with his wife and son, Emile. There, he is commissioned to build dams and canals necessary to provide the city of Aix with an adequate water supply.</td></tr>
<tr><td>1847</td><td>Francesco is stricken with pleurisy and dies, leaving his wife and son with little more than shares in the Canal Company and debts of ninety thousand francs. The company goes bankrupt and Emilie becomes embroiled in interminable and futile lawsuits. Eventually, she is left with no income. As he grows older, Zola will be profoundly affected by his impoverished background. He develops a lifelong compassion for the poor, a longing for social justice and a rejection of charity and disdain for what he considers to be middle-class hypocrisy and pride.</td></tr>
<tr><td>1852</td><td>After receiving his First Communion, Zola is enrolled as a scholarship student at the town's official preparatory</td></tr>
</table>

school, the College Bourbon (now the lycée d'Aix). Although Zola is poorly prepared and begins at the bottom of his class, he soon improves. Almost every year, he will win prizes in Latin, history, French narration and science.

Among his schoolmates are Paul Cézanne and Baptistin Baille, with whom he makes frequent excursions into the idyllic and picturesque Provençal countryside. Zola acquires a love of nature and a deep respect for life that will later pervade his writings. With these two inseparable companions, he also discovers the writings of Victor Hugo and Alfred de Musset, whose verses they would often bring during their jaunts in the country.

1857   Zola's grandmother, Aubert, dies in the fall. Zola, who is temperamentally somber, nervous and high-strung, must now face the terrible reality of death, a reality which will become one of his most obsessive literary themes. Shortly thereafter, the family's financial situation worsens and they move to Paris, where Emilie will seek the support of her husband's powerful friends. As a result of their help, she obtains a scholarship for her son at the lycée Saint-Louis. But Zola is homesick and disoriented at school and instead of paying attention in science, he furtively reads Hugo, Alphonse de Lamartine, Jules Michelet and other authors. At the same time, he writes a comedy, some poems and short stories, while composing long letters to Cézanne and Baille.

1858   At the beginning of his second academic year in Paris, Zola almost dies from what is probably typhoid fever. When he does return to school, it is much the same as the previous year.

1859   In June, Zola applies for the baccalaureate exam, the one great hurdle that all French students must satisfy before going on to an institution of higher learning. He does very well on the scientific part of the orals, but fails in literature, partly due to a disagreement with his examiner regarding an interpretation of a Jean de La Fontaine fable. In November, he takes the exam again, in Marseille, but does not make it through the written part.

Nevertheless, from the fall of this year, until January 1862, Zola will remain deeply involved in artistic activities that will become central to his literary work. He will spend hours browsing the bookstalls along the Seine, follow various left-wing publications and read Dante, Shakespeare, George Sand, André Chénier, Sainte-Beuve, and Montaigne. he accepts the Romantic conception of the poet as a prophet in the tradition of the Bible and aspires to follow in their footsteps.

1860   Zola is forced to take a job as a copy clerk in the Excise Office on the Paris docks. Hating his job, which he finds dehumanizing, He quits in June. For the next nineteen months, Zola will be mostly unemployed. Timid, thin, and hungry, his bourgeois education yields him nothing of practical value. He must pawn everything and borrow money from his friends.

He composes a long poem, *Paolo*, in which, he is inspired, as he tells Cezanne, to exalt Platonic love over carnal love, and demonstrate that in their skeptical century love can serve as faith. He is also now developing the general aesthetic doctrines that will underlie his naturalistic theories.

1862   Zola's destitution ends early in the year when, through the offices of another of his father's friends, he is hired as a clerk at Hatchette's publishing house, founded and run by the brilliant and liberal Louis Hatchette. Although Zola begins in the shipping department, he is soon put in charge of publicity, where he can study the workings of the literary marketplace. Michelet, Sainte-Beuve, and Taine become his friends.

1864   Toward the end of March, Zola has published enough short stories to make up a small book. He manages to get them published under the title *Contes à Ninon* (translated as *Stories for Ninon* in 1895).

1865   Zola publishes his first novel, based on his affair with a prostitute named Berthe, *La Confession de Claude* (translated as *Claude's Confession* in 1882). In general, the novel receives a warm reception, though some critics accuse Zola of depicting shameful and degrading love and a "hideous realism." As Zola continues to progress throughout his mid and late twenties, he is developing the essential elements of his literary naturalism. He is convinced that the right literary formula for his times requires a marriage of art and science. Under Taine's influence, he becomes enthusiastic about Flaubert, Stendahl, and Balzac. He also discovers Dickens, Thackeray, Poe, Hawthorne, and Edmond and Jules de Goncourt. On July 26 and August 31, he publishes two installments of his essay, "Proudhon et Courbet."

1866   In January, Zola leaves Hatchette in order to devote himself exclusively to journalism and creative writing. He is often in the company of a group of revolutionary artists, several of them future impressionists, at the Café Guerbois, all of whom are rebelling against the state-supported artistic tradition. On the occasion of the official exhibition that year, the Salon, Zola publishes a series of articles in the *Evénement* in which he promotes the painter Manet and attacks the current art establishment. In response, the newspaper's publisher, Henri de Villemessant, forces Zola to end this series. Zola also publishes *Mes haines* (My Hates), his first volume of collected essays, mostly on art and literature; *Mon Salon* (My Salon), a collection of art essays; and a potboiler novel, *Le Voeu d'une morte* (translated as *A Dead Woman's Wish* in 1902).

1867   Zola publishes another potboiler novel, *Les Mystères de Marseille* (translated as *The Mysteries of Marseille: A Love Story* in 1882) and a long brochure on Manet, *Edouard Manet: Etude biographique et critique*, which Manet included in his famous portrait of Zola. Zola also publishes another novel, *Thérèse Raquin* (translated in 1881).

1868   Second edition of *Thérèse Raquin* is published with a historically famous preface in which he applies the term "naturalist" to designate a group of contemporary writers to which he belonged. Publishes *Madeleine Férat* (translated as *Magdalen Ferat* in 1880). Joins the staff of the *Tribune*, a major liberal republican weekly. Throughout the year, he is diligently working on plans for his masterpiece, *Les Rougon-*

Macquart, a multi-volume work which would largely take up the next twenty-five years of his career.

1869   Early in the year, Lacroix agrees to publish this project and Zola is contracted to receive a meager but adequate income of five hundred francs per month.

1870   Zola turns thirty. In June, he marries Gabrielle Eléonore Alexandrine Meley, a former seamstress and the woman with whom he had been living for more than five years. On July 19, France declares war on Prussia and Zola is outspoken about Napoleon's criminal folly. In September, the French empire falls and Zola, Gabrielle and his mother flee Paris, first to Marseilles, and then to Bordeaux—the seat of the Government of National Defense. He founds a short-lived newspaper, the *Marseillaise*, serves as a private secretary of a government minister, and after the war serves as a parliamentary correspondent for the new National Assembly.

1871   The first of volume of *Les Rougon-Macquart*, entitled *La Fortune des Rougon*, is published (translated as the *Rougon-Macquart Family* in 1879). Back in Paris in March, Zola witnesses the civil war of the Commune and the horrible carnage brought about by its fall. Meanwhile, his personal life and circle of friends resumes much as it had been before the war started. In March, the *Siècle* finishes serializing *La Fortune des Rougon*. The novel begins to appear in bookshops in October. Zola publishes the second volume, *La Curée* (translated as *In the Whirlpool* in 1879.)

1873   Zola publishes the third novel, *Le Ventre de Paris* (translated as *The Markets of Paris* in 1879). His theatrical version of *Thérèse Raquin* has only a brief run.

1874   Zola publishes the fourth novel of the series, *La Conquête de Plassans* (translated as *The Conquest of Plassans: A Tale of Provincial Life* in 1879). Another one of his plays, *Les Héritiers Rabourdin* (*The Rabourdin Heirs*), is applauded by the audience on its first night, but critics tear it apart. Starting in April, Flaubert, Edmond de Goncourt, Turgenev, Daudet and Zola begin to meet once a month for an elaborate dinner, dubbed the "Dinner of the Hissed Authors."

1875   Zola publishes his fifth novel of the series, *La Faute de l'abbé Mouret* (translated as *The Abbé's Temptation*; or *La Faute de l'abbé Mouret*). Before year-end, this novel has already gone through four editions and is one of Zola's most popular reads.

1876   Zola publishes his sixth novel of the series, *Son Excellence Eugène Rougon* (translated as *Clorinda or the Rise and Reign of His Excellency Eugène Rougon, the Man of Progress* in 1880). In April, Zola begins the serial publication of *L'Assommoir*, which is both a great international success and the cause of a great public scandal in its depiction of the working class of mid-nineteenth-century Paris.

1877   As a result of his success with *L'Assommoir*, Zola and Alexandrine move to an elegant apartment on the rue de Boulogne. In January, *L'Assommoir* comes out in book form.

1878   Zola publishes the eighth novel in the series, *Une Page d'amour* (translated as *Hélène, a Love Episode*, in 1878). He and Alexandrine buy a second residence, a small farmhouse at Médan, in the Seine valley. May 28 is the premier performance of William Busnach and Octave Gastineau's adaptation of *L'Assommoir* at the Ambigu Theater. It is a smash hit with 250 performances in Paris and several tours in the provinces and abroad.

1879   In September, Zola's most famous literary review, "Le Roman expérimental" (translated as "The Experimental Novel" in *The Experimental Novel, and Other Essays*, 1894) is first published in the Saint Petersburg literary review, *Messager de l'Europe*. In this essay, Zola identifies naturalism with the experimental scientific method proposed by Claude Bernard. It is then republished in the *Voltaire* between October 16 and 20.

1880   Zola publishes the ninth novel in the series, *Nana*, which is both a tremendous success, with a first edition consisting of fifty-five thousand copies, and the cause for great public scandal in its depiction of the Parisian demi-monde of the Second Empire. Also published is a collection of stories by Zola and five of his younger naturalist friends, *Les Soirees de Médan* (*Evenings in Médan*), which includes Zola's masterpiece, "L'Attaque du Moulin." But the year is also one of great loss and bereavement—in April, his friend, Louis Duranty, an older writer and one of the leaders of the realist schools in the 1850s, dies; in May, Zola learns of Flaubert's death; and in October, Zola's mother dies.

1882   Haunted by death and distressed by spiritual and intellectual conflict within himself, Zola suffers a nervous breakdown in October. He publishes *Pot-Bouille*, a dryly satirical novel on the theme of middle-class licentiousness.

1883   Zola publishes the tenth novel in the series, *Au Bonheur des Dames* (translated as *The Ladies' Paradise; or, The Bonheu des Dames*, 1883).

1884   Zola publishes the eleventh novel in the series, *La Joie de vivre* (translated as *Joys of Life*, 1884).

1885   In February, the twelfth novel in the series, *Germinal*, comes out in book form. A sequel to *L'Assommoir*, *Germinal* is both another great success and cause for scandal.

1886   Zola publishes the thirteenth novel in the series, *L'Oeuvre* (translated as *Masterpiece; or, Claude Lantier's Struggle for Fame: A Realistic Novel*, in 1886).

1887   Zola publishes the fourteenth novel in the series, *La Terre*. For several years now, many of the younger generation of naturalist writers have been branching off in new directions. Some of the younger writers, Paul Bonnetain, J.H. Rosny, Lucien Descaves, Paul Margueritte and Gustave Guiches, write a scathing attack on the novel and on Zola as well. This document is published in the *Figaro* on August 18, is quickly baptized "Le Manifeste des cinq." Nevertheless, Zola's fame continues to grow.

1888   Zola publishes the fifteenth novel in the series, *Le Rêve* (translated as *The Dream* in 1888). Nearly fifty and childless, Zola takes on a young mistress, Jeanne Rozerot, whom his wife had engaged to help with the sewing and mending.

1889   In the fall, Jeanne gives birth to a baby girl, Denise.

1890   Jeanne gives birth to a second child, a son named Jacques. Shortly after Jacques birth, Alexandrine learns of Zola's mistress. Months later, Alexandrine becomes resigned to the situation. Zola's publishes the sixteenth novel in the series, *La Bête humaine* (translated as *Human Brutes* in 1890).

1891   Zola publishes the seventeenth novel in the series, *L'Argent* (translated as *Money* in 1891).

1892   Zola publishes the eighteenth novel in the series, *La Débâcle* (translated as *The Downfall: A Story of the Horrors of War* in 1892).

1893   Zola publishes his last volume of the Rougon-Macquart series, *Le Docteur Pascal* (translated as *Doctor Pascal; or, Life and Heredity*).

1894   On December 22, Capt. Alfred Dreyfus, a Jewish officer in the French army, is falsely convicted by a court-martial of having sold military secrets to Germany. Thus began the infamous Dreyfus Affair. It was later discovered that the real criminal was Maj. Ferdinand Walsin-Esterhazy, not Dreyfus. Between 1894 and 1898, Zola set to work on a new series of novels, *Les Trois Villes* (*The Three Cities*), a sequel to the Rougon-Macquart series. The first novel of *Les Trois Villes*, *Lourdes*, is published.

1896   *Rome*, the second novel of *Les Trois Villes*, is published and translated.

1898   *Paris*, the third novel of *Les Trois Villes*, is published (and translated in 1900). Zola finally becomes convinced of Dreyfus's innocence and when, on January 11, Esterhazy is acquitted, Zola decides to challenge the government and military authorities to keep the case alive. On January 13, Zola publishes the famous open letter to the president of the Republic in the Parisian newspaper *Aurore*. That letter, entitled "J'accuse," accuses various high officers of a cover-up. In a celebrated trial, Zola is found guilty and sentenced to a year in prison and a fine of three thousand francs. On appeal on April 2, the proceedings are quashed. On July 18, a second trial takes place at Versailles, but Zola flees to England before knowing the outcome.

1899   Between 1899 and 1903, Zola is working on a new series of novels, *Les Quatre Evangiles* (*The Four Gospels*). The first novel of this series, *Fécondité* is published (translated as *Fruitfulness* in 1900). Zola remains in England until June 4, 1899 when he learns that there is to be a review of the first Dreyfus trial, and returns to Paris. The French president pardons Dreyfus on September 19, but Dreyfus will not be completely exonerated until 1906. Indeed, Zola will never have the satisfaction of witnessing the final and happy conclusion to the tragic Dreyfus affair.

1901   Zola publishes *Travail*, (translated as *Work* in 1901), the second novel in *Les Quatre Evangiles*.

1902   On September 28, Zola and Alexandrine take up their autumn and winter quarters on the Rue de Bruzells. It is chilly and a fire in the room burns badly, filling it with carbon monoxide as they sleep. The next morning, one of the servants finds Alexandrine unconscious and Zola dead. On October 5, there is a gigantic public funeral, with a delegation of miners marching in procession, shouting "Germinal! Germinal!"

1903   *Vérité* (*Truth*), the last novel in the series, *Les Quatre Evangiles*, is published posthumously.

1908   On the evening of June 4, Zola's coffin is solemnly removed from its tomb in the Montmarte Cemetery and transported to the Paris Pantheon. After a second funeral, his remains are placed not far from Voltaire's and Jean-Jacques Rousseau's sarcophagi, in the crypt below.

Contributors

HAROLD BLOOM is Sterling Professor of the Humanities at Yale University and Henry W. and Albert A. Berg Professor of English at the New York University Graduate School. He is the author of over 20 books, including *Shelley's Mythmaking* (1959), *The Visionary Company* (1961), *Blake's Apocalypse* (1963), *Yeats* (1970), *A Map of Misreading* (1975), *Kabbalah and Criticism* (1975), *Agon: Toward a Theory of Revisionism* (1982), *The American Religion* (1992), *The Western Canon* (1994), *Omens of Millenium: The Gnosis of Angels, Dreams, and Resurrection* (1996), *Shakespeare: the Invention of the Human*, a 1998 National Book Award finalist, *How to Read and Why* (2000), *Genius* (2002) and *Hamlet: Poem Unlimited* (2003). In 1999, Professor Bloom received the prestigious American Academy of Arts and Letters Gold Medal for Criticism.

ANGUS WILSON was a respected British novelist. His works include *The Wrong Set* (1949) and *Such Darling Dodos and Other Stories* (1950), *Hemlock and After* (1952), *Anglo-Saxon Attitudes* (1956), *The Old Men at the Zoo* (1961), *Late Call* (1965), *No Laughing Matter* (1967), and *Setting the World on Fire* (1980).

F.W.J. HEMMINGS was a respected scholar and critic. In addition to his contributions to Zola scholarship, he has written on Charles Baudelaire, Alexandre Dumas, and Stendhal. His other books include *Culture and Society in France, 1848–1898; Dissidents and Philistines* (1971), *The Age of Realism* (1974), *The Theatre Industry in Nineteenth-Century France* (1993), and *Theatre & State in France, 1760–1905* (1994).

WILLIAM J. BERG is a Professor in the Department of French and Italian at the University of Wisconsin-Madison. He is the author of *Emile Zola Revisited* (1992) and *Gustave Flaubert* (1997).

ROBERT E. ZIEGLER is a Professor in the Department of Humanities at Montana Tech. He is the author of *Beauty Raises the Dead: Literature and Loss in the Fin de Siècle* (2002) and "Huysmans' *En ménage* and the Unwritable Naturalist Text" (1993).

JONATHAN F. KRELL is an Associate Professor of French at the University of Georgia. He is the author of "Between Demon and Divinity: Mélusine Revisited" (2000) and "Michel Tournier's 'Degenerate Art'" (1995).

In addition to numerous articles published in *The New Republic, The New York Review of Books, Harper's,* and *The New York Times Book Review,* FREDERICK BROWN's books include *An Impersonation of Angels: A Biography of Jean Cocteau* (1968), *Pere-Lachaise: Elysium as Real Estate* (1973), *Theater and Revolution: The Culture of the French Stage* (1980), and *Zola, A Life* (1995).

HOLLIE MARKLAND HARDER is a Lecturer at Brandeis University. She is the author of "Proust's Human Comedy" (2001) and "Proust's Novel Confections: Françoise's Cooking and Marcel's Book" (1999).

P.M. WETHERILL has been a Professor in the Department of French at the University of Manchester.. He is the author of *The Literary Text: An Examination of Critical Methods* (1974) and "A Reading of *Eugénie Grandet*" (1971).

NICHOLAS RENNIE is an Assistant Professor of German at Rutgers. He is the author of "Between Pascal and Mallarmé: Faust's Speculative Moment" (2000) and "'Schilderungssucht' and 'historische Krankheit': Lessing, Nietzsche, and the Body Historical" (2001).

MARIE-SOPHIE ARMSTRONG is an Associate Professor of French at Lehigh University. She is the author of "Les 'Hugoglyphes' des Misérables" (2000) and "Hugo's 'égouts' and *Le Ventre de Paris*" (1996).

MICHELLE E. BLOOM is Assistant Professor of Comparative Literature and French at the University of California, Riverside. She is the author of "Les Silences de Maeterlinck et Sarraute" (1996) and "Waxing Eccentrically in Champfleury's 'L'Homme aux figures de cire': Naturalism with a Balzacian Twist" (1993).

ANTHONY SAVILE is Professor of Philosophy at King's College, London. He is the author of *Kantian Aesthetics Pursued* (1993) and *Aesthetic Reconstructions* (1987).

HENRI MITTERAND's vast teaching appointments include the Sorbonne and Columbia University. He is the author of "The Scarlet Vision of the Revolution" (1998) and *L'illusion réaliste: de Balzac a Aragon* (1994).

Bibliography

Baguley, David, ed. *Critical Essays on Emile Zola*. Boston: G.K. Hall & Co., 1986.

———. "Parody and the Realist Novel." In *University of Toronto Quarterly* 55, no. 1 (Fall 1985): 94–108.

Berg, William J. and Laurey K. Martin. *Emile Zola Revisited*. New York: Twayne Publishers, 1992.

Brooks, Peter. "Storied Bodies, or *Nana* at Last Unveil'd." In *Critical Inquiry* 16, no. 1 (Autumn 1989): 1–32.

Brown, Frederick. *Zola: A Life*. New York: Farrar, Strauss, Giroux, 1995.

Carter, Lawson A. *Zola and the Theater*. New Haven: Yale University Press, 1963.

Chaitin, Gilbert. "Transposing the Dreyfus Affair: The Trauma of Identity in Zola's *Vérité*." *Australian Journal of French Studies*, vol. XXXVIII, no. 3 (September–December 2001): 430–44.

Chitnis, Bernice. *Reflecting on* Nana. London and New York: Routledge, 1991.

Colatrella, Carol. "Representing Liberty: Revolution, Sexuality, and Science in Michelet's Histories and Zola's Fiction." In *Nineteenth-Century French Studies* 20, nos. 1–2 (Fall–Winter 1991–1992): 27–43.

Evenhuis, Anthony John. *Messiah or Antichrist?: A Study of the Messianic Myth in the Work of Zola*. London and Newark, N.J.: Associated University Presses, 1998.

———. "Mythic Prefiguration of Zola's Worldview in *La Confession de Claude*." *AMULA* 77 (May 1992): 20–31.

Fuller, Carol S. "The Infertile Rabbit: Ambiguities of Creation and Destruction in *Germinal.*" In *Nineteenth-Century French Studies*, vol. 10, nos. 3–4 (Spring–Summer 1982): 340–59.

Furst, Lilian R. *L'Assommoir: A Working Woman's Life.* Boston: Twayne Publishers, 1980.

———. "A Medical Reading of Gervaise in *L'Assomoir.*" In *Symposium* 46, no. 3 (Fall 1992): 195–207.

Gilman, Sander L. "Black Bodies, White Bodies: Toward an Iconography of Female Sexuality in Late Nineteenth-Century Art, Medicine and Literature." In *Critical Inquiry* 12, no. 1 (Autumn 1985): 204–42.

Grant, Elliott Mansfield. *Zola's* Germinal: *A Critical and Historical Study.* New York: Humanities Press, 1962.

Haavik, Kristof H. *In Mortal Combat: The Conflict of Life and Death in Zola's Rougon-Macquart.* Birmingham, Alabama: Summa Publications, Inc., 2000.

Hemmings, Frederick W. J. *Emile Zola.* Oxford: Clarendon Press, 1966.

Hollier, Denis. "Bloody Sundays." Trans. Betsy Wing. In *Representations* 28 (Fall 1989): 77–89.

Kamm, Lewis. "The Structural and Functional Manifestation of Space in Zola's *Rougon-Macquart.*" In *Nineteenth-Century French Studies*, vol. 3, nos. 3 and 4 (1975): 224–36.

———. "Zola's Object and the Surrealistic Image. In *Nineteenth-Century French Studies* 11, nos. 3–4 (Spring–Summer 1983): 321–33.

———. "Emile Zola: Time, History, and Myth Reviewed." In *Nineteenth-Century French Studies* 20, nos. 3–4 (Spring–Summer 1992): 384–96.

King, Graham. *Garden of Zola: Emile Zola and His Novels for English Readers.* New York: Barnes & Noble Books, 1978.

Lehan, Richard. "American Literary Naturalism: The French Connection." In *Nineteenth-Century Fiction* 38, no. 4 (March 1984): 529–57.

Lethbridge, Robert and Terry Keefe, eds. *Zola and the Craft of Fiction: Essays in Honor of F.W.J. Hemmings.* London: Leicester University Press, 1990.

———. "A Visit to the Louvre: *L'Assomoir* Revisited. In *The Modern Language Review* 87, no. 1 (January 1992): 41–55.

———. "Reading the Songs of *L'Assommoir.*" In *French Studies* 45, no. 4 (October 1991): 435–47.

Maurin, Mario. "Zola's Labyrinths." In *Yale French Studies* 42 (1969): 89–104.

McClendon, Wendell E. "Red on Gray: *Thérèse Raquin.*" In *Nineteenth-Century French Studies* 19, no. 2 (Winter 1991): 304–16.

McGovern, Anne. "From Romantic Genius to Committed Intellectual: The Emergence of Zola's Conception of the Intellectual. *Journal of European Studies* 15, no. 3 (September 1985): 191–207.

Minogue, Valerie. "Zola's Mythology: that forbidden tree." In *Forum for Modern Language Studies*, vol. 14, no. 3 (July 1978): 217–30.

Mitterand, Henri. "The calvary of Catherine Maheu: the description of a page in *Germinal.*" In *Yale French Studies*, vol. 42 (1969): 115–25.

Moore, Mary Jane Evans. "The Spatial Dynamics of *L'Assommoir.*" In *Kentucky Romance Quarterly*, vol. 29, no. 1 (1982): 3–14.

Mossman, Carol A. "Etchings in the Earth: Speech and Writing in *Germinal.*" *L'Esprit Createur* 25, no. 4 (Winter 1985): 30–41.

Nelson, Brian. "Zola and the Ambiguities of Passion: *Une Page d'amour.*" *Essays in French Literature*, vol. 10 (1973): 1–22.

Niess, Robert J. *Zola, Cezanne, and Manet: A Study of L'Oeuvre.* Ann Arbor: University of Michigan Press, 1968.

Pasco, Allan H. "Literary History and Quinet in the Meaning of *La Faute de l'abbe Mouret.*" In *Forum for Modern Language Studies*, vol. 14, no. 3 (July 1978): 208–16.

———. "Myth, Metaphor and Meaning in *Germinal.*" In *The French Review* 46 (1973): 739–49.

Pope, Barbara Corrado. "Emile Zola's *Lourdes*: Land of Healing and Rupture. In *Literature and Medicine* 8 (1989): 22–35.

Richardson, Joanna. *Zola.* London: Weidenfeld and Nicolson, 1978.

Schor, Naomi. "Zola: from window to window." In *Yale French Studies* 42 (1969): 52–67.

Spencer, Michael. "Poetics and Pedagogy: Study of a Short Story by Zola." *Australian Journal of French Studies* 23, no. 2 (May–August 1986): 185–94.

Tilby, Michael. "Emile Zola and His First English Biographer." In *Laurels* 59, no. 1 (Spring–Summer 1988): 33–56.

Viti, Robert M. "The Cave, the Clock and the Railway: Primitive and Modern Time in *La Bête humaine.*" In *Nineteenth-Century French Studies* 19, no. 1 (Fall 1990): 110–21.

Vizetelly, Ernest Alfred. *Emile Zola, Novelist and Reformer: An Account of His Life.* Freeport, N.Y.: Books for Libraries Press, 1971.

Walker, Philip D. *Germinal and Zola's Philosophical and Religious Thought.* Amsterdam and Philadelphia: J. Benjamins Publishing Company, 1984.

———. *Emile Zola.* London: Routledge & K. Paul; New York: Humanities Press, 1968.

————. "Prophetic Myths in Zola." In *Publications of the Modern Language Association*, vol. 74 (1959): 444–52.

————. "The mirror, the window, and the eye in Zola's fiction." In *Yale French Studies* 42 (1969): 38–51.

————. "*Germinal* and Zola's Youthful 'New Faith' Based on Geology." In *Symposium* 36 (1982): 257–72.

Williams, Adelia V. "Cezanne, Manet, and the Genesis of Zola's L'Oeuvre." In *Nineteenth- Century Studies* 6 (1992): 37–49.

Wilson, Angus. *Emile Zola: An Introductory Study of His Novels*. New York: Morrow, 1952.

Zamparelli, Thomas. "Zola and the quest for the absolute in art." In *Yale French Studies* 42 (1969): 143–58.

Zarifopol-Johnston, Ilinca. "'Ceci tuera cela': The Cathedral in the Marketplace." In *Nineteenth-Century French Studies* 17, nos. 3–4 (Spring–Summer 1989): 355–68.

Acknowledgments

"Les Rougon-Macquart: The Form of Expression" by Angus Wilson. From *Emile Zola: An Introductory Study of his Novels*, pp. 51–68. © 1952 by Angus Wilson. Reprinted by permission.

"Cry From the Pit" by F.W.J. Hemmings. From *Emile Zola*, pp. 175–197. © 1953 by F.W.J. Hemmings. Reprinted by permission.

"A Poetics of Vision: Zola's Theory and Criticism" by William J. Berg. From *The Visual Novel: Emile Zola and the Art of His Times*, pp. 29–60. © 1992 by William J. Berg. Reprinted by permission.

"Interpretation as Awakening from Zola's *Le Rêve*" by Robert E. Ziegler. From *Nineteenth-Century French Studies*, vol. 21, nos. 1-2 (Fall–Winter 1992–93): 130–41. © 1993 by The University of Nebraska Press. Reprinted by permission.

"Nana: Still Life, *Nature morte*" by Jonathan F. Krell. From *French Forum*, vol. 19, no. 1 (January 1994): 65–79. © 1994 by the University of Nebraska Press. Reprinted by permission.

"The Master Plan" from *Zola, A Life* by Frederick Brown. Copyright © 1995 by Frederick Brown. Reprinted by permission of Farrar, Straus and Giroux, LLC.

"The Woman Beneath: The *femme de marbre* in Zola's *La Faute de l'abbé Mouret*" by Hollie Markland Harder. From *Nineteenth-Century French Studies*, vol. 24, nos. 3–4 (1996 Spring–Summer): 426–39. © 1996 by The University of Nebraska Press. Reprinted by permission.

"Flaubert, Zola, Proust and Paris: An Evolving City in a Shifting Text" by P.M. Wetherill. From *Forum for Modern Language Studies*, vol. 32, no. 3 (July 1996): 228–39. © 1996 by Oxford University Press. Reprinted by permission.

Nicholas Rennie, "Benjamin and Zola: Narrative, the Individual, and Crowds in an Age of Mass Production," in *Comparative Literature Studies*, vol. 33, no. 4 (1996): 396–413. © 1996 by The Pennsylvania State University. Reproduced by permission of the publisher.

"The Opening Chapter of *La fortune des Rougon*, or the Darker Side of Zolian Writing" by Marie-Sophie Armstrong. From *Dalhousie French Studies*, vol. 44 (Fall 1998): 39–53. © 1998 by Dalhousie University. Reprinted by permission.

"'Zola Fantastique': An Analysis of the Story 'La mort d'Olivier Bécaille'" by Michelle E. Bloom. From *Symposium*, vol. 53, no. 2 (Summer 1999): 69–81. Reprinted by permission of the Helen Dwight Reid Educational Foundation. Published by Heldref Publications, 1319 Eighteenth St., NW, Washington, DC 20036–1802. Copyright © 1999.

"Naturalism and the Aesthetic" by Anthony Savile. From *The British Journal of Aesthetics*, vol. 40, no. 1 (January 2000): 46–63. © 2000 by Oxford University Press. Reprinted by permission.

"Zola, 'ce rêveur définitif'" by Henri Mitterand. French version first appeared in *Melusine*, XXI, 2001, pp. 133–147. Translated by Fiona Wilson. From the *Australian Journal of French Studies*, vol. 38, no. 3 (September–December 2001): 321–35. © 2001 by Monash University. Reprinted by permission.

Index